0279335

700.1

-0 ... 1987

1.85
BW

Modernism
Criticism
Realism.
6.95.

Please renew/return this item by the last date shown.

So that your telephone call is charged at local rate, please call the numbers as set out below:

	From Area codes 01923 or 0208:	From the rest of Herts:
Renewals:	01923 471373	01438 737373
Enquiries:	01923 471333	01438 737333
Minicom:	01923 471599	01438 737599

L32b

9/12

M
C
R

MODERNISM
CRITICISM
REALISM

Hertfordshire
COUNTY COUNCIL
Community Information

1 0 FEB 2001

1 1 APR 2002

- 9 MAY 2002

1 2 NOV 2003

1 2 JAN 2004

2 9 APR 2004

L32a

1 0 OCT 2006

3 0 NOV 2006

0 7 DEC 2007

1 2 APR 2005

LOAN

1 5 NOV 2005

2 5 FEB 2006

1 8 MAY 2006

Born in 1949, **Fred Orton** studied Fine Art at Coventry College of Art, and History of Art at the Courtauld Institute. He is now a lecturer in the Department of Fine Art at the University of Leeds. He is the author of various articles on nineteenth and twentieth century art, and Reviews Editor of *Art History*, journal of the Association of Art Historians. He is co-author, with Griselda Pollock, of *Vincent van Gogh* (Phaidon 1978) and, with Charles Harrison, of *A Provisional History of Art & Language* (Editions Eric Fabre 1982).

Born in 1942, **Charles Harrison** studied Art History at Cambridge University and the Courtauld Institute. Since 1965 he has lectured in Art and Art History at various universities and colleges of art. He has been employed by the Open University since 1977. He is a member of the Art & Language group, and was Durning-Lawrence Lecturer, University of London, 1982–3. He is the author of: *Ben Nicholson* (Tate Gallery 1969); *English Art and Modernism 1900–1939* (Allen Lane and Indiana University Press 1981); and articles in *Studio International, Artforum, Art History, Art-Language* and other publications. He is co-editor, with Francis Frascina, of *Modern Art and Modernism* (Harper and Row 1982).

MODERNISM, CRITICISM, REALISM

Charles Harrison and Fred Orton
(Editors)

Harper & Row, Publishers
London

Cambridge
Hagerstown
Philadelphia
New York

San Francisco
Mexico City
São Paulo
Sydney

Selection and editorial material copyright © Charles
Harrison and Fred Orton 1984

First published 1984

Harper & Row Ltd
28 Tavistock Street
London WC2E 7PN

British Library Cataloguing in Publication Data
Modernism, criticism, realism.
  1. Aesthetics
  I. Harrison, Charles, 1942-
  II. Orton, Fred
  700'.1   N66

  ISBN 0-06-318289-0

Typeset by BookEns, Saffron Walden, Essex
Printed and bound by Butler & Tanner Ltd,
Frome & London

Front cover illustration: Art & Language; Index the Studio at 3
Wesley Place in the Dark (III) and illuminated by an explosion
nearby. (V, VI; drawing (III), acrylic on paper.

Acknowledgements

This publication would not have been possible without the co-operation of those various authors, publishers and copyright-holders who have agreed to inclusion of their material within what must have seemed to some a relatively exotic context. For suggestions and other assistance in compiling this anthology we would like particularly to thank Michael Baldwin, J. R. R. Christie and Mel Ramsden. We would also like to record our gratitude to those students at Leeds University, the Open University and Birmingham Polytechnic Department of Fine Art (MA course) with whom some of the texts have been discussed. Their responses have supported our view of the potential usefulness of this publication. Lastly we would like to express our appreciation of the contributions to the realization of this project made by Marianne Lagrange and Louise Edwards of Harper & Row.

The idea of this anthology, and of the functions it might fulfil, was in part suggested by *Modern Art and Modernism: A Critical Anthology,* edited by Francis Frascina and Charles Harrison and also published by Harper & Row (1982). We have avoided overlap with this collection. The two books are complementary at least in the sense that each furnishes a kind of context for the other. Our introduction offers some discussion of how and why this is the case.

Charles Harrison
Fred Orton

Contents

Acknowledgements

Introduction: Modernism, Explanation and
Knowledge   xi

I Aesthetics and Sensibility

1   *Clement Greenberg:* Complaints of an Art Critic   3

2   *Richard Wollheim:* The Work of Art as Object   9

3   *John Passmore:* The Dreariness of Aesthetics   19

4   *Beryl Lake:* A Study of the Irrefutability of two
Aesthetic Theories   25

5   *Alasdair MacIntyre:* Emotivism   37

II Knowledge and Representation

6   *Jaakko Hintikka:* Knowing How, Knowing That,
and Knowing What . . .   47

7   *Ludwig Wittgenstein:* Seeing and Seeing as   57

8   *N. R. Hanson:* Observation   69

9   *Nelson Goodman:* Seven Strictures on
Similarity   85

10   *Noam Chomsky:* On Cognitive Capacity   93

11   *Barry Barnes:* Conceptions of Knowledge   101

12   *Alison Assiter:* Philosophical Materialism or the
Materialist Conception of History   113

III Representation and Art

13 *William M. Ivins Jnr.:* The Blocked Road to Pictorial Communication *and* The Road Block Broken   125

14 *Michael Baxandall:* The Cognitive Style   139

15 *Art & Language:* Portrait of V. I. Lenin   145

IV Expression

16 *Nelson Goodman:* Expression   173

17 *Thomas S. Szasz:* Hysteria as Communication   181

18 *Art & Language:* Abstract Expression   191

V Communities and Interests

19 *C. B. Macpherson:* The Twentieth-Century Dilemma   207

20 *Alasdair MacIntyre:* The Idea of a Social Science   213

21 *Thomas S. Kuhn*: Paradigms, Tacit Knowledge and Incommensurability   229

22 *Barry Barnes:* Culture and History   243

23 *Art & Language:* Author and Producer Revisited   251

24 *Noam Chomsky:* Some General Features of Language   261

Index   270

Introduction: Modernism, Explanation and Knowledge

> With the new indifference to representation we have become much less interested in skill and not at all interested in knowledge.
> (Roger Fry, 'Art and Life', 1917[1])

Challenging though they may have been at the time they were first made—and challenging they were certainly intended to be—such statements as this have become so familiar in the history of modern art theory and criticism that we tend now to let them pass unremarked. They go unremarked, perhaps, for either of two reasons, according to the different dispositions of those interested in such things. By some they are accorded the status of basic and unquestionable axioms within a now secure and continuous theory of modern art. By others they are noticed simply as typical quotations—perlocutionary acts—to be contextualized in historical and cultural terms and characterized by reference to interests now superseded or always marginal.

The first of these positions may be associated with what is now referred to as the Modernist tradition in art history and art criticism.[2] Fry himself played a decisive part in the entrenchment of Modernism as the dominant tradition in English-language writing about art, though those emphatic changes in priority by which the 'modern' in art was first distinguished and represented as such are now conventionally located in mid-nineteenth-century France. Perhaps the most significant of these changes was the establishment as an overriding critical principle that works of art should be judged according to their coherence as *art*, rather than by their correspondence to some naturalistic canon. Fry's 'new indifference to representation' was not simply a response to the development of 'abstract art' in the previous decade. It testified more significantly to the belief that naturalistic correspondence should be rejected as a measure of competence or quality in art. 'Representation' was re-identified with *descriptive* representation and with illustrative subject-matter, and these were devalued relative to 'expression' and to 'form'. According to conventional Modernist wisdom, it was on such issues that the 'moderns' in later nineteenth-century France had divided themselves off from the 'academics', and it is in terms of such differences that they have remained divided for the past hundred years or more.

Certain kinds of change may be seen as having characterized the separate development of the modern in art. It was the achievement of the American critic Clement Greenberg to recover what was apparently systematic in these kinds of change, and to organize and represent them in terms of a theory of 'Modernist Art'.[3] However one moralizes the development of Greenberg's criticism through the late thirties into the sixties, it has to be said that no art critic at the time did more to preserve the integrity of the modern tradition. It has also to be said that a high price was paid. The purging of talk about subject-matter was no great immediate loss, particularly where what was most often at issue was the valuation to be placed on types of abstract art. Such talk has generally in the twentieth century been easy to generate and often exciting, but almost entirely uninformative; which is to say that it has rarely been of critical interest. The more troubling restrictions that were imposed upon criticism by Greenberg's relatively systematic Modernism were these: firstly that aesthetic judgements had to be represented as involuntary and disinterested; and secondly that consideration of the causal conditions of art had largely to be restricted to a consideration of artistic causes as the only cognitively significant ones for the purpose of criticism. These two restrictions can be traced back to the writings of Roger Fry and Clive Bell, and to earlier writers on the continent (if not, as Greenberg himself would have it, to Immanuel Kant), but it was Greenberg, however disingenuously he may have disclaimed any role as a historian, who first implemented them in art criticism in the interests of an apparently consistent form of historical explanation.

The argument goes like this.[4] The modern tendency within the arts—as supposedly within philosophy and science—is towards the entrenchment of each distinct pursuit within its own specific area of competence, which, within the arts, is defined in part by orientation to specific senses. Greenberg describes this as the pursuit of purity and self-definition. For example, what painting shares with no other art form is its flatness and the fact that it addresses itself to 'eyesight alone'; the dynamic of development in Modernist painting is thus explained as the intensification of flatness and 'opticality',[5] or, as Richard Wollheim would have it, in terms of the conceptual priority accorded to painting's 'possession of a surface' (see text 2). This will inevitably entail the squeezing out of mimetic, descriptive and narrative content, which are anyway properly within literature's area of competence. Substantive change is seen as technical change in relation to other art. If true, this is a rationale for restricting criticism and explanation to discussion of formal and technical change and development. It is a measure of the adequacy of Greenberg's account of change that it can be reconciled with Karl Popper's.[6] That same observation should encourage us to look to the work of such writers as Thomas Kuhn (text 21) and Barry Barnes (texts 11 and 22) for alternative viewpoints from which to scrutinize the Modernist position.

It is important to recognize that Modernist theory—at least as represented by Greenberg, who remains its typical and most influential exponent—is a theory about high art and the autonomy of its forms.[7] It is not to be confused with those types of theory within which art is treated as no more than an exemplary type of design, where 'design' is seen both as the global material of aesthetic diagnosis and as the ideal form of planning in social life and production. The two types of theory have aspects of their histories in common, and they tend to overlap where each is least coherent, but they are fundamentally opposed and irreconcilable. This has become increasingly clear of late. If the aesthetic diagnosis of design has mutated into the semiological analysis of all 'visual production', the Modernist version of the distinction between 'Avant-Garde' and 'Kitsch', formulated by Greenberg in 1939,[8] has been pursued with increasing militancy in attempts to safeguard the 'highest' of technical and aesthetic categories. The accelerating tendency of the former is to 'uncover' the interests at work in visual representation. The tendency of the latter is to uphold the value of aesthetic experience and aesthetic production precisely because they are seen as disinterested.

The second typical disposition in relation to such assertions as Fry's—that which represents them as mere quotations within a transcended discourse—entails the assumption either that we are living in a 'Post-Modernist' culture,[9] or that our culture need accord Modernism no more than marginal historical status and interest whether it is still theoretically current or not. Such texts as Fry's are treated accordingly either as 'literature' in the history of art criticism or as the items of an autonomous and specialized area of interest with no theoretical power or relevance for the uninitiated or unenthusiastic. From such positions scrutiny of the conceptual components of relevant assertions is rendered otiose by the status accorded to the whole, as historical document or idiomatic inconsequence respectively. The first position, that Modernism is over, *passé*, transcended, tends to rest on an empirical identification of Modernism as culture or theory with certain styles associated with 'Modernist Art'. An apparent change in fashion from relatively 'flat' abstract painting to relatively modelled figurative painting— or a 'radical' combination (photographic or otherwise) of figurative imagery and text—is thus interpreted as signalling the 'end of Modernism'. The category mistakes on which such interpretations rest are clear enough not to need spelling out here (though for a critique of the types of assumption involved see Goodman's 'Seven Strictures on Similarity', text 9). As for the second position, in so far as Modernism has been, or is, the dominant culture of art, a belief that Modernism has always been and is marginal must follow from an assumption that art itself is marginal. From the point of view of an interest in political and economic change it may well be, but the resolute layman is in no position to know why. His or her assumption of the marginality of art is neither here nor there in so far as it is made under conditions of indifference to or ignorance of art's potential *cognitive* significance.

Our interest in compiling this anthology rests upon a series of interrelated assumptions variously distinct from those attributed above. (1) That Modernism is still the dominant culture of art, or at least that the dominant representations of that culture are still constituted on the basis of assumptions compatible with Modernist beliefs—which may be to say the same thing. It follows that claims to 'Post-Modernist' status for any theory will be treated with extreme scepticism. (2) That the dominance of Modernism is not necessarily in virtue of its adequacy as *theory*. It follows that an unquestionable or merely documentary status cannot be accorded to any component text. Indeed, a combination of reinterpretation with causal and historical analysis may be the only means to trace and to unpack the confusion of agency with adequacy. (3) That the status of Modernism is not marginal but structural to our culture. It follows that assessment of the theoretical adequacy and range of Modernism is a matter of some importance.

If we reconsider our opening quotation in the light of the above assumptions, it may be somewhat harder to see how it could be allowed to pass unremarked. Like so many of the typical assertions of Modernist criticism, Fry's statement makes an evaluative claim with theoretical underpinnings and implications. Assent to the judgement assumes assent to the ways in which the relations within a certain set of concepts are theoretically established. Representation, interest, skill and knowledge—these are *important* concepts, as we hope our selection of texts will serve to demonstrate. (For a discussion of the conceptual relations between skill and knowledge, for instance, see Hintikka, text 6.) *Any* theory which aims to establish a certain relationship between them—and particularly one which does so in the interests of evaluation—is likely to have implications well outside any immediate context of application or specialization.

It might seem strange—for instance to someone educated in the natural sciences—that such a point should need making at all. Would it not normally be *assumed* that any strong claim about the relationship between natural scientific representation, natural scientific knowledge and the interests of natural science (between how the world is described, what can be known about it, and how much these matter) must have implications well beyond the more specialized professional interests of science—and this *despite* any assumptions that might be made about the autonomy of scientific knowledge or scientific practice? To explain why we should need to stress the significance of such claims as Fry's is to reconstruct a process of learning, or of attempting to learn, within a culture determined by the power of Modernism.

To start from conclusions, we assert the following: (1) that art is *cognitively* (and not simply culturally) significant; (2) that its cognitive significance is misrepresented in Modernist theory (as it is also in many critiques of Modernist theory); and (3) that the Modernist misrepresentation of art's cognitive significance is effectively a means to insulate Modernism itself against substantive critical and historical examination. Or, to put all this more simply: Modernist theory gets away with it, when it does, by imposing restricting conditions of relevance upon any potential criticism; the price it pays in doing this is to apply partial and restrictive (ontological) definitions to its own subject matter (see Lake, text 4). Fry's statement of disinterest, for instance, could be explained and perhaps defended by making explicit the implied restrictions on the meanings of 'representation', 'skill' and 'knowledge': 'representation' means *descriptive* representation; 'skill' means skill in descriptive and imitative draughtsmanship; and 'knowledge' means knowledge of observed topographical particulars or knowledge consistent with the interests of natural science. His negative can now easily enough be translated into its positive: 'With the new commitment to expressive representation we have become far more interested in the skills of formal and chromatic organization and extremely interested in the kinaesthetic intuition and critical contemplation of sensuous experience.' At which point, however, the grand theoretical claim collapses into a mere persuasive prescription: a guide to the correct position from which to consume current art. And this in an essay on the theme of 'Art and Life' written by one of this century's major and most influential critics of art. (For a critical explanation of Fry's dependence upon 'Emotivism' see MacIntyre, text 5.) If Fry's statement is typical, it seems that the more ambitious claims of modern art criticism are sustained in conditions of hiatus: on the one hand by their *apparent* theoretical range, on the other by the *actual* restriction on their field of application.[10]

As Beryl Lake observes with regard to the related theories of Benedetto Croce and Clive Bell (text 4), under these conditions what seem like exceptions to the more general theoretical pronouncements may be ruled out of court as irrelevant; ie they are said to be excluded from the range of items which the theories implicitly include in their own descriptions. According to the means of operation of these descriptions, the exceptions are not included in what was meant by 'art'. A less than complete exclusion will in fact be required if the theory is a theory about the distinguishing characteristics of 'high' or 'major' art (as Greenberg's is). All that will then be needed is that the troublesome exceptions be relegated to secondary or 'minor' status. If the determining tendency of major painting is said to be that modelling and shading have to be progressively eliminated in favour of an intensification of the actual surface (see Wollheim, text 2), then some highly modelled and shaded modern painting need only be said to fall short of 'major quality' to be disqualified as an exception.

It is a persistent claim of Modernist critics—and notably of Greenberg (see text 1)—that the theoretical aspect of their work is never more than the representation of a retrospective logic in history: the hindsight which connects what involuntary, disinterested and untheorized judgements have singled out.[11] However, given the determining effect of concepts of art upon the practice of art (see Wollheim, text 2) we might ask how coherent and how current such a set of articulated preferences would have to become before retrospective logic became effectively indistinguishable from self-fulfilling prescription. In the event of their becoming indistinguishable we might feel justified in using the term 'Modernist Art' with a somewhat different inflection from Greenberg's own, and in a spirit inconsistent with his belief that 'Art is a matter strictly of experience, not of principles.'[12] To paraphrase Art & Language (text 23), theories don't just find their objects, they constitute them; which is to say that the *agents employing those theories* do the constituting. By reference to Kuhn's terminology (text 21) we might say that Modernism acts as a resource of 'metaphysical paradigms', 'values' and 'exemplars' for a loose community of practitioners of art and art criticism, curators, spectators and so on.

'Modernism' refers literally to the property of 'being modern'. But this is not a simply chronological property or category. It is contingent upon the interests and evaluations of those who employ it. On the other hand Modernism takes as its material the actual substance of a historical situation. It refers to and uses this substance. It conveys information about it and theorizes this information both explicitly and implicitly. It will both identify some real historical properties and ascribe, value and constitute these properties and others as 'culture'. In so far as it does this, Modernism has cognitive content. Arguments over the typical or significant properties of the 'modern' are likely to turn on the complex relationships between identification, constitution and evaluation. One important aspect of such an argument will centre both upon the degree of autonomy to be accorded to any formation, specialization, area of interest or art form in assessing its modernism, and upon the grounds on which this autonomy is to be established and defended. For instance, can a practically regulative theory of art be confidently considered 'modern' if it can be shown to be included within a larger body of theory which has already been redescribed and effectively abandoned in some other area of practice or intellectual interest? One answer to this question often furnished within the Modernist critical tradition is that 'theory' is more-or-less accidentally and opportunistically used in the practice of art. It is the end result and only the end result—the finished work—that requires assessment. If that assessment is positive it follows that the *use* of any theory or idea is justified, however discredited it may be or have been in other contexts of interest and application.

We would reply that any assessment of what a work of art is must rest at some level upon a base of knowledge or assumptions about *how* it is what it is; ie upon acknowledged or unacknowledged consideration of causal factors. Among these causal factors will be beliefs, theories etc. Assessment will involve some matching of the spectator's beliefs etc against those beliefs implicitly or explicitly seen as implicated in the production of the work. Under these circumstances it seems reasonable to expect that the assessment of Modernism in art should not *assume* the autonomy of artistic practice; ie that assessment should be made with an eye to the adequacy of any artistic practice with respect to the state of knowledge and theory in other practices. From this position we can recognize art's forms of autonomy and specialization where we are obliged to. We see no good grounds for privileging art relative to other practices or formations; ie taking as basic a set of *assumptions* about its autonomy, thus rendering it immune from certain forms of scrutiny.

It should be acknowledged, however, that many of the changes in art which are emphasized in Modernist art history are both clearly significant and well described in Modernist accounts. If these accounts are to be seen as somehow inadequate or flawed it will have to be because the *explanations* of those changes, the reasons given for them, for their significance and for the relations between them, can be seen to be partial or unsatisfactory. A concept of autonomy, for instance, is only suspect if it can be seen to put illegitimate closures, rather than merely methodological limits, on inquiry and explanation. We need to distinguish between the different forms of autonomy hypothesized in different types of Modernist practice. The Modernist account of art history (and the more so its journalistic derivatives) rests largely on the assumption of a high degree of autonomy in the conditions of production of art. This may be grounded in either of two related sets of assumptions. In the first, the artist is seen as a self-determined 'creator' rather than as a producer bound within certain social and historical relations of production (for a critique of this view see Art & Language, text 23). In the second, art is seen as significantly provoked or fired or inspired by other art, by insight, intuition, emotion etc, rather than as caused within some open system of causal relations compatible with the project of historical materialism (see Assiter, text 12). What will be required of any critique of the findings of Modernist art history is that it should derive from an independent conceptual framework—one, that is to say, which secures emancipation from the closed system within which agent (artist) and action (work of art) are joined by a set of assumptions regarding the adequacy of ('artistic') *reasons* as explanations.[13] (For a critique of similar types of assumptions see MacIntyre, text 20.)

What has been said above regarding Modernist art history may also be said of Modernist art criticism. Modernist critics appear to have been more successful than others in drawing attention to those artists and individual works which have achieved prominence and maintained interest. One's own independence of evaluative judgement from the authority vested in powerful judges is by no means easy to scrutinize. We can certainly say that there is no point in taking issue with the evaluations unless a critique can be mounted of the theoretical bases on which the judgements rest. In the case of the judgements of Modernist criticism, this will require a critique of various claims for the autonomy of art and for the autonomy of 'disinterestedness' and 'involuntariness' in aesthetic response. And this in turn will require that these claims be themselves redescribed and explained. (For an assertion of the disinterestedness of aesthetic judgement, see Greenberg, text 1. For various critiques of claims to disinterestedness see Lake, text 4, MacIntyre, text 5, Baxandall, text 14, introduction to Goodman, text 16, and Art & Language, texts 18 and 23.) The question of the autonomy of art, literature, warfare, carpentry, football etc remains and will remain not a matter of theoretical prescription, but of substantive *open* inquiry.

The various versions of autonomy are differently stressed in variants of the Modernist tradition. The concept of autonomy of aesthetic experience formulated by Benedetto Croce (see Lake, text 4) has had a surprisingly long currency. The formal and technical autonomy of art was stressed by Clive Bell (see text 4) and has received its most elegant exposition in the criticism of Greenberg. A belief in the autonomy of the conditions of production of art has served to establish the limits of inquiry in the normal profession of art history. The concept of autonomy is not in itself a bar to inquiry. Indeed it is hard to see how any historical investigation could proceed without some means to connect possible causal explanations to explananda within a coherent intellectual system. This is no less true of historical materialism, for instance, than of any other form of history. There are ways to consider the problem of autonomy, for example, which might assist in explaining how and why it is feasible to talk of an 'art world' and an 'art market'. But the concepts of autonomy variously employed in the Modernist tradition appear to operate so as to produce consistent kinds of hermeneutic circles: sets of reciprocal restrictions which effectively bind into one world of thought and sensibility what is to be accounted for and what is allowed as *relevant* in interpretation and explanation. It needs to be said that there is no Archimedean point outside the constraining circles of a determining culture. The task is to open them from within, by recourse to relatively independent concepts and explanations. It is to the nature of this task and of these resources that the 'criticism' of our main title is intended to refer.

We are aiming in very general terms to characterize and partially to account for a range of problems and issues in the present state of discourse about art. One way to think of this discourse is as a lattice of beliefs and interests, the separate laths of which can most easily be identified and contrasted when they converge around certain aspects of an identifiable subject; for instance when different points of view, judgements and interpretations are expressed in relation to a specific work of art or of criticism. Such contrasts in the discourses of art are the occasions of specific professional controversies and they assist in the tracing of different genealogies, different causal histories, for distinct theories or beliefs or procedures. So long as modern art history and art criticism are considered in professional isolation, we would say that the *genealogy* of Modernist points of view is indubitably more authentic than that of many apparent alternatives, which often take their colour more from their oppositional character with respect to Modernist theory and method than from the independence of their own genealogies and concepts.

The foregoing is, as it were, a microscopic sample of the conditions of controversy in art. On the other hand anyone with intellectual work to do needs to find themselves in relation to certain broader areas of knowledge and concern. Such issues as those raised by expression, interpretation, explanation, representation, culture, interest and knowledge map out a large field within which many of the microscopic controversies may be perceived as mere incidences, details, fragments or tangents. To what extent they *are* so perceived will depend on the kinds of relations one allows or establishes between art and any other forms of practice or interest, and on the degree to which the concerns of art are seen as comparable to or subsumed under other concerns. This is the basic methodological problem of compiling an anthology such as this one: how does one establish and defend the *relevance* of what is offered? This bears on what we have found to be a chronic condition in art teaching and the teaching of art history: the first problem is how to persuade students that there is a problem; the second problem is how to persuade them that you may be talking about it. The reliance of art discourse upon certain terms and concepts would indeed seem to offer some secure means to establish a relationship of reference between different realms. We can return to Fry's assertion about knowledge and representation. To consider art as a form of representation in the wider sense—to open the reference of Fry's concepts to a wider understanding than that which protects the validity of his statement—is to enable the bringing to bear of critical and theoretical competences from other areas in which the problems of representation have been addressed (see for examples Hanson, text 8, Barnes, text 11, Ivins, text 13, and Kuhn, text 21). The intellectual advantages of such recourse seem to us far to outweigh any strategic advantages gained by restricting the open question of art's autonomy.

It should be said that our aim in mounting this argument is not to demonstrate that Modernism is wicked, or a conspiracy or whatever. We are simply trying to locate it in terms of some wider intellectual interests and concerns than those by which its own boundaries are protected. Exposure to such interests and concerns serves to remind us that there are no foundations to knowledge nor any absolutely secure theories and methods, but also that there may be more or less adequate knowledge, theories and methods to be going on with. That 'more or less?' is the relevant question to address to Modernist theories and procedures. To avoid a common misunderstanding we should also stress that in presenting this anthology we do not seek to clear the critical ground for a return to academic values and competences, or to 'social realism', or to 'subject-matter' or to anything else. Nor do we seek to justify a revision of the canon of high art. If, as we suggest (see our introduction to text 22), the concept of 'quality' might fruitfully be replaced by some more potentially open and explanatory designation for merit in art, it would not necessarily follow that the latter would have to be applied to any different range of objects. We are interested in art, and in the art which has proved most interesting. We do not claim to have a sufficient theory as to why some art proves more interesting than other art, but nor do we seek to redefine or extend that interest in terms of an interest in 'cultural production', or 'visual ideology' or 'signifying practices' or whatever.

The above series of reservations should not, however, be taken as a plea for *laissez-faire* or for pluralism or for fatalism as regards the prospects for thinking to some purpose about the production of art, art criticism or art history. We are trying to consider the conditions of realism, and to do so in recognition both that 'art' is an unstable concept and that response to art is more than a matter of 'reading' artworks. To quote Art & Language, 'the being of art is in virtue of its doing . . . something' (text 23). We must ask: what is done; how and why and in relation to what conditions and to what perception of those conditions? And we must do so independently of any preferential assumptions about end results. Of course the 'end results', the works of art, are of central interest and importance. But (*pace* Goodman, text 9) the critical process of matching concepts against empirical perceptions may achieve nothing so much as the reaffirmation of an existing conceptual framework. Realism as we understand it requires that the inadequacy and contingency of such frameworks be *presupposed*, not because there is no 'real world' or no empirical evidence, but because (*pace* Barnes, text 22) we have no reason to expect convergence in any linguistic account or pictorial representation of that world. Realism is not a matter of correspondence, or even of *conventions* of correspondence. On this point Modernist theory has always been correct. It is a matter of *how*, on what basis, one goes about the process of criticism and correction of *any* representation.[14] It is in terms of such an understanding of realism that the three terms of our overall title are conjoined.

The majority of the texts included in this anthology represent intellectual materials which have proved useful to us. On the one hand they have availed us of a description of the conditions under which we have attempted to learn about art, art criticism and art history. On the other they have suggested means to break the hermeneutic circles of Modernist culture and to open its objects and constituents to inquiry. This has seemed to require a search for materials outside the immediate discourses of art. Any account of how one comes to recognize the limits on learning, and of how one does learn, must take account of contingent dissatisfactions, embarrassing mistakes, accidental encounters, individual psychology and so on. To compile a selection of texts such as this one, however, is to be confronted with what *may* be coherent or consistent, not only as perceived in what gets included, but perhaps more significantly in the character of material excluded. The anthology in its final form, that is to say, has a perceptible tenor which we could not adequately have described in advance of its compilation, but which now seems defensible in relation to substantive issues and not simply in autobiographical terms. (This is to make no claim for the comprehensiveness of our selection.)

One autobiographical acknowledgement is in order however. In considering the need to learn and the possibility of learning, we have had a certain artistic practice in view. Since the late 1960s Art & Language has generated works of art and of art theory which have been significant and interesting anomalies with respect to the normal interests and priorities of art history and art criticism. Our selection of texts may provide some intellectual materials for an understanding of how and why these anomalies are significant and interesting. If it does so, this is not because we have aimed to ratify any specific practice or set of art works, but rather because many of these materials were first introduced to us in the context of Art & Language's own practical search beyond the normal discourses of art for resources of description and analysis. The authority of Modernism was subject to some considerable scrutiny and opposition in the later 1960s, as was the authority of many other intellectual, cultural and political régimes. During the 1970s the dust settled again upon a surface apparently little changed. The supposed revolution in thought has left the institutions of cultural and intellectual life relatively untransformed. Those who have attempted to persist with the work of redescription and criticism have had to do so either outside those institutions or in an uneasy relationship with them, a relationship in which the learning of tolerances is not always easy to distinguish from their exploitation, or the critical exercise of competences from their effective disablement.

This scenario perhaps goes some way to put into context and to explain our inclusions and exclusions. Since the late 1960s two principal resources of theory and method have been widely seen as availing the critical analysis of cultural forms of production. Neither was altogether novel at the time—indeed they had their origins in nineteenth- and early twentieth-century Europe and their importation may largely be timed in relation to the availability of translations— but each was perceived as newly relevant by the supposedly dissenting intellectuals of a certain generation. The first is the Marxist theory and method of historical materialism (discussed by Assiter in text 12). The second is the specifically French tradition of structuralism and semiological analysis as derived principally from the linguistic theories of Ferdinand de Saussure, the social theories of Louis Althusser, the literary theory of Roland Barthes and the psychology of Jacques Lacan, variously amplified or modified by the anthropological theories of Claude Lévi-Strauss, by Michel Foucault's writings on power and intellect, and more recently by the work of Jacques Derrida and Julia Kristeva. [15]

It is often supposed—particularly by those attracted to neither framework of ideas—that these two resources of theory are united in a single tradition. This identification is the more plausible for those persuaded that Gramsci's and

Althusser's revisions of Marx's work constitute either defensible readings or progressive reinterpretations.[16] (On this issue see Chomsky, text 24.) The determinist element in Marx's theory—the axiom that humans as historical beings are defined by the need to produce the means of their subsistence, which underwrites his economic determinism—was transformed by Althusser's response to Gramsci's work and by his hypothesizing of three *interacting* 'levels' in social formations: the political, the economic and the ideological. For Marx, the critique of ideology involved the attribution of beliefs to agents, and the attribution among different sets of agents—classes—of different material interests which explained why certain beliefs might be held by some or inculcated in others. This was a work of historical description and redescription. For Althusser, to study ideology was to study the structure and operation of a *system:* the modes of combination and disposition of those apparatuses of family, law, politics, labour, communication, culture and education which 'represent the *form* in which the ideology of the ruling class must *necessarily* be realised'.[17] There is no independence from this system, which is *mythical* rather than rational, and thus no practice except by and in ideology. Any theory of ideology, for Althusser, addresses 'an omni-present reality, in the sense in which that structure and functioning are immutable, present in the same form throughout what we can call history'.[18]

The structuralist revision of Marx which Althusser thus performed entailed the replacement of historical and causal inquiry by procedures for making comparative (and often, in fact, metaphorical) relationships between different 'structures': between one culture and another, between one institution and another, and between language and more or less anything which can be seen as composed of a system of representations.

Of Althusser's three 'levels' it is the ideological, reinterpreted by the application of post-Freudian theories about the 'formation of the subject', which has achieved priority in semiological and 'Post-Structuralist' literature.

> The importance of understanding ideological practice in the way suggested by the articulation of Marxism and psychoanalysis is very great. The politics which flow from radical and Marxist thought can then be free from any economic determinism, that is, the idea that economic practice is more important than political or ideological processes in the social process. As long as Marxists still think of ideological practice as somehow subservient to the economy (as a 'super-structure' built on the economic 'base'), then their politics will always stress the economy as the principal determinant, and see economic crisis as the principal (or only) cause of social crisis.[19]

According to the viewpoint represented here 'reality' is 'a world which is produced by the whole ensemble of social activities, including that of conceptualizations in language' (the latter embracing art, since 'Art is a practice of language').[20]

In addressing those specific problems and materials in relation to which they were developed, structuralist and semiological methods have often been critically informative. They have done much, for instance, to emphasize the potential artificiality of distinctions between description and expression, or between denotations and connotations. There is now an intellectual and professional fashion, however, for extending their application in pursuit of a general critique of all 'cultural forms (and it seems that more or less anything can be considered as a cultural form, if only by virtue of its inclusion in the 'conceptualizations in language'). Trying-on *applications* of theories can be critical work. But where the process of application *constitutes* the material it treats and professes to explain, it deserves to be viewed with scepticism. By many of those claiming 'radical' explanatory potential for their own applications, aspects of structuralist literary theory, aspects of structuralist anthropology, aspects of structuralist revisions of psychoanalysis, and aspects of 'philosophical' Marxism have all been wrenched from their practical and theoretical contexts and combined into what Jonathan Rée has felicitously dubbed the *nouveau mélange.*[21] The resulting analyses are highly vulnerable to the competent exercise of those specialized (and admittedly often conservative) disciplines whose limits they were perhaps originally intended to transcend.

Substance for a critique of such analyses may be found in the present anthology (for example, see Goodman, text 9, Chomsky, texts 10 and 24, Assiter, text 12, Art & Language, text 15, and MacIntyre, text 20). Two particular objections may be noted: (1) (*pace* Goodman) that the finding of similarities—for example between structures or systems under comparison—may testify rather to the assumptions under which items are viewed as comparable than to the possession of significant common characteristics by the objects (or systems) compared; and (2) (*pace* Chomsky) that the empiricist concept of man as a blank tablet open to being 'imprinted' with ideology is anti-rationalist, anti-scientific and potentially manipulative.

We have perhaps said enough to explain what might seem—in the intellectual climate of these times—like a significant series of omissions from our anthology. We have seen no adequate reason so far to abandon those historical-materialist interests and methods which first fulfilled a pressing need: which availed us (like many others) of a relatively independent description of Modernism as a historically contingent and potentially explicable set of beliefs and procedures. To achieve an independent description is one thing, cognitively to assess the truth of beliefs and the value of procedures is quite another however, though it is a common error within the Marxist tradition to assume that if one has done the former the latter requirement has also somehow been discharged or removed. For the Manichean 'Marxist', for example, a theory identified as 'bourgeois' is assumed to be cognitively empty by virtue of the blanket condemnation which that identification carries. This is silly stuff. Marx may have said, in effect, that philosophers' interpretations don't change the world[22] (a point also made by Ludwig Wittgenstein). He did not, however, say that critical analyses and prescriptions should be regarded as immune from the requirements of philosophical adequacy.

Historical materialism, as Assiter asserts (text 12), is not a philosophy. 'Marxism' still less so. It also needs to be recognized that historical-materialist and Marxist cultural theory is largely based on interpretations of and extrapolations from a body of work primarily addressed to the economic sphere. Marx offered no theory of art, though there has been no lack of subsequent volunteers to debate

'Marxist art theory'. He did sometimes seem to puzzle over the problems apparently posed by art for the materialist thesis.[23] Historical materialism is certainly compatible with those forms of causal analysis for which we are concerned to argue. Such analysis is always liable to misidentify its object, however, or to track arbitrary pathways through any potential constellation of conditions, if it is not constrained by some theoretical conditions of relevance. The problem seems to be on the one hand how to avoid that confusion of ratification with explanation which is common to the weaker derivatives of Modernist history and criticism (and, for example, endemic to the 'monograph'), and on the other how to avoid that proliferation of 'contextual' detail and innuendo which characterizes certain earnest endeavours and economistic 'exposés' in some enterprises associated with the social history of art.

We have argued for the need for examination of certain concepts. Logical and linguistic analysis in the Anglo-Saxon philosophical tradition provides the conventional tools for such work, and we see no reason to reject them. They are required for a critique of the *theoretical power* of Modernism, and we need to use them alongside those forms of historical-materialist analysis which avail us of a critique of Modernism's *non-cognitive agency*. 'Not Marx *or* Wittgenstein, but Marx *and* Wittgenstein', to paraphrase an early Art & Language slogan (and this is not to assume that we can forget the uncomfortable legacies of Freud's 'critique of the etiology of civilization' or of Nietzsche's commentaries on the history of culture[24]). We opened this introduction with a quotation in which the concepts of skill, interest, representation and knowledge were conjoined, and we have suggested that Modernist criticism and art history impose strategic restrictions upon the interpretation of such concepts. The answer to the first part of the above problem seems to be to address these closures as they can be seen to operate in the dominant discourse, to *explain* them, and to relax them where possible by recourse to more open forms of inquiry and explanation in which relevant concepts are employed and discussed. The examination of changes in representational systems, for example, is pursued in the philosophy of science (see Hanson, text 8, and Kuhn text 21) with due respect for the importance of empirical test and observation, but without the need for that commitment to empiricistic notions of 'style' which cripples the history of art. On the subject of representation, we would see it as confirmation of the methodological interest of the work of Ivins (for all his casualness about certain historical conditions; see text 13) and of Gombrich's *Art and Illusion*[25] that they are also of interest to the general epistemological inquiries of Barnes (see text 11). Not much work has yet been done in the history and theory of art which can be said to have been accorded a similar validation. This seems surprising given the role in learning played by our visual faculties, and given also the status of works of art as complex testaments to the skills and interests of visual representation.

The second part of the problem—how to establish strong conditions of relevance in inquiry into and explanation of works of art—is perhaps harder to address. One important suggestion may be derived from Chomsky's work on language (see texts 10 and 24). Recognition of the genetic, biological and epistemological limits on human cognitive capacities imposes conditions of relevance on any explanation of the supposed realization of those capacities. We do *want* to be able to talk about 'creativity', but only so long as we can do so without presupposing either a sect of artistic beings with no basic biological needs or limitations, or some type of primitive intuition necessarily opaque to all rational epistemological, psychological or historical inquiry. (Nor can we assent to a concept of the creative which is categorically distinguished from the critical, even if it follows that we cannot then comfortably restrict the objects and practices over which they must range. It will have to be acknowledged, that is to say, that 'the art which has proved most interesting' is not itself a secure or sufficient interest.)

If we think of fifteenth-century Italy or sixteenth-century Holland or even late eighteenth- and early nineteenth-century England we might be able to see how assessments of merit or 'originality' in art could have been made more or less compatible with a rational and natural-scientific interest in the world. There has been a shift since then towards empiricist rather than rationalist concepts of experience and knowledge, and towards evaluation with respect to a psychological and/or sociological interest in ourselves and our species. A self-conscious confusion in concepts of Nature can be perceived in late nineteenth-century French art and criticism. Mallarmé, for instance, wrote of nature 'revealing herself' through 'new and impersonal men placed directly in communion with the sentiment of their time'.[26] We don't advocate any surrender of the gains of empiricism in combatting superstitious beliefs, but nor do we recommend subjugation either to the concept of the artist as a medium for what cannot be independently considered, or to a concept of the viewing subject as a malleable construct of social forces. Consideration of both the production and the experience of art needs to be as rational as it can be.

It may be that there is indeed some actual and independent quantity or property realized in some relationships between the conditions of production of a work of art and the conditions of response of some observers (though neither 'work of art' nor 'observer' is an easily circumscribed concept). It may also be that this is what the concept of 'aesthetic quality' has sometimes referred to. We would say that relevance to the intuition (or even to the possibility) of this independent quantity or property is properly to be taken as a constraining condition on all explanation and interpretation of works of art—social, historical, critical or whatever; and this because that intuition, that possibility, of actuality and independence, is after all what is most difficult and therefore most *interesting* about art. It may be thought—for instance by those who notice our reluctance to talk of 'quality' in direct speech—that our ambition is to strip art of some necessary mystery. The opposite is the case. What can be explained and understood ought to be explained and understood, albeit no explanation is ever sufficient and no understanding ever secure. Closures protect *mystiques*. If 'mysteries' can be explained they are no longer mysteries, and that's that. But they remain mysteries, if they do, by virtue of their capacity to elude *open* inquiry. The problem with the concept of 'quality' lies in the opportunities its use provides. In the sphere of culture the ground of mysteries is all too easily appropriated by those empowered to *enclose* what they can't explain.

Of one thing we are sure. Neither the actual independence nor the mysteries of art are relative to the arbitration of matters of abstraction and figuration, or of expressiveness and descriptiveness (see Goodman, text 16), or to simple judgements of political or moral content or purport. It does seem as if the independent cognitive functions of art itself have become relatively restricted and that this condition might be causally related to some diagnosis of social and historical conditions. But of this we cannot be sure so long as it is a condition of criticism and interpretation that those cognitive functions are systematically misrepresented and undervalued. We don't know what is to be known from art. This circumstance can be addressed in sustained critical activity which yet acknowledges the implausibility of any secure foundations for knowledge. It will not be overcome, however, by wishful thinking, by the privileging of false beliefs, by a self-serving relativism or by the parading of sensibility. Ironically, perhaps, the Modernist claim for the disinterestedness of intuition and of aesthetic judgement is worth considering at least for its *corrective* value, so long as it is itself open to causal explanation. We may have need of it so long as people go on reading *in* to works of art the morals and meanings they are anxious to find in themselves or in the world.

The majority of the following articles and extracts have been abbreviated as appropriate to the overall themes and purposes of this collection. Substantial excisions are marked [. . .]. Minor excisions which leave the flow of the text unchanged are marked . . . Specific details of the editing of individual texts, together with bibliographical information, will be found at the foot of the relevant introductory discussions.

Notes

1 Based on notes of a lecture given to the Fabian Society, printed in Roger Fry, *Vision and Design* (Chatto & Windus, London, 1920) pp. 1–15.

2 For a historical selection of writing in this tradition, see F. Frascina and C. Harrison (eds), *Modern Art and Modernism: A Critical Anthology* (Harper & Row, London, 1982).

3 See Clement Greenberg, *Art and Culture: Critical Essays* (Beacon Press, Boston, 1961).

4 See Greenberg, 'Modernist Painting', first published in *Arts Yearbook,* (New York, 1961); reprinted in Frascina and Harrison, 1982.

5 Michael Fried was largely responsible for pursuing this implication of Greenberg's reductive theory of Modernism. The concepts of an art which addresses itself 'to eyesight alone' and of relative 'opticality' as a measure of development in Modernism are most militantly employed in the former's criticism of the mid to late 1960s, as published in the journal *Artforum.* See also Fried's *Three American Painters: Kenneth Noland, Jules Olitski, Frank Stella* (Fogg Art Museum, Harvard University, Cambridge, Mass., 1965).

6 See, for instance, Karl Popper, *The Logic of Scientific Discovery* (Hutchinson, London, 1959; Basic Books, New York, 1959).

7 Greenberg's theorizing developed from an early interest in the revolutionary nature of avant-garde art and literature to an identification of avant-gardism with 'major quality'. In his 1940 essay 'Towards a Newer Laocöon' (*Partisan Review,* II: 4, July–August) he wrote that 'purity in art consists in the acceptance, willing acceptance of the limitations of the medium of the specific art.' He has recently said of this article, 'I was too short and dogmatic in my apotheosizing of the abstract without emphasizing that I was focussing on the major *alone*' (Trish Evans (ed), 'A Conversation with Clement Greenberg Part II', *Art Monthly,* 74, London, March 1984, p. 14). For a contextualized discussion of Greenberg's earlier theoretical writings see Fred Orton and Griselda Pollock, '*Avant-Gardes* and Partisans Reviewed', *Art History,* 4: 4, September 1981, pp. 305–327.

8 See Greenberg, 'Avant-Garde and Kitsch', *Partisan Review,* VI: 6, Fall 1939, pp. 24–29; reprinted in Greenberg, 1961. The concepts of 'vanguardism' and 'kitsch' had been used by Ernst Bloch in his essay 'Discussing Expressionism', addressed in opposition to the ideas of Georg Lukács and published in *Das Wort,* 1938. Greenberg's essay may have been written in awareness of the debate on Expressionism, Realism and popular art recently conducted in *Das Wort.* For an English translation of Bloch's text and of Lukács' response, see *Aesthetics and Politics: Debates between Bloch, Lukács, Brecht, Benjamin, Adorno* (New Left Books, London, 1977).

9 Concepts of Modernism are not easily transferrable across the critical discourses of different art forms. An 'Anti-Modernist' phase in English literature, for instance, is associated by David Lodge with such writers as George Orwell in the 1930s. It may be relevant to note that in 1940 Greenberg implicitly claimed a role for visual art as 'the dominant art form' and suggested that 'when it happens that a single art is given the dominant role, it becomes the prototype of all art: the others try to shed their proper characters and imitate its effects' ('Towards a Newer Laocöon', loc. cit., p. 297). Announcements of 'Post-Modernist' phases in art did not really commence until the mid-1960s, when they can perhaps be timed as responses to the publication of Greenberg's 'Modernist Painting' in 1961, offering as this did the first articulate and theorized exposition of artistic Modernism as such. It has been a recurrent feature of subsequent claims to 'Post-Modernist' status that foregoing phases of 'Post-Modernism' are incorporated among the supposedly transcended models.

10 In fairness to Fry it should be acknowledged that the specific reference of his terminology is made quite clear within the context of his article. In taking one assertion out of context we have to some extent served the ends of our argument. This procedure can be defended on two grounds. (1) Fry was writing in support of the thesis that the 'special spiritual activity of art [is] determined much more by its own internal forces—and by the readjustment within it, of its own forces—than by external forces'; ie he assumed a basically constant and transcendental 'spiritual activity' irrespective of changes in representational *functions* (which must be largely contingent upon 'external forces'). (2) In observing the confusion of agency (power and effectiveness) with adequacy in Modernist theories and procedures, we mean to draw attention to the tendency for specific influential critical responses to prescribe the grounds

for 'spiritual activity' or 'aesthetic contemplation' in general.

11 See Evans (ed), 'A Conversation with Clement Greenberg', *Art Monthly,* 73, London, February 1984, p. 8: '. . . if you're going to deal with the past you have to see some logic in the way one event follows another . . .'; and, 'Consensus of taste decides . . . What the people who've seen most, read most, heard most—and who've worked most on what they've seen, read, heard—decide in the way of value judgements proves in the long run to be right.'

12 'Abstract, Representational and so forth', version of a lecture of 1954, published in Greenberg, 1961, p. 133.

13 For a consideration of this issue with respect to the history of abstract art, see Charles Harrison, 'The Ratification of Abstract Art', in M. Compton (ed), *Towards a New Art: Essays on the Background to Abstract Art 1910–20* (The Tate Gallery, London, 1980) pp. 146–155.

14 In this connection, consider the prescription for a 'strong programme' in the sociology of knowledge, as given in D. Bloor, *Knowledge and Social Imagery* (Routledge & Keegan Paul, London, Henley and Boston, 1976) pp. 4–5.

(i) It would be causal, that is, concerned with the conditions which bring about belief or states of knowledge. Naturally there will be other types of causes apart from social ones which will co-operate in bringing about belief.

(ii) It would be impartial with respect to truth and falsity, rationality or irrationality, success or failure. Both sides of these dichotomies will require explanation.

(iii) It would be symmetrical in its style of explanation. The same types of cause would explain, say, true and false beliefs.

(iv) It would be reflexive. In principle its patterns of explanation would have to be applicable to sociology itself. Like the requirement of symmetry this is a response to the need to seek for general explanations. It is an obvious requirement of principle because otherwise sociology would be a standing refutation of its own theories.

In citing Bloor's 'four tenets' we do not intend to suggest that the problems of art are to be subsumed under the sociology of knowledge.

15 We give some relevant publications and dates, with first English-language editions in parentheses. Saussure: *Course in General Linguistics* (post-humously compiled from notes of lectures given 1907–11), 1915 (New York 1959, London 1960). Barthes: *Writing Degree Zero,* 1953 (1967); *Mythologies,* 1957 (1972); *Elements of Semiology,* 1964 (1967); 'The Rhetoric of the Image', 1964 (1971); *S/Z,* 1970 (1975). Althusser: 'On the Young Marx', 1961 (1969, in *For Marx*); 'Contradiction and overdetermination', 1962 (1969, in *For Marx*); 'Freud and Lacan', 1964 (1971 in *Lenin and Philosophy and Other Essays*); 'Marxism and humanism', 1964 (1969 in *For Marx); For Marx,* 1966 (1969). Lacan: 'The mirror-phase as formative of the function of the "I" ', 1949 (1968); *Ecrits,* 1966 (1977, a selection); *The Four Fundamental Concepts of Psychoanalysis,* 1973 (1977). Lévi-Strauss: *Structural Anthropology,* 1958 (1968); *The Savage Mind,* 1962 (1966); *The Raw and the Cooked,* 1964 (1970). Foucault: *The Order of Things,* 1966 (1970); *The Archaeology of Knowledge,* 1969 (1972); 'What

is an Author?', 1969 (1979). Compilations, guides and introductions proliferated in the early 1970s, among them: Ehrmann (ed), *Structuralism* (New York, 1970, reprint of a special edition of *Yale French Studies,* 36–37, 1966); Lane (ed), *Structuralism: A Reader* (London, 1970); Piaget, *Structuralism* (London, 1971, translated from French text of 1968); Robey (ed), *Structuralism: An Introduction* (Oxford, 1973). English-language journals publishing relevant material included *Twentieth-Century Studies* (University of Kent at Canterbury), 1970 and 1972; *Working Papers in Cultural Studies* (University of Birmingham), 1971–2; *Screen,* 1973; *Times Literary Supplement,* 1973. Jameson, *The Prison-House of Language: A Critical Account of Structuralism and Russian Formalism* (Princeton and London, 1972) represented an early critical reaction from the English-speaking Marxist left. It might be said that to talk of a continuous tradition in terms of the various names we have cited is to ride rough-shod over the supposed distinction between 'Structuralism' and 'Post-Structuralism'.

16 For a sensible account of this issue see Jorge Larrain, *Marxism and Ideology* (Macmillan, London, 1983). For an exuberant critique of Althusser see E. P. Thompson, 'The Poverty of Theory' in *The Poverty of Theory and Other Essays* (Merlin Press, London, 1978) pp. 192–397. It needs to be acknowledged that for Gramsci and Althusser respectively, the job in hand was largely one of opposition to and revision of Stalinist interpretations of Marx's determinism.

17 Louis Althusser, 'Ideology and Ideological State Apparatuses (Notes towards an Investigation)', in *Lenin and Philosophy and Other Essays* (London, New Left Books, 1971) p. 172.

18 Althusser, loc. cit., pp. 151–2.

19 Rosalind Coward and John Ellis, *Language and Materialism: Developments in Semiology and the Theory of the Subject* (Routledge & Kegan Paul, London, Henley and Boston, 1977) p. 69.

20 Coward and Ellis, 1977, p. 36 and p. 35.

21 Jonathan Rée, 'Marxist Modes', *Radical Philosophy,* 23, Winter 1979, p. 2. This article was written as a sustained—and vivid—critique of Coward and Ellis, 1977.

22 'The philosophers have only *interpreted* the world differently, the point is, to *change* it.' Karl Marx and Friedrich Engels, 'Theses on Feuerbach', XI, in *The German Ideology* (International Publishers, New York, 1968) p. 199.

23 See, for instance, the notorious discussion of Greek art and epic poetry and the unsatisfactory answer Marx gives to the 'difficulty' that 'they still give us aesthetic pleasure and are in certain respects regarded as a standard and unattainable ideal', in Karl Marx, *A Contribution to the Critique of Political Economy* (Lawrence & Wishart, London, 1971) pp. 215–217.

24 J. P. Stern, *Nietzsche* (Fontana, London, 1978) p. 17. Of Nietzsche, Marx and Freud, Stern writes that their 'standing as modern masters is undisputed: had they not lived the life of modern Europe would be different ... the influence of their speculative thinking touches on every aspect of our experience' (p. 13).

25 E. H. Gombrich, *Art and Illusion: A study in the Psychology of Pictorial Representation* (Phaidon Press, London, 1960).

26 Stéphane Mallarmé, 'The Impressionists and Edouard Manet', *Art Monthly,* 1: 9, London, 1876; reprinted in Frascina and Harrison, 1982, p. 43.

I
AESTHETICS AND SENSIBILITY

1   Complaints of an Art Critic

Clement Greenberg

Since the 1940s Clement Greenberg has been the most important critic associated with the dominant exposition of Modernist art. This exposition rests upon three basic tenets: (1) that the development of Modernist art is characterized by a self-critical and self-defining tendency in each of its forms; (2) that this tendency is inexorable, at least as regards 'major' art; (3) that judgements of quality in art are disinterested and involuntary, whether made by critics or by artists in respect of their own work. These three tenets are mutually implicated. If aesthetic judgement is the disinterested recognition of quality, the Modernist critic's set of aesthetic judgements will simply pick out the 'major' works and artists over a given period. In then connecting these in terms of an observed tendency, Greenberg can claim merely to be identifying what happens to be or have been the case. It was necessarily so, he claims. The evidence for that necessity is the observable tendency which connects all that is presented to judgement as 'major' modern art. The confirmation that what he identifies as major is major—ie the evidence for the disinterestedness of his judgement—is that an 'inexorable' tendency connects it. His response is represented as intuitive and ungoverned by theory. He will thus see himself as proof against accusations that he is engaged on the assembly of evidence in support of any a priori assumptions, beliefs, hypotheses or sets of preferences.

In the article which follows, Greenberg seeks to defend himself against just such accusations. He draws particular attention to those aspects of art which are 'impervious to discursive thinking' (and thus to rational explanation). Response to 'quality', for Greenberg, is response to just these aspects which are, for him, the identifying conditions of art. According to this view art is recognized as such in terms of its effect, where the relevant type of effect is intuitive and beyond rational specification. There is a legacy here from the Italian aesthetician Benedetto Croce (discussed in text 4), for whom works of art, in Beryl Lake's paraphrase, 'are not physical objects at all . . . but exist in the minds of all who truly appreciate them'. In so far as this legacy has a determining effect upon

3

Greenberg's ideas about art, these ideas will be subject to the critique which Lake offers of Croce's aesthetic theories.

In defending himself against accusations of 'formalism', however, Greenberg has a reasoned case to offer. In concentrating upon the effect of works of art, and in asserting that 'content' is not to be prised apart from 'form' in discussion both of 'quality' and of 'effect', he identifies himself rather with the dominant Western tradition in criticism of the modern arts, which is first and foremost addressed to the idea of art as expression.

Source: *Artforum* vol. VI no. 2, New York, October, 1967, pp. 38–39. (Series: Problems of Criticism). Reprinted by permission of the author.

I

Esthetic judgments are given and contained in the immediate experience of art. They coincide with it; they are not arrived at afterwards through reflection or thought. Esthetic judgments are also involuntary: you can no more choose whether or not to like a work of art than you can choose to have sugar taste sweet or lemons sour. (Whether or not esthetic judgments are honestly reported is another matter.)

Because esthetic judgments are immediate, intuitive, undeliberate, and involuntary, they leave no room for the conscious application of standards, criteria, rules, or precepts. That qualitative principles or norms are there somewhere, in subliminal operation, is certain; otherwise esthetic judgments would be purely subjective, and that they are not is shown by the fact that the verdicts of those who care most about art and pay it the most attention converge over the course of time to form a consensus. Yet these objective qualitative principles, such as they are, remain hidden from discursive consciousness: they cannot be defined or exhibited. This is why such a thing as a position or standpoint cannot be maintained in the judging of art. A position, a point of view, depends on definable or exhibitable qualitative criteria, and the entire experience of art shows that there are none. Art can get away with anything because there is nothing to tell us what it cannot get away with—and there is nothing to tell us what it cannot get away with because art has, and does, get away with anything.

Of all the imputations to which this art critic has been exposed, the one he minds most is that his esthetic judgments go according to a position or 'line'. There are various reasons for this imputation, not least among them being, I suppose, the flat, declarative way in which he tends to write. But there is also a general reluctance, or even inability, to read closely, and an equally general tendency to assign motives. The only way to cope with this is the tedious one of disclaiming explicitly and repeatedly all the things you, the writer, are not actually saying or implying. And maybe in addition to that you have to call attention repeatedly to the rules of inference. And also pause to give little lessons in elementary esthetics, like the one I have just recited.

To impute a position or line to a critic is to want, in effect, to limit his freedom. For a precious freedom lies in the very involuntariness of esthetic judging: the freedom to be surprised, taken aback, have your expectations confounded, the freedom to be inconsistent and to like anything in art as long as it is good—the freedom, in short, to let art stay open. Part of the excitement of art, for those who attend to art regularly, consists, or should, in this openness, in this inability to foresee reactions. You don't expect to like the busyness of Hindu sculpture, but on closer acquaintance become enthralled by it (to the point even of preferring it to the earlier Buddhist carving). You don't, in 1950, anticipate anything generically new in geometrical-looking abstract painting, but then see Barnett Newman's first show. You think you know the limits of nineteenth-century academic art, but then come across Stobbaerts in Belgium, Etty and Dyce in England, Hayez in Italy, Waldmueller in Austria, and still others. The very best art of this time continues to be abstract, but the evidence compels you to recognize that below this uppermost level success is achieved, still, by a far higher proportion of figurative than of abstract painting. When jurying you find yourself having to throw out high-powered-looking abstract pictures and keeping in trite-looking landscapes and flower pieces. Despite certain qualms, you relish your helplessness in the matter, you relish the fact that in art things happen of their own accord and not yours, that you have to like things you don't want to like, and dislike things you do want to like. You acquire an appetite not just for the disconcerting but for the state of being disconcerted.

This does not mean that the situation of art at any moment is one of disorder. Time and place always impose a certain kind of order in the form of negative probabilities. Thus it appears unlikely that illusionist painting will be any more capable in the near future than in the recent past of creating truly major art. But the critic cannot proceed *confidently* on this probability, and least of all can he have a *stake* in it, so that he will be embarrassed or disappointed if it should chance to be violated (which it happens to be my very private prejudice to want to see happen). You cannot legitimately want or hope for anything from art except quality. And you cannot lay down conditions for quality. However and wherever it turns up, you have to accept it. You have your prejudices, your leanings and inclinations, but you are under the obligation to recognize them as that and keep them from interfering.

Art has its history as a sheer phenomenon, and it also has its history as quality. Order and logic can be discerned in both, and there is nothing illegitimate in the effort to discern them. But it is illegitimate to believe in, advocate, and prescribe such order and logic as you discern, and another frequent imputation this writer minds is that he is *for* the order and logic *he* discerns. Because he has seen 'purity' (which he always puts between quotes) and 'reduction' as part of the immanent logic of modernist art, he is taken to believe in and advocate 'purity' and 'reduction'. As if 'purity', however useful it may have been as an illusion, were anything more than an illusion in his eyes, and as if he ever wrote anything to indicate otherwise. Because this writer has dwelled on the fact that the most original sculpture of the recent past opens up the monolith in a radical way, he is also taken to be for 'open' sculpture and against the monolithic kind. Yet there is nothing in what he has written that can be interpreted as even implying this. That analysis and description without anything more should so often be inferred to be a program reveals something like bad faith on the part of those who do such inferring—not just laziness, obtuseness, or illiteracy. I can't help thinking this. The bad faith derives from the need to pin a critic down so that you can say, when you disagree with him, that he has motives, that he likes this and not that work of art because he wants to, or because his program forces him to, not because his mere ungovernable taste won't let him do otherwise.

Last and worst, however, is that most art-lovers do not believe there actually is such a thing as ungovernable taste. It is taken for granted that esthetic judgments are voluntary. This is why disagreements about art, music, literature so 'naturally' become personal and rancorous. This is why positions and lines and programs are brought in. But it is one thing to have an esthetic judgment or re-action, another thing to report it. The dishonest reporting of esthetic experience is what does most to accustom us to the notion that esthetic judgments are voluntary. Not only are you ashamed to say that a Norman Rockwell may move you more than a Raphael does (which can happen); you are also afraid simply to sound inconsistent—this because it is also taken for granted that esthetic judgments are rational as well as voluntary, that they are weighed and pondered. Yet rational conclusions can no more be chosen than esthetic ones can. Thus even if esthetic judgments could be arrived at through ratiocination, they would still be in-voluntary—as involuntary as one's acceptance of the fact that 2 plus 2 equals 4.

II

The only definition of 'formalism' with regard to art that my unabridged Webster gives is: 'Emphatic or predominant attention to arrangement *esp.* to prescribed or traditional rules of composition, in painting and sculpture.' My impression is that the word acquired its present broader, and different, meaning when it became the name of an avant-garde Russian literary movement of the time of the First World War that proclaimed 'form' as the main thing in verse and prose. Soon afterwards it became another of the 'isms' in the Bolshevik lexicon of abuse, where it means modernist and avant-garde art and literature in general. Whatever its connotations in Russian, the term has acquired ineradicably vulgar ones in English. This is why I was surprised to see it come into currency not so long ago in American art writing. No proper literary critic would dream of using it. More recently certain artists have been referred to as belonging to a 'formalist' school for no other reason than their having been championed by certain critics whom some other critics call 'formalist'. This is vulgarity with a vengeance.

One reason among others why the use of the term 'formalism' is stultifying is that it begs a large part of the very difficult question as to just what can be sensibly said about works of art. It assumes that 'form' and 'content' in art can be adequately distinguished for the purposes of discourse. This implies in turn that discursive thought has solved just those problems of art upon whose imperviousness to discursive thinking the very possibility of art depends.

Reflection shows that anything in a work of art that can be talked about or pointed to automatically excludes itself from the 'content' of the work, from its import, tenor, gist, or 'meaning' (all of which terms are but so many stabs at a generic term for what works of art are ultimately 'about'). Anything in a work of art that does not belong to its 'content' has to belong to its 'form'—if the latter term means anything at all in this context. In itself 'content' remains indefinable, unparaphraseable, undiscussable. Whatever Dante or Tolstoy, Bach or Mozart, Giotto or David intended his art to be about, or said it was about, the works of his art go beyond anything specifiable in their effect. That is what art, regardless of the intention of artists, *has* to do, even the worst art; the unspecifiability of its 'content' is what constitutes art as art.

All this has been said before, and there is no getting around it. Nor is there anything mystical about it. What has also been said before, but maybe not emphatically enough, is that the quality of a work of art inheres in its 'content', and vice versa. Quality is 'content'. You know that a work of art has content because of its effect. The more direct denotation of effect is 'quality'. Why bother to say that a Velasquez has 'more content' than a Salvador Rosa when you can say more simply, and with directer reference to the experience you are talking about, that the Velasquez is 'better' than the Salvador Rosa? You cannot say anything truly relevant about the content of either picture, but you can be specific and relevant about the difference in their effect on you. 'Effect' like 'quality', is 'content', and the closer reference to actual experience of the first two terms makes 'content' virtually useless for criticism.

There are different kinds of anti-'formalism'. I am not sure but that those more ambitious critics who try to deal with 'content' in abstract as well as representational art are not less sophisticated intellectually than those whose anti-'formalism' compels them to deprecate abstract art in general. To say that Pollock's 'all-over' art reflects the leveling tendencies of a mass society is to say something that is ultimately indifferent in the context of art criticism—indifferent because it has nothing to do with Pollock's quality. To say (as Robert Goldwater does) that Kline's art offers an 'image . . . of optimistic struggle of an entirely unsentimental "grace under pressure"' is to say something that is both indifferent and wanton. Good art is by definition unsentimental, and of what good art can it be said, moreover, that it does not show grace under pressure? And if I choose to feel that Kline is pessimistic rather than optimistic, who can say me nay? Where is the evidence on the basis of which Dr Goldwater and I can argue about that? There is not even the evidence of taste. For you do not have to be able to *see* painting in order to say or not say that Kline's art shows either optimism or pessimism. I, who am considered an arch-'formalist', used to indulge in that kind of talk about 'content' myself. If I do not do so any longer it is because it came to me, dismayingly, some years ago that I could always assert the opposite of whatever it was I did say about 'content' and not get found out; that I could say almost anything I pleased about 'content' and sound plausible.

The anti-'formalist' whom I regard as more intellectually sophisticated concedes the case of abstract art but accuses the 'formalist' of neglecting the crucial importance to pictorial and sculptural art, when it is representational, of the illustrated subject, whether as 'form' or 'content'. I myself, as a reputed 'formalist', would deny this charge. It is quite evident that the illustrated subject—

or let's say 'literature'—can play, does, and has played, a crucial part in figural art. Photography (which my experience tells me is not necessarily inferior to painting in its capacity for art) achieves its highest qualities by 'story-telling'. Nonetheless, it remains peculiarly difficult to talk with relevance about the literary factor in painting or sculpture.

The meaning of an illustrated subject *qua* subject—the prettiness, say, of a girl, her coloring, her expression, her attitude, etc, etc—delivers itself to any eye, not just the one attuned to pictorial or sculptural art. The person who cannot tell the qualitative difference between a portrait by Ingres and one on the cover of *Time* perceives just as much of the subject *qua* subject as the person who can. Iconography is brilliantly practiced by people largely blind to the non-literary aspects of art. It does seem that literary meaning as such seldom decides the qualitative difference between one painting or sculpture and another. Yet I say 'seem' advisedly. For at the same time the illustrated subject can no more be thought away, or 'seen away', from a picture than anything else in it can. The thing imaged does, somehow, impregnate the effect no matter how indifferent you may be to it. The problem is to show something of how this happens, and that is what I cannot remember having seen any art writer do with real relevance—with relevance to the quality of the effect. And I notice that even those fellow-critics who nowadays complain most about 'formalism' will again and again in the showdown fall back on 'formalism' themselves because otherwise they find themselves condemned to repeat commonplaces or irrelevancies.

The art of Edvard Munch is a case in point. I know of nothing in art that affects me in anything like the way that his 'literature' does. Yet the purely pictorial impact of his art (leaving his drawings and prints aside) remains something else, something less. His paintings, as successful as many of them are in their own pictorial terms, do not startle my eyes again and again the way great paintings do. Compared, say, with Matisse, Munch never looks more than minor. How then does his illustration manage to carry so strongly and convey so intensely? I wish some non-'formalist' critic would enlighten me here, if only a little bit. I am eager to be instructed by example.

I am all the readier to be instructed by an example of this kind because it is otherwise so much easier to deal in words with literary considerations than with 'abstract' or 'formal' ones. It is easier to write plausible literary criticism than plausible art criticism. You can write at length about the questions raised by the kind of life depicted in an indifferent novel or even poem, and whether or not you make a contribution to general wisdom, the chances are that your failure to deal with the novel or poem as art won't be noticed. Ruskin, murmuring at a picture he otherwise liked, because it showed children drinking wine, would not sound half so silly were it a piece of fiction he was talking about. Not that literary critics, properly speaking, get away with their irrelevance in the long run. But men of letters do, and so do iconographers. Nor do I object to this—as long as men of letters and iconographers do not claim to be critics.

2   The Work of Art as Object

Richard Wollheim

Wollheim, author of Art and its Objects *(1968), writes as a philosopher interested in aesthetics, psychology and modern art. His argument in the following text starts from the observation that 'in the making of art a concept enters into, and plays a crucial role in, the determination of what is made'. He seeks to characterize what he terms 'the dominant theory' at work in modern art by identifying those concepts which appear to determine modern artistic practice. His measure of the adequacy of any such characterization (for example a piece of art criticism) is that 'in it the concepts that have helped fashion the work reappear'. In the activity of art a range of concepts will be involved, and these will form a certain hierarchy. Though, in Wollheim's view, 'the relations that hold within a given set of concepts are timeless' (for example the relations between 'painting', 'representation of light' and 'spotting of the canvas'), 'these relations can at different periods or under different conditions be thought or felt to change, largely because the concepts themselves can be differently experienced'.*

What Wollheim has in mind is that a painter, for instance, might under certain conditions so perceive the relations between 'painting' and 'spotting of the canvas' that in order to produce something which counted as a painting at all *he or she would feel required to work the surface of the canvas with small even touches of paint. What would then be required of adequate criticism would be that the conceptual importance of such technical features and concerns should be understood and represented as determining upon the concept of painting. (The example might be seen as referring to the later phases of Impressionism in France during the last quarter of the nineteenth century.)*

The account which Wollheim proceeds to give of the 'conceptual hierarchy' of modern art is one compatible with the findings of Modernist criticism, with the judgements of Clement Greenberg in particular, and with the work of Greenberg's follower Michael Fried. It should be noted that Wollheim is not concerned to explain *how or why shifts take place in a conceptual hierarchy.*

9

(For a text which is concerned with such explanation, see the excerpt from Kuhn, text 21.) It should also be noted that Wollheim's apparent means of testing and confirming his identification of the 'dominant theory' is compatible with the means by which Greenberg tests and confirms his account of the dominant tendency of modern painting (this notwithstanding Greenberg's assertion elsewhere that 'art is a matter strictly of experience, not of principles'): ie by means of an assertion of value, as expressed in the concluding paragraph of the following text. In both Greenberg's and Wollheim's cases the judgement of aesthetic merit is represented as an ineluctable confirmation of a certain view of art, ungoverned by any a priori assumptions or beliefs which holding to that view might be thought to imply.

Various possible critical positions in respect of Wollheim's argument are represented in this anthology. Following Lake (text 4) we might ask whether the judgement of aesthetic merit can be considered an empirical test. We might also ask (pace MacIntyre, text 5) whether the 'theory' might not rather be considered as an irrefutable rationalization of preference. In the latter case the objection, 'But the art I most admire doesn't conform to the theory', would be likely to be countered by Greenberg or Wollheim with disqualification of the objector's taste. Wollheim's means of identification of 'expressive quality' (for example in his concluding account of Rothko's painting) might also be critically considered in the light of the causal account of expression in Art & Language's 'Abstract Expression' (text 18). From another point of view Wollheim's measure of the adequacy of critical descriptions of art might be considered in relation to Baxandall's notion of a 'period cognitive style' (text 14). Can we justifiably identify Greenberg and Wollheim, for instance, as possessing the individual knowledge and skills of interpretation, the categories and model patterns, the training in a range of representational conventions, and the experience distinctively appropriate to modern art, and thus as exemplifying a socially significant match between 'pictorial skills' and 'visual skills'?

Source: *On Art and the Mind* (Harvard University Press, 1973), pp. 112–119. An earlier version of this paper was published in *Studio International* vol. 180, no. 928, London, December, 1970. This material has been edited by the author and is reprinted by permission of the author and Harvard University Press.

If we wanted to say something about art that we could be quite certain was true, we might settle for the assertion that art is intentional. And by this we would mean that art is something we do, that works of art are things that human beings make. And the truth of this assertion is in no way challenged by such discoveries, some long known, others freshly brought to light, as that we cannot produce a work of art to order, that improvisation has its place in the making of a work of art, that the artist is not necessarily the best interpreter of his work, that the spectator too has a legitimate role to play in the organization of what he perceives. [. . .]

Though much is unclear about the notion of activity, one thing seems clear. From the fact that art is something that we do, it follows that in the making of art a concept enters into, and plays a crucial role in, the determination of what is made: or, to put it another way, that when we make a work of art, we make it under a certain description—though, of course, unless our attention is drawn to the question, we may not be in a position to give the description. Indeed [. . .] the truth seems to me to be that, on any given occasion, or in the case of any given work, there will be more than one concept involved, and the concepts that are involved will form some kind of hierarchy, with some concepts falling under others, either more or less organized. In the existence of such a conceptual hierarchy, regulative in the production of works of art, we find, I maintain, the justification for talking of a theory of art. In this lecture I want to look at the matter rather more generally, and I shall ask you to consider with me a theory of modern art. The theory I have in mind could not be called *the* theory of modern art, for there is evidently no such thing, but I would claim that it is the dominant theory. [. . .]

My suggestion is this: that for the mainstream of modern art, we can postulate a theory that emphasizes the material character of art, a theory according to which a work of art is importantly or significantly, and not just peripherally, a physical object. Such a theory, I am suggesting, underlies or regulates much of the art activity of our age, and it is it that accounts for many of the triumphs and perhaps not a few of the disasters of modern art. Within the concept of art under which most of the finest, certainly most of the boldest, works of our age have been made, the connotation of physicality moves to the fore.

The evidence for such a theory at work is manifold, the inspiration of the theory can be seen in a wide variety of phenomena which it thereby unifies: the increasing emphasis upon texture and surface qualities; the abandonment of linear perspective, at any rate as providing an overall grid within which the picture can be organized; the predilection for large areas of undifferentiated or barely fluctuating colour; the indifference to figuration; the exploitation of the edge, of the shaped or moulded support, of the unprimed canvas; and the physical juxtaposition of disparate or borrowed elements, sometimes stuck on, sometimes freestanding, to the central body of the work, as in collage or assemblages. These devices have, beyond a shadow of a doubt, contributed decisively to the repertoire of European art since, say, 1905: and any dispute about the presence of some such theory as I have produced would, I imagine, confine itself to the issue of how central these devices, and the modifications in art that they have brought about, are thought to be.

I want therefore to turn away from any central discussion of the theory to the qualifications that need to be entered if the theory, or the formulation of it, is to be adequate. I shall bring what I have to say under three general considerations. But in doing so, I shall give the theory itself a small twist towards greater specificity. I shall consider it exclusively in relation to painting, and I shall understand it as insisting upon the surface of a painting. In the context of a painting, for 'physicality' read 'possession of a surface'.

The first consideration, is this: The theory that I have been suggesting emphasizes or insists upon the physicality of the work of art, or the surface of the painting—emphasizes or insists upon them, but (this is the point) the theory did not discover or invent them. I am not, of course, making the self-evident point that even before 1905 paintings had surfaces. I am making the somewhat less evident point that before 1905 the fact that a painting had a surface, or the more general fact that works of art were physical, were not regarded as accidental or contingent facts about art.

For to read certain critics, certain philosophers of art, even certain contemporary artists, one might well think that before the beginning of the twentieth century the concept of art was totally without any connotation of materiality. Of course—it is conceded—in making their pictures earlier artists recognized that they were making physical objects. But for them the picture and the physical object were not equated, and the manipulation of the medium was seen more as a preliminary to the process of making art rather than as that process itself. For the picture was conceived of as something immaterial that burgeoned or billowed out from the canvas, panel or frescoed wall that provided its substrate. These things—canvas, panel, wall—were necessary for its existence, but it went beyond them, and the concept of it bore no reference to them.

Such a view of the past, which is artificially sustained by the very careless and utterly misleading use of the term 'illusionism' to characterize all forms of figurative painting, indeed all forms of representational painting, seems supported neither by empirical nor by theoretical considerations. Furthermore, there is a body of evidence against it. There are various moments in the history of European painting since the high Renaissance, when artists have shown a clear predilection for the values of surface, and they have employed selected means to bring out the physical quality of what they were working on or with. Take, for instance, the emergence of the brush-stroke as an identifiable pictorial element in sixteenth-century Venetian painting; the free sketching in of landscapes in the background of seventeenth- and eighteenth-century painting; or the distinctive use of cropped figures set up against the edge of the support in late nineteenth-century Parisian art. Now, of course, there is this difference: that to the earlier paintings these devices were no more than a *possible* employment of painting, and for them the constraints of art lay elsewhere. It was, for instance, optional for Velazquez or for Gainsborough whether they expressed their predilection for the medium. What was necessary within their theory of art was that, if they did, it found expression within the depiction of natural phenomena. For, say, Matisse or Rothko, the priorities are reversed. But none of this suggests that the earlier painters thought that what they were doing was ancillary to painting. Between them and us what has happened is that some connotations of art that were previously recessive have moved to the fore, and vice versa.

The second consideration that touches upon the theory of modern art I have proposed seems to strike somewhat deeper. It is this: The theory emphasizes the physicality of art; it insists upon the fact that a painting has a surface. Indeed, by a ready trick of exaggeration the insisted-upon fact that a painting *has* a surface — a fact which, as we have seen, earlier generations did not overlook—can convert itself into the thesis that a painting *is*, or is no more than, a surface. Which gives us an extreme version of the theory, though not one unknown. However, a necessary modification is effected—once it is recognized that, in talking of a surface, the theory is irreducibly or ineliminably referring to *the surface of a painting*. In formulating the theory we can safely drop the phrase 'of a painting' only when the dropped phrase is understood. If the phrase is not merely dropped, but drops out of mind, the theory becomes incoherent. For to talk of a surface, without specifying what kind of surface it is, which means in effect what it is a surface of, picks out no kind of object of attention.

Perhaps one way of bringing out this consideration is to go back to the nature of the theory. For the theory, as we have seen, provides us, if it is adequate, with those concepts under which a certain form of art—the art of our day—has been produced. However, it is clear that no one could set himself to produce a surface, unless he had some answer to the question what it was the surface of: nor could he endeavour to accentuate or work up a surface unless, once again, he thought of himself as accentuating or working up the surface of this or that kind of thing. To put it another way round: the instruction 'Make us aware or conscious of the surface' given in the studio, would take on quite different significances, if said, to someone throwing a stoneware pot, to someone painting in oil on primed canvas, to someone carving in marble, or to someone working in fresco. (Think, for instance, whether, in conformity to the instruction, the surface should be made smooth or rough.) Each of the recipients of the instruction would, in effect, fill it out from his knowledge of what he was doing, before he obeyed it. And, if he didn't know what he was doing, if, for instance, he was a complete beginner who hadn't as yet grasped the nature of the activity on which he had launched himself, he could not obey the instruction at all. It wouldn't be, simply, that he wouldn't know how to do what he had been asked to do: he wouldn't know what he had been asked to do. For him the instruction would mean about as much as 'Make it average-sized'.

The examples I have given might be misleading in one respect: for they might suggest that the further specification that is required before it becomes clear how the surface is to be worked refers exclusively to the material. The artist, in other words, needs to know what the surface is of just in the sense of what it is made of. This, however, would be erroneous. Not merely is this no more than part of what is required, but it is misleading even as to that. The distinction we need here is that between *a material* and *a medium*. A medium may embrace a material, though it may not, but, if it does, a medium is a material worked in a characteristic way, and the characteristics of the way can be understood only in the context of the art within which the medium arises.[1] 'Fidelity to material' is not so much an inadequate aesthetic, as some have thought, it is rather an inadequate formulation of an aesthetic. Bernini and Rodin were not faithful to marble, though they may have been faithful to marble as a material of sculpture. Given this distinction, the barest specification of the surface must be by reference to the medium which makes up or is laid on the surface. [. . .]

The third consideration that I want to raise in connection with the theory of modern art is this: The theory insists upon the physicality of the work of art—

upon for instance, the surface of the painting. And this I have equally put by saying that the theory insists upon the fact that the painting has a surface. But from this it does not follow that a painting produced in conformity with this theory will insist upon the fact that it has a surface. Yet this is sometimes thought to follow both by critics and by artists: and consequential distortions are produced both in criticism—so that for instance, it is thought good enough to say of a painting that it insists upon the fact of its surface—and in art itself—so that we are confronted by objects which seek to acquire value from this insistence. [. . .]

Perhaps the best way of bringing out this consideration is to show how the theory, as it stands, can lead to anything but boring art. For the theory, in asserting that a painting has a surface, draws the painter's attention to the surface in a way or to a degree not contemplated by his predecessors. But if the theory were that the painting should assert that it has a surface, then not merely would no premium be placed on the use of the surface but the effect of the theory might well be to work against the use of the surface. For it might be felt that any such use would only interfere with the clarity or the definitiveness of the painting's assertion. The *fact* of the surface might become eclipsed, wholly or partially, by the *use* of the surface. And in an aesthetic situation where the fact of the surface is reckoned the important thing, the use of the surface begins to look diversionary at best and probably hazardous.

To talk of the use of the surface and to contrast this with the fact of the surface, and to identify the former rather than the latter as the characteristic preoccupation of modern art, attributes to modern art a complexity of concern that it cannot renounce. For it is only if we assume such a complexity that there is any sense in which we can think of the surface as being used. Used, we must ask, for what? And the answer to this has to lie in that complexity of concern.—The point, I must emphasize, would not be worth making were it not for the widespread confusion which equates the autonomy of modern art with its single-mindedness, even with its simple-mindedness. To talk of the autonomy of art is to say something about where its concerns derive from, it is to say nothing about their number or their variety.

To talk of the surface being used, rather than of its existence being asserted, as a characteristic of modern painting, is not a point to make in the abstract. The point cannot be grasped without some kind of incursion into the substantive issue. What therefore I should like to do for the rest of this lecture is to consider three paintings, and try to make the point in relation to them. It is no accident that these paintings are amongst the masterpieces of twentieth-century art.

The first painting is *La Fenêtre Ouverte* (Plate I) painted by Matisse in Tangiers in 1913. Some of the things that I shall say about it will apply to the other great open-window paintings of Matisse, for instance the sombre *La Porte-fenêtre* of 1914 or the painting entitled *La Fenêtre*, or *Le Rideau Jaune*. In this painting we discern, amongst other things, Matisse's recurrent concern with the nature of the ground. Now, if we consider what is not so much the earliest painting we have, though it is often called that, as the precursor of painting—I refer to the cave art of the early Stone Age—there is no ground, there is simply the image.[2] With the introduction of the ground, the problem arises, How are we to conceive

14

of the ground in a way that does not simply equate it with the gap between the figures or the absence of depiction? In the history of European painting we can see various answers to this question. One answer is for the painter to equate the ground with the background or, if this term is taken broadly enough, with the landscape, and then to organize the detail that this equation is likely to impose upon him in a hierarchical fashion, detail subsumed within detail, in a Chinese box-like fashion. This answer we can see as given in some of the finest achievements of European art—for instance, in such different kinds of work as the masterpieces of Van Eyck and Poussin. Another answer is to regard the ground as providing, still through representation, not so much content additional to the central figures, but a space in which the central figures are framed. Now for a variety of reasons neither of these two classic answers is open to Matisse. For Matisse—and here he exhibits two of the main thrusts of twentieth-century art— dispenses both with the notion of detail in the traditional sense and also with the commitment to a unitary and ordered spatial framework. And so the question returns, How is the ground to be conceived of except in purely negative terms? How—which is an extension of this question—is the frontier of the ground, of the line which encloses it, not to seem quite arbitrary? And it is at this point, to find an answer to this question, that Matisse resorts to the surface. It is here that he *uses* the surface. For what he does is to associate the ground so closely with the surface—by which I mean that he charges the surface in such a way that it barely involves a shift of attention for us to move from seeing a certain expanse as ground to seeing it as surface—that we fully accept the size of the surface as determining the extent of the ground. To understand Matisse's use of the surface, we might say that through it he reconciles us to the ground without our hankering after any of the classic ways of treating the ground that Matisse has forsworn.

There is perhaps another line of thought in *La Fenêtre Ouverte* which is worth pursuing. What we see through the open window is a view. Now, at any rate for a painter there is, perhaps, a certain absurdity in thinking of a view as a view on to— well, a view on to nothing, which is rather what treating what is depicted through the frame of the window as mere ground implies. The view is—of course in a rather special, one might say in a rather professional, sense—an object. And now we can see a secondary use that Matisse makes of the surface. For by emphasizing the surface where it coincides with the ground, he leads us towards this painter's way of looking at or considering the view. Of course, Matisse isn't a clumsy painter, and he avoids that use of the surface which would make it look as though the open window were filled with a solid object. It is made clear, at one and the same time, that the view isn't an object but that it is as though it were.

The second painting I want to consider is one of Morris Louis's later canvases (Plate III). Louis's work at this stage was largely dominated by one pre-occupation—apart, that is, from his interest in the physical look of the picture or how the surface looks. And this preoccupation can be described from two different points of view. From one point of view, it is a concern with colour: from another point of view it is a concern with patches—where patches are contrasted both with volumes, which are three-dimensional, and with shapes, which, though two-dimensional, are seen as suspended in, or visibly inhabit, three-dimensional space. Louis, in other words, wanted to introduce colour into the content of his paintings but to as great a degree as is humanly possible—or, better, visibly possible—he wanted consideration of the spatial relations between the coloured elements, or the bearers of colour, to recede. Now, I do not think that it is quite correct to say—as Michael Fried does in his otherwise perceptive account of these paintings[3]— that Louis's patches are non-representational: that is to say, I do not think that Louis wants us exclusively to see stained parts of the canvas. He seeks a form of representation where the representation of space or of anything spatial is at a minimum. And to achieve this effect, he uses the surface in such a way that so long as we look centrally at one of the patches we see it representationally. But, as our eyes move towards the edge of the patch, the representational element diminishes, and we become dominantly, then exclusively, aware of the canvas. In other words, representation gets negated at the very point where questions of spatiality—how does this patch stand to the next?—would begin to arise. The overall effect is that, in looking at Louis's patches, we seem aware of them as though they were embedded in, or pressed down upon, the surface—an effect, which, incidentally, we find, in a highly figurative context, in some of Goya's paintings. The surface, then, is used to control or to limit the operation of representation, so that colour can be encountered in what we might call a 'pure' mode: as predicated of extended but non-spatial elements.

The third painting that I want to consider is one of Rothko's canvases from the Four Seasons series, now hanging in the Tate (Plate II): to my mind, one of the sublimest creations of our time. In comparison with Louis, even with Matisse, Rothko uses the surface in a highly complex way. And I shall only give one hint of how we might think of this. The greatness of Rothko's painting lies ultimately, I am quite sure, in its expressive quality, and if we wanted to characterize this quality—it would be a crude characterization—we would talk of a form of suffering and of sorrow, and somehow barely or fragilely contained. We would talk perhaps of some sentiment akin to that expressed in Shakespeare's *Tempest*—I don't mean expressed in any one character, but in the play itself. However, the immediacy of Rothko's canvas derives from the way in which this expressive quality is provided with a formal counterpart: and that lies in the uncertainty that the painting is calculated to produce, whether we are to see the painting as containing an image within it or whether we are to see the painting as itself an image. Whether we are to see it as containing a ring of flame or shadow— I owe this description of the fugitive image to the brilliant description of the Four Seasons paintings by Michel Butor in his essay 'Rothko: The Mosques of New York'[4]—or whether we are to look upon it as somewhat the equivalent of a stained glass window.[5]

Now, it is to bring about this uncertainty, as well as to preserve it from, or to prevent it from degenerating into, a mere oscillation of perception, which could, if I am right, be highly inimical to Rothko's expressive purpose, that he uses the surface as he does. For the use of the surface, or the way it manifests itself to us, simultaneously suggests forms within the painting and imposes unity across the painting. It suggests light falling upon objects and light shining through a translucent plane. Wherever a definitive reading begins to form itself, the assertion of surface calls this in doubt.

It is only now, when we have taken note of other, or more working, aspects of the theory of modern art as I have suggested it, that it seems to me appropriate to observe an aspect that might have seemed to some worthy of earlier attention: I mean the way it is likely to give rise to objects that manifest the only kind of beauty we find acceptable today.

Notes

1 Stanley Cavell, *Must We Mean What We Say?* (1969)
2 On this, see Meyer Schapiro, 'On Some Problems in the Semiotics of Visual Art: Field and Vehicle in Image-Signs', *Semiotica*, vol. I, no. 3 (1969), pp. 223–42.
3 Michael Fried, *Three American Painters* (Boston, 1965), pp. 19–20.
4 Michael Butor, *Inventory,* trans. Richard Howard (London, 1970).
5 I have benefited greatly from conversations with Peter Larisey, S.J.

3   The Dreariness of Aesthetics

John Passmore

The following text offers a critique of one tendency in modern criticism and aesthetics which has persisted from earlier theorizing: the tendency towards generalization about aesthetic quality in the arts. Passmore begins his article by seeking explanation for the comparative lack of interest shown in aesthetics in the British philosophical tradition, as contrasted with the intense cultivation of the field 'in France, in Germany, in Italy, in the Americas'. He notes the tendency to regard aesthetics as 'a poor relation of ethics' and to accept 'the view that aesthetic judgements are subjective (and hence, by implication, not worth discussing, suitable only for proclamation) which contrasts oddly with the concern that morals should have some more secure foundation'.

Passmore attributes the dullness of aesthetics in part to a failure to distinguish between 'technical points', which may be settled by the application of rules (for example the question of whether or not a given poem is a sonnet) and 'formal points', which 'can only be made with difficulty, after the closest scrutiny of the specific work of art', and which involve aesthetic considerations. He finds a comparable woolliness—a desire 'to retain "mystery" rather than to dispel it'—in education, in sociology and in metaphysics, and attributes this to 'the attempt to impose a spurious unity on things, the spuriousness being reflected in the emptiness of the formulae in which that unity is described'.

Passmore notes the problem for anyone attempting to establish common features in a selection of admired works of art (his examples are Alice in Wonderland, Crime and Punishment *and* The Decline and Fall of the Roman Empire*), and, by contrast, our common-sense inclination to judge on the basis of quite distinct criteria and categories (for example a 'good thriller' may without inconsistency be judged as 'bad literature'). He takes issue with the view represented by Carritt in his* Introduction to Aesthetics, *that 'rational sensitive beings such as men have a set of experiences pretty clearly distinguishable from others', and that these experiences are 'a set of entities called "aesthetic* experiences" '. *This position, on which the possibility of aesthetic philosophy itself depends, is consistent with 'the Cartesian assumption that there is an inner world of "experiences", about whose nature we cannot be mistaken, provided only that we are reasonably careful in examining them. . .' Passmore continues, 'The outcome, as usual, is scepticism; we know our own experiences so thoroughly because they are ours, but we have no possible way of knowing other people's experiences.' Our excerpt continues from this point.*

Source: William Elton (ed.) *Aesthetics and Language* (Basil Blackwell, Oxford, 1967), pp. 48–55. Footnotes have been deleted.

[. . .] It is my view that unless we can discover properties in good works of art which are not present in bad ones, we are inevitably led into this, or some comparable, species of scepticism; and, further, that if we try to include in our theory whatever works are for any reason accounted 'good', no such properties can be found. Just at what point distinctions ought to be made is, of course, the serious question; the proof, I should say, that a distinction lies here rather than there . . . is that a particular line of fracture gives rise to interesting generalizations. If it is true . . . that no interesting generalizations (no generalizations which show us something about the distinctive properties of good literature) arise out of the study of 'literature' as the ordinary histories of literature define it; and that, on the other hand, there are interesting properties in such works as *The Brothers Karamazov, Macbeth, Tartuffe,* 'The Love Song of J. Alfred Prufrock', *Ulysses,* and other equally interesting but different properties in *Alice in Wonderland*, 'Kubla Khan', and *The Snow Maiden* then that is the only case that can be made out (and the only case that needs to be made out) in support of the distinction which I have proposed.

To try to avoid such distinctions is like trying to find characteristics common to science and to astrology, and peculiar to the pair of them as compared with other human activities. There are mechanical resemblances—both the astrologer and the scientist make calculations, for example—but these resemblances haven't the same theoretical interest as those which link physics with chemistry, and astrology with palmistry. The astrologer calls us arbitrary if we generalize about science in such a way as to exclude astrology from its ambit; and many people will be indignant if we talk about literature in such a way that *The Decline and Fall* or *Alice in Wonderland* do not have the properties we ascribe to 'good' literature. But this indignation misses the point at issue: the possibility of discovering general and distinctive properties must determine our field.

Now, even if there are things which are worth saying about 'literature' (in the sense in which we have defined it), and other things which are worth saying about music, about architecture, and so on, it still does not follow that there is such a thing as aesthetics, in distinction from literary theory, musical theory, etc; it seems to me possible at least that the dullness of aesthetics arises from the attempt to construct a subject where there isn't one. The alternatives have commonly been posed as if we had to say either that there is aesthetics or else that 'It's all a matter of personal preference', but perhaps the truth is that there is no aesthetics and yet there are principles of literary criticism, principles of musical criticism, etc. We have no real difficulty in saying what is wrong with a cheap novelette, or what is wrong with the Albert Memorial, and we can do both of these things without being dull: the dullness arises if we try to develop a general theory of 'wrongness' in art.

But surely, it may be replied, we speak of any form of art as 'beautiful' or 'ugly'—must there not be general properties which these descriptions convey? I should suggest, on the contrary, that there is something suspect ('phony') about 'beauty'. Artists seem to get along quite well without it: it is the café-haunters, the preachers, the metaphysicians, and the calendar-makers who talk of beauty. We wouldn't feel quite comfortable if we called the etchings of Goya or the engravings of Hogarth beautiful; nor would we naturally employ that word as a description of Joyce's *Ulysses* or of Moussorgsky's *Boris Goudonov*. 'Beauty' is always nice, always soothing; it is what the bourgeoisie pays the artist for; it is truth as compared with facts, goodness as compared with spontaneous creative action. In more professional circles, it is the refuge of the metaphysician finding a home for art in his harmonious universe, attempting to subdue its ferocity, its revelations of deep-seated conflict, its uncompromising disinterestedness, by ascribing to it a 'Beauty' somehow akin to goodness.

When Lessing in his *Laocöon* (Chapter 2) objects to the work of Pyreicus 'who painted, with all the diligence of a Dutch artist, nothing but barbers' shops, filthy factories, donkeys, and cabbages, as if that kind of thing had so much charm in Nature and were so rarely seen', when he demands (Chapter 24) that painting should 'confine herself solely to those visible objects which awaken agreeable sensations' or that 'one should not force expression beyond the bounds of art, but rather subject it to the first law of art, the law of Beauty' (Chapter 2), he has usage on his side. 'Why, when there is so much beauty in the world, does the artist want to paint ugly women, or the novelist depict sordid scenes?'—that is the regular complaint of the Philistine. 'Beauty,' in this sense, is clearly relative to social conventions and individual disgusts; we may attempt to purge the word for the purposes of aesthetics, but certainly we shall be cutting across the grain of usage. The subjectivists are probably right about beauty; but no consequences follow of any importance for aesthetics.

At least, though, we must allow talk about *good* literature, *good* architecture? 'That's really good' is the typical remark of artists and of critics. And it is applied equally to literature and to music, to painting, and to architecture. There's another phrase, often substituted: 'He's really brought that off'; this, I suggest, is what goodness means—'bringing it off'—accomplishing his special task. And in literature this involves something quite different from what it involves in painting; the link between the two sorts of 'goodness' is no closer than that between a good painting and a good theory, or between a good piece of business and a good shot at tennis. It is good because it is well done, but there is no sort of 'well-doing' peculiar to art, although there is a sort of well-doing peculiar to each specific art.

21

The remarks of artists are, of course, often of technical rather than aesthetic interest; 'He's done a good job' may mean 'He has solved a ticklish technical problem'. Unless we insist, again, on the difference between technical and formal considerations, we may be bewildered by the apparent diversity of judgments about 'goodness'; one painter, for example, is praised for the clarity of his colours, and another because the objects on his canvas shade almost imperceptibly into one another. These are not, however, contradictory aesthetic criteria. We are in either case admiring the skill of the painter, but the aesthetic question remains: the question, that is, of the formal relationships between the three-dimensional objects thus depicted. These relationships may sometimes be best conveyed by clear lines, sometimes by fuzzy ones. Similarly, what is a bad style in one context is a good one in another. The turgid rhetoric in which King Claudius explains his conduct to the Danish court is, in that context, precisely right; we condemn Lyly's characters because they speak euphuistically, whatever the occasion, but it would be absurd to object to Osric on the same ground.

We have here distinguished a technical from an aesthetic use of 'good'. How can this be done if there are no aesthetic properties? A good detective story need not be a good work of art; people who 'like to curl up with a good book' aren't passing aesthetic judgments. It is therefore impossible to define 'the aesthetic use of "good"' as 'the use of "good" in which it is applied to works of art', for we can rightly describe a work as 'good' without ascribing aesthetic characters to it. The solution, I think, is that although there are not 'aesthetic properties' common to all good works of art, there is what we may call an aesthetic approach to works of art, just as there is a scientific way of considering a thing, without it being the case that things have scientific characters; or again, there are not technical properties but there is a technical approach. The technical approach raises the question: 'how was this work put together?'; the historical approach: 'when was it done, influenced by what?'; the biographical approach: 'what does it amount to, as an event in its creator's life?'; the aesthetic approach: 'how does this work hang together?' But 'hanging together'—or, to use more genteel expressions, coherence, harmony, integrity, form—is not a special aesthetic property, recognizably the same in various works of art; it is more like a category than a property, suggesting the kinds of question which are to be asked rather than the sort of property that is to be looked for. We only arrive at the level of properties when we ask specific questions about specific works.

This doctrine, that we must seek different properties in different art-forms is not, of course, a new one; Croce attacks it in his *Essence of Aesthetic.* But Croce very much confuses the issue by attacking two quite distinct 'prejudices' at the same time; the first, the doctrine of literary kinds (tragedy, comedy, pastoral, epic, etc), the second, the doctrine of aesthetic kinds (painting, music, literature, etc). To the first one can certainly object, as Croce does, that the boundaries between, say, tragedy and comedy can never be fixed with any precision, but do we ever find ourselves in doubt whether we are confronted by a symphony or by a statue?

What Croce would have us believe is that whether we are contemplating architectural masses, or a Bach fugue, or a play by Shakespeare, or the paintings of Cézanne, what we are in every case *really* contemplating is a certain form of human feeling. This is a particular variety of aesthetics now widely accepted. Whether the feelings we then admire are supposed to be those of the artist, or whether we admire our own feelings anthropomorphically ascribed to inanimate objects—'we transform the inert masses of a building into so many limbs of a living body, a body experiencing inner strains which we transport back into ourselves'[1]—the suggestion is in either case the same, that nothing inanimate can have aesthetic properties in itself, that nothing is 'beautiful' except the human spirit. Art then most eminently plays a metaphysical role: it stands for the animistic as against the scientific view of things, showing what things 'mean' as distinct from what they are. Whatever describes the work itself is dismissed as 'technical'; aesthetics is no longer particularly concerned with works of art.

Such a theory, however, can never show that a work 'means' one thing rather than another; for what a work 'means' will depend upon what it suggests to a particular observer. (And there is nothing here to correspond to the rules of linguistic usage; to call architecture a 'language' in the hope of thus avoiding arbitrariness is to pretend there is a convention where none in fact exists; nor should we seek to establish one.) Mr Carritt's scepticism is the only honest conclusion of all such doctrines. That the *Pastoral Symphony* is more fully expressive of cheerfulness than 'Pop Goes the Weasel' or that Durham Cathedral is more expressive of religious feelings than the Methodist Chapel at Llangollen— these are matters regarding which argument would be absurd; it is as if, to take a strictly comparable case, one person were to argue that Monday is a yellow day and another that it is a red day. Concerning such merely personal associations there can certainly be no dispute. Meanwhile people go ahead with their ordinary aesthetic discussions, criticizing literature as literature, music as music; asking what the work of art *is*, not what it 'means', quite as if they were concerned here, as in science, with particular matters of fact. And if this were not so, criticism, education, controversy, would be impossible.

To return to our main theme, there is no way of *proving* that good works of art have no distinctive properties in common (properties, that is, which are not to be found also in bad works of art or in whatever is well done, whether a work of art or not). One can only draw attention to what happens when aestheticians try to nominate such properties. Sometimes the aesthetician substitutes for aesthetics something quite different; for example, the theory of art. For certainly art (good and bad) may be considered as a social institution; we can ask how it arises, what social effects it has, under what conditions it flourishes; there is a phenomenon, art, which can be studied socially, psychologically, or ethically. Or else, and very commonly, he substitutes metaphysics for aesthetics; or, on the other side, the study of techniques. Sometimes the characteristics which the aesthetician mentions—unity, structure, integrity—are general categories rather than anything at all peculiar to works of art; here, we have suggested, the aesthetician may unwittingly be on the right track, but certainly he has mentioned no aesthetic properties. And sometimes (this also can be illuminating) he stretches modes of criticism which are applicable enough in a particular art in the attempt to make them cover every art. Thus, if it be said that good works of art 'develop a theme',

23

we know what this means in music, we may feel that we can make some sense of the phrase in criticizing literature (although already, I suggest, we really mean something quite different), but how could we possibly apply this critical method to sculpture? Similarly, 'balance' may have a specific meaning in the plastic arts, but can it be non-metaphorically applied to literature and music? And more often than not, the aesthetician does none of these things; he simply talks dreary and pretentious nonsense. The alternative, I suggest, isn't subjectivism but an intensive special study of the separate arts, carried out with no undue respect for anyone's 'aesthetic experiences', but much respect for real differences between the works of art themselves. In this sense—art for art's sake!

Note

1 Lotze, *Microcosmos* (Bk V, Ch. 2) as quoted in Vernon Lee's *Anthropomorphic Aesthetics* (in her *Beauty and Ugliness*, p. 18).

4   A Study of the Irrefutability of two Aesthetic Theories

Beryl Lake

To Benedetto Croce and to Clive Bell respectively may be attributed two aesthetic theories which have exerted a profound influence over the development of modern art criticism and modern aesthetics. Croce was responsible for formulating the view that the essential identity of the work of art lies not in its specific physical character but in the intuitive experience of the sensitive observer. Clive Bell, in seeking to isolate the 'quality peculiar to all objects that provoke. . . aesthetic emotion', hit on the formula 'significant form'. In all objects deserving of the name 'work of art', 'lines and colours combined in a particular way, certain forms and relations of forms, stir our aesthetic emotions' (Bell, Art, 1914). The dominant tendency of modern art criticism has been to conflate these two notions, and implicitly to represent the business of criticism as the identification of subjective impressions with the effects of 'forms and relations of forms'.

Argument with the findings of such criticism has tended to be fruitless and frustrating, for reasons which are made clear by Lake and filled out, by implication, by MacIntyre (text 5). According to Lake's conclusion, 'It is inappropriate to point out counter-facts to such theories as Croce's and Bell's, since the theories are so stated that any such facts are impotent.' MacIntyre points to the irresolvability of competing arguments as a condition of modern moral debate, and to the intellectual dependence of the Bloomsbury circle (of which Bell was a member) upon the moral doctrine of Emotivism. He also, in 'The Idea of a Social Science' (text 20) offers a critical model which may be applicable, by extension, to the procedures of Modernist aesthetics and criticism. The tendency of Modernism to frustrate causal inquiry—for example to rule out as fouls such questions as how, and in accordance with what interests, Croce and Bell came to hold and to promote such theories—may be considered in relation to MacIntyre's critique of the Winchian anthropologist, for whom agents' reasons (however irrational) are taken as adequate explanations.

Both Croce's and Bell's theories rely heavily upon a belief in the unquestionable nature of expressive effects and the incorrigible nature of claims about the consequent 'feelings' of sensitive observers. For an analysis of the concept of expression see Goodman (text 16). See also Art & Language (text 18) for a discussion of the possibility of a causal (and thus corrigible) account of expression and expression claims.

Source: William Elton (ed.) *Aesthetics and Language* (Basil Blackwell, Oxford, 1967), pp. 100–113.

The aim of this paper is to study the linguistic nature of two famous aesthetic theories, those of Benedetto Croce and Clive Bell. I am interested in beginning to understand (at least) what sort of functions statements in aesthetics have. Do they, for example, like the statement 'Living grass is green', describe matter of fact which could be different, and could, therefore, serve to refute them? Or do they, like 'A panther is an animal', assert a classification in a priori terms, that is do we find that 'Art is significant form' is both irrefutable and unconfirmable by reference to any facts about works of art?

The usual assumption seems to be that a theory of aesthetics describes the nature of art and artistic experience, in a way not very different from that in which a scientific theory describes the nature of physical phenomena; that a theory of aesthetics is based upon, and answers to, matter of fact, albeit very special and sacred matters of fact about Art. This is the assumption I am particularly interested in examining.

Croce's Theory about Works of Art

I shall begin by asking what sort of theory this is, and then I shall go on to consider what sort of theory Bell's is. This will involve expounding the theories in so far as they describe the nature of works of art, as briefly as possible, and considering whether they are empirically refutable.

Croce distinguishes between two kinds of knowledge, intuitive or imaginative, and intellectual or conceptual. Works of art are primarily examples of what he calls 'intuitive knowledge', so this is the kind of knowledge which will concern us here. Intuitive knowledge is direct knowledge of individuals, including images. It is also active (not passive reception of sensations); the knower somehow creates what he knows. Intuitions (occasions of intuitive knowledge) are furthermore identified with expressions: 'The spirit only intuits in making, forming, expressing . . .'[1] Intuitions must also be something like perceptions: Croce gives the examples of 'this river, this lake, this brook . . .' as intuitions, to be contrasted with the *concept* water.[2] Croce's emphasis on the similarity between intuitions and perceptions is not so puzzling if one remembers that on his view any perception is an activity; both what we would call perception and imaginative activity are creative.

Now, real works of art are not physical objects at all, in spite of our everyday way of speaking about them, ie despite such comments as 'I saw a Van Gogh hanging on the wall', and 'The Philharmonic Orchestra plays Brahms' second symphony'. Croce insists that real works of art do not hang on the walls of galleries nor are they performed by orchestras, but exist in the minds of all who truly appreciate them. They consist in imaginatively organized non-physical wholes; they are syntheses and clarifications of crude sensory material, that is of the impressions of sense. Sense experience, it is suggested, is given form in intuition: 'The impressions reappear as it were in expression, like water put into a filter, which reappears the same and yet different on the other side.'[3]

Briefly, then, the part of Croce's *Aesthetic* with which we are concerned is that which asserts:

1 The real work of art is an imaginative, or spiritual, or mental, not a physical thing.
2 The real work of art is an intuition which is also an expression and an occasion of intuitive knowledge. This 'knowledge' is not knowledge about anything; it is immediate.

Many difficulties arise, which are frequently pointed out. For one thing, it is hard to see what 'expression' means if it is not expression at least in some sort of physical medium. But we shall not enter into a detailed account of possible flaws in Croce's theory; rather, we shall attempt to understand what sort of theory it is, ie whether or not it is empirical.

Let us suppose that it is empirical. The claim is that a work of art is an imaginative entity, an intuition-expression, existing only in the minds of artists and genuine appreciators. Picasso's 'Guernica' is not really in the New York Museum of Modern Art; only its incidental physical medium is. Picasso's 'Guernica' is what Picasso intuited and what bona fide viewers appreciate. It is unlikely that all such viewers should have the same intuititions as Picasso; for since Croce holds that intuiting is creative, each person will express his own particular synthesis of his own particular impressions in his intuition. If this theory is empirical, then, one thing it claims is that certain physical objects which are usually mistaken for works of art are not works of art at all, but that somehow connected with these physical impostors are the real works of art, the sets of imaginative experiences in the life histories of all sorts of different people. No painted canvas, for example, is a real work of art. Botticelli's 'Birth of Venus', as a work of art, is someone's intuition, and the suggestion is that he had created a work of art quite apart from creating it *in a physical medium* by painting. It is incidental to the work of art proper that it should be made an object for public perception, as it were, by a manipulation of materials.

How are we to decide that it is either true or false to say that real works of art are spiritual entities of some sort and not physical objects? Suppose we find evidence from the writings of critics and artists which indicate that the mere physical-object result of the artist's intuition is not really a work of art. We might interpret, for example, Shelley's statement in his *Defense of Poetry*[4] as a point in favour of Croce's view: 'the most glorious poetry that has ever been communicated to the world is probably a feeble shadow of the original conceptions of the poet . . .'

We might also cite Mozart's descriptions of pre-creative images of his works, descriptions which give the impression that his works of art were created before he set to work in a physical medium. And doubtless there are many other better examples of this kind of thing. Perhaps we could then go on to say that ordinary language (eg statements like 'I have just bought a beautiful Greek vase') misleads, that the common opinion that frescoes are painted walls, and that symphonies are physical sound patterns, is a false one.

But it seems that appeal to the facts relevant to this interpretation goes against Croce's view at least as much as it confirms it. For example, critics speak of colour tones and formal designs in paintings, and seem to take careful note of physical elements like brush strokes. Artists make comments which imply the importance of the nature of the physical medium in which they work. Picasso said: 'I don't know in advance what I am going to put on the canvas, any more than I decide in advance what colours to use.'[5] In the case of literature, words, which are the physical medium, seem to be the vehicle of the artist's inspiration; it does not seem to be the case, as the Crocean view would imply, that a poem is an intuition which is separable from its verbal embodiment. To quote from Collingwood: 'The artistic activity does not use a ready-made language, it "creates" language as it goes along.'[6] A poem uses language in such a way that the use is uniquely fitting for the purpose, and one might be allowed to say that the poem *is* language used creatively. The consequence of interpreting Croce's view about the nature of works of art as empirical then, seems clearly to be that it is false, since his view does not account for the fact that artists, critics and ordinary language unequivocally imply that works of art are *at least* physical objects (in the wide sense of 'physical object' usually associated with 'physical', where 'physical' covers processes as well as objects).

It looks, then, that if we interpret Croce's view as empirical we can point to facts that seem to falsify it as well as to facts that tend to confirm it. And this is not the same as saying that works of art are sometimes physical objects and sometimes not, as, for example, we might say (trivially) that works of art are sometimes paintings and sometimes not. It seems to amount to saying that, depending upon how you look at the matter, works of art are physical objects or they are not. Someone who considers such a fact as that a monkey looking at a Cézanne can *with point* be said not to be seeing a work of art, but only a physical object, may be led to the conclusion that works of art are not physical objects, simply because he is impressed with the differences. On the other hand, someone else who is impressed by the fact that what we appraise and what artists create is at least a physical object, not a mental image (we do not normally count intuitions or beautiful day-dreams as works of art, at least until they are transformed into paintings, music, statues, etc) may be led to the opposite conclusion that works of art are physical, even if they do differ in important respects from ordinary pens and houses and sounds.

The question is, whether Croce intends merely to point out a set of facts about works of art which suggests that they are different from physical objects, and whether he would admit that another set of facts might show that they are nevertheless physical.

What he writes in his book *Aesthetic* suggests strongly that the answer is no. Let us consider his theory again. 'Art' always means primarily 'intuitive knowledge'. 'Intuitive knowledge' is so described that it is 'knowledge by acquaintance' except that it is always imaginative; hence a work of art *must* be imaginative rather than material. On his theory there is no question whatever of admitting that in any sense a work of art could be a physical object, since he insists that a work of art is an intuition, an active creation of the imagination. Even if he did accept the statement that a work of art is a physical object, his admission would have to be reinterpreted in conformity with the rest of his idealist position; for, as we noted above, all perception is in Croce's philosophy essentially creative. Of course, if seeing a chair is to be interpreted as a kind of imagining of a chair, as a psychological contributing to what is seen, this goes as much against the common belief that chairs are there to be seen as Croce's theory goes against the common belief that works of art are there to be seen, or heard, or understood.

It begins to look, then, as if Croce intends his theory to be construed in a way which leaves us at a loss to know what might, even in theory, count against it. If we say: 'But very often indeed people believe that a work of art is *at least* painted canvas, or sculptured marble, or a pattern of sounds, which it makes sense to say many people see or hear in the same way,' Croce can answer either that it makes sense to say that a work of art is only what is appreciated and expressed in the imaginations of artists and sensitive appraisers; or that seeing painted canvas or hearing sounds is essentially creative, ie that the viewer or hearer creates what he sees or hears. In fact, both ways of speaking, Croce's and the opposite, seem to be important and acceptable. Yet if these theories are empirical, one would be false, the other true. But what could be a *conceivable* refutation of Croce? Suppose we urged that if a work of art were not a physical object in the common-sense meaning of 'physical', not, for example, paint on canvas which 'is there' for everyone to see, then there would seem to be no point whatsoever in people flocking to art galleries and concert halls, no point in summer pilgrimages to Florence or attendance at Art Festivals. For surely all that is located in Florence or concert halls that could be relevant is a collection of physical statues, buildings, paintings, or a collection of musicians, instruments, scores producing sounds, also physical. If works of art are intuitions which anyone with sufficient imagination can create, why do people not sit in the seclusion of the humblest homes to enjoy them? This as a criticism of Croce's theory, seems simply absurd; one can imagine a number of ways in which he could answer it. He might say that of course what we are calling material works of art are the occasions for intuitions, or the guides to recreating in the imagination the artists' intuitions. It is at this point that it seems clear that Croce's view is irrefutable. We can refuse to agree, we can give reasons for our refusal along the lines indicated above, but we cannot prove him wrong, as we could prove someone wrong who wished to hold that all works of art were paintings. In the latter case we could appeal to common language and opinion: the dictionary could be our arbiter. Croce does not seem merely to be denying what is commonly said by way of criticism, since what is commonly said can be used to back his theory as well as an opposing one.

Let us suppose someone says: 'All works of art are paintings.' He will be immediately corrected: 'Oh no, some are statues, some are buildings, some are musical compositions, and so on. Look in your dictionary.' If he resists, either he will be considered obstinate in the face of refutation, or else we shall think he means something like: 'I think only paintings deserve the name of works of art.' In the latter case no rational argument is possible. We might, perhaps, try to persuade him that he does not *really* think any such thing; but it is to be presumed he knows what he thinks. Suppose, now, someone says: 'All works of art are really objects of the imagination.' We might say, 'Oh no, they are really physical objects.' Reasons can be produced on both sides, but it seems that at no point could we say that we have shown to Croce's satisfaction that his view is false. The way people talk about works of art provides evidence for both sides, but neither side will accept the opposing evidence. The Crocean could always say, 'Of course, works of art are often talked about as if they were physical objects, but this is the fault of language and does not show my view to be mistaken.'

Neither, it may be observed, will any amount of scrutinizing works of art provide us with a possible way of refuting Croce's view. Attempting to conduct the experiment of looking long and hard at a Whistler with the idea of seeing whether it is really a material or an imaginative object would not yield any result. Both Croce and a critic who holds the common belief that it is paint on canvas (albeit expertly put on and very pleasing, etc) would have the same object to scrutinize. No facts known to the one would be unknown to the other, and there is nothing which one could point out which would convince the other that the view of which he was convinced was wrong.

We can imagine no situation in which Croce would appear irrational if he refused to give up his theory. There is no imaginable change in the world which he would grant would falsify 'Works of art are objects of the imagination.' Suppose there was a world in which there was nothing which answered to any descriptions now given of human imagination. Would Croce in this case admit that the only remaining account of works of art would be that they are physical objects? Indeed not, since without imagination, on his view, there could not be any works of art at all. The claim, 'Works of art are objects of the imagination,' stands in sharp contrast to a genuine empirical assertion, like 'Works of art are paintings.' The latter, though in fact false, could conceivably be true, eg in a world where there was no other artistic activity besides painting.

It seems that we are justified in concluding that Croce's account of the nature of works of art is not empirical, or that it is in an important way irrefutable; and it does not seem to describe a matter of fact characteristic of such works, as we tried to suggest it might when we were supposing it empirical. It does not seem to do this because counter-evidence would not turn the view into a merely probable one, nor would it refute it by showing that the view held only for a limited class of works of art.

It now looks as if Croce's theory is couched in a priori terms, stated in such a way that no counter-evidence can possibly be brought against it which would make him modify or reject his conclusion. It looks as if Croce is insisting that the word 'Art' *should* be restricted to the kind of intuitions he describes, although normally it is not. 'Art is Intuitive Knowledge' becomes, on this interpretation, *a priori* true, irrefutably true.

I shall go on to discuss Clive Bell's theory before considering what more (besides creating necessary propositions) these aestheticians are doing; obviously there is something more, or else aesthetics would not be the intriguing subject it is.

Clive Bell's Theory about Works of Art

Clive Bell is his own best brief expositor:

> The starting point for all systems of aesthetics must be the personal experience of a peculiar emotion. The objects which provoke this emotion we call works of art.[7] This emotion is called the aesthetic emotion; and if we can discover some quality peculiar to all the objects that provoke it, we shall have solved what I take to be the central problem of aesthetics. We shall have discovered the essential quality in a work of art. . . .[8]

This essential quality of works of art, Bell decides, is 'significant form'. Certain relations between forms, forms themselves, lines and colours are what stir our aesthetic emotions. If we ask which relations, etc, do this, the answer is, the significant ones. And if we ask, 'Significant of what?' the answer is given by Bell's 'metaphysical hypothesis', that they are significant ultimately of the reality of things, of 'that which gives to all things their individual significance, the thing in itself, the ultimate reality'.[9]

The claim is first made that there exist aesthetic emotions which are only aroused by works of art. Then it is claimed that what is common to all works of art, or objects which arouse aesthetic emotions, is 'significant form'.

The assertion that sensitive people have aesthetic emotions is surely empirical. We should confirm or falsify this by asking those who are acknowledged to be sensitive people whether they experience an emotion which is unique to situations in which they are appraising works of art. We are not concerned here with the truth of this claim, but simply with its semantic type, ie its empirical or a priori character. And it certainly seems to be empirical. Many people would be prepared to admit that there is an aesthetic emotion, although some may wish to say that natural objects as well as works of art arouse it. We can believe that if Clive Bell had been confronted with constant denials of the existence of the aesthetic emotion he could still sincerely claim that he frequently experienced it. His experience at least would back his claim that such experiences do exist, and as a matter of fact many others admit having emotions of this sort. Yet we believe that Bell would say that if he had never had such an experience, his aesthetic theory would not have arisen; he insists that this personal emotion is the starting point. Bell's theory, then, seems to have what we might call empirical feet on the ground. But from there it soars into what we might call metaphysical heights, and the same suspicion assails us as in the case of Croce's view.

What is common to all works of art, or objects which arouse the aesthetic emotion, is significant form. Bell never explains clearly what significant form is; the 'metaphysical hypothesis' suggests that it is not merely a certain (unspecified) combination of lines and colours. (Bell concerns himself, as is evident, primarily with painting.) Roger Fry, who shared Bell's view, commented that significant form is more than pleasing and so on, but that an attempt at full explanation would land him 'in the depths of mysticism': 'On the edge of that gulf I stop.'[10] As Wittgenstein's famous comment advises, 'Whereof one cannot speak, thereof one must be silent.'[11]

Whatever significant form is, the questions here are 'What are we to make of the view that it is the common denominator of works of art?' 'In what position would a person be if he denied it?'

This is a way of asking if the view is empirical. How could someone convince Clive Bell that works of art (supposing, for the sake of argument, they have a common feature) do not have significant form as an essential feature, or never have significant form at all? Someone might say that Frith's 'Paddington Station' is a work of art which, because it is purely descriptive of reality, has no significant form, and therefore Bell's view is false. But we know what Bell's answer would be; he gives it himself. 'Paddington Station' is *not* a work of art precisely because it does not have significant form, precisely because it is merely descriptive painting.[12] His critical judgments and his aesthetic theory seem to be in line. Apropos of the frequent praise he bestows on Cézanne in his critical works, he writes:

> Cézanne carried me off my feet before I ever noticed that his strongest characteristic was an insistence on the supremacy of significant form. When I noticed this, my admiration for Cézanne and some of his followers confirmed me in my aesthetic theories.[13]

Bell is impressed with the formal qualities of paintings. He says:

> The pure mathematician rapt in his studies knows a state of mind which I take to be similar, if not identical ... [with the aesthetic emotion aroused by significant form].[14]

Any painting, then, which someone might try to point out as an example of art which does not have significant form, would be denied to be a work of art for this very reason. No instance could possibly be produced of a work of art which did not have significant form, for anything which did not have significant form would not be counted as a work of art. 'Paddington Station' has not significant form; therefore, in spite of popular belief to the contrary, 'Paddington Station' is not a work of art. Likewise, since 'Paddington Station', Bell judges, is not worthy of the title 'work of art', it cannot have significant form. The upshot of the theory is that nothing can count as a work of art unless it has significant form. It begins to look as if 'Works of art have significant form' is like 'Squares have four sides'. 'Is a work of art' and 'has significant form' seem to mean the same, so that the latter does not say what anything must answer to in order to count as a work of art, except that it must be a work of art.

Certainly someone who wishes to deny that all works of art have significant form would not be able to produce any evidence to convince Bell. He might point to a Hogarth and say that it lacked significant form but was a work of art, but Bell would reply that either it has significant form or it is not a work of art. He might point to a Ben Nicholson and say that it had significant form but was not a work of art, or, for that matter, to a tree. But Bell is committed to the view that if something has significant form it is a work of art, and if something is a work of art, it has significant form. No exceptions are theoretically possible once his view is adopted. This is not the characteristic of an empirical view.

We can imagine water running uphill, but we cannot begin to imagine, according to Bell, a work of art which has no significant form. Adopting his view clearly amounts to deciding not to call anything which we do not also call 'significant form', 'work of art'. We are reminded of the way in which we refuse to call anything 'square' which we do not also call 'four-sided'. It looks as if 'only those paintings, etc, are works of art which have significant form' is irrefutable, therefore non-empirical, and therefore in some sense a priori.

Of course, such sentences as 'Works of art have significant form' do not in ordinary language express a priori propositions. But then the expression 'significant form' is not an ordinary expression. There is reason for supposing that aestheticians have, in one sense, a special language adapted to the purposes of their own theories. Bell, for example, coined this phrase to establish his point that there is something which is very important to him about works of art. But he goes on to make it impossible to give an instance of even a purely imaginable thing which is both a work of art and lacks significant form.

Conclusions

I have tried to show that Croce's and Bell's theories are not refutable by reference to matters of fact. It seems to me that Croce will allow nothing to count as an example of a work of art which is not what he calls an intuition, and Clive Bell will allow nothing to count as an example of a work of art which has not what he calls significant form. While it certainly sounds as if both these writers are describing an objective characteristic which all works of art have, study of their theories reveals that this is not true, since no imaginable instance will count against their descriptions.

Let us suppose that Croce and Clive Bell disagree together about whether a work of art is an intuition or something which has significant form. One point of disagreement would be that while Croce would emphasize that a painting is a product of the aesthete's imagination, Clive Bell would emphasize that its formal characteristics, the relation of its lines and shapes as they are painted on the canvas, are Significant. Suppose Croce tried to convince Bell that the paint on the canvas was incidental, that what was appreciated was something in the imagination of the appreciator; he might point out that this is the difference between a physical object and a work of art. Bell would undoubtedly retort that the difference between a physical object and a work of art is that a work of art is a physical object which has a certain sort of form, significant form. We can easily see that the argument would be interminable, neither being able to convince the other. This does not happen in empirical disputes. For example, a dispute about whether or not the word 'art' is, as a matter of fact, used only for paintings would be terminated by consulting a dictionary. A dispute about whether more people went to plays in England than in France would be terminated by making a survey and getting statistics. In the case of an argument between Croce and Bell, it seems to me that no appeal to facts, linguistic or about experiences, canvases, paints or anything else, would settle it to the satisfaction of both sides.

Croce is impressed by the role of the Imagination in creating and appreciating works of art; so he declares that Art *is* Intuition, something mentally created rather than painted, sculptured, or written. He is so impressed by this aspect that he regards the physical medium of a work of art as irrelevant. In this way his theory can be said to be prompted by an important aesthetic fact, but he so forms it that it transcends the facts until they can no longer count against it. He will not allow, for example, the importance most other people attach to the physical aspect of works of art to count against his view that they are purely non-physical. It becomes pointless to talk about 'refuting Croce's theory'. It can be valued, enjoyed, said to make an interesting point, but not factually refuted. For it is made in the a priori medium.

Clive Bell, on the other hand, is impressed by the value of formal relationships of line and colour in certain kinds of painting, Cézanne's, for example. He is so impressed by this aspect of a certain kind of art that he declares that 'Art is Significant Form'. This statement, too, arising from an aesthetic fact (namely, that in some works it is the formal designs that arouse aesthetic emotion) transcends the other facts about other sorts of art which go against it. Descriptive painting, for example, he declares to be 'not Art'. Although Bell claims to have isolated what is a common characteristic of all works of art, as someone might isolate alcohol as the common characteristic of all cocktails, what he has really done is to restrict the use of the word 'Art' to a certain sort of painting which seems to him very important and exciting. And of course it is impossible to refute someone who decides to restrict the meaning of a word. All we can do is sympathize with or regret his usage.

I conclude that very probably many conclusions in aesthetics are fabricated a priori statements, which originally arise from a desire to emphasize one fact about aesthetic objects and experience to the firm exclusion of the rest. A trivial example of the sort of statement I believe aesthetic statements to be like would be 'The only universities in England are Oxford and Cambridge,' made by a person who was so impressed by the virtues (and by none of the drawbacks) of the ancient universities that he is utterly unconvinced by having pointed out to him the facts which show that London, Liverpool, Manchester, etc also have Universities. He has made 'The only universities in England are Oxford and Cambridge' a priori true in so far as he refuses to say of any other educational institution in England that it is a 'university', refuses to admit any possible counter-instance. He has restricted the use of the phrase 'English university'. Such a person has said nothing interesting, valuable, or exciting, of course, but the parallel with the aesthetician who says that 'Art is such and such' is one of linguistic mechanism.

If what I believe about the nature of some aesthetic theories is correct, it is inappropriate to ask whether such theories are true or false, since they cannot be refuted empirically. It is inappropriate to point out counter-facts, since the theories are so stated that any such facts are impotent. It is only appropriate to sympathize with, or to feel opposed to, aesthetic theories, and to understand the artistic prejudices which have caused them.

Notes

1   Benedetto Croce, *Aesthetic* (London, 1922) p. 8.
2   Croce, 1922, p. 22.
3   Croce, 1922, p. 15.
4   Percy Bysshe Shelley, *The Defense of Poetry* (London, 1906) p. 193.
5   Quoted by Herbert Read, *Art Now* (New York, 1934) p. 123.
6   R. G. Collingwood, *The Principles of Art*, p. 275.
7   Clive Bell, *Art* (London, 1927) p. 6.
8   Bell, 1927, p. 7.
9   Bell, 1927, pp. 69–70.
10 Roger Fry, *Vision and Design* (Chatto & Windus, London, 1920) p. 302.
11 Ludwig Wittgenstein, *Tractatus Logico-Philosophicus* (London, 1947) p. 189.
12 Bell, 1927, pp. 17–18.
13 Bell, 1927, pp. 40–1.
14 Bell, 1927, p. 25.

5 Emotivism

Alasdair MacIntyre

The typical Modernist critic claims that his aesthetic judgements are involuntary and disinterested. This claim has been interpreted by some opponents of Modernist criticism as an attempt to naturalize, and thus to privilege and protect, what are in fact the contingent tastes of a powerful minority (see, for example, Art & Language's 'Author and Producer Revisited', text 23). Such opposition tends to be associated with the interests of historical-materialist and related versions of social history and, more recently, of cultural studies. The context of MacIntyre's critique of Emotivism, by contrast, is an historical and critical account of moral theory and moral debate. It nevertheless addresses issues pertinent to a critique of Modernist aesthetics, both because the development of the latter can be historically associated with the doctrine of Emotivism at certain points, and because the status of evaluative judgements is a critical issue for Modernism and Emotivism alike.

MacIntyre departs from three connected observations about contemporary moral debate. He notes: (1) the 'conceptual incommensurability [see Kuhn, text 21] of rival arguments: . . . from our rival conclusions we can argue back to our rival premises; but when we do arrive at our premises argument ceases and the invocation of one premise against another becomes a matter of pure assertion and counter-assertion'; (2) the claims for impersonality and rationality which are nevertheless made for these arguments; and (3) 'that the concepts which inform our moral discourse were originally at home in larger totalities of theory and practice in which they enjoyed a role and function supplied by contexts of which they have now been deprived'.

In face of these observations MacIntyre points to the need for a historical treatment of moral philosophy, to furnish, as it were, an explanatory genealogy of our present condition. This project would be fruitless, however, if it could be held that the impossibility of rational resolution was a feature of all moral disagreements at all times, rather than a contingent feature of modern moral debate. According to MacIntyre, the doctrine of Emotivism is 'one philosophical theory which this challenge specifically invites us to confront'. He therefore addresses Emotivism as a means to dispose of the challenge and to justify his project.

Source: After Virtue: a study in moral theory (University of Notre Dame Press, 1981), Ch. 2, 'The Nature of Moral Disagreement Today and the Claims of Emotivism', pp. 11–21. Copyright © 1981 University of Notre Dame Press, Notre Dame, Indiana, 46556 U.S.A. This material has been edited.

[. . .] Emotivism is the doctrine that all evaluative judgments and more specifically all moral judgments are *nothing but* expressions of preference, expressions of attitude or feeling, in so far as they are moral or evaluative in character. Particular judgments may of course unite moral and factual elements. 'Arson, being destructive of property, is wrong' unites the factual judgment that arson destroys property with the moral judgment that arson is wrong. But the moral element in such a judgment is always to be sharply distinguished from the factual. Factual judgments are true or false; and in the realm of fact there are rational criteria by means of which we may secure agreement as to what is true and what is false. But moral judgments, being expressions of attitude or feeling, are neither true nor false; and agreement in moral judgment is not to be secured by any rational method, for there are none. It is to be secured, if at all, by producing certain non-rational effects on the emotions or attitudes of those who disagree with one. We use moral judgments not only to express our own feelings and attitudes, but also precisely to produce such effects in others.

Emotivism is thus a theory which professes to give an account of *all* value judgments whatsoever. Clearly if it *is* true, *all* moral disagreement *is* rationally interminable; and clearly if that is true then certain . . . features of contemporary moral debate do indeed have nothing to do with what is specifically contemporary. But is it true?

Emotivism has been presented by its most sophisticated protagonists hitherto as a theory about the meaning of the sentences which are used to make moral judgments. C. L. Stevenson, the single most important exponent of the theory, asserted that the sentence 'This is good' means roughly the same as 'I approve of this; do so as well,' trying to capture by this equivalence both the function of the moral judgment as expressive of the speaker's attitudes and the function of the moral judgment as designed to influence the hearer's attitudes. [1] Other emotivists suggested that to say 'This is good' was to utter a sentence meaning roughly 'Hurrah for this!' But as a theory of the meaning of a certain type of sentence emotivism plainly fails for at least three very different reasons.

The first is that, if the theory is to elucidate the meaning of a certain class of sentences by referring to their function, when uttered, of expressing feelings or attitudes, an essential part of the theory will have to consist in an identification and characterisation of the feelings or attitudes in question. On this subject proponents of the emotive theory are in general silent, and perhaps wisely. For all attempts so far to identify the relevant types of feelings or attitudes have found it impossible to avoid an empty circularity. 'Moral judgments express feelings or attitudes,' it is said. 'What kind of feelings or attitudes?' we ask. 'Feelings or attitudes of approval,' is the reply. 'What kind of approval?' we ask, perhaps remarking that approval is of many kinds. It is in answer to this question that every version of emotivism either remains silent or, by identifying the relevant kind of approval as moral approval—that is, the type of approval expressed by a specifically moral judgment—becomes vacuously circular.

It becomes easy to understand why the theory is vulnerable to this first type of criticism, if we consider two other reasons for rejecting it. One is that emotivism, as a theory of the meaning of a certain type of sentence, is engaged in an impossible task from the beginning, because it is dedicated to characterising as equivalent in meaning two kinds of expression which, as we have already seen, derive their distinctive function in our language in key part from the contrast and difference between them. I have already suggested that there are good reasons for distinguishing between what I called expressions of personal preference and evaluative (including moral) expressions, citing the way in which utterances of the first kind depend upon who utters them to whom for any reason-giving force that they may have, while utterances of the second kind are not similarly dependent for their reason-giving force on the context of utterance. This seems sufficient to show that there is some large difference in meaning between members of the two classes; yet the emotive theory wishes to make them equivalent in meaning. This is not just a mistake; it is a mistake that demands explanation. A sign of where explanation should be sought is found in a third defect of the emotive theory, considered as a theory of meaning.

The emotive theory, as we have seen, purports to be a theory about the meaning of sentences; but the expression of feeling or attitude is characteristically a function not of the meaning of sentences, but of their use on particular occasions. The angry schoolmaster, to use one of Gilbert Ryle's examples, may vent his feelings by shouting at the small boy who has just made an arithmetical mistake, 'Seven times seven equals forty-nine!' But the use of this sentence to express feelings or attitudes has nothing whatsoever to do with its meaning. This suggests that we should not simply rely on these objections to reject the emotive theory, but that we should rather consider whether it ought not to have been proposed as a theory about the *use*—understood as purpose or function—of members of a certain class of expressions rather than about their *meaning*—understood as including all that Frege intended by 'sense' and 'reference'.

Clearly the argument so far shows that when someone utters a moral judgment, such as 'This is right' or 'This is good', it does not mean the same as 'I approve of this; do so as well' or 'Hurrah for this!' or any of the other attempts at equivalence suggested by emotive theorists; but even if the meaning of such sentences were quite other than emotive theorists supposed, it might be plausibly claimed, if the evidence was adequate, that in using such sentences to *say* whatever they mean, the agent was in fact *doing* nothing other than expressing his feelings or attitudes and attempting to influence the feelings and attitudes of others. If the emotive theory thus interpreted were correct it would follow that the meaning and the use of moral expressions were, or at the very least had become, radically discrepant with each other. Meaning and use would be at odds in such a way that meaning would tend to conceal use. We could not safely infer what someone who uttered a moral judgment was doing merely by listening to what he said. Moreover the agent himself might well be among those for whom use was concealed by meaning. He might well, precisely because he was self-conscious about the meaning of the words that he used, be assured that he was appealing to independent impersonal criteria, when all that he was in fact doing was expressing his feelings to others in a manipulative way. How might such a phenomenon come to occur?

Let us in the light of such considerations disregard emotivism's claim to universality of scope; and let us instead consider emotivism as a theory which has been advanced in historically specific conditions. In the eighteenth century Hume embodied emotivist elements in the large and complex fabric of his total moral theory; but it is only in this century that emotivism has flourished as a theory on its own. And it did so as a response to a set of theories which flourished, especially in England, between 1903 and 1939. We ought therefore to ask whether emotivism as a theory may not have been both a response to, and in the very first instance, an account of *not*, as its protagonists indeed supposed, moral language as such, but moral language in England in the years after 1903 as and when that language was interpreted in accordance with that body of theory to the refutation of which emotivism was primarily dedicated. The theory in question borrowed from the early nineteenth century the name of 'intuitionism' and its immediate progenitor was G. E. Moore.

'I went up to Cambridge at Michaelmas 1902, and Moore's *Principia Ethica* came out at the end of my first year . . . it was exciting, exhilarating, the beginning of a renaissance, the opening of a new heaven on a new earth.' So wrote John Maynard Keynes,[2] and so in their own rhetorical modes Lytton Strachey and Desmond McCarthy and later Virginia Woolf, who struggled through *Principia Ethica* page by page in 1908, and a whole network of Cambridge and London friends and acquaintances. What opened the new heaven was Moore's quiet but apocalyptic proclamation in 1903 that after many centuries he had at last solved the problems of ethics by being the first philosopher to attend with sufficient care to the precise nature of the questions which it is the task of ethics to answer. What Moore believed that he had discovered by attending to the precise nature of these questions was threefold.

First that 'good' is the name of a simple, indefinable property, a property different from that named by 'pleasant' or 'conducive to evolutionary survival' or any other natural property. Hence Moore speaks of good as a non-natural property. Propositions declaring this or that to be good are what Moore called 'intuitions'; they are incapable of proof or disproof and indeed no evidence or reasoning whatever can be adduced in their favour or disfavour. Although Moore disclaims any use of the word 'intuition' which might suggest the name of a faculty of intuition comparable to our power of vision, he none the less does compare good as a property with yellow as a property in such a way as to make verdicts that a given state of affairs is or is not good comparable to the simplest judgments of normal visual perception.

Secondly, Moore takes it that to call an action right is simply to say that of the available alternative actions it is the one which does or did as a matter of fact produce the most good. Moore is thus a utilitarian; every action is to be evaluated solely by its consequences, as compared with the consequences of alternative possible courses of action. And as with at least some other versions of utilitarianism it follows that no action is ever right or wrong *as such*. Anything whatsoever may under certain circumstances be permitted.

Thirdly, it turns out to be the case, in the sixth and final chapter of *Principia Ethica*, that 'personal affections and aesthetic enjoyments include *all* the greatest, and *by far* the greatest goods we can imagine . . .' This is 'the ultimate and fundamental truth of Moral Philosophy'. The achievement of friendship and the contemplation of what is beautiful in nature or in art become certainly almost the sole and perhaps the sole justifiable ends of all human action.

We ought to notice immediately two crucial facts about Moore's moral theory. The first is that his three central positions are logically independent of each other. There would be no breach in consistency if one were to affirm any one of the three and deny the other two. One can be an intuitionist without being a utilitarian; most English intuitionists came to hold the view that there was a non-natural property of 'right' as well as of 'good' and held that to perceive that a certain type of action was 'right' was to see that one had at least a prima facie obligation to perform that type of action, independently of its consequences. Likewise a utilitarian has no necessary commitment to intuitionism. And neither utilitarians nor intuitionists have any necessary commitment to the values of Moore's sixth chapter. The second crucial fact is easy to see retrospectively: the first part of what Moore says is *plainly* false and the second and third parts are at the very least highly contentious. Moore's arguments at times are, it must seem now, *obviously* defective—he tries to show that 'good' is indefinable, for example, by relying on a bad dictionary definition of 'definition'—and a great deal is asserted rather than argued. And yet it is this to us plainly false, badly argued position which Keynes treated as 'the beginning of a renaissance', which Lytton Strachey declared to have 'shattered all writers on ethics from Aristotle and Christ to Herbert Spencer and Mr Bradley' and which Leonard Woolf described as 'substituting for the religious and philosophical nightmares, delusions, hallucinations in which Jehovah, Christ and St Paul, Plato, Kant and Hegel had entangled us, the fresh air and pure light of commonsense'.[3]

This is great silliness of course; but it is the great silliness of highly intelligent and perceptive people. It is therefore worth asking if we can discern any clues as to why they accepted Moore's naive and complacent apocalypticism. One suggests itself. It is that the group who were to become Bloomsbury had already accepted the values of Moore's sixth chapter, but could not accept these as merely their own personal preferences. They felt the need to find objective and impersonal justification for rejecting all claims except those of personal intercourse and of the beautiful. What specifically were they rejecting? Not in fact the doctrines of Plato or St Paul or any other of the great names in Woolf's or Strachey's catalogue of deliverance, but those names as symbols of the culture of the late nineteenth century. Sidgwick and Leslie Stephen are being dismissed along with Spencer and Bradley, and the whole of the past is envisaged as a burden that Moore has just helped them to cast off. What was it about the moral culture of the late nineteenth century which made it a burden to be escaped from? That is a question to which an answer ought to be deferred, precisely because it is going to be forced on us more than once in the course of the argument and later on we shall be better equipped to answer it. But we ought to notice how dominant the theme of that rejection is in the lives and writings of the Woolfs, of Lytton Strachey, of Roger Fry. Keynes emphasised the rejection not only of the Benthamite version of utilitarianism and of Christianity, but of all claims on behalf of social action conceived as a worthwhile end. What was left?

The answer is: a highly impoverished view of how 'good' may be used. Keynes gives examples of central topics of discussion among Moore's followers: 'If A was in love with B and believed that B reciprocated his feelings, whereas in fact B did not, but was in love with C, the state of affairs was certainly not as good as it would have been if A had been right, but was it worse or better than it would become if A discovered his mistake?' Or again: 'If A was in love with B under a misapprehension as to B's qualities, was this better or worse than A's not being in love at all?' How were such questions to be answered? By following Moore's prescriptions in precise fashion. Do you or do you not discern the presence or absence of the non-natural property of good in greater or lesser degree? And what if two observers disagree? Then, so the answer went, according to Keynes, either the two were focusing on different subject matters, without recognising this, or one had perceptions superior to the other. But, of course, as Keynes tells us, what was really happening was something quite other: 'In practice, victory was with those who could speak with the greatest appearance of clear, undoubting conviction and could best use the accounts of infallibility'. . .

There is evident here precisely that gap between the meaning and purport of what was being said and the use to which utterance was being put to which our reinterpretation of emotivism drew attention. An acute observer at the time and Keynes himself retrospectively might well have put matters thus: these people take themselves to be identifying the presence of a non-natural property, which they call 'good'; but there is in fact no such property and they are doing no more and no other than expressing their feelings and attitudes, disguising the expression of preference and whim by an interpretation of their own utterance and behaviour which confers upon it an objectivity that it does not in fact possess. [. . .]

What makes emotivism convincing as a thesis about a certain kind of moral utterance at Cambridge after 1903 are certain features specific to that historical episode. Those whose evaluative utterances embodied Moore's interpretations of those utterances could not have been doing what they took themselves to be doing because of the falsity of Moore's thesis. But nothing whatsoever seems to follow about moral utterance in general. Emotivism on this account turns out to be an empirical thesis, or rather a preliminary sketch of an empirical thesis, presumably to be filled out later by psychological and sociological and historical observations, about those who continue to use moral and other evaluative expressions, as if they were governed by objective and impersonal criteria, when all grasp of any such criterion has been lost. We should therefore expect emotivist types of theory to arise in a specific local circumstance as a response to types of theory and practice which share certain key features of Moore's intuitionism. Emotivism thus understood turns out to be, as a cogent theory of use rather than a false theory of meaning, connected with one specific stage in moral development or decline, a stage which our own culture entered early in the present century. [. . .]

The scheme of moral decline which these remarks presuppose would, as I suggested earlier, be one which required the discrimination of three distinct stages; a first at which evaluative and more especially moral theory and practice embody genuine objective and impersonal standards which provide rational justification for particular policies, actions and judgments and which themselves in turn are susceptible of rational justification; a second stage at which there are unsuccessful attempts to maintain the objectivity and impersonality of moral judgments, but during which the project of providing rational justifications both by means of and for the standards continuously breaks down; and a third stage at which theories of an emotivist kind secure wide implicit acceptance because of a general implicit recognition in practice, though not in explicit theory, that claims to objectivity and impersonality cannot be made good. [. . .]

The appearance of emotivism in [a] variety of philosophical guises suggests strongly that it is indeed in terms of a confrontation with emotivism that my own thesis must be defined. For one way of framing my contention that morality is not what it once was is just to say that to a large degree people now think, talk and act *as if* emotivism were true, no matter what their avowed theoretical standpoint may be. Emotivism has become embodied in our culture. But of course in saying this I am not merely contending that morality is not what it once was, but also and more importantly that what once was morality has to some large degree disappeared—and that this marks a degeneration, a grave cultural loss. [. . .]

Notes

1 C. L. Stevenson, *Ethics and Language* (1945) Chapter 2.
2 Quoted in S. P. Rosenbaum (ed), *The Bloomsbury Group* (1975) p. 52.
3 Quoted in David Gadd, *The Loving Friends* (1974).

II

KNOWLEDGE
AND
REPRESENTATION

6 Knowing How, Knowing That, and Knowing What: Observations on their Relation in Plato and Other Greek Philosophers

Jaakko Hintikka

Despite his apparent concern with the restricted question of meaning in classical philosophy, Hintikka offers a useful exposition of issues relevant to the practice, interpretation, criticism and teaching of art. This is not simply because so many of our relevant linguistic concepts—epistemology, technique, sophistication, empiricism, teleology, pedagogy—have their roots in the Greek language, and because their usage at times implies an authorization from classical culture, but also because the problems of interrelationships between the concepts he discusses are problems of practical moment. From the writings of Clive Bell ('Art is not to be learned; at any rate it is not to be taught') to the clichés of post-war studio teaching ('Our students are doers not thinkers') or the pronouncements of Modernist criticism ('Art is a matter strictly of experience, not of principles') it has been assumed in influential quarters that the relationship between technique and achievement in art is ineffable; that it is not open to scrutiny by reference to available procedures of inquiry or to well-grounded considerations of knowledge.

Hintikka is not concerned to explain the production or merit of art, but rather to examine the relations between such concepts as virtue, knowledge, skill, technique and telos (the notion of an end or aim for a given activity), within the context of a specific literature and period. In the process, though, he encourages a critical consideration of the ways in which such concepts are employed and related in modern usage. Of particular relevance is the distinction made between empeiria, *as referring to skills learnable by rote, habit or training, and* episteme, *as referring to skills governed by rational principles, which are teachable and*

47

learnable, requiring as a necessary condition the ability to give an account of one's relevant beliefs. The Platonic definition of a craftsman as one who unites knowing how to produce x with knowing (in principle) what x is, also has application to our means of relating skill, planning and imagination. Finally we may note the relevance of the concept of the Socratic elenchus, understood as a form of rational questioning, aimed at the correction of false statements and definitions and at the achievement or inculcation of virtue. Within the context of an interest in art, and of a discussion of the relations between knowing how, knowing that and knowing what, we might understand the elenchus as a means by which critical assessments of competence might be related to assessments of merit.

Source: Modality, Morality and other problems of sense and nonsense: Essays dedicated to Sören Halldén (Lund, CWK Gleerup Bokförlag, 1973), pp. 1–12. Some references have been deleted. Reprinted by permission of Liber Grafiska AB.

The first problem I shall address myself to in this essay has been the subject of lively debate in recent literature. It is the question: how did Plato conceive of the idea of knowledge (ἐπιστήμη, *episteme*, sometimes also translated as 'science')? Similar questions can of course be asked concerning other Greek philosophers, especially concerning Socrates. One reason why this question is important is the paradoxical Socratic identification of virtue with knowledge, ἀρετή (*arete*) with *episteme*. Does the precise meaning of the term *episteme* throw any light on why Socrates (and the young Plato) assimilated the two to each other? What kind of knowledge did they have in mind, anyway?

These questions are not immediately answered by the known facts of Greek usage. Rather, it is this usage that gives rise to the hard problems. It is easily seen that *episteme* meant something not quite identical with our knowledge, and the same is true to some extent of the other Greek words for knowledge, such as σοφία (*sophia*), τέχνη (*tekhne*), etc. One of the most important differences was that *episteme* could mean both knowledge and skill, both knowing that and knowing how. 'It signifies both knowledge and ability, and is used more particularly to denote experience in manual skills', writes Bruno Snell (*The Discovery of the Mind*[1]). Each of the artisans, a smith, a shoemaker, a sculptor, even a poet exhibited *episteme* in practising his trade. The word *episteme*, 'knowledge', was thus very close in meaning to the word *tekhne*, 'skill'. The basic use of the corresponding verb ἐπίσταμαι (*epistamai*) is said to be to express, in connection with an infinitive, an ability or a skill, ie 'knowing how to do something'. This, we are told, is the only meaning of the verb in the *Iliad*.

In Plato, too, *episteme* is frequently assimilated to *tekhne* or otherwise used in the same sense as the latter term. (See, eg *Ion* 537 d, 538 a ff; *Charmides* 165 d; *Euthyphro* 14 c; *Republic* I, 342 c, IV, 428 b-c; *Euthydemus* 289 c.) Nor is this due to any accidental ambiguity of the word. No attentive reader of the early Platonic dialogues can doubt that the knowledge so tenaciously sought after by Socrates is there thought of as being in some respects essentially similar to the skills of the craftsmen. In fact, Socrates says of them that 'I was conscious that I knew practically nothing, but I knew I should find that they knew many fine things (πολλὰ καὶ καλὰ ἐπισταμένους). And in this I was not deceived; they did know what I did not, and in this way they were wiser than I' (*Apologia* 22d). Nor can this be dismissed as an instance of Socratic irony, for the sequel shows that Socrates' main criticism of craftsmen was not that their *tekhne* was not genuine knowledge, but rather that its applicability was restricted to one field. It is sometimes said that the ideal of knowledge of the Greek philosophers was abstract, impractical, and unrelated to anything like technology. As far as Socrates and the young Plato are concerned almost the opposite is the case. One of their most important conceptual paradigms was that of a craftsman who is bringing forth a concrete product. (Cf Snell.) This is a recurring model in the early Platonic dialogues. The serious limitations of the major Greek philosophers' conception of knowledge cannot be blamed on their alienation from technology. Rather, it seems to me that these very same limitations were shared by the Greek idea of a craftsman or artisan, that is, by the Greek idea of technology.

This makes all the more burning our question of the precise meaning of this Socratic *episteme* which was so closely related to *tekhne*. What kind of knowledge was identified by Socrates with virtue?

A sweeping answer to this question has been given by John Gould in his interesting book *The Development of Plato's Ethics*. According to him the moral *episteme* Socrates was talking about was not propositional knowledge, not *knowing that*, but moral skill, *knowing how*. If Gould is right it is not enough to say that there was an element of knowledge in addition to an element of skill in the Socratic *episteme*; according to him, in the field of morality it is manifested *only* as a skill. '... ἐπιστήμη, as we have seen, is expressed only in action', he writes.[2] If this is the case, then it follows that the Socratic paradox does not identify virtue with *knowledge* of moral values, but with moral *skill*. To think otherwise is to be seduced by what Gould calls 'the intellectualistic legend'.

Gould's views have found supporters, and they are worth being discussed with some care. It seems to me that, in their unqualified form, they in any case prove too much. For what was the *arete* which Socrates claimed to amount to *episteme*? It is well known that it was not precisely an ethical 'virtue' in our sense. Tentatively, we might say that it was a configuration of those attributes that commanded the greatest admiration. They included prominently, and sometimes well-nigh exclusively, the attribute of political skill and more generally the attributes needed for competitive social excellence. (Cf eg Snell;[3] Adkins, *Merit and Responsibility*.[4]) But if so, one cannot maintain that the right-hand side of the *arete* = *episteme* equation simply meant skill without making it into a trivial generalization of that particular skill which the left-hand side denoted. Although we must make a due allowance to the fact that the Socratic paradox was less paradoxical to the Greeks than it is to us, we can scarcely wish to reduce it to the tautology 'moral skill is moral skill' or 'moral skill is a skill'.

This general criticism may be slightly unfair to Gould, however, and in any case it has to be supplemented by a more detailed discussion of the evidence. Telling detailed criticisms of Gould's main thesis have in fact been provided by Gregory Vlastos (among others). One cannot hope to do better than to quote Vlastos:

> Try the 'know how' sense in that sentence and see what you can make of it: 'To fear death is nothing but to think oneself wise while one is not; for it is to think one knows the unknown' (*Apologia* 29 a). And there is more at issue here than mere linguistics. Think of the doctrine Socrates is expounding. If 'virtue is knowledge' meant that 'for the achievement of *arete* what is required is a form of ability', Socrates would be saying here that people fear death only because they do not have the ability not to fear it, and what could be more trivial than that? Or, to continue the citation from Gould, 'ability, comparable in some respects to the creative or artistic ability of potters, shoemakers, and the like'; the analogy with these particular acts would imply that the reason we fear death is that we have not acquired skill in meeting it, and what could be further from Socrates' thought? What Socrates wants us to understand is that we fear death because we have mistaken beliefs: we think we know death to be a great evil, greater than disgrace; if we so much as knew our ignorance, our fear of death would leave us. There is no getting away from 'intellectualism' here.

Vlastos goes on to argue that Gould's interpretation misses the whole point of the Socratic art of questioning: the Socratic *elenchus* which clearly 'tests statements, not actions', and that this 'intellectualistic' *elenchus* was tied essentially to Socrates' strive to inculcate virtue. 'The daily practice of the *elenchus* would have been irrelevant to this aim unless Socrates did not believe that to do the only thing *elenchus* could hope to do—to correct false beliefs, confused ideas, and wrong ways of thinking—was of itself to produce a necessary condition of good moral conduct.'

It may be added that long before Plato's time *epistamai* occasionally served to express knowledge of facts not knowing how. For instance, in the *Odyssey* (δ 730) *epistamai* is used to express Penelope's servant girl's awareness of the fact that her son had gone 'on board of the hollow blackship'. 'Knowing how' interpretation does not apply here by any stretch of imagination. Hence the general facts about Greek usage do not force us to adopt Gould's interpretation, either.

Gould's thesis is thus wrong. Or, rather, it is oversimplified, for there is no doubt that he is fully right to the extent that there is an element of 'know how' in the concept of *episteme* which distinguishes it from our concept of 'knowing that' in the Greek idea.

This does not solve but instead reinforces our problem of the precise nature of *episteme*. Now the problem largely becomes a query as to how the (from our modern point of view) disparate elements of knowledge and skill could coexist in the idea of *episteme* and also how they were related to each other. It is perhaps not so very difficult to see on what kinds of occasions the term *episteme* was used in ancient Greece. The real difficulty is to see what these several occasions had in common, what enabled the Greeks to classify them under the same heading. The problem, we might say, is not in determining the extension of the concept of *episteme*, but rather in determining its intension.

A partial answer is obtained by seeing what *episteme* was contrasted with. We have already seen that *episteme* did not exclude practical skill. However, not any human ability, not any manual dexterity could be called *episteme*. Many of them could be referred to by the much less honorific title of ἐμπειρία (*empeiria*). The contrast between *episteme* and *empeiria* was not a contrast between knowing that and knowing how. It was a contrast between such skills as are governed by general rational principles and hence could be taught and learned by recipes and rules and those which only could be assimilated by example and rote. *Episteme* could be conceptualized; *empeiria* turned completely on past experiences and training and was therefore comparable to mere habit. Occasionally *empeiria* is translated as 'experience' (a case in point is Sir David Ross' translation of the beginning of Aristotle's *Metaphysics*), which is somewhat misleading because the difference between *episteme* and *empeiria* does not turn on a different origin of the knowledge or skill in question, but rather on the level of conceptualization involved. It even appears that *empeiria*, like *episteme*, could be more like knowing that than knowing how. For a typical move in Greek philosophy was to emphasize the connection between *empeiria* and memory. 'From memory *empeiria* is produced in men', Aristotle writes, 'for the several memories of the same thing produce finally the capacity for a single *empeiria*. And *empeiria* seems pretty much like *episteme* and *tekhne*, but in truth *episteme* and *tekhne* come to men through *empeiria* ... Art arises when from many notions gained by *empeiria* one universal judgement about a class of objects is produced' (*Met.* I 980b27— 981a7). Plato, too, gives as an example of *empeiria* a mere memory of what has happened. The *episteme-empeiria* distinction thus cuts completely across the *knowing that – knowing how* distinction.

Another way of emphasizing the same or closely related point was for the Greek philosophers to say that *episteme*, unlike *empeiria*, presupposed *awareness* of what one was doing and ability to give an account (*logos*) of it. In the *Theaetetus, episteme* was even identified tentatively with true belief accompanied by *logos*. (Cf also *Rep.* VII, 533c.) Even though this is in the course of the dialogue rejected as a *sufficient* characterization of knowledge (in the sense of *episteme*), ability to give a rational account of one's belief was clearly thought by Plato as a *necessary* condition of knowledge. In his bitter criticism of popular wisdom Xenophanes says that 'even if one chanced to say the complete truth, oneself knows it not' (fragment 34). It seems to me that this is the spirit in which we must also understand Plato's (Socrates') statement that poets, like oracles, 'say many fine things, but know none of the things they say' (*Apologia* 22c), not as an expression of mild disapproval, but as a bitter criticism. This bitterness is perhaps more clearly in evidence when the same criticism is applied in the *Meno* (99c—d) to ordinary statesmen: their being 'like soothsayers and diviners' is ground for condemning them as having 'no knowledge of anything they say'. My point here is not belied by the fact that later the ageing and increasingly pessimistic Plato came to associate more and more importance to mere true belief and mere *empeiria* as a vehicle of that non-rational persuasion which is needed to maintain the social order.

Thus we are led to a more specific question in our quest of the meaning of *episteme*. For speaking of awareness or account immediately prompts the question: Awareness of what? Account of what? If even a skill could be *episteme* provided it was accompanied by 'one universal judgement about a class of objects', what was this judgement supposed to be about?

Here we come to the main specific suggestion I propose to put forward in this paper. So far my discussion has followed fairly conventional lines; now I shall venture a thesis which obviously needs all kinds of qualifications but which perhaps may be understood most easily in a blunt and unqualified form.

We have already noted that the activity of a craftsman was an important conceptual model for the Greeks, especially for Socrates and for the early Plato. What is the knowledge about that enables an artisan to practice his trade? The simple-minded answer is 'knowledge of his own products, of their nature'. A shoemaker's knowledge of shoes is what enables him to produce them, and the same holds for any other craftsman. According to Plato, what makes the activity of a craftsman a real *episteme* is that he is not acting 'at random' (οὐκ εἰκῇ), to use Plato's own formulation (*Gorgias* 503d—e), but 'with a view to some object', that is, 'with the purpose of giving a certain form to whatever he is working upon'. Awareness of this form is then thought of as the gist of a craftsman's skill.

Thus the essence of a productive skill and, by a tacit generalization, of any rational skill is seen in the awareness of its end and of the nature of this end. In so far as we can generalize this, we immediately have an answer to our earlier question as to the connection link between 'knowing that' and 'knowing how' in the concept of *episteme*. In any craftsman's activity, *knowing how to produce* (or bring about) x and *knowing what x is* were inseparably connected with each other. (Perhaps it is hopeless in principle to try to separate them sharply in the Greek usage.) We can thus see that typically the 'knowing that' aspect that there is to the *episteme* is of a certain very special kind: it is knowledge of essences or definitions, knowing *what* rather than (unspecified) knowing *that*.

For instance, the doctor's art, the art of healing, is from this point of view nearly identical with his knowledge of what health is, which of course implies the secondary capacity of telling the healthy from the sick. This somewhat surprising conclusion is in fact explicitly assented to in the Platonic dialogues. In the *Laches* (195c) it is in so many words denied that 'doctors know any thing more, in treating sick persons, than how to tell what is healthy and what is diseased' and asserted that 'this is all that they know'. It is worth noticing that what is here identified with 'knowing what' is not any species of abstract, propositional knowledge, but that art or skill which is exhibited by a doctor 'in treating sick persons'.

One passage is of course not conclusive. Nor do I want to claim that there is a great deal more to be said of the matter. It is clear, nevertheless, that there are many indications in the same direction in the early Platonic dialogues. To give you some flavor of them, let me call your attention to the *Charmides* (170a), where Plato asks whether 'a science of science (ie *episteme* of *episteme*), if such exists, be able to do more than determine that one of two things is science (*episteme*), and the other is not science'. This question receives an unqualified 'no, only that' as an answer. This answer obviously is nothing but another application of the same general principle we found operative also in the *Laches:* Knowledge of *x* equals ability to tell what is *x* and what is not *x*. It is also likely that in the *Laches* practical skills are almost as close to Plato's mind as they are in the *Charmides*: in the very next sentence 'knowledge of health' is explicitly mentioned.

The point of view we have reached here seems to me extremely interesting in several respects, I cannot do much more here, however, than to indicate some of the most promising lines of future investigation.

As against Gould, Vlastos was seen to emphasize that if we do not recognize the intellectual, 'knowing that' aspect of Socratic *episteme*, the whole point of the Socratic *elenchus* (ελεγχος) is lost sight of. From the point of view we have reached, we can now understand much more than just the intellectual character of the Socratic *elenchus*: we can understand the specific character it took in Plato's Socratic dialogues, which typically were but as many searches for the *definition* of some philosophically important concept, for instance, of this or that virtue.

The kind of what-knowledge that the definition of a virtue presumably gives us was above seen to be virtually identified by Socrates with a skill in bringing about that virtue in oneself and in others. The definition of a virtue was apparently supposed to present us with a 'form', or a plan, almost a 'blueprint' of that particular virtue, a blueprint would have enabled us to realize it in the same way a shoemaker's knowledge of the *eidos* of a shoe enables him to work, not at random, but in the way best calculated to bring about a shoe. Small wonder, therefore, that definitions played such an overwhelmingly important role in the Socratic method, and small wonder also that the quest turned out to be such a difficult enterprise. Small wonder, for that matter, that Plato could in the *Meno* infer from the failure of contemporary Athenian statesmen to make their contemporaries or even their own sons virtuous that the questions of these statesmen 'were not an effect of knowledge'—that is, apparently, not an effect of that definition of *arete* to the search of which this dialogue was dedicated.

The Socratic assimilation of virtue to knowledge becomes a natural corollary to the general view we have reached. Possessing a virtue, in the normal sense of being able to practice it, will be inseparably tied to knowing the nature and perhaps even the definition of that particular virtue: virtue, indeed, becomes knowledge. But this equation is not a tautology, as it easily was on the interpretation that identified the relevant *episteme* with moral 'knowhow'. However unparadoxical the Socratic paradox may become from our point of view, we can see that in any case it presents a mighty challenge to a theoretical thinker to spell out that definitory what-knowledge with which virtue is identified in the 'paradox'.

Another doctrine which prima facie may appear somewhat far-fetched but which we can now appreciate better is Aristotle's idea of a close connection between knowing the nature of something and being able to bring it about. Or, rather, what may appear far-fetched is not this idea itself but the length to which Aristotle sometimes pushes it. Again a doctor's art of healing serves as an example: 'the medical art is in some sense identical with health', Aristotle writes. The context of this kind of statement shows how Aristotle arrived at it and also how he qualified it: 'Evidently then there is not necessity, on this ground at least, for the existence of forms (Ideas). For man is begotten by man, and a given man by an individual father; and similarly in the arts, for the medical art is the formal cause of health' (*Metaphysics* XII, 3, 1070a28—31). Aristotle's point in the last sentence is that in the same way as each man is begotten by a man, the instances of health that a doctor brings about when he cures his patients are derived from the presence of the form of health (as embodied in its definition) in the doctor's mind. The same point is made by Aristotle in pretty much the same terms in *Met.* XII, 4, especially 1070b33—36, which is the passage I first quoted from.

The familiar Aristotelian theory of a definition as expressing the immediate cause of the thing defined is obviously a part of the same syndrome.

I could go on giving examples. This would be a virtually endless task, however, if I am right. For it seems to me that we have much more here than an epistemological peculiarity of the Socratic school. The central role which the concept of an end or limit (*telos*) of an activity plays in the concept of an *episteme* governing this activity in Socrates and Plato seems to me a special case of a much more general tendency of the Socratic philosophers. Not only in their discussions of knowledge, but in discussing almost any phenomenon, they tended to drag in, wittingly or unwittingly, the *telos* of that activity. It is as though they could not conceptually master a situation without subsuming it somehow under the concept of a process with an end, *telos*. We might thus call the tendency in question 'conceptual teleology' and speak of the underlying way of thinking as 'telic'. It is important to realize that explicitly teleological doctrines are not what is meant here. At best, they are particular manifestations of the conceptual or implicit teleology which is being described here.

The prominence of the paradigm of a craftsman which we have already registered is not unconnected with the fact that of all human activities the activity of a craftsman is likely to have the most concrete and clearly definable product.

This general 'telic' tendency has sometimes been noted in the literature, though apparently its different manifestations have never been studied systematically. For instance R. G. Collingwood writes (*Principles of Art*[5]):

> Once the Socratic school had laid down the main lines of a theory of craft, they were bound to look for instances of craft in all sorts of likely and unlikely places. To show how they met this temptation, here yielding to it and there resisting it, or first yielding to it and there laboriously correcting their error, would need a long essay.

Clearly, this is not an occasion for the long essay Collingwood envisaged but which he never executed. Elsewhere, I have ventured to offer a few suggestions along similar lines. A few general comments may nevertheless be in order here in connection with Collingwood's remark. First of all, it seems to me that in one sense Collingwood's suggestion is far too intellectualistic. The temptation to discuss all and sundry phenomena in terms of their ends and outcomes did not arise just from the success of the Socratic school in their conscious attempts to develop a 'theory of craft' as Collingwood says. It was deeply ingrained in the very concepts with which the Greeks were wont to operate. The 'theory of craft' which the Socratic school elaborated was made a natural conceptual paradigm by this broader tendency, which largely remained tacit and even unconscious.

On the other hand, Collingwood is entirely right in the idea that conceptual preferences of the kind he describes do not predetermine a philosopher's views. He spoke, as we saw, of the Socratic philosophers as sometimes successfully 'resisting' the temptations of the craftsman-model. I want to emphasize very strongly that even any further claims that the temptations were predominantly unconscious and conceptual does not commit me to what I like to call the Whorfian fallacy, that is to say to the view that the concepts a thinker inherits and the conceptual preferences he has somehow make it impossible for him to avoid certain views, impossible for him to develop his theories in more than one way. If my suggestion concerning the general nature of the Greek conceptual system is correct, Collingwood's remarks provide us with beautiful counter-examples to the Whorfian fallacy. For Collingwood is certainly right in saying that a large part of the philosophical activity of the Socratic school consisted in attempts, and sometimes not entirely unsuccessful attempts, to free themselves of the implications of their conceptual presuppositions. Understanding these presuppositions nevertheless remains a vital part of the task of a historian, for without appreciating these presuppositions he will never understand why certain problems were so problematic to the old philosophers as they obviously were. However, this appreciation of certain presuppositions does not imply belief of their inevitability.

Although I cannot elaborate the point here, it seems to me that this telic way of thinking colored Plato's concept of knowledge also in other ways than in connection with the relation of knowing how to knowing that. It also colored his ideas of the relation of knowledge to its objects. These ideas, in turn, were special cases of Plato's general ways of looking at the relation of such 'mental acts' as knowledge and belief (even saying) to their objects. It seems to me that, in some slightly vague sense, these relations were thought of by Plato in telic terms, somehow as attempts of the knowledge or belief or statement to realize itself in its objects. This is reflected in Plato's classification of knowledge and belief as powers or capacities (*dynameis*) each of which is characterized by its characteristic objects (*Rep.* V, 477). One area where this immediately led Plato into trouble was to ask when an act of saying is successful. On one hand, we all agree that this is the case whenever something meaningful is uttered. However, in telic terms a statement is successful only if it 'hits its objects', ie reaches the objects which it is about. And what can this mean but that the statement in question is *true*? Thus it becomes a tremendous problem for Plato to account for the possibility of a meaningful falsity, of the possibility of 'false saying'. If I am not mistaken, Plato devotes to this subject more space than to the explicit explanation of his theory of forms.

I cannot here go into the details of the solution Plato gave to this problem. I have mentioned it only as an illustration of how a historian's awareness of the conceptual presuppositions of some old philosopher enables him, not so much to predict the opinions of this philosopher, but to appreciate the difficulty and depth of some of the problems with which this philosopher was wrestling—appreciate what Collingwood called his 'laboriously correcting' his conceptual biases.

Some small supplementary examples of the implicit teleology that I have mentioned might help to make my suggestion clearer. A nice illustration of my point is the double meaning of that word Werner Jaeger has tried to raise to the status of the key word of the Greek culture, the word *paideia*. Originally, it meant just children's education, but it came to mean the totality of the Greek cultural ideas. What connects the two is just the telic point of view: The ideals of a culture determine the ends of education in that culture.

Another illustration is somewhat closer to our central topic of Plato's philosophy and the Platonic concept of knowledge. If the end or aims of any activity is the most important aspect of that activity, all activities are assimilated conceptually to the production of certain results, to making. (This is just what is involved in the conceptual preponderance of the craftsman-paradigm.) But if so, the line between *doing* and *making* is apt to remain unclear and unimportant. I cannot here discuss at any greater length the intricate problems that arise in connection with the concepts of doing and making in ancient Greece—one is for instance reminded of Hannah Arendt's remarks on the subject. I shall nevertheless register both the general claim that the doing–making distinction was under-developed in ancient Greece and also the specific claim that no clear doing–making distinction was ever made by Plato, notwithstanding the claims of many scholars.

The absence of a clear doing–making distinction also helped to emphasize the telic element in *episteme*. We saw that what was characteristic of *episteme* was knowledge (rational awareness) of *what one is doing*, which thus early became *knowledge of what one is making* (*bringing about*). One can perhaps say that the generality of my earlier analysis of the relationship of knowing that and knowing how in Socrates and Plato presupposes the assimilation of all kinds of *episteme* to the special kind of *episteme* which pertained to processes with a more or less clearly defined end. Now we can see that this presupposition was fulfilled, if it was fulfilled, in virtue of the implicit teleology of the ancient Greek way of thinking.

I do not think it would be necessary to emphasize that many *caveats* are needed here. However, I believe they come to mind rather more easily than the bold unqualified claims I have made.

Notes

1   Bruno Snell, *The Discovery of the Mind,* p. 185.
2   John Gould, *The Development of Plato's Ethics,* p. 52.
3   Snell, Chapter 8.
4   Adkins, *Merit and Responsibility.*
5   R. G. Collingwood, *Principles of Art*, pp. 17–18.

7   Seeing and Seeing as

Ludwig Wittgenstein

Wittgenstein's Philosophical Investigations *was published in 1953, two years after his death. Unlike his* Tractatus Logico-Philosophicus *of 1921 it is not ordered as a coherent and sequential argument building from premise to conclusion. Wittgenstein himself, in his Preface of 1945, wrote that he had intended 'that the thoughts should proceed from one subject to another in a natural order and without breaks'. He continued:*

> *After several unsuccessful attempts to weld my results together into such a whole, I realized I should never succeed. The best that I could write would never be more than philosophical remarks; my thoughts were soon crippled if I tried to force them on in any single direction against their natural inclination.—And this was, of course, connected with the very nature of the investigation. For this compels us to travel over a wide field of thought criss-cross in every direction.—The philosophical remarks in this book are, as it were, a number of sketches of landscapes which were made in the course of these long and involved journeyings. The same or almost the same points were always being approached afresh from different directions, and new sketches made.*

The starting and ending points of Wittgenstein's 'journeyings' were common language utterances, the middle a potential clarification of the puzzle or illusion involved in the utterance—a 'sketch' made from a certain direction—and so on.

   In the following extract from the Philosophical Investigations *Wittgenstein collects together interrelated linguistic materials on 'seeing' and 'seeing as', and presents them in such a way that the reader is invited to take part as if in dialogue with the aphorisms. He wrote from the conviction that the meanings of terms and concepts are not to be viewed abstractly, but according to the actual contexts in which those terms and concepts were used. (Just what counts as 'use' in Wittgenstein's philosophy is not exactly clear.) 'Philosophy may in no way interfere with the actual use of language', he wrote elsewhere in the* Philosophical Investigations, *'it can in the end only describe it' (124). This process of description, however, is also a means to diagnosis of the reasons for confusion and misunderstanding.*

> *It is the business of philosophy, not to resolve a contradiction by means of a mathematical or logico-mathematical discovery, but to make it possible for us to get a clear view of the state of mathematics that troubles us: the state of affairs* before *the contradiction is resolved. (And this does not mean that one is sidestepping a difficulty).*
>
> *The fundamental fact here is that we lay down rules, a technique, for a game, and that then when we follow the rules, things do not turn out as we had assumed. That we are therefore as it were entangled in our own rules.*
>
> *This entanglement in our rules is what we want to understand (ie get a clear view of).*
>
> *It throws light on our concept of meaning something. For in those cases things turn out otherwise than we had meant, foreseen. That is just what we say when, for example, a contradiction appears: 'I didn't mean it like that.'*
>
> *The civil status of a contradiction, or its status in civil life: there is the philosophical problem. (125)*

To read Wittgenstein's discussion is to be made aware of how easily we can mislead or be misled, for instance if our accounts of what we see are governed by assumptions which others do not share. Later in the same section of the Philosophical Investigations *as that from which our extract is taken, Wittgenstein discusses what he calls 'aspect-blindness'.*

> *Could there be human beings lacking in the capacity to see something as something—and what would that be like? What consequences would it have?*

'The "aspect-blind"', he concludes, 'will have an altogether different relationship to pictures from ours.' Though it lies outside the scope of Wittgenstein's own philosophical concerns, we might consider the consequences of broadening the concept of an aspect—and of 'aspect-blindness'—to include the symbolic and signifying features of pictures. Could we consider as in some sense aspect-blind a person who claimed to 'see' a painting of a repulsive murder as a certain arrangement of 'forms and relations of forms'? Though not in this direction, the concept of 'seeing as' is extended by N. R. Hanson in text 8. From another point of view, the concept of 'aspect-blindness' might be considered in relation to Kuhn's discussion of the problems attendant on acceptance of new 'paradigms' in science (text 21).

Source: Philosophical Investigations (Basil Blackwell, Oxford, 1968), pp. 193e–204e. Reprinted with permission.

XI

Two uses of the word 'see'.

The one: 'What do you see there?'—'I see *this*' (and then a description, a drawing, a copy). The other: 'I see a likeness between these two faces'—let the man I tell this to be seeing the faces as clearly as I do myself.

The importance of this is the difference of category between the two 'objects' of sight.

The one man might make an accurate drawing of the two faces, and the other notice in the drawing the likeness which the former did not see.

I contemplate a face, and then suddenly notice its likeness to another. I *see* that it has not changed; and yet I see it differently. I call this experience 'noticing an aspect'.

Its *causes* are of interest to psychologists.

We are interested in the concept and its place among the concepts of experience.

You could imagine the illustration

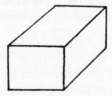

appearing in several places in a book, a text-book for instance. In the relevant text something different is in question every time: here a glass cube, there an inverted open box, there a wire frame of that shape, there three boards forming a solid angle. Each time the text supplies the interpretation of the illustration.

But we can also *see* the illustration now as one thing now as another.— So we interpret it, and *see* it as we *interpret* it.

Here perhaps we should like to reply: The description of what is got immediately, ie of the visual experience, by means of an interpretation—is an indirect description. 'I see the figure as a box' means: I have a particular visual experience which I have found that I always have when I interpret the figure as a box or when I look at a box. But if it meant this I ought to know it. I ought to be able to refer to the experience directly, and not only indirectly. (As I can speak of red without calling it the colour of blood.)

I shall call the following figure, derived from Jastrow, the duck-rabbit. It can be seen as a rabbit's head or as a duck's.

And I must distinguish between the 'continuous seeing' of an aspect and the 'dawning' of an aspect.

The picture might have been shewn me, and I never have seen anything but a rabbit in it.

Here it is useful to introduce the idea of a picture-object. For instance

would be a 'picture-face'.

In some respects I stand towards it as I do towards a human face. I can study its expression, can react to it as to the expression of the human face. A child can talk to picture-men or picture-animals, can treat them as it treats dolls.

I may, then, have seen the duck-rabbit simply as a picture-rabbit from the first. That is to say, if asked 'What's that?' or 'What do you see here?' I should have replied: 'A picture rabbit'. If I had further been asked what that was, I should have explained by pointing to all sorts of pictures of rabbits, should perhaps have pointed to real rabbits, talked about their habits, or given an imitation of them.

I should not have answered the question 'What do you see here?' by saying: 'Now I am seeing it as a picture-rabbit.' I should simply have described my perception: just as if I had said 'I see a red circle over there.'—

Nevertheless someone else could have said of me: 'He is seeing the figure as a picture-rabbit.'

It would have made as little sense for me to say 'Now I am seeing it as . . .' as to say at the sight of a knife and fork 'Now I am seeing this as a knife and fork.' This expression would not be understood.—Any more than: 'Now it's a fork' or 'It can be a fork too.'

One doesn't *'take'* what one knows as the cutlery at a meal *for* cutlery; any more than one ordinarily tries to move one's mouth as one eats, or aims at moving it.

If you say 'Now it's a face for me,' we can ask: 'What change are you alluding to?'

I see two pictures, with the duck-rabbit surrounded by rabbits in one, by ducks in the other. I do not notice that they are the same. Does it *follow* from this that I *see* something different in the two cases?—It gives us a reason for using this expression here.

'I saw it quite differently, I should never have recognized it!' Now, that is an exclamation. And there is also a justification for it.

I should never have thought of superimposing the heads like that, of making *this* comparison between them. For they suggest a different mode of comparison.

Nor has the head seen like *this* the slightest similarity to the head seen like *this*—although they are congruent.

I am shewn a picture-rabbit and asked what it is; I say 'It's a rabbit.' Not 'Now it's a rabbit.' I am reporting my perception.—I am shewn the duck-rabbit and asked what it is; I *may* say 'It's a duck-rabbit.' But I may also react to the question quite differently.—The answer that it is a duck-rabbit is again the report of a perception; the answer 'Now it's a rabbit' is not. Had I replied 'It's a rabbit,' the ambiguity would have escaped me, and I should have been reporting my perception.

The change of aspect. 'But surely you would say that the picture is altogether different now!'

But what is different: my impression? my point of view?—Can I say? I *describe* the alteration like a perception; quite as if the object had altered before my eyes.

'Now I am seeing *this*,' I might say (pointing to another picture, for example). This has the form of a report of a new perception.

The expression of a change of aspect is the expression of a *new* perception and at the same time of the perception's being unchanged.

I suddenly see the solution of a puzzle-picture. Before, there were branches there; now there is a human shape. My visual impression has changed and now I recognize that it has not only shape and colour but also a quite particular 'organization'.—My visual impression has changed;—what was it like before and what is it like now?—If I represent it by means of an exact copy—and isn't that a good representation of it?—no change is shewn.

And above all do *not* say 'After all my visual impression isn't the *drawing*; it is *this*—which I can't shew to anyone.'—Of course it is not the drawing, but neither is it anything of the same category, which I carry within myself.

The concept of the 'inner picture' is misleading, for this concept uses the '*outer* picture' as a model; and yet the uses of the words for these concepts are no more like one another than the uses of 'numeral' and 'number'. (And if one chose to call numbers 'ideal numbers', one might produce a similar confusion.)

If you put the 'organization' of a visual impression on a level with colours and shapes, you are proceeding from the idea of the visual impression as an inner object. Of course this makes this object into a chimera; a queerly shifting construction. For the similarity to a picture is now impaired.

If I know that the schematic cube has various aspects and I want to find out what someone else sees, I can get him to make a model of what he sees, in addition to a copy, or to point to such a model; even though *he* has no idea of my purpose in demanding two accounts.

But when we have a changing aspect the case is altered. Now the only possible expression of our experience is what before perhaps seemed, or even was, a useless specification when once we had the copy.

And this by itself wrecks the comparison of 'organization' with colour and shape in visual impressions.

If I saw the duck-rabbit as a rabbit, then I saw: these shapes and colours (I give them in detail)—and I saw besides something like this: and here I point to a number of different pictures of rabbits.—This shews the difference between the concepts.

'Seeing as . . .' is not part of perception. And for that reason it is like seeing and again not like.

I look at an animal and am asked: 'What do you see?' I answer: 'A rabbit'.—I see a landscape; suddenly a rabbit runs past. I exclaim 'A rabbit!'

Both things, both the report and the exclamation, are expressions of perception and of visual experience. But the exclamation is so in a different sense from the report: it is forced from us.—It is related to the experience as a cry is to pain.

But since it is the description of a perception, it can also be called the expression of thought.—If you are looking at the object, you need not think of it; but if you are having the visual experience expressed by the exclamation, you are also *thinking* of what you see.

Hence the flashing of an aspect on us seems half visual experience, half thought.

Someone suddenly sees an appearance which he does not recognize (it may be a familiar object, but in an unusual position or lighting); the lack of recognition perhaps lasts only a few seconds. Is it correct to say he has a different visual experience from someone who knew the object at once?

For might not someone be able to describe an unfamiliar shape that appeared before him just as *accurately* as I, to whom it is familiar? And isn't that the answer?—Of course it will not generally be so. And his description will run quite differently. (I say, for example, 'The animal had long ears'—he: 'There were two long appendages,' and then he draws them.)

I meet someone whom I have not seen for years; I see him clearly, but fail to know him. Suddenly I know him, I see the old face in the altered one. I believe that I should do a different portrait of him now if I could paint.

Now, when I know my acquaintance in a crowd, perhaps after looking in his direction for quite a while,—is this a special sort of seeing? Is it a case of both seeing and thinking? or an amalgam of the two, as I should almost like to say?

The question is: *why* does one want to say this?

The very expression which is also a report of what is seen, is here a cry of recognition.

What is the criterion of the visual experience?—The criterion? What do you suppose?

The representation of 'what is seen'.

The concept of a representation of what is seen, like that of a copy, is very elastic, and so *together with it* is the concept of what is seen. The two are intimately connected. (Which is *not* to say that they are alike.)

How does one tell that human beings *see* three-dimensionally?—I ask someone about the lie of the land (over there) of which he has a view. 'Is it like *this*?' (I shew him with my hand)—'Yes.'—'How do you know?'—'It's not misty, I see it quite clear.'—He does not give reasons for the surmise. The only thing that is natural to us is to represent what we see three-dimensionally; special practice and training are needed for two-dimensional representation whether in drawing or in words. (The queerness of children's drawings.)

If someone sees a smile and does not know it for a smile, does not understand it as such, does he see it differently from someone who understands it?—He mimics it differently, for instance.

Hold the drawing of a face upside down and you can't recognize the expression of the face. Perhaps you can see that it is smiling, but not exactly what *kind* of smile it is. You cannot imitate the smile or describe it more exactly.

And yet the picture which you have turned round may be a most exact representation of a person's face.

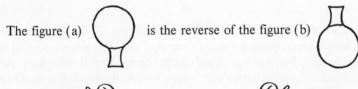

The figure (a) is the reverse of the figure (b)

As (c) is the reverse of (d) *Pleasure*

But—I should like to say—there is a different difference between my impressions of (c) and (d) and between those of (a) and (b). (d), for example, looks neater than (c). (Compare a remark of Lewis Carroll's.) (d) is easy, (c) hard to copy.

Imagine the duck-rabbit hidden in a tangle of lines. Now I suddenly notice it in the picture, and notice it simply as the head of a rabbit. At some later time I look at the same picture and notice the same figure, but see it as the duck, without necessarily realizing that it was the same figure both times.—If I later see the aspect change—can I say that the duck and rabbit aspects are now seen quite differently from when I recognized them separately in the tangle of lines? No.

But the change produces a surprise not produced by the recognition.

If you search in a figure (1) for another figure (2), and then find it, you see (1) in a new way. Not only can you give a new kind of description of it, but noticing the second figure was a new visual experience.

But you would not necessarily want to say 'Figure (1) looks quite different now; it isn't even in the least like the figure I saw before, though they are congruent!'

There are here hugely many interrelated phenomena and possible concepts.

Then is the copy of the figure an *incomplete* description of my visual experience? No.—But the circumstances decide whether, and what, more detailed specifications are necessary.—It *may* be an incomplete description; if there is still something to ask.

Of course we can say: There are certain things which fall equally under the concept 'picture-rabbit' and under the concept 'picture-duck'. And a picture, a drawing, is such a thing.—But the *impression* is not simultaneously of a picture-duck and a picture-rabbit.

'What I really *see* must surely be what is produced in me by the influence of the object'—Then what is produced in me is a sort of copy, something that in its turn can be looked at, can be before one; almost something like a *materialization*.

And this materialization is something spatial and it must be possible to describe it in purely spatial terms. For instance (if it is a face) it can smile; the concept of friendliness, however, has no place in an account of it, but is *foreign* to such an account (even though it may subserve it).

If you ask me what I saw, perhaps I shall be able to make a sketch which shews you; but I shall mostly have no recollection of the way my glance shifted in looking at it.

The concept of 'seeing' makes a tangled impression. Well, it is tangled.—I look at the landscape, my gaze ranges over it, I see all sorts of distinct and indistinct movement; *this* impresses itself sharply on me, *that* is quite hazy. After all, how completely ragged what we see can appear! And now look at all that can be meant by 'description of what is seen'.—But this just is what is called description of what is seen. There is not *one genuine* proper case of such description—the rest being just vague, something which awaits clarification, or which must just be swept aside as rubbish.

Here we are in enormous danger of wanting to make fine distinctions.—It is the same when one tries to define the concept of a material object in terms of 'what is really seen'.—What we have rather to do is to *accept* the everyday language-game, and to note *false* accounts of the matter *as* false. The primitive language-game which children are taught needs no justification; attempts at justification need to be rejected.

Take as an example the aspects of a triangle. This triangle

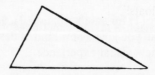

can be seen as a triangular hole, as a solid, as a geometrical drawing; as standing on its base, as hanging from its apex; as a mountain, as a wedge, as an arrow or pointer, as an overturned object which is meant to stand on the shorter side of the right angle, as a half parallelogram, and as various other things.

'You can think now of *this* now of *this* as you look at it, can regard it now as *this* now as this, and then you will see it now *this* way, now *this*.'—*What* way? There *is* no further qualification.

But how is it possible to *see* an object according to an *interpretation*?—The question represents it as a queer fact; as if something were being forced into a form it did not really fit. But no squeezing, no forcing took place here.

When it looks as if there were no room for such a form between other ones you have to look for it in another dimension. If there is no room here, there *is* room in another dimension.

(It is in this sense too that there is no room for imaginary numbers in the continuum of real numbers. But what this means is: the application of the concept of imaginary numbers is less like that of real numbers than appears from the look of the *calculations*. It is necessary to get down to the application, and then the concept finds a different place, one which, so to speak, one never dreamed of.)

How would the following account do:'What I can see something *as*, is what it can be a picture of'?

What this means is: the aspects in a change of aspects are those ones which the figure might sometimes have *permanently* in a picture.

A triangle can really be *standing up* in one picture, be hanging in another, and can in a third be something that has fallen over.—That is, I who am looking at it say, not'It may also be something that has fallen over,' but'That glass has fallen over and is lying there in fragments.' This is how we react to the picture.

Could I say what a picture must be like to produce this effect? No. There are, for example, styles of painting which do not convey anything to me in this immediate way, but do to other people. I think custom and upbringing have a hand in this.

What does it mean to say that I '*see the sphere floating in the air*' in a picture?

Is it enough that this description is the first to hand, is the matter-of-course one? No, for it might be so for various reasons. This might, for instance, simply be the conventional description.

What is the expression of my not merely understanding the picture in this way, for instance, (knowing what it is *supposed* to be), but *seeing* it in this way?— It is expressed by: 'The sphere seems to float,' 'You see it floating,' or again, in a special tone of voice, 'It floats!'

This, then, is the expression of taking something for something. But not being used as such.

Here we are not asking ourselves what are the causes and what produces this impression in a particular case.

And *is* it a special impression?—'Surely I see something *different* when I see the sphere floating from when I merely see it lying there.'—This really means: This expression is justified!—(For taken literally it is no more than a repetition.)

(And yet my impression is not that of a real floating sphere either. There are various forms of 'three-dimensional seeing'. The three-dimensional character of a photograph and the three-dimensional character of what we see through a stereoscope.)

'And is it really a different impression?'—In order to answer this I should like to ask myself whether there is really something different there in me. But how can I find out?—I *describe* what I am seeing differently.

Certain drawings are always seen as flat figures, and others sometimes, or always, three-dimensionally.

Here one would now like to say: the visual impression of what is seen three-dimensionally is three-dimensional; with the schematic cube, for instance, it is a cube. (For the description of the impression is the description of a cube.)

And then it seems queer that with some drawings our impression should be a flat thing, and with some a three-dimensional thing. One asks oneself 'Where is this going to end?'

When I see the picture of a galloping horse—do I merely *know* that this is the kind of movement meant? Is it superstition to think I *see* the horse galloping in the picture?—And does my visual impression gallop too?

What does anyone tell me by saying 'Now I see it as .....'? What consequences has this information? What can I do with it?

People often associate colours with vowels. Someone might find that a vowel changed its colour when it was repeated over and over again. He finds *a* 'now blue—now red', for instance.

The expression 'Now I am seeing it as . . .' might have no more significance for us than: 'Now I find *a* red.'

(Linked with physiological observations, even this change might acquire importance for us.)

Here it occurs to me that in conversation on aesthetic matters we use the words: 'You have to see it like *this*, this is how it is meant'; 'When you see it like *this*, you see where it goes wrong'; 'You have to hear this bar as an introduction'; 'You must hear it in this key'; 'You must phrase it like *this*' (which can refer to hearing as well as to playing).

This figure

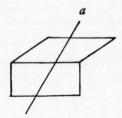

is supposed to represent a convex step and to be used in some kind of topological demonstration. For this purpose we draw the straight line *a* through the geometric centres of the two surfaces.—Now if anyone's three-dimensional impression of the figure were never more than momentary, and even so were now concave, now convex, that might make if difficult for him to follow our demonstration. And if he finds that the flat aspect alternates with a three-dimensional one, that is just as if I were to shew him completely different objects in the course of the demonstration.

What does it mean for me to look at a drawing in descriptive geometry and say: 'I know that this line appears again here, but I can't *see* it like that'? Does it simply mean a lack of familiarity in operating with the drawing; that I don't 'know my way about' too well?—This familiarity is certainly one of our criteria. What tells us that someone is seeing the drawing three-dimensionally is a certain kind of 'knowing one's way about'. Certain gestures, for instance, which indicate the three-dimensional relations: fine shades of behaviour.

I see that an animal in a picture is transfixed by an arrow. It has struck it in the throat and sticks out at the back of the neck. Let the picture be a silhouette.—Do you *see* the arrow—or do you merely *know* that these two bits are supposed to represent part of an arrow?

(Compare Köhler's figure of the interpenetrating hexagons.)

'But this isn't *seeing*!'—'But this is seeing!'—It must be possible to give both remarks a conceptual justification.

But this is seeing! *In what sense* is it seeing?

'The phenomenon is at first surprising, but a physiological explanation of it will certainly be found.'—
Our problem is not a causal but a conceptual one.

If the picture of the transfixed beast or of the interpenetrating hexagons were shewn to me just for a moment and then I had to describe it, *that* would be my description; if I had to draw it I should certainly produce a very faulty copy, but it would shew some sort of animal transfixed by an arrow, or two hexagons interpenetrating. That is to say: there are certain mistakes that I should *not* make.

The first thing to jump to my eye in this picture is: there are two hexagons.
Now I look at them and ask myself: 'Do I really see them *as* hexagons?'— and for the whole time they are before my eyes? (Assuming that they have not changed their aspect in that time.)—And I should like to reply: 'I am not thinking of them as hexagons the whole time.'

Someone tells me: 'I saw it at once as two hexagons. And that's the *whole* of *what* I saw.' But how do I understand this? I think he would have given this description at once in answer to the question 'What are you seeing?', nor would he have treated it as one among several possibilities. In this his description is like the answer 'A face' on being shewn the figure

The best description I can give of what was shewn me for a moment is *this*: . . .

'The impression was that of a rearing animal.' So a perfectly definite description came out.—Was it *seeing*, or was it a thought?

Do not try to analyse your own inner experience.

Of course I might also have seen the picture first as something different, and then have said to myself 'Oh, it's two hexagons!' So the aspect would have altered. And does this prove that I in fact *saw* it as something definite?

'Is it a *genuine* visual experience?' The question is: in what sense is it one?

Here it is *difficult* to see that what is at issue is the fixing of concepts.
A *concept* forces itself on one. (This is what you must not forget.) [. . .]

8   Observation

N. R. Hanson

Hanson's book Patterns of Discovery *was first published in 1958
and the following excerpt from his first chapter shows the strong and immediate
influence exerted by Wittgenstein's* Philosophical Investigations. *The book is
concerned with the philosophical aspects of research and discovery in science,
with the dependence of imaginative discovery upon rational procedure, and with
the dependence of rational procedure upon conceptual clarity in language.
'There is a sense ... in which seeing is a "theory-laden" undertaking. Observation of* x *is shaped by prior knowledge of* x. *Another influence on observations
rests in the language or notation used to express what we know, and without
which there would be little we could recognize as knowledge.'*

*To Wittgenstein's 'seeing' and 'seeing as', Hanson adds 'a further element in
seeing and observation', 'seeing that', which he suggests 'may be the logical
element which connects observing with our knowledge, and with our language'.
By 'seeing that', Hanson intends to refer to 'the conceptual organization' of the
visual field; ie to the ways in which observations cohere in the context of
knowledge, for example knowledge of tendencies, processes and mechanisms—
of how things behave under certain conditions. In order to bring out the
importance of 'seeing that', Hanson draws attention to the differences between
pictorial and linguistic representation, and to the ways in which observations
and pictures, which are not themselves 'true' or 'false', may be* significant *and
may provide the grounds for statements which can be assessed as true or false
('for what is it for things to make sense other than for descriptions of them to be
composed of meaningful sentences?').*

*It is of course easier to understand how Hanson's discussion might be
applied to a landscape by John Constable than, say, to an abstract painting. But
it might be considered that both the painter and the observer of an abstract
painting must attempt to get their observations 'to cohere against a background
of established knowledge', just as do the painter and viewer of a landscape. In
the case of the abstract painting, deprived of the possibility of matching against*

some actual or imagined scene, we could expect that 'established knowledge' would be defined less by reference to natural science, or even to general or artistic conventions of representation, and more by established paradigms of 'abstract painting' and by a set of appropriate linguistic descriptions. It follows that abstract painting may be more conceptually dependent upon language— and indeed upon a specific discourse about painting—than figurative painting, and not less so as some enthusiasts would have it.

This is not to say either that abstract painting is intrinsically uninteresting or that we can or should put the clock back and start again from Constable. Hanson's book raises a more substantial issue concerning the apparent separation of science and visual representation. It also suggests a partial explanation for this separation. In a later chapter on 'Elementary Particle Physics' he gives an account of how and why geometrical and picturing models and procedures as the paradigms of scientific theory-formation were finally replaced in the early twentieth century by mathematical models and procedures. Of the 'present situation in fundamental physics', he writes:

> *This is unpicturability-in-principle: to picture particles is to rob oneself of what is needed to explain ordinary physical objects. Though intrinsically unpicturable and unimaginable, these mathematically described particles can explain matter in the most powerful manner known to physics. Indeed, only when the quest for picturability ended was the essence of explanation within all natural philosophy laid bare.*

Notwithstanding the idealism of talk about 'essences of explanation', Hanson's suggestion reverses the normal art-historical presupposition that it was 'art' which moved away from 'science'. It also raises the tantalizing speculation that the Modernist emphasis on feeling, sensitivity and expression, and the militant distinguishing of these from knowledge and information, may at some level have been a retreat misrepresented as an advance. That is to say this emphasis may have been a response at some level to the final displacement of visual representation from its formerly central function as a source of significant naturalistic discriminations, on the basis of which descriptions could be made that were open to judgement of their truth or falsity. (For examples of the earlier performance of this function in pictorial representation, see Ivins, text 13.)

Source: *Patterns of Discovery: an inquiry into the conceptual foundations of science* (Cambridge University Press, London, 1972), ch. 1, pp. 5–30. This material has been edited. Footnotes and illustrations have been re-numbered and some have been omitted.

A

[. . .] Let us consider Johannes Kepler: imagine him on a hill watching the dawn. With him is Tycho Brahe. Kepler regarded the sun as fixed: it was the earth that moved. But Tycho followed Ptolemy and Aristotle in this much at least: the earth was fixed and all other celestial bodies moved around it. *Do Kepler and Tycho see the same thing in the east at dawn?*

We might think this an experimental or observational question . . . Not so in the sixteenth and seventeenth centuries. Thus Galileo said to the Ptolemaist '. . . neither Aristotle nor you can prove that the earth is *de facto* the centre of the universe . . .'[1] 'Do Kepler and Tycho see the same thing in the east at dawn?' is perhaps not a *de facto* question . . . but rather the beginning of an examination of the concepts of seeing and observation.

The resultant discussion might run:

'Yes, they do.'

'No, they don't.'

'Yes, they do!'

'No, they don't!'. . .

That this is possible suggests that there may be reasons for both contentions. Let us consider some points in support of the affirmative answer.

The physical processes involved when Kepler and Tycho watch the dawn are worth noting. Identical photons are emitted from the sun; these traverse solar space, and our atmosphere. The two astronomers have normal vision; hence these photons pass through the cornea, aqueous humour, iris, lens and vitreous body of their eyes in the same way. Finally their retinas are affected. Similar electro-chemical changes occur in their selenium cells. The same configuration is etched on Kepler's retina as on Tycho's. So they see the same thing.

Locke sometimes spoke of seeing in this way: a man sees the sun if his is a normally-formed retinal picture of the sun. Dr Sir W. Russell Brain speaks of our retinal sensations as indicators and signals. Everything taking place behind the retina is, as he says, 'an intellectual operation based largely on non-visual experience. . .'.[2] What we *see* are the changes in the *tunica retina* . . . Often, talk of seeing can direct attention to the retina. Normal people are distinguished from those for whom no retinal pictures can form: we may say of the former that they can see whilst the latter cannot see. Reporting when a certain red dot can be seen may supply the oculist with direct information about the condition of one's retina.

This need not be pursued, however . . . Seeing the sun is not seeing retinal pictures of the sun. The retinal images which Kepler and Tycho have are four in number, inverted and tiny. Astronomers cannot be referring to these when they say they see the sun. If they are hypnotized, drugged, drunk or distracted they may not see the sun, even though their retinas register its image in exactly the same way as usual.

Seeing is an experience. A retinal reaction is only a physical state—a photochemical excitation. Physiologists have not always appreciated the differences between experiences and physical states. People, not their eyes, see. Cameras, and eyeballs, are blind. Attempts to locate within the organs of sight (or within the neurological reticulum behind the eyes) some nameable called 'seeing' may be dismissed. That Kepler and Tycho do, or do not, see the same thing cannot be supported by reference to the physical states of their retinas, optic nerves or visual cortices: there is more to seeing than meets the eyeball.

Naturally, Tycho and Kepler see the same physical object. They are both visually aware of the sun. If they are put into a dark room and asked to report when they see something—anything at all—they may both report the same object at the same time. Suppose that the only object to be seen is a certain lead cylinder. Both men see the same thing: namely this object—whatever it is. It is just here, however, that the difficulty arises, for while Tycho sees a mere pipe, Kepler will see a telescope, the instrument about which Galileo has written to him.

Unless both are visually aware of the same object there can be nothing of philosophical interest in the question whether or not they see the same thing. Unless they both see the sun in this prior sense our question cannot even strike a spark.

Nonetheless, both Tycho and Kepler have a common visual experience of some sort. This experience perhaps constitutes their seeing the same thing. Indeed, this may be a seeing logically more basic than anything expressed in the pronouncement 'I see the sun' (where each means something different by 'sun'). If what they meant by the word 'sun' were the only clue, then Tycho and Kepler could not be seeing the same thing, even though they were gazing at the same object.

If, however, we ask, not 'Do they see the same thing?' but rather 'What is it that they both see?', an unambiguous answer may be forthcoming. Tycho and Kepler are both aware of a brilliant yellow-white disc in a blue expanse over a green one. Such a 'sense-datum' picture is single and uninverted. To be unaware of it is not to have it. Either it dominates one's visual attention completely or it does not exist.

If Tycho and Kepler are aware of anything visual, it must be of some pattern of colours. What else could it be? We do not touch or hear with our eyes, we only take in light. This private pattern is the same for both observers. Surely if asked to sketch the contents of their visual fields they would both draw a kind of semi-circle on a horizon-line. They say they see the sun. But they do not see every side of the sun at once; so what they really see is discoid to begin with. It is but a visual aspect of the sun. In any single observation the sun is a brilliantly luminescent disc, a penny painted with radium.

So something about their visual experiences at dawn is the same for both: a brilliant yellow-white disc centred between green and blue colour patches. Sketches of what they both see could be identical—congruent. In this sense Tycho and Kepler see the same thing at dawn. The sun appears to them in the same way. The same view, or scene, is presented to them both.

In fact, we often speak in this way. Thus the account of a recent solar eclipse: 'Only a thin crescent remains; white light is now completely obscured; the sky appears a deep blue, almost purple, and the landscape is a monochromatic green . . . there are the flashes of light on the disc's circumference and now the brilliant crescent to the left. . .'[3] Newton writes in a similar way in the *Opticks*: 'These Arcs at their first appearance were of a violet and blue Colour, and between them were white Arcs of Circles, which . . . became a little tinged in their inward Limbs with red and yellow . . .'[4] Every physicist employs the language of lines, colour patches, appearances, shadows. In so far as two normal observers use this language of the same event, they begin from the same data: they are making the same observation. Differences between them must arise in the interpretations they put on these data.

Thus, to summarize, saying that Kepler and Tycho see the same thing at dawn just because their eyes are similarly affected is an elementary mistake. There is a difference between a physical state and a visual experience. Suppose, however, that it is argued as above—that they see the same thing because they have the same sense-datum experience. Disparities in their accounts arise in *ex post facto* interpretations of what is seen, not in the fundamental visual data. If this is argued, further difficulties soon obtrude.

B

[. . .] How do visual experiences become organized? How is seeing possible? Consider Fig 1 in the context of Fig 2:

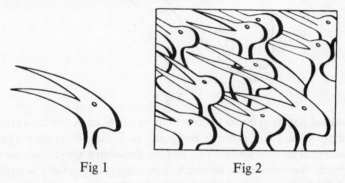

Fig 1   Fig 2

The context gives us the clue. Here, some people could not see the figure as an antelope. Could people who had never seen an antelope, but only birds, see an antelope in Fig 1?

In the context of Fig 3 the figure may indeed stand out as an antelope. It might even be urged that the figure seen in Fig 2 has no similarity to the one in Fig 3 although the two are congruent. Could anything be more opposed to a sense-datum account of seeing?

Fig 3

[. . .] The appropriate aspect of the illustration is brought out by the . . . context in which it appears. It is not an illustration of anything determinate unless it appears in some such context . . . I must talk and gesture around Fig 1 to get you to see the antelope when only the bird has revealed itself. I must provide a context. The context is part of the illustration itself.

Such a context, however, need not be set out explicitly. Often it is 'built into' thinking, imagining and picturing. We are set to appreciate the visual aspect of things in certain ways. Elements in our experience do not cluster at random.

Fig 4

A trained physicist could see one thing in Fig 4: an X-ray tube viewed from the cathode. Would Sir Lawrence Bragg and an Eskimo baby see the same thing when looking at an X-ray tube? Yes, and no. Yes—they are visually aware of the same object. No—the *ways* in which they are visually aware are profoundly different. Seeing is not only the having of a visual experience; it is also the way in which the visual experience is had.

At school the physicist had gazed at this glass-and-metal instrument. Returning now, after years in University and research, his eye lights upon the same object once again. Does he see the same thing now as he did then? Now he sees the instrument in terms of electrical circuit theory, thermodynamic theory, the theories of metal and glass structure, thermionic emission, optical transmission, refraction, diffraction, atomic theory, quantum theory and special relativity. [. . .]

If one must find a paradigm case of seeing it would be better to regard as such not the visual apprehension of colour patches but things like seeing what time it is, seeing what key a piece of music is written in, and seeing whether a wound is septic.

Pierre Duhem writes:

> Enter a laboratory; approach the table crowded with an assortment of apparatus, an electric cell, silk-covered copper wire, small cups of mercury, spools, a mirror mounted on an iron bar; the experimenter is inserting into small openings the metal ends of ebony-headed pins; the iron oscillates, and the mirror attached to it throws a luminous band upon a celluloid scale; the forward-backward motion of this spot enables the physicist to observe the minute oscillations of the iron bar. But ask him what he is doing. Will he answer 'I am studying the oscillations of an iron bar which carries a mirror'? No, he will say that he is measuring the electric resistance of the

spools. If you are astonished, if you ask him what his words mean, what relation they have with the phenomena he has been observing and which you have noted at the same time as he, he will answer that your question requires a long explanation and that you should take a course in electricity.[5]

The visitor must learn some physics before he can see what the physicist sees. Only then will the context throw into relief those features of the objects before him which the physicist sees as indicating resistance.

This obtains in all seeing. Attention is rarely directed to the space between the leaves of a tree, save when a Keats brings it to our notice. (Consider also what was involved in Crusoe's seeing a vacant space in the sand as a footprint.) Our attention most naturally rests on objects and events which dominate the visual field. What a blooming, buzzing, undifferentiated confusion visual life would be if we all arose tomorrow without attention capable of dwelling only on what had heretofore been overlooked. [. . .]

C

There is a sense . . . in which seeing is a 'theory-laden' undertaking. Observation of x is shaped by prior knowledge of x. Another influence on observations rests in the language or notation used to express what we know, and without which there would be little we could recognize as knowledge. . .

I do not mean to identify seeing with *seeing as*. Seeing an X-ray tube is not seeing a glass-and-metal object as an X-ray tube. However, seeing an antelope and seeing an object as an antelope have much in common. Something of the concept of seeing can be discerned from tracing uses of 'seeing . . . as . . .' Wittgenstein[6] is reluctant to concede this, but his reasons are not clear to me. On the contrary, the logic of 'seeing as' seems to illuminate the general perceptual case. Consider again the footprint in the sand. Here all the organizational features of *seeing as* stand out clearly, in the absence of an *'object'*. One can even imagine cases where 'He sees it as a footprint' would be a way of referring to another's apprehension of what actually is a footprint. So, while I do not identify, for example, Hamlet's seeing of a camel in the clouds with his seeing of Yorick's skull, there is still something to be learned about the latter from noting what is at work in the former.

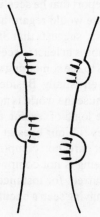

Fig 5

There is, however, a further element in seeing and observation. If the label 'seeing as' has drawn out certain features of these concepts, 'seeing that . . .' may bring out more. Seeing a bear in Fig 5 [is] to see that were the 'tree' circled we should come up behind the beast. Seeing the dawn was for Tycho and Simplicius to see that the earth's brilliant satellite was beginning its diurnal circuit around us, while for Kepler and Galileo it was to see that the earth was spinning them back into the light of our local star. Let us examine 'seeing that' in these examples. It may be the logical element which connects observing with our knowledge, and with our language.

Of course there are cases where the data are confused and where we may have no clue to guide us. In microscopy one often reports sensations in a phenomenal, lustreless way: 'It is green in this light; darkened areas mark the broad end. . .' So too the physicist may say: 'The needle oscillates, and there is a faint streak near the neon parabola. Scintillations appear on the periphery of the cathodescope. . .' To deny that these are genuine cases of seeing, even observing, would be unsound, just as is the suggestion that they are the only genuine cases of seeing.

These examples are, however, overstressed. The language of shapes, colour patches, oscillations and pointer-readings is appropriate to the unsettled experimental situation, where confusion and even conceptual muddle may dominate. The observer may not know what he is seeing: he aims only to get his observations to cohere against a background of established knowledge. This seeing is the goal of observation. It is in these terms, and not in terms of 'phenomenal' seeing, that new inquiry proceeds. Every physicist forced to observe his data as in an oculist's office finds himself in a special, unusual situation. He is obliged to forget what he knows and to watch events like a child. These are non-typical cases, however spectacular they may sometimes be.

First registering observations and then casting about for knowledge of them gives a simple model of how the mind and the eye fit together. The relationship between seeing and the corpus of our knowledge, however, is not a simple one.

What is it to see boxes, staircases, birds, antelopes, bears, goblets, X-ray tubes? It is (at least) to have knowledge of certain sorts. (Robots and electric eyes are blind, however efficiently they react to light. Cameras cannot see.) It is to see that, were certain things done to objects before our eyes, other things would result. How should we regard a man's report that he sees x if we know him to be ignorant of all x-ish things? Precisely as we would regard a four-year-old's report that he sees a meson shower. 'Smith sees x' suggests that Smith could specify some things pertinent to x. To see an X-ray tube is at least to see that, were it dropped on stone, it would smash. To see a goblet is to see something with concave interior. We may be wrong, but not always—not even usually. Besides, deceptions proceed in terms of what is normal, ordinary. Because the world is not a cluster of conjurer's tricks, conjurers can exist. Because the logic of 'seeing that' is an intimate part of the concept of seeing, we sometimes rub our eyes at illusions.

'Seeing as' and 'seeing that' are not components of seeing, as rods and bearings are parts of motors: seeing is not composite. Still, one *can* ask logical questions. What must have occurred, for instance, for us to describe a man as having found a collar stud, or as having seen a bacillus? Unless he had had a visual sensation and knew what a bacillus was (and looked like) we would not say that he had seen a bacillus, except in the sense in which an infant could see a bacillus. 'Seeing as' and 'seeing that', then, are not psychological components of seeing. They are logically distinguishable elements in seeing-talk, in our concept of seeing.

Fig 6

To see Fig 6 as a transparent box, an ice-cube, or a block of glass is to see that it is six-faced, twelve-edged, eight-cornered. Its corners are solid right angles; if constructed it would be of rigid, or semi-rigid material, not of liquescent or gaseous stuff like oil, vapour or flames. It would be tangible. It would take up space in an exclusive way, being locatable here, there, but at least somewhere. Nor would it cease to exist when we blinked. Seeing it as a cube is just to see that all these things would obtain.

This is knowledge: it is knowing what kind of a thing 'box' or 'cube' denotes and something about what materials can make up such an entity. 'Transparent box' or 'glass cube' would not express what was seen were any of these further considerations denied. Seeing a bird in the sky involves seeing that it will not suddenly do vertical snap rolls; and this is more than marks the retina. We could be wrong. But to see a bird, even momentarily, is to see it in all these connexions. As Wisdom would say, every perception involves an aetiology and a prognosis.[7]

Sense-datum theorists stress how we can go wrong in our observations, as when we call aeroplanes 'birds'. Thus they seek what we are right about, even in these cases. Preoccupation with this problem obscures another one, namely, that of describing what is involved when we are right about what we say we see; and after all this happens very often. His preoccupation with mistakes leads the phenomenalist to portray a world in which we are usually deceived; but the world of physics is not like that. Were a physicist in an ordinary laboratory situation to react to his visual environment with purely sense-datum responses—as does the infant or the idiot—we would think him out of his mind. We would think him *not* to be seeing what was around him.

'Seeing that' threads knowledge into our seeing; it saves us from re-identifying everything that meets our eye; it allows physicists to observe new data as physicists, and not as cameras. We do not ask 'What's that?' of every passing bicycle. The knowledge is there in the seeing and not an adjunct of it. (The pattern of threads is there in the cloth and not tacked on to it by ancillary operations.) We rarely catch ourselves tacking knowledge on to what meets the eye. Seeing this page as having an opposite side requires no squeezing or forcing, yet nothing optical guarantees that when you turn the sheet it will not cease to exist. This is but another way of saying that ordinary seeing is corrigible, which everybody would happily concede. The search for incorrigible seeing has sometimes led some philosophers to deny that anything less than the incorrigible is seeing at all.

Seeing an object x is to see that it may behave in the ways we know x's do behave: if the object's behaviour does not accord with what we expect of x's we may be blocked from seeing it as a straightforward x any longer. Now we rarely see dolphin as fish, the earth as flat, the heavens as an inverted bowl or the sun as our satellite. '. . .what I perceive as the dawning of an aspect is not a property of the object, but an internal relation between it and other objects.'[8] To see in Fig 4 an X-ray tube is to see that a photo-sensitive plate placed below it will be irradiated. It is to see that the target will get extremely hot, and as it has no water-jacket it must be made of metal with a high melting-point—molybdenum or tungsten. It is to see that at high voltages green fluorescence will appear at the anode. Could a physicist see an X-ray tube without seeing that these other things would obtain? Could one see something as an incandescent light bulb and fail to see that it is the wire filament which 'lights up' to a white heat? The answer may sometimes be 'yes', but this only indicates that different things can be meant by 'X-ray tube' and 'incandescent bulb'. Two people confronted with an x may mean different things by x. Must their saying 'I see x' mean that they see the same thing? A child could parrot 'X-ray tube', or 'Kentucky' or 'Winston', when confronted with the figure above, but he would not see that these other things followed. And this is what the physicist does see.

If in the brilliant disc of which he is visually aware Tycho sees only the sun, then he cannot but see that it is a body which will behave in characteristically 'Tychonic' ways. These serve as the foundation for Tycho's general geocentric-geostatic theories about the sun. They are not imposed on his visual impressions as a tandem interpretation: they are 'there' in the seeing. (So too the interpretation of a piece of music is there in the music. Where else could it be? It is not something superimposed upon pure, unadulterated sound.)

Similarly we see Fig 6 as from underneath, as from above, or as a diagram of a rat maze or a gem-cutting project. However construed, the construing is there in the seeing. One is tempted to say 'the construing *is* the seeing'. The thread and its arrangement *is* the fabric, the sound and its composition *is* the music, the colour and its disposition *is* the painting. There are not two operations involved in my seeing Fig 6 as an ice-cube; I simply see it as an ice-cube. Analogously, the physicist sees an X-ray tube, not by first soaking up reflected light and then clamping on interpretations, but just as you see this page before you.

Tycho sees the sun beginning its journey from horizon to horizon. He sees that from some celestial vantage point the sun (carrying with it the moon and planets) could be watched circling our fixed earth. Watching the sun at dawn through Tychonic spectacles would be to see it in something like this way.

Kepler's visual field, however, has a different conceptual organization. Yet a drawing of what he sees at dawn could be a drawing of exactly what Tycho saw, and could be recognized as such by Tycho. But Kepler will see the horizon dipping, or turning away, from our fixed local star. The shift from sunrise to horizon-turn is analogous to the shift-of-aspect phenomena already considered; it is occasioned by differences between what Tycho and Kepler think they know.

These logical features of the concept of seeing are inextricable and indispensable to observation in research physics. Why indispensable? That men do see in a way that permits analysis into 'seeing as' and 'seeing that' factors is one thing; 'indispensable', however, suggests that the world must be seen thus. This is a stronger claim, requiring a stronger argument. Let us put it differently: that observation in physics is not an encounter with unfamiliar and unconnected flashes, sounds and bumps, but rather a calculated meeting with these as flashes, sounds and bumps of a particular kind—this might figure in an account of what observation is. It would not secure the point that observation could not be otherwise. This latter type of argument is now required: it must establish that an alternative account would be not merely false, but absurd. To this I now turn.

D

Fortunately, we do not see the sun and the moon as we see the points of colour and light in the oculist's office; nor does the physicist see his laboratory equipment, his desk, or his hands in the baffled way that he may view a cloud-chamber photograph or an oscillograph pattern. In most cases we could give further information about what sort of thing we see. This might be expressed in a list: for instance, that x would break if dropped, that x is hollow, and so on.

To see Fig 5 as a bear on a tree is to see that further observations are possible; we can imagine the bear as viewed from the side or from behind. Indeed, seeing Fig 5 as a bear is just to have seen that these other views could all be simultaneous. It is also to see that certain observations are not possible: for example, the bear cannot be waving one paw in the air, nor be dangling one foot. This too is 'there' in the seeing.

'Is it a question of both seeing and thinking? or an amalgam of the two, as I should almost like to say?'[9] Whatever one would like to say, there is more to seeing Fig 5 as a bear, than optics, photochemistry or phenomenalism can explain.

Notice a logical feature: 'see that' and 'seeing that' are always followed by 'sentential' clauses. The addition of but an initial capital letter and a full stop sets them up as independent sentences. One can see an ice-cube, or see a kite as a bird. One cannot see that an ice-cube, nor see that a bird. Nor is this due to limitations of vision. Rather, one may see that *ice-cubes can melt*; that *birds have 'hollow' bones*. Tycho and Simplicius see that *the universe is geocentric;* Kepler and Galileo see that *it is heliocentric.* The physicist sees that *anode-fluorescence will appear in an X-ray tube at high voltages.* The phrases in italics are complete sentential units.

Pictures and statements differ in logical type, and the steps between visual pictures and the statements of what is seen are many and intricate. Our visual consciousness is dominated by pictures; scientific knowledge, however, is primarily linguistic. Seeing is, as I should almost like to say, an amalgam of the two—pictures and language. At the least, the concept of seeing embraces the concepts of visual sensation and of knowledge.

The gap between pictures and language locates the logical function of 'seeing that'. For vision is essentially pictorial, knowledge fundamentally linguistic. Both vision and knowledge are indispensable elements in seeing; but differences between pictorial and linguistic representation may mark differences between the optical and conceptual features of seeing. This may illuminate what 'seeing that' consists in.

Not all the elements of statement correspond to the elements of pictures: only someone who misunderstood the uses of language would expect otherwise. There is a 'linguistic' factor in seeing, although there is nothing linguistic about what forms in the eye, or in the mind's eye. Unless there were this linguistic element, nothing we ever observed could have relevance for our knowledge. We could not speak of significant observations: nothing seen would make sense, and microscopy would only be a kind of kaleidoscopy. For what is it for things to make sense other than for descriptions of them to be composed of meaningful sentences?

We must explore the gulf between pictures and language, between sketching and describing, drawing and reporting. Only by showing how picturing and speaking are different can one suggest how 'seeing that' may bring them together; and brought together they must be if observations are to be *significant* or *noteworthy*.

Knowledge here is of what there is, as factually expressed in books, reports, and essays. How to do things is not our concern. I know how to whistle; but could I express that knowledge in language? Could I describe the taste of salt, even though I know perfectly well how salt tastes? I know how to control a parachute— much of that knowledge was imparted in lectures and drills, but an essential part of it was not *imparted* at all; it was 'got on the spot'. Physicists rely on 'know-how', on the 'feel' of things and the 'look' of a situation, for these control the direction of research. Such imponderables, however, rarely affect the corpus of physical truths. It is not Galileo's insight, Newton's genius and Einstein's imagination which have *per se* changed our knowledge of what there is: it is the true things they have said. 'Physical knowledge', therefore, will mean 'what is reportable in the texts, reports and discussions of physics.' We are concerned with *savoir*, not *savoir faire*.

The 'foundation' of the language of physics, the part closest to mere sensation, is a series of statements. Statements are true or false. Pictures are not at all like statements: they are neither true nor false; retinal, cortical, or sense-datum pictures are neither true nor false. Yet what we see can determine whether statements like 'The sun is above the horizon' and 'The cube is transparent', are true or false. Our visual sensations may be 'set' by language forms; how else could they be appreciated in terms of what we know? Until they *are* so appreciated they do not constitute observation: they are more like the buzzing confusion of fainting or the vacant vista of aimless staring through a railway window. Knowledge of the world is not a *montage* of sticks, stones, colour patches and noises, but a system of propositions.

Fig 4 . . . asserts nothing. It could be inaccurate, but it could not be a lie. This is the wedge between pictures and language.

Significance, relevance—these notions depend on what we already know.

Objects, events, pictures, are not intrinsically significant or relevant. If seeing were just an optical-chemical process, then nothing we saw would ever be relevant to what we know, and nothing known could have significance for what we see. Visual life would be unintelligible; intellectual life would lack a visual aspect. Man would be a blind computer harnessed to a brainless photoplate.

Pictures often copy originals. All the elements of a copy, however, have the same kind of function. The lines depict elements in the original. The arrangement of the copy's elements shows the disposition of elements in the original. Copy and original are of the same logical type; you and your reflection are of the same type. Similarly, language might copy what it describes.

Consider Fig 5 alongside 'The bear is on the tree.' The picture contains a bear-element and a tree-element. If it is true to life, then in the original there is a bear and a tree. If the sentence is true *of* life, then (just as it contains 'bear' and 'tree') the situation it describes contains a bear and a tree. The picture combines its elements, it mirrors the actual relation of the bear and the tree. The sentence likewise conjoins 'bear' and 'tree' in the schema 'The —— is on the ——.' This verbal relation signifies the actual relation of the real bear and the real tree. Both picture and sentence are true copies: they contain nothing the original lacks, and lack nothing the original contains. The elements of the picture stand for (represent) elements of the original: so do 'bear' and 'tree'. This is more apparent when expressed symbolically as $b \ R \ t$, where $b =$ bear, $t =$ tree and $R =$ the relation of being on.

By the arrangement of their elements these copies show the arrangement in the original situation. Thus Fig 5, 'The bear is on the tree', and 'bRt' show what obtains with the real bear and the real tree; while 'The tree is on the bear', and 'tRb', and a certain obvious cluster of lines do not show what actually obtains.

The copy is of the same type as the original. We can sketch the bear's teeth, but not his growl, any more than we could see the growl of the original bear. Leonardo could draw Mona Lisa's smile, but not her laugh. Language, however, is more versatile. Here is a dissimilarity between picturing and asserting which will grow to fracture the account once tendered by Wittgenstein, Russell and Wisdom. Language can encapsulate scenes and sounds, teeth and growls, smiles and laughs; a picture, or a gramophone, can do one or the other, but not both. Pictures and recordings stand for things by possessing certain properties of the original itself. Images, reflections, pictures and maps duplicate the spatial properties of what they image, reflect, picture or map; gramophone recordings duplicate audio-temporal properties. Sentences are not like this. They do not stand for things in virtue of possessing properties of the original; they do not *stand for* anything. They can state what is, or could be, the case. They can be used to make assertions, convey descriptions, supply narratives, accounts, etc, none of which depend on the possession of some property in common with what the statement is about. We need not write 'THE BEAR is bigger than ITS CUB' to show our meaning.

Images, reflections, pictures and maps in fact copy originals with different degrees of strictness. A reflection of King's Parade does not copy in the same sense that a charcoal sketch does, and both differ from the representation of 'K.P.'

on a map of Cambridge and from a town-planner's drawing. The more like a reflection a map becomes, the less useful it is as a map. Drawings are less like copies of originals than are photographs. Of a roughly sketched ursoid shape one says either 'That's a bear' or 'That's supposed to be a bear.' Similarly with maps. Of a certain dot on the map one says either 'This is Cambridge' or 'This stands for Cambridge.'

Language copies least of all. There are exceptional words like 'buzz', 'tinkle' and 'toot', but they only demonstrate how conventional our languages and notations are. Nothing about 'bear' looks like a bear; nothing in the sound of 'bear' resembles a growl. That b-e-a-r can refer to bears is due to a convention which co-ordinates the word with the object. There is nothing dangerous about a red flag, yet it is a signal for danger. Of Fig 5 we might say 'There is a bear.' We would never say this of the word 'bear'. At the cinema we say 'It's a bear', or 'There's K.P.'—not 'That stands for a bear', or 'That denotes K.P.' It is words that denote; but they are rarely like what they denote.

Sentences do not show, for example, bears climbing trees, but they can state that bears climb trees. Showing the sun climbing into the sky consists in representing sun and sky and arranging them appropriately. Stating that the sun is climbing into the sky consists in referring to the sun and then characterizing it as climbing into the sky. The differences between representing and referring, between arranging and characterizing—these are the differences between picturing and language-using.

These differences exist undiminished between visual sense-data and basic sentences. Early logical constructionists were inattentive to the difficulties in fitting visual sense-data to basic sentences. Had they heeded the differences between pictures and maps, they might have detected greater differences still between pictures and language. One's visual awareness of a brown ursoid patch is logically just as remote from the utterance '(I am aware of a) brown, ursoid patch now,' as with any of the pictures and sentences we have considered. The picture is of x; the statement is to the effect that x. The picture shows x; the statement refers to and describes x. The gap between pictures and language is not closed one millimetre by focusing on sense-data and basic sentences.

The prehistory of languages need not detain us. The issue concerns differences between *our* languages and *our* pictures, and not the smallness of those differences at certain historical times. Wittgenstein is misleading about this: '...and from [hieroglyphic writing] came the alphabet without the essence of representation being lost.'[10] This strengthened the picture theory of meaning, a truth-functional account of language and a theory of atomic sentences. But unless the essence of representation had been lost, languages could not be used in speaking the truth, telling lies, referring and characterizing.

Not all elements of a sentence do the same work. All the elements of pictures, however, just represent. A picture of the dawn could be cut into small pictures, but sentences like 'The sun is on the horizon' and 'I perceive a solaroid patch now' cannot be cut into small sentences. All the elements of the picture show something; none of the elements of the sentences state anything. 'Bear!' may serve as a statement, as may 'Tree!' from the woodcutter, or 'Sun!' in eclipse-observations. But 'the', 'is' and 'on' are not likely ever to behave as statements.

Pictures are of the picturable. Recordings are of the recordable. You cannot play a smile or a wink on the gramophone. But language is more versatile: we can describe odours, sounds, feels, looks, smiles and winks. This freedom makes type-mistakes possible: for example, 'They found his pituitary but not his mind,' 'We surveyed his retina but could not find his sight.' Only when we are free from the natural limitations of pictures and recordings can such errors occur. They are just possible in maps; of the hammer and sickle which signifies Russia on a school map, for instance, a child might ask 'How many miles long is the sickle?' Maps with their partially conventional characters must be read (as pictures and photographs need not be); yet they must copy.

There is a corresponding gap between visual pictures and what we know. Seeing bridges this, for while seeing is at the least a 'visual copying' of objects, it is also more than that. It is a certain sort of seeing of objects: seeing that if *x* were done to them *y* would follow. This fact got lost in all the talk about knowledge arising from sense experience, memory, association and correlation. Memorizing, associating, correlating and comparing mental pictures may be undertaken *ad indefinitum* without one step having been taken towards scientific knowledge, that is, propositions known to be true. How long must one shuffle photographs, diagrams and sketches of antelopes before the statement 'antelopes are ungulates' springs forth?

When language and notation are ignored in studies of observation, physics is represented as resting on sensation and low-grade experiment. It is described as repetitious, monotonous concatenation of spectacular sensations, and of school-laboratory experiments. But physical science is not just a systematic exposure of the senses to the world; it is also a way of thinking about the world, a way of forming conceptions. The paradigm observer is not the man who sees and reports what all normal observers see and report, but the man who sees in familiar objects what no one else has seen before.

Notes

1   Galileo, *Dialogue Concerning the Two Chief World Systems* (California, 1953), 'The First Day', p. 33.
2   W. Russell Brain (with Strauss), *Recent Advances in Neurology* (London, 1929) pp. 88ff.
3   From the BBC report, 30 June 1954.
4   Isaac Newton, *Opticks*, II:I.
5   Pierre Duhem, *La théorie physique* (Paris, 1914) p. 218.
6   ' "Seeing as" is not part of perception. And for that reason it is like seeing and again not like.' Ludwig Wittgenstein, *Philosophical Investigations,* p. 197.
7   'Is the pinning on of a medal merely the pinning on of a bit of metal?' Wisdom, 'Gods', *Proceedings of the Aristotelian Society*, 1944–5.
8   Wittgenstein, *Philosophical Investigations,* p. 212; cf *Tractatus Logico-Philosophicus* 2.0121.
9   Wittgenstein, *Philosophical Investigations,* p. 197.
10 Wittgenstein, *Tractatus Logico-Philosophicus*, 4.016.

9   Seven Strictures on Similarity

Nelson Goodman

Goodman's book The Languages of Art *(see text 16) offers one of the most sensible analyses yet published of systems of artistic representation. The following essay should give some pause for thought to those by whom compare-and-contrast exercises are seen as basic tools and tests of art historical teaching and learning, as also to those by whom degrees of artistic 'naturalism' and 'realism' are assessed in respect of some descriptive or iconic similarity to features of the world.*

More generally Goodman is concerned to alert us to the possibility that while we normally take similarity as offering empirical evidence on which to form metaphors or principles of classification and discrimination, judgements of similarity may actually follow *from metaphorical modes or principles of classification and discrimination already established. Such judgements, that is to say, may merely affirm those types of relationship we have already established as means to organize our observations and deliberations. Classification of works of art, for instance, is often supposed to be established on the basis of stylistic similarities. Following Goodman, we might suspect that the 'finding' of stylistic similarities is occasionally a sign that some principle of classification has* already *been applied or that some interest is already at work. In this context, we might also consider Wittgenstein's notion of 'family resemblances' as holding between items falling under the same concept (such as those which might count as 'games'). There will be times when we may find ourselves classifying together things which defeat our strenuous efforts to find them similar.*

Goodman asserts that similarity is relative to culture, to purposes and interests, to inductive practices and principles, to significance and to circumstance.

It is not a reliable basis upon which to form a picture of any of these, since similarity 'tends ... to require for its explanation just what it purports to explain'.

Source: Problems and Projects (Hackett Publishing Company, 1972), pp. 437–446. Footnotes have been deleted. Reprinted by permission of Nelson Goodman and Hackett Publishing Company Inc., Indianapolis, Indiana.

Similarity, I submit, is insidious. And if the association here with invidious comparison is itself invidious, so much the better. Similarity, ever ready to solve philosophical problems and overcome obstacles, is a pretender, an impostor, a quack. It has, indeed, its place and its uses, but is more often found where it does not belong, professing powers it does not possess.

The strictures I shall lay against similarity are none of them new, but only recently have I come to realize how often I have encountered this false friend and had to undo his work.

First Stricture: Similarity does not make the difference between representations and descriptions, distinguish any symbols as peculiarly 'iconic', or account for the grading of pictures as more or less realistic or naturalistic.

The conviction that resemblance is the necessary and sufficient condition for representation is so deeply ingrained that the evident and conclusive arguments to the contrary are seldom considered. Yet obviously one dime is not a picture of another, a girl is not a representation of her twin sister, one printing of a word is not a picture of another printing of it from the same type, and two photographs of the same scene, even from the same negative, are not pictures of each other.

All that this proves, of course, is that resemblance alone is not enough for representation. But where reference has been established—where a symbol does refer to some object—is not similarity then a sufficient condition for the symbol's being a representation? Plainly *no*. Consider a page of print that begins with 'the final seven words on this page' and ends with the same seven words repeated. The first of these seven-word inscriptions surely refers to the second, and is as much like it as can be, yet is no more a picture of it than is any printing of a word a picture of another printing.

Still, once pictures are somehow distinguished from other denotative symbols—and this must be by some other means than similarity—does not comparative naturalism or realism among pictures depend upon their degree of resemblance to what they represent? Not even this can be maintained. For pictures of goblins and unicorns are quite easily graded as more or less realistic or naturalistic or fantastic, though this cannot depend upon degree of resemblance to goblins and unicorns

The most we can say is that among pictures that represent actual objects, degree of realism correlates to some extent with degree of similarity of picture to object. But we must beware of supposing that similarity constitutes any firm, invariant criterion of realism; for similarity is relative, variable, culture-dependent. And even where, within a single culture, judgments of realism and of resemblance tend to coincide, we cannot safely conclude that the judgments of realism follow upon the judgments of resemblance. Just the reverse may be at least equally true: that we judge the resemblance greater where, as a result of our familiarity with the manner of representation, we judge the realism greater.

Second Stricture: Similarity does not pick out inscriptions that are 'tokens of a common type', or replicas of each other.

Only our addiction to similarity deludes us into accepting similarity as the basis for grouping inscriptions into the several letters, words, and so forth. The idea that inscriptions of the same letter are more alike than inscriptions of different letters evaporates in the glare of such counter-examples as those in Fig 1. One might argue that what counts is not degree of similarity but rather similarity

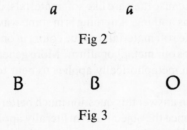

Fig 1

in a certain respect. In what respect, then, must inscriptions be alike to be replicas of one another? Some who should know better have supposed that the several inscriptions of the same letter are topologically equivalent, but to show how wrong this is we need only note that the first inscription in Fig 2 is not topologically equivalent to the second, and that the second mark in Fig 3 is topologically equivalent not to the first but to the third.

$$a \qquad\qquad ɑ$$

Fig 2

$$B \qquad\qquad ß \qquad\qquad O$$

Fig 3

We have terrible trouble trying to say how two inscriptions must be alike to be replicas of one another—how an inscription must resemble other inscriptions of the letter *a* to be itself an *a*. I suspect that the best we can do is to say that all inscriptions that are *a*'s must be alike in being *a*'s. That has the solid ring of assured truth, but is hardly electrifying. Moreover, notice that to say that all *a*'s are alike in being *a*'s amounts simply to saying that all *a*'s are *a*'s. The words 'alike in being' add nothing; similarity becomes entirely superfluous.

Third Stricture: Similarity does not provide the grounds for accounting two occurrences performances of the same work, or repetitions of the same behavior or experiment.

In other words, what I have said about replicas of inscriptions applies also to events. Two performances of the same work may be very different. Repetitions of the same behavior, such as hitting a tennis ball against a barn door, may involve widely varying sequences of motions. And if we experiment twice, do the differences between the two occasions make them different experiments or only different instances of the same experiment? The answer, as Sir James Thomson stresses, is always relative to a theory—we cannot repeat an experiment and look for a covering theory; we must have at least a partial theory before we know whether we have a repetition of the experiment. Two performances are of the same symphony if and only if, however unlike they may be, they comply with the same score. And whether two actions are instances of the same behavior depends upon how we take them; a response to the command, 'Do that again,' may well be the question: 'Do what again? Swat another fly or move choreographically the same way?'

In each of these cases, the grouping of occurrences under a work or an experiment or an activity depends not upon a high degree of similarity but upon the possession of certain characteristics. In the case of performances of a Beethoven symphony, the score determines what those requisite characteristics are; in the case of repetitions of an experiment, the constitutive characteristics must be sought in the theory or hypothesis being tested; in the case of ordinary actions, the principle of classification varies with our purposes and interests.

Fourth Stricture: Similarity does not explain metaphor or metaphorical truth.

Saying that certain sounds are soft is sometimes interpreted as saying in effect that these sounds are like soft materials. Metaphor is thus construed as elliptical simile, and metaphorical truths as elliptical literal truths. But to proclaim that certain tones are soft because they are like soft materials, or blue because they are like blue colors, explains nothing. Anything is in some way like anything else; any sounds whatever are like soft materials or blue colors in one way or another. What particular similarity does our metaphor affirm? More generally, what resemblance must the objects a term metaphorically applies to bear to the objects it literally applies to?

I do not think we can answer this question much better than we can answer the question what resemblance the objects a term literally applies to must bear to each other. In both cases, a reversal in order of explanation might be appropriate: the fact that a term applies, literally or metaphorically, to certain objects may itself constitute rather than arise from a particular similarity among those objects. Metaphorical use may serve to explain the similarity better than—or at least as well as—the similarity explains the metaphor.

Fifth Stricture: Similarity does not account for our predictive, or more generally, our inductive practice.

That the future will be like the past is often regarded as highly dubious—an assumption necessary for science and for life but probably false, and capable of justification only with the greatest difficulty if at all. I am glad to be able to offer you something positive here. All these doubts and worries are needless. I can assure you confidently that the future will be like the past. I do not know whether you find this comforting or depressing. But before you decide on celebration or suicide, I must add that while I am sure the future will be like the past, I am not sure in just what way it will be like the past. No matter what happens, the future will be in some way like the past.

Let me illustrate. Suppose in investigating the relationship of two variables—say pressure and volume, or temperature and conductivity—for a given material, we obtain the data plotted as unlabelled dots in Fig 4. Where shall we expect the next point to be? Perhaps at *a*, since *a* is like all preceding points in falling on the same straight line. But *b* is like all earlier points in falling on the same curve (the broken line—and many others), and in fact *every* value of *y* where *x* = *k* will be like all earlier points in falling on some—and indeed many a—same curve.

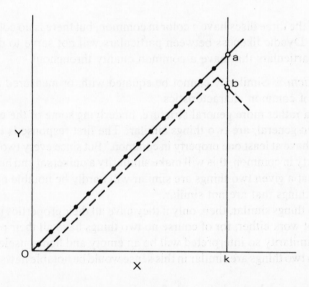

Fig 4

Thus our predictions cannot be based upon the bald principle that the future will be like the past. The question is *how* what is predicted is like what has already been found. Along which, among countless lines of similarity, do our predictions run? I suspect that rather than similarity providing any guidelines for inductive practice, inductive practice may provide the basis for some canons of similarity.

Sixth Stricture: Similarity between particulars does not suffice to define qualities.

Many a good philosopher has supposed that, given particulars and a relation of likeness that obtains between two particulars if and only if they share at least one among certain qualities, he can readily define such qualities and so avoid admitting them as additional undefined entities. If several particulars are all alike, the reasoning runs, they will all share some one quality or other; and qualities can thus be identified with the most comprehensive classes of particulars that are all alike.

The flaw here went unnoticed for a long time, simply for lack of logical scrutiny. Just how do we go from likeness between two particulars to likeness among several? Several particulars are all alike, we are tempted to say, if and only if each two of them are alike. But this will not work. Each two among three or more particulars may be alike (that is, have a quality in common) without all of them having any quality in common. Suppose, for example, we have three discs, the first one half red and half blue, the second one half blue and half yellow, and the third one half yellow and half red:

	rb	by	yr
	1	2	3

Each two of the three discs have a color in common, but there is no color common to all three. Dyadic likeness between particulars will not serve to define those classes of particulars that have a common quality throughout.

Seventh Stricture: Similarity cannot be equated with, or measured in terms of, possession of common characteristics.

This is a rather more general stricture, underlying some of the earlier ones.

When, in general, are two things similar? The first response is likely to be: 'When they have at least one property in common.' But since every two things have some property in common, this will make similarity a universal and hence useless relation. That a given two things are similar will hardly be notable news if there are no two things that are not similar.

Are two things similar, then, only if they have all their properties in common? This will not work either; for of course no two things have all their properties in common. Similarity so interpreted will be an empty and hence useless relation. That a given two things are similar in this sense would be notable news indeed, but false.

By now we may be ready to settle for a comparative rather than a categorical formula. Shall we say that two things *a* and *b* are more alike than two others *c* and *d* if *a* and *b* have more properties in common than do *c* and *d*? If that has a more scientific sound and seems safer, it is unfortunately no better; for any two things have exactly as many properties in common as any other two. If there are just three things in the universe, then any two of them belong together in exactly two classes and have exactly two properties in common: the property of belonging to the class consisting of the two things, and the property of belonging to the class consisting of all three things. If the universe is larger, the number of shared properties will be larger but will still be the same for every two elements. Where the number of things in the universe is *n*, each two things have in common exactly 2^{n-2} properties out of the total of $2^n - 1$ properties; each thing has 2^{n-2} properties that the other does not, and there are $2^{n-2} - 1$ properties that neither

90

has. If the universe is infinite, all these figures become infinite and equal.

I have, indeed, been counting only first-order extensional properties. Inclusion of higher-order properties will change the arithmetic but not the argument. The inevitable suggestion that we must consider intensional properties seems to me especially fruitless here, for identifying and distinguishing intensional properties is a notoriously slippery matter, and the idea of measuring similarity or anything else in terms of number of intensional properties need hardly be taken seriously.

More to the point would be counting not all shared properties but rather only *important* properties—or better, considering not the count but the overall importance of the shared properties. Then *a* and *b* are more alike than *c* and *d* if the cumulative importance of the properties shared by *a* and *b* is greater than that of the properties shared by *c* and *d*. But importance is a highly volatile matter, varying with every shift of context and interest, and quite incapable of supporting the fixed distinctions that philosophers so often seek to rest upon it.

Here, then, are seven counts in an indictment against similarity. What follows? First, we must recognize that similarity is relative and variable, as undependable as indispensable. Clear enough when closely confined by context and circumstance in ordinary discourse, it is hopelessly ambiguous when torn loose. In this, similarity is much like motion. Where a frame of reference is tacitly or explicitly established, all is well; but apart from a frame of reference, to say that something moves is as incomplete as to say that something is to the left of. We have to say what a thing is to the left of, what it moves in relation to, and in what respects two things are similar.

Yet similarity, unlike motion, cannot be salvaged merely by recognizing its relativity. When to the statement that a thing moves we add a specification of the frame of reference, we remove an ambiguity and complete our initial statement. But when to the statement that two things are similar we add a specification of the property they have in common, we again remove an ambiguity; but rather than supplementing our initial statement, we render it superfluous. For, as we have already seen, to say that two things are similar in having a specified property in common is to say nothing more than that they have that property in common. Similarity is not definitionally eliminated here; we have neither a definiens serving as an appropriate replacement for every occurrence of 'is similar to' nor a definitional schema that will provide an appropriate replacement for each occurrence. Rather we must search for the appropriate replacement in each case; and 'is similar to' functions as little more than a blank to be filled.

Furthermore, comparative judgments of similarity often require not merely selection of relevant properties but a weighting of their relative importance, and variation in both relevance and importance can be rapid and enormous. Consider baggage at an airport check-in station. The spectator may notice shape, size, color, material, and even make of luggage; the pilot is more concerned with weight, and the passenger with destination and ownership. Which pieces of baggage are more alike than others depends not only upon what properties they share, but upon who makes the comparison, and when. Or suppose we have three glasses, the first two filled with colorless liquid, the third with a bright red liquid. I might be likely to say the first two are more like each other than either is like the third. But it happens that the first glass is filled with water and the third with water colored by a drop of vegetable dye, while the second is filled with hydrochloric acid—and I am thirsty. Circumstances alter similarities.

But have I overlooked the residual and most significant kind of similarity—similarity between qualities as measured by nearness of their positions in an ordering? We are no longer speaking of concrete things, with their countless properties, but of qualities like hues or pitches, which are ordinarily treated as undimensional. Is not such similarity free of variations resulting from different selections and weightings of relevant properties? Surely, pitches are the more alike as they differ by fewer vibrations per second. But are they? Or is middle *C* more like high *C* than like middle *D*? The question is argument enough. Similarity of so-called simple qualities can be measured by nearness of their positions in an ordering, but they may be ordered, with good reason, in many different ways.

What, then, shall we say of the orderings of sensory qualities as mapped by psychophysicists on the basis of paired comparisons, fractionations, matching, and so forth? If many such methods yield closely congruent maps, relative nearness of position on such a map amounts to similarity under the general conditions and in the general context of the laboratory experiments, and has good title to be taken as a standard measure of similarity among the qualities in question. But can we test the validity of the methods used by examining how well similarity so measured agrees with ordinary judgments of likeness? I think there is no satisfactory way of stabilizing ordinary, as against laboratory, conditions and context to obtain judgments of sensory similarity that are qualified to stand as criteria for appraising the laboratory results. The laboratory results create rather than reflect a measure of sensory similarity. Like most systems of measurement, they tend to govern ordinary judgments at least as much as to be governed by them. And we have seen that the relative weighting of the different qualities of objects is so variable that even reliable measures of similarity for qualities of each kind will give no constant measure of overall similarity for the objects themselves.

Relativity, even volatility, is not a fatal fault. Physics does not stop talking of motion merely because motion is not absolute. But similarity, as we have seen, is a much more slippery matter. As it occurs in philosophy, similarity tends under analysis either to vanish entirely or to require for its explanation just what it purports to explain.

You may feel deprived, depressed, or even angry at losing one more handy tool from the philosopher's dwindling kit. But the rejection of similarity is not, as in the case of classes, rejection of some logical hanky-panky on grounds of philosophical distaste, nor, as in the case of intensions, modalities, analyticity, and synonymy, the rejection of some philosophical tomfoolery on grounds of utter obscurity. If statements of similarity, like counterfactual conditionals and four-letter words, cannot be trusted in the philosopher's study, they are still serviceable in the streets.

10   On Cognitive Capacity

Noam Chomsky

Chomsky's work on linguistics has been of considerable importance for the study and understanding of language. His book Reflections on Language, *from the beginning of which the following passage is taken, is both a defence of his own theories of language and linguistics and a demonstration of the relevance of these theories to considerations of intelligence, knowledge and experience. The tendency of the book is to support the values of science and rationality. For all the difficulty and specialization of Chomsky's more technical work, the application of his own findings is made in consciousness of the present and historical contexts of human activity and of the need for emancipation from reactionary social doctrines.*

A notable feature of Chomsky's theory of language is that he sees the cognitive capacity to which language testifies as the distinctive characteristic of the human species. Through the study of language we may come to a better understanding of 'other domains of human competence and action'. Chomsky opposes the prevailing modern tendency to approach physical and mental development in different ways and proposes rather that the faculty of language acquisition and use should be seen as biologically and genetically determined. Against the typically empiricist view that 'social environment is the dominant factor in development of personality, behaviour patterns, and cognitive structures', he points to the limitations on the possible variety of human languages and to the consequent implication that 'highly restrictive principles guide the construction of grammar'. His suggestion is that the growth of language, and also of the visual perceptual system, should be regarded as 'analogous to the development of a bodily organ'.

The attraction of this view is not simply that it justifies the application of such rational procedures as those which govern inquiry in the natural sciences, but also that it encourages a view of human intellectual capacities which takes cognizance of the genetic, biological and epistemological limits on those capacities. Some critical implications of Chomsky's theory of language are developed in the second excerpt from his book (text 24).

Source: Reflections on Language (Fontana, London, 1976), Ch. 1, 'On Cognitive Capacity', pp. 3–12. Reprinted by permission of William Collins Sons & Company Limited, and Random House Inc. Footnotes have been abbreviated, and one sentence deleted.

[. . .] Why study language? There are many possible answers, and by focusing on some I do not, of course, mean to disparage others or question their legitimacy. One may, for example, simply be fascinated by the elements of language in themselves and want to discover their order and arrangement, their origin in history or in the individual, or the ways in which they are used in thought, in science or in art, or in normal social interchange. One reason for studying language—and for me personally the most compelling reason—is that it is tempting to regard language, in the traditional phrase, as 'a mirror of mind'. I do not mean by this simply that the concepts expressed and distinctions developed in normal language use give us insight into the patterns of thought and the world of 'common sense' constructed by the human mind. More intriguing, to me at least, is the possibility that by studying language we may discover abstract principles that govern its structure and use, principles that are universal by biological necessity and not mere historical accident, that derive from mental characteristics of the species. A human language is a system of remarkable complexity. To come to know a human language would be an extraordinary intellectual achievement for a creature not specifically designed to accomplish this task. A normal child acquires this knowledge on relatively slight exposure and without specific training. He can then quite effortlessly make use of an intricate structure of specific rules and guiding principles to convey his thoughts and feelings to others, arousing in them novel ideas and subtle perceptions and judgments. For the conscious mind, not specially designed for the purpose, it remains a distant goal to reconstruct and comprehend what the child has done intuitively and with minimal effort. Thus language is a mirror of mind in a deep and significant sense. It is a product of human intelligence, created anew in each individual by operations that lie far beyond the reach of will or consciousness.

By studying the properties of natural languages, their structure, organization, and use, we may hope to gain some understanding of the specific characteristics of human intelligence. We may hope to learn something about human nature; something significant, if it is true that human cognitive capacity is the truly distinctive and most remarkable characteristic of the species. Furthermore, it is not unreasonable to suppose that the study of this particular human achievement, the ability to speak and understand a human language, may serve as a suggestive model for inquiry into other domains of human competence and action that are not quite so amenable to direct investigation.

The questions that I want to consider are classical ones. In major respects we have not progressed beyond classical antiquity in formulating clear problems in this domain, or in answering questions that immediately arise. From Plato to the present time, serious philosophers have been baffled and intrigued by the question that Bertrand Russell, in one of his later works,[1] formulated in this way: 'How comes it that human beings, whose contacts with the world are brief and personal and limited, are nevertheless able to know as much as they do know?' How can we gain such rich systems of knowledge, given our fragmentary and impoverished experience? A dogmatic skeptic might respond that we do not have such knowledge. His qualms are irrelevant to the present point. The same question arises, as a question of science, if we ask how comes it that human beings with such limited and personal experience achieve such convergence in rich and highly structured systems of belief, systems which then guide their actions and interchange and their interpretation of experience.

In the classical tradition, several answers were suggested. One might argue, along Aristotelian lines, that the world is structured in a certain way and that the human mind is able to perceive this structure, ascending from particulars to species to genus to further generalization and thus attaining knowledge of universals from perception of particulars. A 'basis of pre-existent knowledge' is a prerequisite to learning. We must possess an innate capacity to attain developed states of knowledge, but these are 'neither innate in a determinate form, nor developed from other higher states of knowledge, but from sense-perception'. Given rich metaphysical assumptions, it is possible to imagine that a mind 'so constituted as to be capable of this process' of 'induction' might attain a rich system of knowledge.[2]

A more fruitful approach shifts the main burden of explanation from the structure of the world to the structure of the mind. What we can know is determined by 'the modes of conception in the understanding';[3] what we do know, then, or what we come to believe, depends on the specific experiences that evoke in us some part of the cognitive system that is latent in the mind. In the modern period, primarily under the influence of Cartesian thought, the question of what we can know became again a central topic of inquiry. To Leibniz and Cudworth, Plato's doctrine that we do not attain new knowledge but recover what was already known seemed plausible, when this doctrine was 'purged of the error of preexistence'.[4] Cudworth argued at length that the mind has an 'innate cognoscitive power' that provides the principles and conceptions that constitute our knowledge, when provoked by sense to do so. '*But sensible things themselves* (as, for example, light and colors) *are not known and understood either by the passion or the fancy of sense, nor by anything merely foreign and adventitious, but by intelligible ideas exerted from the mind itself, that is, by something native and domestic to it . . .*'[5] Thus knowledge 'consisteth in the awakening and exciting of the inward active powers of the mind', which 'exercise[s] its own inward activity upon' the objects presented by sense, thus coming 'to know or understand, . . . actively to comprehend a thing by some abstract, free and universal ratios, reasonings . . .' The eye perceives, but the mind can compare, analyze, see cause-and-effect relations, symmetries, and so on, giving a comprehensive idea of the whole, with its parts, relations, and proportions. The 'book of nature', then, is 'legible only to an intellectual eye', he suggests, just as a man who reads a book in a language that he knows can learn something from the 'inky scrawls'. 'The primary objects of science and intellection', namely, 'the intelligible essences of things', 'exist no where but in the mind itself, being its own ideas . . . And by and through these inward ideas of the mind itself, which are its primary objects, does it know and understand all external individual things, which are the secondary objects of knowledge only.'

Among the 'innate ideas' or 'common notions' discussed in the rich and varied work of seventeenth-century rationalists are, for example, geometrical concepts and the like, but also '*relational* ideas or categories which enter into every presentation of objects and make possible the unity and interconnectedness of rational experience',[6] including such 'relative notions' as 'Cause, Effect, Whole and Part, Like and Unlike, Proportion and Analogy, Equality and Inequality, Symmetry and Asymmetry', all '*relative* ideas . . . [that are] . . . no material impresses from without upon the soul, but *her own active conception proceeding from herself whilst she takes notice of external objects*'.[7] Tracing the development of such ideas, we arrive at Kant's rather similar concept of the 'conformity of objects to our mode of cognition'. The mind provides the means for an analysis of data as experience, and provides as well a general schematism that delimits the cognitive structures developed on the basis of experience.

Returning to Russell's query, we can know so much because in a sense we already knew it, though the data of sense were necessary to evoke and elicit this knowledge. Or to put it less paradoxically, our systems of belief are those that the mind, as a biological structure, is designed to construct. We interpret experience as we do because of our special mental design. We attain knowledge when the 'inward ideas of the mind itself' and the structures it creates conform to the nature of things.

Certain elements of the rationalist theories must be discarded, but the general outlines seem plausible enough. Work of the past years has shown that much of the detailed structure of the visual system is 'wired in', though triggering experience is required to set the system in operation. There is evidence that the same may be true of the auditory structures that analyze at least some phonetic distinctive features. (Cf Eimas *et al.*, 1971.[8]) As techniques of investigation have improved, Bower argues, 'so has the apparent sophistication of the infant perceptual system'. He reviews evidence suggesting that 'the infant perceptual system seems capable of handling all of the traditional problems of the perception of three-dimensional space'—perception of solidity, distance, size-distance invariants, and size constancy. Thus 'contrary to the Berkeleian tradition the world of the infant would seem to be inherently tridimensional'.[9] There is evidence that before infants are capable of grasping, they can distinguish graspable from ungraspable objects, using purely visual information (Bruner) and Koslowski, 1972[10]).

Gregory observes that 'the speed with which babies come to associate the properties of objects and go on to learn how to predict hidden properties and future events would be impossible unless some of the structure of the world were inherited—somehow innately built into the nervous system'.[11] He suggests further that there may be a 'grammar of vision', rather like the grammar of human language, and possibly related to the latter in the evolution of the species. Employing this 'grammar of vision'—largely innate—higher animals are able to 'read from retinal images even hidden features of objects, and predict their immediate future states', thus 'to classify objects according to an internal grammar, to read reality from their eyes'. The neural basis for this system is gradually coming to be understood . . .

Despite the plausibility of many of the leading ideas of the rationalist tradition and its affinity in crucial respects with the point of view of the natural sciences, it has often been dismissed or disregarded in the study of behavior and cognition. It is a curious fact about the intellectual history of the past few centuries that physical and mental development have been approached in quite different ways. No one would take seriously a proposal that the human organism learns through experience to have arms rather than wings, or that the basic structure of particular organs results from accidental experience. Rather, it is taken for granted that the physical structure of the organism is genetically determined, though of course variation along such dimensions as size, rate of development, and so forth will depend in part on external factors. From embryo to mature organism, a certain pattern of development is predetermined, with certain stages, such as the onset of puberty or the termination of growth, delayed by many years. Variety within these fixed patterns may be of great importance for human life, but the basic questions of scientific interest have to do with the fundamental, genetically determined scheme of growth and development that is a characteristic of the species and that gives rise to structures of marvelous intricacy.

The species characteristics themselves have evolved over long stretches of time, and evidently the environment provides conditions for differential reproduction, hence evolution of the species. But this is an entirely different question, and here too, questions can be raised about the physical laws that govern this evolution. Surely too little is known to justify any far-reaching claims.

The development of personality, behavior patterns, and cognitive structures in higher organisms has often been approached in a very different way. It is generally assumed that in these domains, social environment is the dominant factor. The structures of mind that develop over time are taken to be arbitrary and accidental; there is no 'human nature' apart from what develops as a specific historical product. According to this view, typical of empiricist speculation, certain general principles of learning that are common in their essentials to all (or some large class of) organisms suffice to account for the cognitive structures attained by humans, structures which incorporate the principles by which human behavior is planned, organized, and controlled. I dismiss without further comment the exotic though influential view that 'internal states' should not be considered in the study of behavior.[12]

But human cognitive systems, when seriously investigated, prove to be no less marvelous and intricate than the physical structures that develop in the life of the organism. Why, then, should we not study the acquisition of a cognitive structure such as language more or less as we study some complex bodily organ?

At first glance, the proposal may seem absurd, if only because of the great variety of human languages. But a closer consideration dispels these doubts. Even knowing very little of substance about linguistic universals, we can be quite sure that the possible variety of languages is sharply limited. Gross observations suffice to establish some qualitative conclusions. Thus, it is clear that the language each person acquires is a rich and complex construction hopelessly underdetermined by the fragmentary evidence available. This is why scientific inquiry into the nature of language is so difficult and so limited in its results. The conscious mind is endowed with no advance knowledge (or, recalling Aristotle, with only insufficiently developed advance knowledge). Thus, it is frustrated by the limitations of available evidence and faced by far too many possible explanatory theories, mutually inconsistent but adequate to the data. Or—as unhappy a state—it can devise no reasonable theory. Nevertheless, individuals in a speech community have developed essentially the same language. This fact can be explained only on the assumption that these individuals employ highly restrictive principles that guide the construction of grammar. Furthermore, humans are, obviously, not designed to learn one human language rather than another; the system of principles must be a species property. Powerful constraints must be operative restricting the variety of languages. It is natural that in our daily life we should concern ourselves only with differences among people, ignoring uniformities of structure. But different intellectual demands arise when we seek to understand what kind of organism a human really is.

The idea of regarding the growth of language as analogous to the development of a bodily organ is thus quite natural and plausible. It is fair to ask why the empiricist belief to the contrary has had such appeal to the modern temper. Why has it been so casually assumed that there exists a 'learning theory' that can account for the acquisition of cognitive structures through experience? Is there some body of evidence, established through scientific inquiry, or observation, or introspection, that leads us to regard mental and physical development in such different ways? Surely the answer is that there is not. Science offers no reason to 'accept the common maxim that there is nothing in the intellect which was not first in the senses', or to question the denial of this maxim in rationalist philosophy.[13] Investigation of human intellectual achievements, even of the most commonplace sort, gives no support for this thesis.

Empiricist speculation and the 'science of behavior' that has developed within its terms have proved rather barren, perhaps because of the peculiar assumptions that have guided and limited such inquiry. The grip of empiricist doctrine in the modern period, outside of the natural sciences, is to be explained on sociological or historical grounds. The position itself has little to recommend it on grounds of empirical evidence or inherent plausibility or explanatory power. I do not think that this doctrine would attract a scientist who is able to discard traditional myth and to approach the problems afresh. Rather, it serves as an impediment, an insurmountable barrier to fruitful inquiry, much as the religious dogmas of an earlier period stood in the way of the natural sciences. [. . .]

Notes

1 Bertrand Russell, *Human Knowledge: Its Scope and Limits* (Simon & Schuster, New York, 1948) p. 5.
2 Aristotle, *Posterior Analytics*, 2.19 (ed McKeon, 1941) pp. 184–6.
3 Ralph Cudworth, *Treatise Concerning Eternal and Immutable Morality*, Andover, New York, 1838) p. 75.
4 Leibniz, *Discourse on Metaphysics* (trans Montgomery, 1902) p. 45.
5 Cudworth, *True Intellectual System of the Universe*, cited by Arthur O. Lovejoy, 'Kant and the English Platonists', in *Essays Philosophical and Psychological, in Honor of William James* (Columbia University, Longmans, Green & Co., New York, 1908).
6 Lovejoy, 1908.
7 Henry More, 'Antidote Against Atheism', cited by Lovejoy, 1908.
8 Peter D. Eimas, Einar R. Signeland, Peter Jusczyk and James Vigorito, 'Speech Perception in Infants', *Science*, 171, 1971, pp. 303–6.
9 T. G. R. Bower, 'Object Perception in Infants', *Perception*, 1, 1972, pp. 15–30.
10 J. S. Bruner and Barbara Koslowski, 'Visually Preadapted Constituents of Manipulatory Action', *Perception*, 1, 1972, pp. 8–14.
11 Richard Gregory, 'The Grammar of Vision', *The Listener*, 19 February 1970.
12 This view, popularized in recent years by B. F. Skinner, is foreign to science or any rational inquiry. The reasons for its popularity must be explained on extrascientific grounds. . .
13 Antoine Arnauld, *The Art of Thinking: Port-Royal Logic* (Bobbs-Merrill, Indianapolis, 1964) p. 36.

Notes

1. Bertrand Russell, *Mysticism and Logic and Other Essays* (London: Allen & Unwin, 1918), p. 4.

2. Nicholas F. Gier, ... (Madison, 1987), pp. 154-5.

3. Philip Crawford, *Trauma: Uncovering Ethical and Interpretive Motifs* (Aronson, New York, 1990), p. 13.

4. Aaron ... Directions in ...

5. O'Leary, *The Theological System of ...* (New York, 1995), p. 4.

6. ... Rorty, Kant and the English Platonists ...

7. F. Copleston, ...

8. J. T. Snow, ...

9. Henri Ellenberger, ... Review, 1904.

10. Peter D. Kramer, Time ... Rinehart, Winston, New York, 1990.

11. J. C. ... Bauer, *Object Relations in ...*

12. L. S. ... Kirshner ... Gestalt ... on Intimacy

13. Maturana-Varela, *Mexperences*, 1, 1972, pp. 4-14.

14. Richard Metzgar, "The Grammar of Vision," *The Review of ...*, 1970.

15. His view, popularized in recent years by B. F. Skinner, is for the most part antipsychological ...

16. Arthur Amiel, *The Art of ..*, Bobbs-Merrill, Indianapolis, 1961, p. 14.

11   Conceptions of Knowledge

Barry Barnes

The title of Barnes' Interests and the Growth of Knowledge *refers to the publication of a symposium,* Criticism and the Growth of Knowledge *(eds I. Lakatos and T. Musgrave, Cambridge University Press, 1970), devoted to a discussion of the competing views of Karl Popper and Thomas Kuhn (see text 21) on the philosophy of scientific discovery (views flagged in the titles of their respective studies:* The Logic of Scientific Discovery *and* The Structure of Scientific Revolutions). *The issues raised in these various publications are of fundamental concern for all theories of knowledge, scientific knowledge in particular. Is there a body of systematic and disinterested knowledge, modified in response to rational criticism, to which we can accord the title 'science', and which can then be distinguished from such non-scientific hypotheses as those which follow from the interested inquiries of sociology, history and psychology? Or is the apparent autonomy of science, as of other practices, itself a matter rather of social and historical convention? In the latter case the status of scientific knowledge as* paradigmatic *knowledge will be open to question, as will the nature of relations between science and other areas of human interest. Alternatively, can it be argued that the principles of inquiry of a well-conducted sociology, or history or psychology, are systematic and disinterested, and that they therefore qualify as actual or potential 'sciences'?*

Since the mid nineteenth century the 'sociology of knowledge' has grown into a flourishing subject in itself. As Barnes observes in his Introduction, work in this area 'has predominantly been carried out by politically active men, more familiar with political thought than with any other kind'. Barnes himself was trained as a natural scientist and employs 'forms of argument and explanation which . . . are avowedly naturalistic'. As he asserts, 'the experience of a scientific training can reveal how ludicrously misconceived polemics against science from intellectuals and social theorists sometimes are. But, equally, it can give the lie to idealisations of science, and alleged demonstrations of the special status of its knowledge.'

II Knowledge and Representation

In this first excerpt from his book (the second appears in Section V, text 22), Barnes contrasts the 'comtemplative' and 'sociological' accounts of knowledge. He suggests that the former account relies heavily upon an analogy with visual apprehension and pictorial representation. Barnes' procedure is not to undermine the analogy but rather, by emphasizing that visual representation is an 'active and socially mediated process', to connect it rather to the sociological account. In support of his thesis he cites the work of Ivins (see text 13) on the 'syntax of pictorial statements' and of Gombrich (specifically his Art and Illusion*) on the importance of* conventions *of representation. Further support to Barnes' assertion that 'observing is a typical kind of learning' is supplied by the excerpt from Hanson printed in the present anthology (text 8).*

Barnes treats representations as 'actively manufactured renderings of their referents, produced from available cultural resources' and as 'constructs for use in activity', where 'activity' can embrace the exercise of cognitive functions, and where such functions are related to the 'objectives of some social group'. According to this view, it is in terms of their role in activity that representations are to be understood and assessed. If works of art can be included in this account of representation—and there seems no clear reason why they should not be— Barnes' text may be seen as a strong argument against any claim for disinterestedness in aesthetic judgement (which must somehow be dependent upon 'the exercise of cognitive functions'). It also provides grounds for a consideration of the changing social functions of art which avoids the kinds of simplification or abstraction risked in talk of 'socially produced meanings' or of 'visual ideologies' or of culturally determined 'ways of seeing'.

Source: *Interests and the Growth of Knowledge*, (London, Routledge & Kegan Paul, PLC, 1977), Ch. 1, 'The Problem of Knowledge', Section 1, 'Conceptions of Knowledge', pp. 1–10. Footnotes have been deleted.

An immediate difficulty which faces any discussion of the present kind is that there are so many different conceptions of the nature of knowledge. Some of these can be set aside, for sociological purposes, by taking knowledge to consist in accepted belief, and publicly available, shared representations. The sociologist is concerned with the naturalistic understanding of what people take to be knowledge, and not with the evaluative assessment of what deserves so to be taken; his orientation is normally distinct from that of the philosopher or epistemologist. But this still leaves a daunting number of alternative conceptions of knowledge, and how it is related to thought and activity on the one hand, and the external world on the other. Although detailed consideration of all these possibilities is out of the question, some such conception, however loose and informal, is essential if we are to proceed. Perhaps the best compromise is briefly to examine two general accounts of knowledge which have been of some sociological significance, and to advocate a working conception developed from one of them. This will involve setting aside many issues, and almost entirely ignoring the important question of how people *learn*. Hopefully, however, it will be found acceptable as a mode of presentation, rather than a justification, of the position advanced, and a setting of the scene for later, more concrete discussion.

One common conception of knowledge represents it as the product of contemplation. According to this account, knowledge is best achieved by disinterested individuals, passively perceiving some aspect of reality, and generating verbal descriptions to correspond to it. Such descriptions, where valid, match reality, rather as a picture may match in appearance some aspect of the reality it is designed to represent. Invalid descriptions, on the other hand, distort reality and fail to show a correspondence when compared with it; often they are the products of social interests which make it advantageous to misrepresent reality, or social restrictions upon the investigation of reality which make accurate perception of it impossible.

This contemplative account, as it can be called, unites a number of notions. It describes knowledge as the product of isolated individuals. And it assumes that the individuals intrude minimally between reality and its representation: they apprehend reality *passively,* and, as it were, let it speak for itself; their perception is independent of their interests, their expectations or their previous experience. Hence the knowledge they produce is essentially only a function of reality itself. It can be tested by any individual who is able to compare it with reality, since its property of correspondence with reality is entirely independent of the situation wherein it was produced. These various notions tend to be associated because they are all indicated by a simple, memorable, concrete model: learning and knowledge generation are thought of in terms of visual apprehension, and verbal knowledge by analogy with pictorial representation. Indeed, it is probably our intuitive sense of correspondence between a picture and the appearance of something real, which sustains much of the credibility of the contemplative account, at least at the everyday level.

Certainly, our everyday epistemological notions appear to be thoroughly permeated with this conception, and the analogy between learning and passive visual apprehension. We talk of understanding as 'seeing', or 'seeing clearly'; we are happy to talk of valid descriptions giving us a 'true picture'. Similarly, we are able to characterise inadequate knowledge as 'coloured', 'distorted', 'blind to relevant facts', and so on. The overall visual metaphor is a resource with which we produce accounts of the generation and character of truth and error. And in many ways these accounts serve us well. Nonetheless, in sociology, the contemplative account has always co-existed with a sharply contrasted alternative, and at the present time it is the latter toward which the general trend of thought is moving. Increasingly, knowledge is being treated as essentially social, as a part of the culture which is transmitted from generation to generation, and as something which is actively developed and modified in response to practical contingencies.

Such a conception stands in polar opposition to most of the elements of the contemplative account. Knowledge is not produced by passively perceiving

103

individuals, but by interacting social groups engaged in particular activities. And it is evaluated communally and not by isolated individual judgments. Its generation cannot be understood in terms of psychology, but must be accounted for by reference to the social and cultural context in which it arises. Its maintenance is not just a matter of how it relates to reality, but also of how it relates to the objectives and interests a society possesses by virtue of its historical development. An appropriate concrete model which integrates these various themes can be provided by considering a society's knowledge as analogous to its techniques or its conventional forms of artistic expression, both of which are readily understood as culturally transmitted, and as capable of modification and development to suit particular requirements.

The relationship of these two opposed conceptions has always been an uneasy one within the context of sociology, with the tension between the two always apparent, but with individual writers rarely situating themselves consistently and unambiguously on one side or the other. Thus, Karl Mannheim's *Ideology and Utopia* (1936) opens with a clear indication of its commitment to the second, active conception:

> Strictly speaking it is incorrect to say that the single individual thinks. Rather it is more correct to insist that he participates in thinking further what other men have thought before him. He finds himself in an inherited situation with patterns of thought which are appropriate to this situation and attempts to elaborate further the inherited modes of response or to substitute others for them in order to deal more adequately with the new challenges which have arisen out of the shifts and changes in his situation. (Chapter 1.1)

But, although these points are reasserted a number of times throughout the work, a great part of its argument and much of its concrete discussion is, in fact, predicated upon the contemplative model. Natural science and mathematics, Mannheim tells us, are forms of knowledge which bear no mark of the context of their production and which can properly be assessed entirely in terms of their correspondence with reality. Moreover, precisely *because* they are the products of disinterested contemplation, they are *preferable* to other kinds of knowledge, to sociology or history or political thought.

In his treatment of these latter kinds of knowledge Mannheim continues to be inconsistent. Sometimes he insists that this knowledge can in no way be assessed in context-independent, contemplative terms. Then he develops an argument which implies the opposite. He states that such knowledge, knowledge of social reality, is always in practice related to social standpoints and interests, and thus context-dependent. This makes the knowledge inadequate or, at best, of restricted validity. However, under ideal but realisable conditions, context-independent knowledge, corresponding to social reality, could be produced. A class of disinterested intellectuals, able to take a properly contemplative approach, could produce it.

It is true that some of this inconsistency is the product of Mannheim's combining essays written at different times. Chapters 1 and 5 are those most inclined to an active, contextual and social treatment of knowledge, and they were the last written. But these are also the least concrete chapters of the book. And even in these chapters, the contemplative account and its associated metaphors remain important components, without which the results of Mannheim's thinking would be bereft of all plausibility and coherence. It is clear that in spite of himself, Mannheim produced a work largely based upon the contemplative account. Although he explicitly rejected it, he apparently could not help but think in terms of it. Even the most original and insightful points in *Ideology and Utopia* are conceptualised in terms of contemplation, and the associated visual metaphors.

Thus, Mannheim's work reveals just how difficult it can be to move away from a contemplative position. The associated pictorial metaphor for knowledge is so pervasive, intuitively attractive and, indeed, valuable as an explanatory resource, that it can be difficult in practice to structure one's thought independently of it. Mannheim knew, and advanced, many good arguments against the contemplative account, and in favour of the alternative he explicitly advocated, but this did not suffice to reorient his practical approach. Hence, given that a form of the active, social conception of knowledge is to be put forward as a working orientation here, it seems appropriate to present it in a way which is designed to counteract the appeal of the pictorial metaphors incorporated in the contemplative account. Such a presentation cannot hope to count in any way as a justification; it merely offers a model for consideration, and for use in following the subsequent discussion. But there is in any case no space in which to develop a detailed discussion of the problems involved.

It might be thought that the best procedure for moving away from the contemplative account would be to break the equivalence of pictorial and verbal representations and emphasise the differences between passive-visual apprehension and understanding generally. If verbal statements cannot be matched against reality like pictures are, then the need for an alternative metaphor to characterise the nature of verbal knowledge is indicated. In fact, the opposite strategy is the more expedient. We should emphasise the equivalence of all representations, pictorial or verbal, and accept observing as a typical kind of learning. It is the treatment of visualisation and depiction as *passive* processes which mars contemplative conceptions in the sociology of knowledge, and makes their visual and pictorial metaphors unsatisfactory. Our strategy should be to reveal pictorial representation, the most favourable case for the contemplative conception, as essentially an active and a socially mediated process, and in this respect typical of representation and knowledge generation generally.

In fact, this is something that has been done for us already by those academic fields directly concerned with the study of pictorial representations and their creation. Work in fields as different as the psychology of perception and the history of art could be used to make the points we need. Let us take the latter field, where the close relationship, if not the complete equivalence, of pictorial and verbal representation is more or less taken for granted, and references to the 'language' or 'vocabulary' of an artist or illustrator are commonplace. A particularly relevant work is that of Ivins (1953) on the history of prints and engravings. Here language is looked to as a model on the basis of which to understand pictures. Ivins devotes his extremely concrete and well-illustrated book to showing how the 'syntax' of 'pictorial statements' has changed from the

Renaissance to the present day. And he makes it clear that the 'pictorial statements' he considers simply cannot be treated as passive reflections of real appearances; rather they render scenes and objects in terms of conventions.

Gombrich's important study *Art and Illusion* (1959) makes similar points. It reveals the difficulties which arise in talking of the extent to which a representation can correspond to reality or the direct appearance of reality. And it makes clear that, at least for intuitively straightforward conceptions of correspondence, representations not only do not correspond with appearances but they cannot (not even if they are photographs). Representations may, when viewed under particular conditions in particular contexts, achieve a *trompe l'oeil*, but such deceptions are generally produced by conventions of representation which involve obvious distortions of what the painter or illustrator sees. The capacity to produce 'realistic' representations tends to depend upon the study of existing paintings which use appropriate conventions, rather than upon an open observant attitude to what is depicted.

In Gombrich, Ivins and similar work, we find an account of the construction of pictorial representations which serves admirably as an informal working model for the construction of knowledge. Pictorial representations are actively constructed from conventions available as the resources of some culture or subculture. The successful realisation of paintings, for example, depends upon familiarity with existing paintings and illustrations and the conventions implicit in them. Such conventions are meaningful as words are meaningful, and are actively manipulated and organised in the light of particular aims or interests.

Extending this account, when a representation conveys knowledge or information about, say, an object, it is by classifying it, by making it an instance of one or more kinds of entity recognised by the culture whose resources are drawn upon. In this way the representation makes it possible for existing knowledge to be applied to its referent, and it makes the referent a source of meaningful information, a potential check upon existing knowledge. Knowledge and object are connected by the representation. (We can, admittedly, deploy knowledge directly as we act, but this is because our perception organises and pre-classifies what we perceive; we read the world, rather as we read handwriting, as an assemblage of symbols.)

All representations are indeed then, as Ivins says, kinds of statement. They must be distinguished both from the objects they represent and from the appearances of those objects. Any representation is one of numerous possibilities which the resources of a culture make available. And the resources of a culture are themselves reasonably treated as a particular selection from an endless number of possibilities. In both cases, we are entitled to seek an explanation of why some possibilities rather than others are actually encountered.

It may well be that particular individuals frequently notice resemblances between aspects of their environment in a random, undirected way, and build up particular beliefs and representations in a fashion which cannot be explained systematically. But public knowledge typically evolves much more coherently, and the people who contribute representations to it operate in what is cumulatively a much more orderly way. Typically they are concerned, directly or indirectly, in the performance of some institutionalised activity, designed to further particular aims or ends. This means that the knowledge they produce is designed from the start to facilitate certain kinds of prediction, or function in the performance of particular kinds of competence. And its evaluation is pre-structured to an extent by these design requirements; to anticipate Habermas's term, ... it is pre-structured by a situated technical 'interest in prediction and control'.

Representations are not assessed with any particular stress on their rendering of appearances, but instrumentally, in conjunction with whatever the activities are with which they function. Hence, the growth of knowledge should not be thought of as the result of random learning about reality, but as the correlate of the historical development of procedures, competences and techniques relevant in various degrees to the ends or objectives of cultures or sub-cultures. Of course, many such competences and associated representations find such wide instrumental applicability that once introduced into practically any culture they are almost guaranteed an enduring position therein.

Representations are actively manufactured renderings of their referents, produced from available cultural resources. The particular forms of construction adopted reflect the predictive or other technical cognitive functions the representation is required to perform when procedures are carried out, competences executed, or techniques applied. Why such functions are initially required of the representation is generally intelligible, directly or indirectly, in terms of the objectives of some social group.

This very informal conception should suffice as a basis for the following discussion, although for many purposes it would be altogether inadequate as it stood. It would need considerable qualification, for example, if activities like scientific research were the central foci of discussion, with their basic orientation to the creative extension of knowledge. It is often pointed out that theories and representations employed for creative scientific work are often not those which have proved the most instrumentally adequate. Scientists often impute instrumental adequacy to one set of representations (say those of classical mechanics or geometrical optics) but regard others, those they use in their work, as having greater ontological adequacy. This is often taken to indicate that knowledge must be, and is, evaluated as a direct rendering of reality and not simply as an aid to activity. Unfortunately yesterday's ontologies have a depressing tendency to become tomorrow's instrumentally adequate representations, and on that basis, and other grounds which cannot be gone into here, the general outlines of the present account can be adequately defended. Nonetheless, the actors' distinction between instrumentally applicable theories and those suitable as guides to research is of great relevance and interest, and would merit extended discussion in other contexts.

Let us however concentrate on our informal conception as it stands, and try to make it a little more concrete by reference to some examples. In order to continue to erode the appeal of a contemplative conception of knowledge, pictorial representations will be used. And so that the representations will be generally accepted as embodying knowledge, the illustrations chosen will be of a kind which have utility in the context of natural science. They will be considered in order, from those which are easily reconciled with the above account, to those which may not immediately appear to be so. Hopefully, the sequence will act as a 'bridge' to the most problematic cases, and indicate the fully general scope of the account.

Imagine then that some students in a physics laboratory are requested to draw some apparatus set out before them, and that the result is Fig 1; such a result is not empirically unreasonable. Presumably, there is no problem in arguing that the figure is a pictorial statement constructed from existing cultural resources; it is assembled from signs meaningful as concepts in physical theories of electricity, and is obviously reminiscent of a verbal statement. Perhaps the commonest

Fig 1

immediate concern of students who construct diagrams like Fig 1 is to conform to expectations, but basically such representations are sustained in our culture as adjuncts to competences. In this case, it scarcely makes sense to ask whether the referent of Fig 1 is truly what the figure indicates it to be: the referent could be a battery and a resistance box wired together, a length of metal, a nerve fibre, a building or indeed practically anything at all. The appropriateness of the figure cannot be assessed in isolation, by examination of its referent. All that can be assessed is the use of the figure, how it is actively employed.

The real problem with Fig 1 is likely to lie in establishing that it is a typical representation. In particular, there is no vestige of resemblance between its appearance and that of what it is used to represent. Let us move then to Fig 2. Maps frequently show an intuitive resemblance to the appearance of reality itself, as, for example, when it is seen from the air; sometimes they are deliberately designed to resemble appearances. But they remain compatible with the above account. They are constructed entirely in terms of conventions. Their particular form depends upon what procedures they are designed to facilitate. Their value is assessed functionally and not by reference to appearance. Maps indeed afford one of the clearest and most accessible contexts in which to examine the connection between the structure of representations and their function. (If ever physics needs to be supplemented as a paradigm of knowledge, there is much to be said for turning to cartography.)

Fig 3 is taken from an anatomy textbook, and depicts some muscles of 'the arm'. It is designed to facilitate recognition and naming in the context of an esoteric activity. *Therefore*, it is not a rendering of a particular arm. Despite being

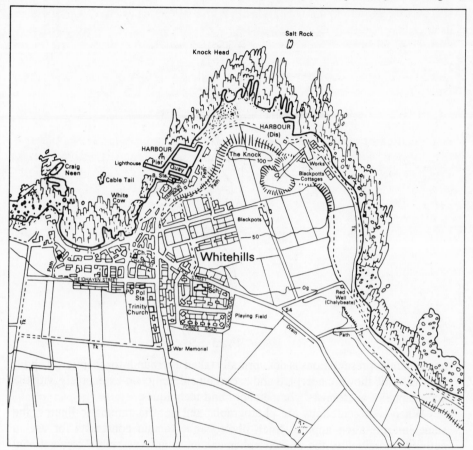

Fig 2

apparently realistic it is intentionally a schemata. It cannot be taken as an attempt passively to imitate reality. Indeed its effect is to *modify* perception so that students can perceive arms in terms of its scheme of representation. As an aid to seeing and naming, its schematic character is accentuated at the expense of its possibilities as a rendition of appearances. There is no particular arm to which it relates as a representation; it is a typification constructed from available symbols. (That it is indeed constructed from symbols can only escape our notice if we forget that symbols are involved in *perception* as well as representation.)

Like all scientific representations, Fig 3 is reliably applicable only to aid particular kinds of procedure. In this case the procedures, together with directly associated instrumental interests, are embodied in the role of the anatomist and his student audience. Those who make practical use of such representations are generally well aware that their reliability and applicability is restricted; this awareness is automatically generated in learning to use the representations. Other instrumental interests and other activities, located in other scientific roles, engender other kinds of representation. But this limitation upon the scope of

109

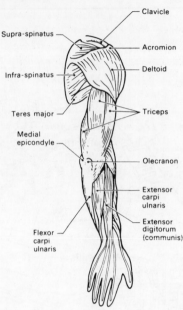

Fig 3

anatomical representations is not normally taken as grounds for scepticism about their validity; they are accepted and accorded credibility co-extensively with the acceptance of anatomists' competences and techniques.

When representations are photographs and not diagrammatic figures, the same interpretation applies. Such photographs remain constructs for use in activity. Admittedly, the photographer cannot simply assemble conventional symbols when he takes a photograph of some real object. But he can work his material so that his finished product can be seen in terms of, or *as*, such an assemblage. Examination of the photographs sometimes used in the teaching of human anatomy illustrates this point convincingly. Their manufacture does, of course, involve the use of particular human bodies, but their representational adequacy is again evaluated in use, and not by comparing them with the particular bodies from which they were manufactured.

The argument is then that all representations, pictorial or verbal, realistic or abstract, are actively constructed assemblages of conventions or meaningful cultural resources, to be understood and assessed in terms of their role in activity. Essentially this amounts to making representations analogous to techniques, artistic conventions or other typical forms of culture, rather than considering them in terms of the contemplative conception. Sociologists have often found it appropriate to adopt this treatment in dealing with everyday knowledge. But, like Mannheim, they have sometimes felt that a special kind of knowledge exists in the natural sciences and mathematics, intelligible only in contemplative terms. Scientific knowledge, however, is always assessed in conjunction with the institutionalised technical procedures of its specialities and is entirely typical of knowledge in general: science is in many ways a constellation of craft skills. As for mathematical knowledge, we have here a developed set of generally utilisable procedures and representations to which no reality can even be said to correspond. It is precisely their extraordinary versatility in furthering a vast range of objectives, which results in their widespread use and sustains their credibility as knowledge.

However, in thus rejecting a contemplative conception of knowledge and adopting a view which emphasises its social dimension, it is important not to lose sight of the connection which does exist between knowledge and the real world. This is properly stressed in the contemplative account, albeit usually in terms of an unclear notion of truth as correspondence. Knowledge is not related to activity rather than reality; it is related to activity which consists precisely in men attempting to manipulate, predict and control the real world in which they exist. Hence knowledge is found useful precisely because the world is as it is; and it is to that extent a function of what is real, and not the pure product of thought and imagination. Knowledge arises out of our encounters with reality and is continually subject to feedback-correction from these encounters, as failures of prediction, manipulation and control occur. We seek to eliminate such failures, but so far reality has sustained its capacity to surprise us and dash our expectations. Indeed, our liability to be surprised in this way, to be confounded in our expectations, constitutes an important argument against a purely idealist theory of knowledge.

12 Philosophical Materialism or the Materialist Conception of History

Alison Assiter

One influential aspect of Karl Marx's work concerns the complex relationships between needs, productive activities and knowledge, or what is represented as knowledge. He thought about these relationships and sought to demonstrate their nature within the context of history. In the first part of this article, originally published in the journal Radical Philosophy, *Assiter argues against the view that Marx's work should be placed within a tradition of materialist philosophy, or indeed 'inside any kind of philosophical tradition. . . On the contrary,' she continues, 'his materialism is an empirical theory about human beings in history.' She takes issue with those Marxists who both rule out of court the idealist's request for a justification of knowledge and claim for Marx's materialism that it is not in need of justification. The first of Marx's 'Theses on Feuerbach' certainly suggests a dissociation from philosophical materialism.*

> *The chief defect of all hitherto existing materialism . . . is that the thing, reality, sensuousness, is conceived only in the form of the object, or of contemplation, but not as human sensuous activity, practice, not subjectively.*

(Cf Hanson's discussion of observation and Barnes' critique of the 'contemplative account' of knowledge in texts 8 and 11 respectively.)

The second part of Assiter's article, which follows, offers both a description and a justification of Marx's materialism, not as a philosophical materialism but as a conception of history. She seeks in particular to resolve the apparent contradiction between Marx's determinism (the belief that 'it is the production and reproduction of real life which is causally responsible for ideas, conceiving and so on') and his view that 'ideas can revolutionize things'. Her solution is to reinterpret the relation between consciousness as determined or conditioned by life and consciousness as conscious existence (within which we can take thought and act). What she suggests is that in certain circumstances a relation of identity (ie where both meanings of 'consciousness' refer to states of the same individual) need not rule out a causal relation (eg where one state influences the other). We can say of one and the same person, for instance, that he or she thinks like a wage-labourer (ie is determined by some role as a producer) but also that he or she may take thought about the conditions of being a wage-labourer and possibly effect some change in those conditions. The 'producer' and the 'thinker' here designate what Assiter calls different 'time slices' of the same individual, yet we can still say that the person-as-producer causally determines the person-as-thinker. Some implications of this argument, relevant to a consideration of the identity and role of the artist, are taken up by Art & Language in 'Author and Producer Revisited' (text 23).

It should be noted that assent to the basic premises of historical materialism rules out assent to any view of artists compatible with Clive Bell's (1914) assertion that 'they do not work to live, they live to work'—unless, that is, artists are to be seen as other than human by virtue of their having no basic needs to be met.

Source: *Radical Philosophy* no. 23, England, Winter, 1979, pp. 12–20. Reprinted by permission of the author and Radical Philosophy Group. This material has been edited and one footnote has been deleted.

[. . .] Before justifying Marx's materialism . . . I must begin by describing it. The subject material of Marx's materialist conception of history is *material life*. What is this? An answer is: '[People], their activity, and the material conditions under which they live'.[1] But why material life? In order to give a general characterisation of materialism one would have to be less specific than this surely? One would, but one might come to capture the essence of materialism by discussing one of its aspects. And, after all, the idealist restricts the domain of his concerns. The Berkleyan idealist began with the question: 'What is it that I can claim to know with the highest possible degree of certainty?' Why begin with what I, the individual, can claim to know?

So let us continue discussing material life. In the *German Ideology* Marx tells us: 'We must begin by stating the first premise of all human existence, the premise, namely, that men must be in a position to live in order to "make history". But life involves, before all else, eating and drinking, a habitation, clothing, and many other things. The first historical act is therefore the production of means to satisfy these needs.'[2] He goes on, in that work, to proffer a distinguishing characteristic of human beings from animals: 'They themselves [men] begin to distinguish themselves from animals as soon as they begin to produce their means of subsistence . . .'[3]

In the *Economic and Philosophical Manuscripts,* Marx tells us that, in contra-distinction to the Hegelian view, 'Man is a natural being' . . . 'he is an active natural being.'[4]

Can one give any of this the kind of justification the idealist claims to be able to offer for his basic premises? One might state Marx's 'basic' premise as follows:

(1) Natural beings have basic needs.

Let us assume that by 'basic need' is meant 'need that must be satisfied before other needs can be'. And, further, a need is, by definition, a want that must be satisfied.

Assuming that there are such things as 'natural beings', (1) may be falsified in one of two ways. The being might have no needs at all, or it might have no basic needs. What would a being with non-basic, but no basic needs be like? It would be a creature with bodily characteristics, and certain high-level wants and capacities, but without, eg the need to eat, to defecate, to breathe, to exhale carbon dioxide. Certainly one can imagine very different forms of life from those we have got—isn't this just what we are being asked to conceive of when we are told to think about the possibility of life on another planet? But to argue that there could be beings with wants but no needs is rather like arguing that there could be a mathematical series that began in the middle, and it really was the middle. Wouldn't we simply redefine what counted as the beginning of the series in such a case? Thus the series of natural numbers might start at number 10; number 10 would be the first member of the series. Similarly, the supposition that there could be beings with high-level wants but no basic needs, ought to be interpreted as a supposition to the effect that there could be beings with different basic needs from ours. Surely, this is part of the point that is made by Marx when he tells us that needs change with changes in the productivity of labour and in the organisation of production.

The mathematical series analogy can be used to show, too, that natural beings must have some needs. The idea that there could be a natural being with no wants or needs is like the notion of a series with no members. The idea of a series contains the notion of something's forming it; similarly, the concept of a 'being' contains the idea of something's making it into a being. What makes it a being is a collection of needs.

Given that there are natural beings, then, it seems to be a sort of necessary truth to say that they have basic needs.

There are two further premises required for the 'foundation' of Marx's materialism. These are:

(2) Basic needs must be satisfied.

and

(3) In order to satisfy their basic needs, some natural beings must produce their means of subsistence.

One might justify (2) in the following manner. If the natural being is to survive, it must satisfy its basic needs. Or, put another way, if the being is to continue to be a being with basic needs, it must satisfy them. We could insert the extra premise:

(1A) Natural beings have basic needs, and they have them for a period of time.

(1A) must be true, because if it is allowed that the being might cease to have basic needs, that would be to contradict (1). (2) then gives one of the necessary conditions of the truth of (1).

(3) can be given a similar kind of justification. If natural beings continually went around consuming everything without producing, they would eventually

have nothing left to consume. So, in order to survive, or to continue to be a natural being, at least some of them must produce. This time, one has to interpret (1) as implying that the being has basic needs for a relatively long period of time. Then (3) becomes a necessary condition for (2). (For the sake of the argument, 'natural being' in (1) and (2) can be taken to include animals, while in (3) those who produce may be construed as the human beings.)

Another way of putting this is 'If (1) is true, than so are (2) and (3).' But (1) is necessarily true.

The justification of (3) depends upon the assumption that nature reproduces itself less rapidly than consumers consume. Certainly this is accepted as true, in fact, but must it be? I think so, for the following reason: if something reproduced itself more quickly than it consumed, it would be producing gradually less and less 'worthy' specimens, specimens that would eventually die out through lack of nourishment. This point can be generalised to support the criterion that nature must reproduce itself less rapidly than consumers consume.

This argument is almost parallel to some arguments against the sceptic about the existence of objects in the external world. The sceptic is taken to doubt or deny that objects continue to exist when not perceived. The argument against this takes the form of proving that the truth of what he doubts or denies is a necessary condition for something that he cannot doubt or deny being true. Similarly, one might imagine some kind of 'sceptic' denying that natural beings must produce. But they must produce if they are to continue to have basic needs, a view we take our 'sceptic' to accept. And the similarity in the argument to some that are used against the sceptic provides some support for the view that this 'materialist' argument is one which the idealist should not take too lightly . . .

What I am arguing effectively, then, is that Marx's materialist conception of history should be construed as a kind of 'naturalism'. It is a theory about human need. Clearly it must be differentiated from other forms of naturalism—one distinguishing mark will be that as well as its being a theory about the way in which human needs are satisfied, it also concerns the production of new needs: people not only reproduce their needs but develop new ones and change themselves in the process.

Upon these roots grow the various strands of Marx's materialist conception of history . . .

The Materialist Conception of History

The idea of natural beings as producers of means of subsistence has been justified. The rest of the theory develops out of this idea—that of natural beings as producers, and in particular from the concept of a 'mode of production'.

I'd like, now, to examine that concept and to attempt to work out a way around a problem that has reared its head at various moments in the history of Marxism. I'll outline the problem by delving a little into the state of 'philosophical Marxism' at the time of Stalin and subsequently.

During the Stalin epoch it was supposed to be commonplace in the Marxist movement that philosophical materialism entailed historical materialism and that, from the philosophical materialist thesis that matter existed first, it followed that it is changes in 'the material life' of society—in the productive forces—that bring about major changes in social life (see J. Stalin, *Dialectical Materialism*[5]). Humanist and other subsequent Marxist thinkers found fault with this. Apart from the dubious political views that were justified in its name, it appeared to lead to fatalism, and to allow no room for an independent culture. And, if ideas were only reflections of things, how could ideas revolutionise things? People were keen, therefore, to disassociate Marx from determinism. They referred to works of the early Marx, and particularly to the Theses on Feuerbach, in support of an anti-determinist position. Here is Sidney Hook on Thesis I:[6]

> Marx sought to save the idealist's insight that knowledge is active. Otherwise his own historical materialism would result in fatalism ... The starting point of perception is not an object on the one hand and a subject opposed to it on the other, but an *interacting process* within which sensations are just as much the resultant of the active mind (the total organism) as the things acted upon. What is beheld in perception, then, depends just as much upon the perceiver as upon the antecedent cause of the perception.

And many others mention Engels' *Letter to Bloch* in support of the view that the 'base' of society does not simply determine the superstructure, rather the two interact. In that letter, Engels tells us:[7]

> According to the materialist conception of history, the determining element in history is *ultimately* the production and reproduction of real life. More than this, neither Marx nor I have ever asserted ...

But, contrary to this, it seems that even the early Marx is some kind of determinist. Here he is in 1852:[8]

> The class struggle *necessarily* leads to the dictatorship of the proletariat. [My italics.]

And, earlier still, in 1844:[9]

> The question is not what this or that proletarian, or even the whole of the proletariat at the moment *considers* as its aim. The question is *what the proletariat is*, and what, consequent on that being, it will be compelled to do.

Engels put forward a determinist viewpoint in *Anti-Duhring*, a work which was written consequent on an agreed division of labour with Marx. And there are other reasons for taking the 'determinist' line. First of all, there are passages in the later works where this view is taken—see, for instance, the *Contribution to the Critique of Political Economy*. There is also a good pragmatic reason for supposing that Marx held some kind of determinist view. According to the materialist conception of history, it is the production and reproduction of real life that is the determining element in history; this is true whether or not one adds the adverb 'ultimately'. In other words, it is the production and reproduction of real life which is causally responsible for ideas, conceiving and so on. And this is a determinism about the production of ideas etc. As yet insufficient has been said for us to know exactly what is determining what; nonetheless it is a determinist theory. If we deny the determinism we must deny the 'determination' of ideas by the production of real life; we must, therefore, deny the materialist conception of history. Any variant of historical materialism which doubts that it is a determinist theory must be a watered-down version; one which, in the end, might just as well be labelled an 'idealist' theory as a 'materialist' one.

So the problem then becomes: given that Marx was some kind of determinist, how is it that, also on his view, ideas can revolutionise things? I propose to introduce two constraints upon a successful account of the part of the materialist conception of history that relates to this problem. First of all, it must be compatible with Marx's determinism. Yet it must allow that the proletariat can revolutionise things; and, secondly, it must retain individuals and classes as pivotal to the theory.

I propose to attempt to uncover a solution to the problem by discussing the relation between 'material life' and 'consciousness'. My argument will not necessarily bear on the question of the relation between the material 'base' of society and the 'superstructure'.

Marx mentions the relation in several places, and offers what appear, on the face of things, to be incompatible accounts of its nature. Here are some examples:

> The production of ideas, of conceptions, of consciousness, is at first directly interwoven with the material activity and the material intercourse of men, the language of real life.

Later in the same passage, we find out that:

> Consciousness *can never be anything else than* conscious existence, and the existence of men is their conscious life process. [My italics][11]

But in the Preface to the *Critique of Political Economy*, we find:

> It is their social being that determines (or *conditions*) their consciousness.[12]

It looks as though there are at least two different accounts of the nature of the relation here. On the one hand, it is identity—consciousness is one and the same thing as conscious existence. On the other, it seems to be some sort of causal relation—consciousness is determined or conditioned by life. I suggest that, rather than charging Marx with inconsistency, we interpret the relation as having a double aspect. There is a relation of identity between the two but the relation is also causal. How can this be? Kripke argues that statements of identity, if true, are necessarily true, because they concern a relation between 'rigid designators': terms which designate the same object in any possible world in which they designate at all.[13] On his view, natural kind terms, as well as names, are rigid designators. Now, if the statement that 'consciousness is conscious existence' were necessarily true, then, for Kripkean reasons, it is highly unlikely that there could be a causal relation of any sort between consciousness and conscious existence. Even if one doubts the truth of some views on the subject, the view that the causal relation between a cause and its effect, if it holds on the actual world, holds in every possible world, is highly implausible. But I don't think we need hold that the statement in question is necessarily true, even if one believes that names and natural kind terms are rigid designators. For the terms in question do not designate rigidly.

To support this point, I'd like to look at a parallel identity statement between singular terms to the one we have been considering. We could take 'the one working on the production line' as a particular instance of the general term 'producer of use values' — taking 'conscious existence' to relate to production of use values. And 'the one discussing wages with the manager' could count as an instance of 'those with consciousness'. If the two descriptions are true of one and the same person, then the one discussing wages is identical with the one working on the production line. But the relation between 'the one working . . .' and 'the one discussing wages' is not a rigid relation. This is because 'the one discussing wages' does not designate the person rigidly; rather it designates the individual for a particular period of his existence. 'The one discussing wages' is one and the same person as 'the one working . . .' but there is a counterfactual situation in which *that person* is not the one discussing wages.

I am not arguing, here, for a view like Frege's — that identity statements are contingent because they hold between items under different descriptions.[14] I'm suggesting, rather, that there is a class of identity statements which are contingent, because the two terms designate different 'time slices' of the one individual. On Frege's view, the statement 'Guirisanker is Everest' is contingent, but it need not be on the view I am advocating. What makes it contingent, on the Fregean view, is the point of view from which one and the same thing is observed. But it is not the relation between observer and person which produces the contingency of the statement I am considering. Rather, it is produced by the two descriptions picking out different 'time slices' of the one individual. So the above argument need not bear on the question whether or not identity statements between names are necessarily true.

If the relation is a contingent identity, it is not ruled out that it is also causal. And I'd like to support the view that it is causal, by looking at an analogy. One might describe a particular policeman either as 'that policeman' or as 'that man'; and there could be the appropriate relation of identity between the person and itself. But one could also suppose it to be true that the man as a man is conditioned or determined by the man as a policeman. The person's life as a man could well be conditioned by his role as a policeman. Similarly, it could be true that people as thinking beings are conditioned or determined by people as producers. The individual qua thinking being is a reflection of the person as producer. To take our example: the one who is discussing wages is conditioned or determined by the person working on the production line.

How does this relate to the determinism problem? It is compatible with Marx's determinism, because the view is that people as thinkers are determined (or conditioned) by people as producers. But since it allows that some thoughts may not be conditioned by the environment, it is also compatible with Marx's view that a person or a class may influence the environment.

A problem that might arise is the following, put by Cohen as an objection to Engels' graveside speech.[15] According to Engels:

> Marx discovered the law of development of all human history; the simple fact that mankind must first of all eat, drink, have shelter and clothing, before it can pursue politics, science, art, religion etc., and that, therefore, the production of the immediate material means of subsistence and consequently the degree of economic development attained by a given people or during a given epoch form the foundation

upon which the state institutions, the legal conceptions, art and even the ideas and religion of the people concerned, have been evolved, and in the light of which they must, therefore, be explained . . .

Cohen comments that this passage is offering us one of two inferences: either that from (a) men must produce food if they are to engage in politics etc, to (b) the activity of material production is the foundation on which those activities rest; or that from (b) to (c) the activity of material production, together with the degree of economic development, explains those activities. And he labels (c) the 'indispensability claim'. Cohen responds: 'The indispensability claim is impregnable, but it cannot make material production prior to mental, as far as explanation is concerned. For mental production is also indispensable to life and indispensability is a transitive relation.' He suggests that there are two ways in which material production requires mental production. First, mental activity enters into material production, and the capacity to perform those activities depends upon mental production and general culture; and, secondly, religion and/or law and/or ideology are essential to secure order in the labour process (to discipline the labouring agents) and an ordering of the labour process (to organise production).

Now Engels' view is different from mine, because I am not explaining mental production by reference to material production; nonetheless if Cohen is right that mental production must enter into material production my thesis would not be compatible with Marx's determinism. But I do not think it must. There are material productions not involving mental activity—for instance, a bee building a hive, or an ant a nest. And there is none involved for particular people who are performing movements in relation to a conveyor belt that they have carried out many times before. Perhaps, too, there was none in the Stone Age character's first rubbing of the two flints together. Maybe it was done by instinct. Moreover, primitive communism required no religion and/or law and/or ideology. I conclude, then, that the objection does not affect my argument.

Another objection that may be levelled against my argument is that I have re-introduced an over-simplified account of the relation between 'material production' and 'consciousness', one which the young Marx might have upheld but which Marx in his maturity would certainly have rejected. It is worth noting that, as this objection would probably be put, it would be phrased in terms of the relation between 'base' and 'superstructure'. For instance, Stuart Hall[16] argues that the young Marx saw the relation between 'base' and 'superstructure' as an identity, the latter simply reflecting the former. He claims that Marx began rejecting this in the *18th Brumaire*, in the light of the non-correspondence of the 'classes in dominance at the economic level and the class factions in power, at the level of politics and state'.[17]

Hall assumes that the immature Marx held three views conjointly: that 'base' and 'superstructure' are identical; that the one reflects the other[18] and simple economic determinism.[19] He does not so much as hint at their incompatibility or suggest that this might be a reason for doubting that Marx held all three. It is apparently obvious to Hall that Marx held all three (though he does not distinguish them one from another) and obvious that each—or, at least, simple economic determinism—is incorrect. I hope I have said enough to dispel the illusion that economic determinism is simply and obviously wrong. My formulation concerns the relation between 'material production' and 'consciousness' and, though it is compatible with determination, it does not lead to the one being nothing but a reflex of the other.

To conclude this section: I have offered an interpretation of the relation between 'material production' and 'consciousness' which is compatible with Marx's determinism, but which allows that people may revolutionize things.

I make no claims to have solved the various problems concerning the relation between the base of society and the 'legal and political superstructure'.

Overall Conclusion

Marx's materialism, I have argued, is not a philosophical materialism of any sort. His materialism is equivalent to his materialist conception of history. Despite its not being a philosophical theory, it does not follow that it cannot be justified in the kind of way an idealist might come to accept.

This is only the beginnings of an account of all that the materialist conception of history has to offer us, but it is one which remains largely within Marx's conceptual territory. To that extent, perhaps unlike Althusser's theory, it can lay claim to being Marxist.

Notes

1 K. Marx, *The German Ideology*, p. 31.
2 Marx, *The German Ideology*, p. 39.
3 Marx, *The German Ideology*, p. 7.
4 Marx, *Economic and Philosophical Manuscripts*, p. 181.
5 J. Stalin, *Dialectical Materialism*, in Stalin, *Works*, Vol. I (Lawrence & Wishart, 1963) pp. 382–6.
6 S. Hook, *Towards an Understanding of K. Marx* (London, 1935) pp. 88–9.
7 F. Engels, *Letter to Bloch*, in *Selected Works*, Vol II, p. 488.
8 Marx, *Selected Works*, Vol II, K. Marx to Weydermeyer, p. 452.
9 Marx, *The Holy Family*, Chapter IV, Section 4.
10 Marx, *The German Ideology*, p. 32.
11 Marx, *The German Ideology*, p. 33.
12 Marx, *Selected Works*, p. 181.
13 See S. Kripke, 'Naming and Necessity', in D. Davidson and F. Harman (eds), *Semantics of Natural Languages* (Reidel, Dordrecht, Holland, 1972) pp. 309–43.
14 See G. Frege, 'On Sense and Reference', in *Translations from Frege* (Blackwell, 1966).
15 See G. A. Cohen, in *Essays in Honor of E. H. Carr,* p. 83.
16 In 'Base and Superstructure', in *Class, Hegemony and Party* (Lawrence and Wishart, 1977).
17 Hall, 1977, p. 57.
18 Hall, 1977, p. 53.
19 Hall, 1977, p. 53.

III
REPRESENTATION AND ART

13 The Blocked Road to Pictorial Communication *and* The Road Block Broken

William M. Ivins Jnr

Ivins—one-time curator of prints at the Metropolitan Museum of Art in New York—departs from a conviction and interest unusual in those for whom works of art are prime objects of study. He is concerned not with what Walter Benjamin called the 'aura' (the authenticity and authority) of the original work, but with the importance of exact repeatability in 'pictorial statements and communications'. His book Prints and Visual Communication *traces the development of printed imagery from the first woodblock illustrations of the fifteenth century to the photographic processes of the twentieth. The book deals not simply with the development of techniques but more significantly with the communication of knowledge and the extension of abilities made possible by this development. 'The importance of being able exactly to repeat pictorial statements is undoubtedly greater for science, technology, and general information than it is for art.' Ivins somewhat overestimates the ability of printing techniques to produce* exact *repeatability and underestimates the significance attached to the printed text. Nevertheless his work is clearly distinguished by its emphasis and interests from the normal practices of connoisseurship and art appreciation, in which the 'aesthetic qualities' of art are always at centre-stage front.*

Ivins opens his study with a critique of the confusion, which he detects in our conventional reverence for the Greeks, between 'what constitutes intelligence' and what is 'thought of, in the Arnoldian sense, as culture'. In opposition to the estimation of classical culture he notes that, 'In the objects that have come down to us from classical times there is little evidence of any actively working and spreading mechanical ingenuity.' By contrast, 'When the Middle Ages had finally produced the roller press, the platen press, and the type-casting mould, they had created the basic tools for modern times.'

In the excerpts which follow, Ivins traces the social, intellectual and technological consequences of such tools having been made available. He also demonstrates the importance for one area of knowledge, the science of botany, of the development of 'exactly repeatable pictorial statements'. In the process he makes clear how the progress of certain studies is frustrated when limited by dependence on linguistic description. Freedom from this dependence requires both skilful care in delineation from original objects and the capacity for 'schematic representation of . . . generalized or theoretical generic forms'. Ivins thus draws attention to the critical nature of the relationship between direct empirical observation and rational classification as it pertains to visual representation.

For an instance of the application of Ivins' work in the wider fields of epistemology and the sociology of knowledge, see the first excerpt from Barnes, text 11.

Source: *Prints and Visual Communication* (London, Routledge & Kegan Paul PLC, 1953) Ch. 1, 'Introduction—the blocked road to pictorial communication', pp. 2–20. and Ch. 2, 'The road block broken—the fifteenth century', pp. 33–46. This material has been edited and illustrations have been re-numbered.

I

[. . .] Although every history of European civilization makes much of the invention in the mid-fifteenth century of ways to print words from movable types, it is customary in those histories to ignore the slightly earlier discovery of ways to print pictures and diagrams. A book, so far as it contains a text, is a container of exactly repeatable word symbols arranged in an exactly repeatable order. Men have been using such containers for at least five thousand years. Because of this it can be argued that the printing of books was no more than a way of making very old and familiar things more cheaply. It may even be said that for a while type printing was little more than a way to do with a much smaller number of proof readings. Prior to 1501 few books were printed in editions larger than that handwritten one of a thousand copies to which Pliny the Younger referred in the second century of our era. The printing of pictures, however, unlike the printing of words from movable types, brought a completely new thing into existence—it made possible for the first time pictorial statements of a kind that could be exactly repeated during the effective life of the printing surface. This exact repetition of pictorial statements has had incalculable effects upon knowledge and thought, upon science and technology, of every kind. It is hardly too much to say that since the invention of writing there has been no more important invention than that of the exactly repeatable pictorial statement.

Our failure to realize this comes in large measure from the change in the meaning and implications of the word 'print' during the last hundred years. For our great grandfathers, and for their fathers back to the Renaissance, prints were no more and no less than the only exactly repeatable pictorial statements they knew. Before the Renaissance there were no exactly repeatable pictorial statements. Until a century ago, prints made in the old techniques filled all the functions that are now filled by our line cuts and half tones, by our photographs and blueprints, by our various colour processes, and by our political cartoons and pictorial advertisements. If we define prints from the functional point of view so indicated, rather than by any restriction of process or aesthetic value, it becomes obvious that without prints we should have very few of our modern sciences, technologies, archaeologies, or ethnologies—for all of these are dependent, first or last, upon information conveyed by exactly repeatable visual or pictorial statements.

This means that, far from being merely minor works of art, prints are among the most important and powerful tools of modern life and thought. Certainly we cannot hope to realize their actual role unless we get away from the snobbery of modern print collecting notions and definitions and begin to think of them as exactly repeatable pictorial statements or communications, without regard to the accident of rarity or what for the moment we may regard as aesthetic merit. We must look at them from the point of view of general ideas and particular functions, and, especially, we must think about the limitations which their techniques have imposed on them as conveyors of information and on us as receivers of that information.

From very ancient times materials suitable for the making of prints have been available, and apposite skills and crafts have been familiar, but they were not brought into conjunction for the making of exactly repeatable pictorial statements in Europe until roughly about AD 1400 [. . .]

Learned men have devoted many large and expensive volumes to the gathering together of all the literary evidence there is about classical painting and drawing and to the reproduction of all the specimens of such drawing and painting as have been found. It appears from these books that there are no surviving classical pictorial statements, except such as were made incidentally in the decoration of objects and wall surfaces. For such purposes as those there was no need or call for methods to exactly repeat pictorial statements. From the point of view of art as expression or decoration there is no such need, but from that of general knowledge, science, and technology, there is a vast need for them. The lack of some way of producing such statements was no less than a road block in the way of technological and scientific thought and accomplishment.

Lest it be thought that in saying this I am merely expressing a personal prejudice, I shall call your attention to what was said about it by a very great and unusually intelligent Roman gentleman, whose writings are held in particularly high esteem by all students of classical times. Some passages in the *Natural History* of Pliny the Elder, a book that was written in the first century of our era, tell the story in the most explicit and circumstantial of manners. As pointed out by Pliny, the Greeks were actually aware of the road block from which they suffered, but far from doing anything about it they accommodated themselves to it by falling back into what can only be called a known and accepted incompetence. More than that, I believe, they built a good deal of their philosophy about this incompetence of theirs. In any case, what happened affords a very apposite example of how life works under the double burden of a pessimistic philosophy and a slave economy. There is nothing more basically optimistic than a new and unprecedented contrivance, even though it be a lethal weapon.

III Representation and Art

Pliny's testimony is peculiarly valuable because he was an intelligent eye-witness about a condition for which, unfortunately, all the physical evidence has vanished. He cannot have been the only man of his time to be aware of the situation and the call that it made for ingenuity. Seemingly his statement has received but slight attention from the students of the past. This is probably due to the fact that those students had their lines of interest laid down for them before the economic revolution that came to England in the late eighteenth and early nineteenth centuries and did not reach Germany until after 1870, at a time when the learned and the gentry knew nothing and cared less about what they regarded as merely mechanical things. The preoccupation of the post-mediaeval schools and universities with classical thought and literature was probably the greatest of all the handicaps to technological and therefore to social advance. It would be interesting to see a chronological list of the establishments of the first professorships of engineering. With rare exceptions the mechanical callings and knowledges were in the past as completely foreign to the thought and life of the students of ancient times as they were to the young elegants who attended the Academy or walked and talked with Aristotle. So far as I have been able to observe they still are.

In any event, according to Bohn, what Pliny said was this:

> In addition to these [Latin writers], there are some Greek writers who have treated of this subject [ie botany] . . . Among these, Crateuas, Dionysius, and Metrodorus, adopted a very attractive method of description, though one which has done little more than prove the remarkable difficulties which attended it. It was their plan to delineate the various plants in colours, and then to add in writing a description of the properties which they possessed. Pictures, however, are very apt to mislead, and more particularly where such a number of tints is required for the imitation of nature with any success; in addition to which, the diversity of copyists from the original paintings, and their comparative degrees of skill, add very considerably to the chances of losing the necessary degree of resemblance to the originals . . . (Chapter 4, Book 25).

> Hence it is that other writers have confined themselves to a verbal description of the plants; indeed some of them have not so much as described them even, but have contented themselves for the most part with a bare recital of their names, considering it sufficient if they pointed out their virtues and properties to such as might feel inclined to make further inquiries into the subject (Chapter 5, Book 25).

> The plant known as 'paeonia' is the most ancient of them all. It still retains the name of him who was the first to discover it, being known also as the 'pentorobus' by some, and the 'glyciside' by others; indeed this is one of the great difficulties attendant on forming an accurate knowledge of plants, that the same object had different names in different districts (Chapter 10, Book 25).

It is to be noted that in his account of the breakdown of Greek botany, Pliny does not fall back upon general ideas of a woolly kind. There is no Zeitgeist explanation, no historicism, no suggestion that things were not done simply because people in their wisdom and good taste preferred not to do them even though of course they could have done them if they had wanted to. Pliny's reason is as hard and brutal a fact as a bridge that has collapsed while being built. This essay amounts to little more than a summary account of the long slow discovery of ways to erect that bridge.

In view of this I shall rephrase what Pliny said: The Greek botanists realized the necessity of visual statements to give their verbal statements intelligibility. They tried to use pictures for the purpose, but their only ways of making pictures were such that they were utterly unable to repeat their visual statements wholly and exactly. The result was such a distortion at the hands of the successive copyists that the copies became not a help but an obstacle to the clarification and the making precise of their verbal descriptions. And so the Greek botanists gave up trying to use illustrations in their treatises and tried to get along as best they could with words. But, with words alone, they were unable to describe their plants in such a way that they could be recognized—for the same things bore different names in different places and the same names meant different things in different places. So, finally, the Greek botanists gave up even trying to describe their plants in words, and contented themselves by giving all the names they knew for each plant and then told what human ailments it was good for. In other words, there was a complete breakdown of scientific description and analysis once it was confined to words without demonstrative pictures.

What was true of botany as a science of classification and recognition of plants was also true of an infinite number of other subjects of the very greatest importance and interest to men. Common nouns and adjectives, which are the materials with which a verbal description is made, are after all only the names of vaguely described classes of things of the most indefinite kind and without precise concrete meanings, unless they can be exemplified by pointing to actual specimens. In the absence of actual specimens the best way (perhaps the only way) of pointing is by exhibiting properly made pictures. We can get some idea of this by trying to think what a descriptive botany or anatomy, or a book on machines or on knots and rigging, or even a sempstress's handbook, would be like in the absence of dependable illustrations. The only knowledges in which the Greeks made great advances were geometry and astronomy, for the first of which words amply suffice, and for the second of which every clear night provides the necessary invariant image to all the world.

All kinds of reasons have been alleged in explanation of the slow progress of science and technology in ancient times and in the ages that succeeded them, but no reference is ever made to the deterrent effect of the lack of any way of precisely and accurately repeating pictorial statements about things observed and about tools and their uses. The revolutionary techniques that filled this lack first came into general use in the fifteenth century. Although we can take it for granted that the making of printed pictures began some time about 1400, recognition of the social, economic, and scientific, importance of the exact repetition of pictorial statements did not come about until long after printed pictures were in common use. This is shown by the lateness of most of the technical illustrated accounts of the techniques of making things. As examples I may cite the first accounts of the mechanical methods of making exactly repeatable statements themselves. Thus the first competent description of the tools and technique of etching and engraving was the little book that Abraham Bosse published in 1645; the first technical account of the tools and processes used in making types and printing from them was that published by Joseph Moxon in 1683; and the first similar account of woodcutting, the oldest of all these techniques, was the *Traité* of J. M.

129

Papillon, which bears on its title page the date 1766. It is not impossible that Moxon's *Mechanick Exercises*, which were published serially in the last years of the seventeenth century, had much to do with England's early start in the industrial revolution.

Anyone who is gifted with the least mechanical ingenuity can understand these books and go and do likewise. But he can do so only because they are filled with pictures of the special tools used and of the methods of using them. Parts of Moxon's account of printing can be regarded as studies in the economy of motion in manipulation . . .

Of many of the technologies and crafts requiring particular manual skills and the use of specialized tools there seem to have been no adequate accounts until the completion of the great and well illustrated *Encyclopaedia* of Diderot and his fellows in the third quarter of the eighteenth century, just before the outbreak of the French Revolution. But the *Encyclopaedia* was a very expensive and very large set of volumes, intended for and limited to the use of the rich. Curiously, the importance of its contribution to a knowledge of the arts and crafts has attracted comparatively little attention as compared to that which has been given to its articles on political matters, although there is good reason to think that they had equally great results.

The last century is still so close to us and we are so busy keeping up with the present one, that it is hard for us to realize the meaning of the fact that the last hundred and fifty years have seen the greatest and most thoroughgoing revolution in technology and science that has ever taken place in so short a time. In western Europe and in America the social, as well as the mechanical, structure of society and life has been completely refashioned. The late Professor Whitehead made the remarkable observation that the greatest invention of the nineteenth century was that of the technique of making inventions. But he did not point out that this remarkable invention was based in very large measure on that century's sudden realization that techniques and technologies can only be effectively described by written or printed words when they are accompanied by adequate demonstrative pictures.

The typical eighteenth-century methods of book illustration were engraving and etching. Etchings and engravings have always been expensive to make and to use as book illustrations. The books that were fully illustrated with them were, with few exceptions, intended for the consumption of the rich and the traditionally educated classes. In the eighteenth century the title pages of these books sometimes described them as being 'adorned with elegant sculptures', or other similar words. The words 'adorned' and 'elegant' tell the story of their limitations, mental and financial alike. Lest it be thought that the phrase I have just quoted came from some polite book of verse or essays, I may say that it has stuck in my memory ever since at the age of ten I saw it on the title page of a terrifying early eighteenth-century edition of *Foxe's Martyrs*, in which the illustrators went all out to show just what happened to the Maryian heretics. Under the circumstances I can think of few phrases that throw more light on certain aspects of eighteenth-century life and thought.

Although hundreds of thousands of legible impressions could be printed at low cost from the old knife-made woodcuts, the technique of woodcutting was not only out of fashion in the eighteenth century, but its lines were too coarse and the available paper was too rough for the woodcut to convey more than slight information of detail and none of texture.

At the end of the eighteenth century and the beginning of the nineteenth century a number of very remarkable inventions were made. I shall mention but three of them. First, Bewick, in the 1780s, developed the technique of using an engravers' tool on the end of the wood, so that it became possible to produce from a wood-block very fine lines and delicately gradated tints, provided it were printed on smooth and not too hard paper. Next, in 1798, Robert, in France, invented, and shortly afterwards, in England, Fourdrinier perfected, a paper-making machine, operated by power, either water or steam, which produced paper by a continuous process. It also made possible the production of paper with a wove surface that was smoother than any that had previously been made in Europe. When fitted with calendar rolls the machine produced paper that was so smooth it was shiny. Finally, just before 1815, Koenig, a German resident in England, devised for the (London) *Times* a printing press that was operated by power and not by the strength of men's backs. In connection with a revival of Ged's earlier invention of stereotyping, these inventions brought about a very complete revolution in the practice of printing and publishing. The historians of printing have devoted their attention to the making of fine and expensive books, and in so doing they have overlooked the great function of books as conveyors of information. The history of the cheap illustrated book and its role in the self-education of the multitude has yet to be written.

It took but a comparatively short time for these three or four inventions to spread through the world. As they became familiar there was such a flood of cheap illustrated informative books as had never before been known. Nothing even approaching it had been seen since the sixteenth century. It took only a few decades for the publishers everywhere to begin turning out books of this kind at very low prices. In a short time the world ceased to talk about the 'art and mystery' of its crafts. In France they said that the Revolutionary law abolishing the guilds opened the careers to the talents, but it was actually these cheap illustrated informative books that opened the crafts to everyone, no matter how poor or unlearned, provided only that he knew how to read and to understand simple pictures. As examples of this I may cite the well-known *Manuels Roret*, the publication of which goes back to 1825, and the English *Penny Cyclopaedia* which began in 1833. It is to be noted that for a long time in the nineteenth century the upper classes and the traditionally educated made few contributions to the rapidly lengthening list of new inventions, and that so many of those inventions were made by what in England until very recent years were condescendingly referred to as 'self-educated men'. The fact was that the classicizing education of the men who were not self educated prevented them from making inventions.

In the Renaissance they had found a solution of the dilemma of the Greek botanists as described by Pliny. In the nineteenth century informative books usefully illustrated with accurately repeatable pictorial statements became available to the mass of mankind in western Europe and in America. The result was the greatest revolution in practical thought and accomplishment that has ever been known. This revolution was a matter as momentous from the ethical and political points of view as from the mechanical and economic ones. The masses had begun to get the one great tool they most needed to enable them to solve their own problems. Today the news counters in our smallest towns are piled with cheap illustrated magazines at which the self-consciously educated turn up their noses, but in those piles are prominently displayed long series of magazines devoted to mechanical problems and ways of doing things, and it would be well for the cultured if they thought a little about the meaning of that. [...]

NOMEN HERBAE ASPARAGI AGRESTIS.

Fig 1 'Asparagus agrestis', woodcut from the herbal of the *Pseudo-Apuleius*, Rome, *c.* 1483. About actual size.

II

[...] Some time just after 1480, there was published at Rome the so-called *Pseudo-Apuleius*, a book that contains much for thought. Its text is that of a ninth-century botanical manuscript which for centuries prior to the last war was in the monastery at Subiaco. Its woodcuts [Fig 1] are careless copies of the illustrations in that manuscript, but they are actually closer to their originals than we should expect in view of the then prevalent attitude towards such things. They were the final step in a long series of copies of copies of copies that went back to original drawings made not impossibly by some of the Greek botanists of whom Pliny talked. They point the moral of his account of why the Greek botanists gave up trying to illustrate their books. In any case, this was the first illustrated botany book to be printed, and it was also the first printed reproduction of both the text and the illustrations in a very ancient volume. It was the Adam from which sprang that line of facsimiles of old manuscripts and drawings that every museum and university library prides itself in having on its shelves.

In 1484 the herbal known as the *Latin Herbarius* was printed at Mainz. It is a large and fully illustrated volume containing many woodcuts of plants, that seem to have been copied from various older sources. It suffers, though not so badly, from the same trouble as the *Pseudo-Apuleius*. The next year, 1485, however, the same printer issued another and completely different herbal in German, which is known as the *Gart der Gesundheit*. Its handsome and well-drawn illustrations [Fig 2] were epoch making in the history of prints as a medium for the conveyance of information in invariant form. It is pleasant to let the author tell the story in his own words. In his brief introduction he says:

> . . . as man has no greater or nobler treasure on this earth than bodily health, I came to believe that I could undertake no more honourable or useful or holier work or labour, than to bring together a book in which the virtue and nature of many herbs and other creations of God, with their true colours and form, were made comprehensible for the consolation and use of all the world. Therefore, I caused this praiseworthy book to be begun by a master learned in medicine, who at my request brought together in a book the virtue and nature of many herbs out of the esteemed masters of medicine, Galen, Avicenna . . . and others. And when I was in the middle of the work of drawing and painting the herbs I noticed that many noble herbs did not grow in this German land, so that, except by hearsay, I could not draw them in their true colours and form. Therefore, I left the work I had begun unfinished and hanging in the pen until I had received grace and dispensation to go to the Holy Sepulchre . . . And so, lest this noble work, begun but not ended, be left undone, and also that my journey should serve not only the salvation of my soul but all the world, I took with me a painter of understanding and with a subtle and practised hand. And so I travelled . . . In journeying through these kingdoms and lands I diligently learned the herbs that were there, and had them painted and drawn in their true colours and form. And afterwards, when, with God's help, I was come again in German land and home, the great love which I had for this work has moved me to finish it . . . And in order that it may be of use to the learned and the lay I have had it turned into German.

The *Gart der Gesundheit* is thus the first printed illustrated account of the results of a journey undertaken with scientific purposes in mind. I know of no earlier statement that a writer on a scientific subject refused to have his book illustrated from hearsay and took care that it be done directly from the original objects represented. Because of this it is one of the greatest monuments in the history of the descriptive sciences. It is to be regretted that we know the names neither of the man who undertook the task, of the learned man who assembled the literary material, nor of the subtle artist who made the drawings. [. . .]

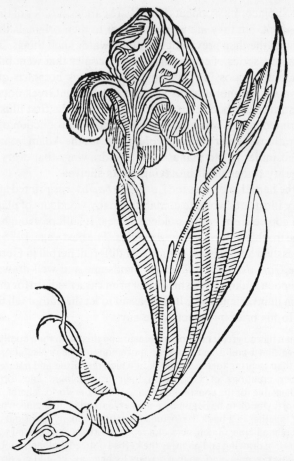

Gladiolus   notten krut oder geel swerteln
Capitulū·rrcv· *19.5.*
Ladiolus latine·grece dt reris·Die meister sprechen
daz diß krut habe keynen stengel vnd hait bletter die
wachsen vß dr würtzeln die glichen eynes swertes
lamel·vn ist zweyer hande·Eyns wechset an druckē
steten vnd hait eyn ble blomen die ist weych vn wōl

Fig 2 'Gladiolus', woodcut from the *Gart der Gesundheit,* Mainz, 1485.
Reduced.

    The publication of the herbals of 1484 and 1485 was followed by that of many
others in many places. For a period of almost fifty years most of these other books
were illustrated with copies of the woodcuts in those two herbals, many of which
were copied from them at second and even third hand, with a steadily decreasing
size in the dimensions of the pictures and a steady increase in the amount of
distortion of the representations. The degradation and distortion thus introduced
into the pictures perhaps reached their culmination in the first English herbal, the
Grete Herbal, of 1526, in which the pictures [Fig 3] have at last become little

134

PLATE I

Henri Matisse *La Fenêtre Ouverte* (1913) $59\frac{1}{2}'' \times 37''$ Paris, Private Collection. © DACS 1984.

PLATE II

Mark Rothko (1903–1970) *Red on Maroon* (The Four Seasons, no. 4) (1969) 105″ × 94″ oil on canvas. London, Tate Gallery.

PLATE III

Morris Louis (1912–1962) *Alpha Phi* (1961) 102″ × 180¾″ acrylic on canvas. London, Tate Gallery.

PLATE IV

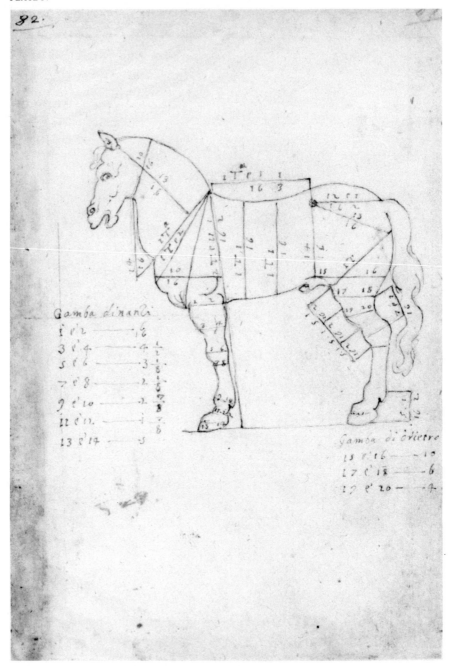

After Leonardo da Vinci *Dimensions of a Horse* pen and chalk, MS M.A. 1139 fol. 82 r., New York, Pierpont Morgan Library.

PLATE V

Jackson Pollock *Mural* (1950) 72" × 96" oil, enamel and aluminium paint on canvas, mounted on wood. Tehran, Museum of Modern Art.

PLATE VI

Art & Language *Portrait of V.I. Lenin by Charangovitch in the style of Jackson Pollock* (1980) oil and enamel paint on paper, mounted on canvas. Courtesy of Galerie Eric Fabre, Paris.

PLATE VII

Art & Language, drawing for '*V.I. Lenin*' *by V. Charangovitch (1970) in the style of Jackson Pollock*, (1980) pencil on paper. Collection Jan Debbaut, Eindhoven.

more than decorative motifs much more suited to serve as cross stitch patterns than for the conveyance of information. They constitute a remarkably sad example of what happens to visual information as it passes from copyist to copyist.

These herbals, beginning with the *Pseudo-Apuleius* of about 1480 and coming down through the *Grete Herbal* of 1526, are extremely interesting from still another point of view. When arranged in families and in a time order they clearly show the operation of what I suppose is one of the basic human characteristics. So long as the illustrators did not return to the original plants as sources of information about their shapes, but confined themselves to such knowledge of the forms as they could extract from pictures made by earlier men— to what may be called hearsay and not first-hand evidence— it was inevitable that they should rationalize their own pictorial accounts and overlook or disregard what appeared to them to be mere irrationalities in the pictorial accounts given by their predecessors. This rationalization most frequently took the form of an endeavour for symmetry which produced regular shapes that not only lost all verisimilitude of lines and edges but introduced a balanced arrangement of parts and forms, which, however satisfying to mental habits, resulted in a very complete misrepresentation of the actual facts. I am sure that all sorts of morals can be drawn from these botanical illustrations, but shall content myself with remarking

Fig 3 Violets. Woodcut from the *Grete Herbal*, London, 1525. About actual size.

that in their almost comic way these pictures raise some of the most desperately serious problems that are known to man, for these problems are those of thought itself rather than of the materials with which it deals. There is a Latin tag which asks who it is that takes care of the caretakers. According to our temperaments we may laugh at these pictures or be condescending or up stage about them, but if we look at them intelligently they contain matter for the most humble prayer. [. . .]

Fig 4 Violets. Woodcut from Brunfels's *Herbarum vivae eicones,* Strassburg, 1530. Reduced.

The first return to nature after the herbal of 1485 came when Brunfels issued, at Augsburg in 1530, the first volume of his celebrated herbal. This was illustrated with sharply observed and sensitively drawn woodcuts by Hans Weiditz [Fig 4]. Weiditz is mentioned only in some laudatory verses in the first edition of the first volume. His remarkable woodcuts have been adversely criticized as being portraits of particular plants, showing not only their personal forms and characters but the very accidents of their growth, such as wilted leaves and broken stems, rather than being schematic statements of the distinguishing characteristics of the species and genera. In view of the fact that there was as yet nothing that could be called a workable classificatory system in botany, this criticism has always seemed to me to be a bit forehanded.

Twelve years later, in 1542, at Basel, Fuchs published his celebrated herbal, in which the abundant woodcut illustrations [Fig 5] no longer represented particular plants but were careful schematic representations of what were considered the generic forms. They contain no indication of either the personalities or the accidents of growth of the plants. The illustrations were drawn from the actual plants by an artist named Albert Mayer, whose drawings were then copied on the blocks, and doubtless given their schematic form, by Heinrich Fullmaurer, after which the woodcutter, Hans Rudolph Speckle, did his work of cutting the blocks. We know this because at the end of the volume there are portraits of the three men at work, with their names and callings. These portraits are the first explicit statement I recall that a set of illustrations, although based on drawings specifically made for the purpose of illustrating a text, were, as actually printed, second-hand and not first-hand reports. This is the first time that both artist and woodcutter are given full recognition in the informational book they concerted to illustrate, and it is the first specific statement of the fact that the drawing on the

Braſsicæ quartum genus.
Rappißkraut.

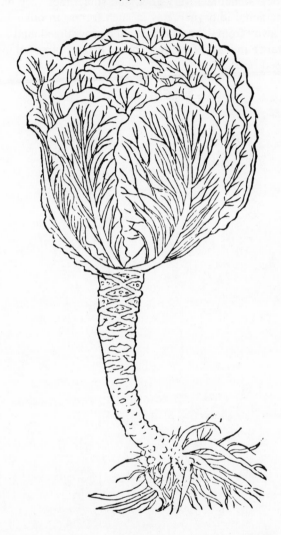

Fig 5 'Kappiskraut', woodcut from Fuchs's *De Stirpium Historia*, Basel, 1545.
Enlarged.

block was not made by the original draughtsman but was a revised version of his drawing made by a specialist whose business it was to draw with lines that were suitable for their technical purpose. I shall have much to say about the inevitable results of this practice and its effects upon the communication of information and ideas. It is important to notice that in this first forthright example the result was no longer a portrait of a particular thing but a schematic representation of its generalized or theoretical generic forms. It thus represents not only one of the most important steps ever consciously taken in the long search for a scientific classification of natural forms, but it also represents, quite unconsciously, one of the great steps in the substitution of rationalized statements of natural forms in place of the older, sometimes very good and sometimes very bad, attempts to represent the personal idiosyncracies of such forms. In other words, it was a deliberate step away from the particular to the generalized, and as such is of the greatest importance in view of the subsequent history of visual information and the thought based on it. [. . .]

14   The Cognitive Style

Michael Baxandall

Michael Baxandall's Painting and Experience in Fifteenth Century Italy *has exercised a considerable influence on art-historical study in general. This is perhaps in part because his evidence is organized by strong hypotheses of the kind which generate interesting research programmes. The book is thus untypical of the main run of art-historical work and publication, in which speculation tends to be constrained by the decorum of deductive method. Baxandall gives his study the subtitle* A Primer in the Social History of Pictorial Style. *(There is perhaps an implicit reference here to the subtitle of E. H. Gombrich's* Art and Illusion: A Study in the Psychology of Pictorial Representation.*) His aim is 'to show how the* style *of pictures is a proper material of social history'. What makes this a feasible aim is that Baxandall's concept of style is underpinned not, in the customary manner, by the collecting together of empirical 'similarities', but more importantly by considerations of the historical conditions of cognitive activity and use.*

> *A society develops its distinctive skills and habits, which have a visual aspect, since the visual sense is the main organ of experience, and these visual skills and habits become part of the medium of the painter: correspondingly, a pictorial style gives access to the visual skills and habits and, through these, to the distinctive social experience. An old picture is the record of visual activity. One has to learn to read it, just as one has to learn to read a text from a different culture, even when one knows, in a limited sense, the language: both language and pictorial representation are conventional activities. (p. 152)*

Baxandall's concept of style unites the representational activity of the artist with the representational skills and interests of typical observers. He thus locates the experience of visual apprehension firmly within the context of interested social activity rather than of disinterested and passive contemplation. His account of his subject may therefore be seen as compatible with the accounts of observation and knowledge furnished by Hanson (text 8) and by Barnes (text 11). In the passage which follows Baxandall argues that the discriminations made within a given culture will be practically limited by the linguistic concepts available to articulate them. (In so far as this is a 'logocentric' view it is open to some dispute.) This will include the discrimination and recognition of skills. The concepts available in use will be largely furnished through other contexts of activity, including the handling of affairs, going to church and the conduct of social life, and will differ to some extent according to individual experience and practice, though certain concepts will be shared among those who form the 'patronizing classes'. It is in terms of the conceptual and linguistic evidence for visual skills that Baxandall seeks to establish a 'Quattrocento cognitive style as it relates to Quattrocento pictorial style'.

In his chapter on 'The Period Eye' Baxandall notes that how we perceive a given graphic configuration (what we see it as) 'will depend on many things— particularly on the context of the configuration. . .—but not least on the inter- preting skills one happens to possess, the categories, the model patterns and habits of inference and analogy: in short, what we may call one's cognitive style'. *And later: 'Much of what we call "taste" lies in this, the conformity between discriminations demanded by a painting and skills of discrimination possessed by the beholder.'*

Though his exposition is well fitted to his chosen subject, Baxandall's work has clear methodological relevance for the study of art in general, both in its sociological and its epistemological aspects. We might consider, for instance, what form of 'cognitive style' on the part of what type of 'patronizing class' can appropriately be connected to the 'pictorial styles' of modern art. It should be pointed out, however, that though Baxandall refers to the realities with which artist and patron were constantly in contact, he does not consider how differences in the nature of that contact might have to be seen as leading to some asymmetries in the relationship between pictorial skill and cognitive style. Both Quattrocento pictorial skill' and 'Quattrocento cognitive style' need to be viewed as abstractions performed in the interests of theoretical elegance.

Source: *Painting and Experience in Fifteenth Century Italy*, Ch. II, 'The Period Eye', Section 3, 'The cognitive style', pp. 36–40. © (Oxford University Press, 1972.) Reprinted by permission of Oxford University Press.

[. . .] Renaissance people were, as has been said, on their mettle before a picture, because of an expectation that cultivated people should be able to make discriminations about the interest of pictures. These very often took the form of a preoccupation with the painter's skill, and we have seen too that this preoccupation was something firmly anchored in certain economic and intellectual conventions and assumptions. But the only practical way of publicly making discriminations is verbally: the Renaissance beholder was a man under some pressure to have words that fitted the interest of the object. The occasion might be one when actual enunciation of words was appropriate, or it might be one when internal possession of suitable categories assured him of his own competence in relation to the picture. In any event, at some fairly high level of consciousness the Renaissance man was one who matched concepts with pictorial style.

This is one of the things that makes the kind of culturally relative pressures on perception we have been discussing so very important for Renaissance perception of pictures. In our own culture there is a class of over-cultivated person who, though he is not a painter himself, has learned quite an extensive range of specialized categories of pictorial interest, a set of words and concepts specific to the quality of paintings: he can talk of 'tactile values', or of 'diversified images'. In the fifteenth century there were some such people, but they had relatively few special concepts, if only because there was then such a small literature of art. Most of the people the painter catered for had half-a-dozen or so such categories for the quality of pictures—'foreshortening', 'ultramarine at two florins an ounce', 'drapery' perhaps, and a few others we shall be meeting—and then were thrown back on their more general resources.

Like most of us now, his real training in consciously precise and complex visual assessment of objects, 'both natural ones and those made by man's art', was not on paintings but on things more immediate to his well-being and social survival:

> The beauty of the horse is to be recognized above all in its having a body so broad and long that its members correspond in a regular fashion with its breadth and length [Fig. 1 & Plate IV]. The head of the horse should be proportionately slender, thin and long. The mouth wide and sharply cut; the nostrils broad and distended. The eyes should not be hollowed nor deeply recessed; the ears should be small and carried like spears; the neck long and rather slender towards the head, the jaw quite slender and thin, the mane sparse and straight. The chest should be broad and fairly round, the thighs not tapering but rather straight and even, the croup short and quite flat, the loins round and rather thick, the ribs and other like parts also thick, the haunches long and even, the crupper long and wide . . . The horse should be taller before than behind, to the same degree a deer is, and should carry its head high, and the thickness of its neck should be proportional with its chest. Anyone who wants to be a judge of horses' beauty must consider all the parts of the horse discussed above as parts related in proportion to the height and breadth of the horse . . .

But there is a distinction to be made between the general run of visual skills and a preferred class of skills specially relevant to the perception of works of art. The skills we are most aware of are not the ones we have absorbed like everyone else in infancy, but those we have learned formally, with conscious effort; those which we have been taught. And here in turn there is a correlation with skills that can be talked about. Taught skills commonly have rules and categories, a terminology and stated standards, which are the medium through which they are teachable. These two things—the confidence in a relatively advanced and valued skill, and the availability of verbal resources associated with them—make such skills particularly susceptible to transfer in situations such as that of a man in front of a picture.

This raises a problem. We have been moving towards a notion of a Quattrocento cognitive style. By this one would mean the equipment that the fifteenth-century painter's public brought to complex visual stimulations like pictures. One is talking not about all fifteenth-century people, but about those whose response to works of art was important to the artist—the patronizing classes, one might say. In effect this means rather a small proportion of the population: mercantile and professional men, acting as members of confraternities

Figure 1. Pisanello. *Studies of a Horse*. Cod. Vallaudi 2468. Paris, Louvre. Pen and chalk.

or as individuals, princes and their courtiers, the senior members of religious houses. The peasants and the urban poor play a very small part in the Renaissance culture that most interests us now, which may be deplorable but is a fact that must be accepted. Yet among the patronizing classes there were variations, not just the inevitable variation from man to man, but variation by groups. So a certain profession, for instance, leads a man to discriminate particularly efficiently in identifiable areas. Fifteenth-century medicine trained a physician to observe the relations of member to member of the human body as a means to diagnosis, and a doctor was alert and equipped to notice matters of proportion in painting too. But while it is clear that among the painter's public there were many subgroups with special skills and habits—the painters themselves were one such subgroup—this book will be concerned with more generally accessible styles of discrimination. A Quattrocento man handled affairs, went to church, led a social life; from all of these activities he acquired skills relevant to his observation of painting. It is true that one man would be stronger on business skills, another on pious skills, another on polite skills; but every man had something of each of these, whatever the individual balance, and it is the highest common factor of skill in his public that the painter consistently catered for.

To sum up: some of the mental equipment a man orders his visual experience with is variable, and much of this variable equipment is culturally relative, in the sense of being determined by the society which has influenced his experience. Among these variables are categories with which he classifies his visual stimuli, the knowledge he will use to supplement what his immediate vision gives him, and the attitude he will adopt to the kind of artificial object seen. The beholder must use on the painting such visual skills as he has, very few of which are normally special to painting, and he is likely to use those skills his society esteems highly. The painter responds to this; his public's visual capacity must be his medium. Whatever his own specialized professional skills, he is himself a member of the society he works for and shares its visual experience and habit [. . .]

15   Portrait of V. I. Lenin

Art & Language

Art & Language is an informal group or organization, founded in England in 1968, the membership of which grew to include various artists, art theorists, critics and art historians in England, America and Australia. Their interests converged on the possibility of overlap between these (and other) functions. The membership was substantially reduced in the late 1970s. The three Art & Language texts included in this anthology originally appeared in the journal Art-Language, *which is written, edited and published by the group.*

It has been a tradition within Art & Language that all relevant forms of production should be issued under the group name. This practice was adopted in recognition of the difficulty or irrelevance of attributing authorship in the context of collaborative projects. In such contexts as this anthology, however, it is conventional to identify arguments with the names of those individuals doing the arguing. As regards the texts included here, Art & Language is to be indentified with the collaborative work of Michael Baldwin, Charles Harrison and Mel Ramsden.

'Portrait of V. I. Lenin' (the title refers to Art & Language's series of painted 'Portraits of V. I. Lenin in the Style of Jackson Pollock' [Ref. Plates V–VII]) departs from David Kaplan's discussion of the relations between names, their objects and the users of those names. A name, Kaplan suggests, may be of its object (for someone) by virtue of a relation of resemblance, or descriptiveness or iconicness (x is like *its object for* p); *or it may be of its object (for someone) by virtue of a causal or genetic connection (x can be* traced *to its object by* p); *a name may also be vivid for someone by virtue of some interest on that person's part, and can be so independently of either descriptive or genetic considerations. Kaplan illustrates his argument by analogy with pictures. The Art & Language text follows up the implications of this analogy and extends them in pursuit of a concept of realism in representation which is sufficiently sophisticated to cover the actual practice of art, and not just those types of pictures which are 'philosophers' objects'.*

As regards any claim that a picture is 'of' something, Art & Language asserts, 'It is an implicit condition of any realistic criticism that genesis be

145

recognized in general as a more powerfully explanatory concept than resemblance.' The argument is generally addressed against those cultural tendencies which suggest that the 'how' of the production of pictures should be inferred from assumptions about the 'what'; for example, the tendency to allow the application of empiricist or stylistic categories to define the grounds of causal inquiry. (Cf Goodman's 'Seven Strictures on Similarity', text 9.) As an interim hypothesis Art & Language suggests that:

> *... there may be a way to regard realistic pictures as, among other things, pictures whose genetic systems contain a 'closed', or rather partially closed system. We may be able to regard a realistic picture as a picture whose termini are that picture and that which it is of [in the genetic sense]. Such a system is not really closed, rather it is differentiated from other non-realist art practice in that it is limited or restricted in some way that is historically or* cognitively significant, *and not just structurally or because of an investment in dominance.*

The argument formulated in this article is extended in Art & Language's 'Abstract Expression' (text 18) in pursuit of an analysis of the expressive aspects of pictures and of the types of claims made for expressive content. In reading these texts the following points need to be borne in mind. They were produced within a collaborative practice. One persistent concern of this practice has been to ask what kind of production the production of art can or should be, given the current state both of 'art' and of interpretation, and the relationship of each to a history *of art and of interpretations. To ask this is also to ask what kinds of resources can be mobilized to address the problem. Some of the resources deployed by Art & Language have been philosophical, focussed on types of logical and causal arguments. Art & Language's usage of these resources involves a critical extension of their range and penetration.*

Source: Art-Language vol. 4, no. 4, Banbury, June 1980, pp. 26–62. Some footnotes have been deleted. © Copyright Art & Language.

It is truistic to say that realist art must be descriptive of something. Realist pictures are also supposed to have something to do with knowledge.

The possible distinction between the descriptive and genetic features of pictures is usually left very fuzzy in the higher reaches of realist theory. As a consequence these notions are subjected to an *ad hoc* synthesis. The problematic and limited character of the How and the What of pictures goes substantially unrecognised. Semiotics clears some of the fog, but the cost is a practical epistemological vacuity—a system for picking out descriptive equivalences.

The conceptual problems of the relations of representation are not all over. The earnest hope of some realists that they are all over embraces a flight from reality. We assert that these relations are, crudely, of two sorts: 'descriptive' or denotative and genetic. These are two main links that a picture can have with reality. We further assert that the genetic 'link' is either neglected or fuzzed into description. This is a pity as it is a very powerful consideration when one is considering the problems of realism. This last contention is problematic. We need to rummage around between pictures and representations and the world before we can go on to explore the consequences for the higher reaches.

It may be contended that some pictures have a link with reality and others do not. Some pictures have a different link with reality than others. This 'link' is genetic.

Discussing names in connection with 'simple' pictures of one person, David Kaplan[1] considers a fundamental relation between a name and an object:

> What we are after . . . is a three part relation between Ralph, a name (which I here use in the broad sense of singular term) *a*, and a person x. For this purpose I will introduce two special notions: that of a name *a* being of x for Ralph, and that of a name being vivid, both of which I will compare with the notion of a name denoting x.
>
> Let us begin by distinguishing the *descriptive content* of a name from the *genetic character* of the name as used by Ralph. The first goes to user-independent features of the name, the second to features of a particular user's acquisition of certain beliefs involving the name. It is perhaps easiest to make the distinction in terms not of names but of pictures, with consideration limited to pictures which show a single person. Those features of a picture, in virtue of which we say it resembles or is a likeness of a particular person, comprise the picture's descriptive content. The genetic character of a picture is determined by the causal chain of events leading to its production. In the case of photographs and portraits we say that the picture is *of* the person who was photographed or who sat for the portrait. The same relation presumably holds between a perception and the perceived object. This relation between picture and person clearly depends entirely on the genetic character of the picture. Without attempting a definition, we can say that for a picture to be *of* a person, the person must serve significantly in the causal chain leading to the picture's production and also serve as object for the picture. The second clause is to prevent all of an artist's paintings from being *of* the artist. I will shortly say a bit more about how I understand this relation, which I designate with italicized '*of*'.
>
> The 'user-independence' of the descriptive content of a picture lies in the fact that 'identical' pictures, such as two prints made from a single negative, will resemble all the same persons. In this sense, the descriptive content of a picture is a function of what we might call the picture-type rather than the picture-token. The 'user-dependent' nature of the genetic character of a picture lies in the fact that 'identical' paintings can be such that they are *of* different persons (eg twins sitting separately for portraits). Thus the genetic character of a picture is a function only of the picture-token. In order to accommodate genesis, I use 'picture' throughout in the sense of 'picture-token'.

Kaplan's three notions, resemblance (ε descriptive content), genesis and vividness are powerfully interconnected. Vividness, for example, may be thought to cope with some of the anomalies and difficulties encountered in trying to deal with the possible relativity of descriptiveness, the culture-bound or instrumentally bound character of resemblance etc. Resemblance and vividness are liable to be shredded by our behaviour in encounters with actual pictures and by our more robust intuitions as to what is to count as a picture.

Genetic *of* may provide a sharp tool with which to criticise some of the excessive inventions of semiotics. It may be that the substantive critical homework problem that Kaplan provides is how to preserve the notion of genesis (with a suitably non-empiricist interpretation) in the light of the fact that the other two notions are easily damaged.

It is tempting to follow Kaplan and try to stick to pictures of single persons or things on analogy with singular names and descriptions, but few pictures are philosophers' objects. Most or all pictures are referentially intractable or complex in some way.

Descriptive Content?

Those features of a picture according to which we are able (under certain conditions) to see it as 'resembling' a person or etc comprise (under certain conditions) the descriptive content of the picture, although these features are in general neither necessary nor sufficient for descriptive or representational content. (For some people these pictures will be seen as comprising the 'representational content'.)

It seems that resemblance comprises the descriptive content of the picture but only with considerable modifications, under some conditions. Resemblance is relative to practice and to other resemblances and cultures, and it is variable in time etc. A judgement of 'high descriptive content', say, will not necessarily follow upon normal judgements of resemblance. What we could perhaps say is that among pictures that *represent actual objects* (or real objects) and within certain cultural constraints (and for pictures, though possibly not for texts, notably within a legacy of nineteenth-century cultural constraints), those features in virtue of which we might say that a picture resembles or is in some sense iconically tied to an object or scene comprise its descriptive content.

We are locating such relations as resemblance within the broad notion of descriptive content. It is more or less normal to say that in some (Western) cultural circumstances judgements of resemblance will consort very intimately with judgements of descriptiveness and that a picture 'p's' resemblance (or something) to an object 'a' will be a possible condition of its descriptiveness at least.[2]

According to Kaplan, the genetic character of a picture is determined by the causal chain leading to its production. The descriptive content of a picture is *comprised by* its resemblance to an object or person. Is 'comprised by' like 'determined by'? This is not clear. A little logical gap. A potential source of less scholastical or captious problems is opened when the following modification is made to Kaplan's formula; viz, that the descriptive content of a picture is *under certain conditions* (in certain contexts) determined by its resemblance to someone or something (or by its isomorphic features), and furthermore that these features are *only relatively* independent of producers and onlookers.

Is even this true? Can it be made true? Are pictures like descriptions? Do they mesh with descriptions? That is, are pictures analogues of descriptions? Do they match descriptions? Are they analogues of sentences in some way; ie are they logically complex? A picture can, under certain circumstances, be distinguished from other denotative things, from other things or symbols with descriptive content, but this distinguishing is not done by adverting to resemblance or similarity (. . . or even isomorphicness?). Little violence is done to our picture of pictures in suggesting that there can be cases such that questions of degree of resemblance will have nothing to do with questions of descriptiveness. Resemblance might have a lot to do with single actual objects, tables and chairs, mayors and mayoresses; the trouble comes when they are made so special, so logically clear, as to obscure the more important features of representational equivalence. For example, we don't have to struggle to think of the wiring diagram of a Morris Marina as a picture. It doesn't *resemble* the wires and connections of a Morris Marina. It is however *descriptive*. It may be more important to consider the problem of the equivalence of such a diagram with the 'Burial at Ornans' than to consider the minutiae of a phenomenalists' colour photograph.

Resemblance is, of course, serviceable as a condition of representation 'on the streets', where a picture might be taken as a representation of that which it resembles, without any sense of the need for consideration of other possible causes of its specific appearance. But it is not open to us to approach the matter in so vulgar (or robust?) a fashion, and we should thus try to avoid the possibility of confusion of 'representation' with 'resemblance'. Presumably, necessary conditions of 'representation' have been concerned with cognitive content and cognitive function; whereas 'resemblance' has traditionally entailed problems in dealing with a non-cognitive background to empirical experience and a-historical user-independence. More specifically: we do know that consideration of genesis can lead to revision of the relation between resemblance and denotation or 'signification'. It is therefore *only in the absence of genetic considerations* that a picture p's resemblance to 'x' can be seen as providing description of 'x' in the sense that the picture represents *in so far* as it resembles.

Obviously, many people are aware that 'resemblance' is not the only feature that pictures can have to link them with the world. Isomorphs and non-iconic models are not resemblances. Conventional symbols, etc are not resemblances. The point is that to treat any of them just as signs ignores genesis. Genetic *of* does not, however, introduce 'straight copying from reality', though it could look that way. *Of* will have to be defended.

> It is fairly obvious, if one pauses to think, that there can be no such thing in painting as straight copying from reality. One cannot observe the world, decide how it is and thereby know exactly what has to be done to the two dimensional surface (the painting in the making) to produce a likeness (any kind of likeness, photographic or not). The problem of producing a likeness is that of working out *what* one has to put down in two dimensions that will produce a sense of equivalence to what one has observed in the scene to be painted. This problem cannot be resolved without resorting to invention.[3]

This much does indeed seem obvious. We shall thus expect to move a long way from the equation of representation with resemblance.

Icons

Faute de mieux, we are trying to establish some conventional quasi-term so as to refer to the locality of 'resemblance'. In order not to seem unduly sure of ourselves, we will call those features of a picture connected with the resemblance-type aspects of its descriptive content its 'iconic features', 'icons' etc. In conventional semiotic wisdom, icons are *supposed* to be symbols whose relationship with their objects is mediated by resemblance or something; non-iconic symbols are *supposed* to be symbols whose relation(s) to their objects is (are) mediated in some other way ... this is usually *supposed* to be by conventions, and indexical signs are *supposed* to be mediated by where the snow lay dinted. We use 'icon' etc with no great confidence. The term is here intended to push discussion towards some main features of some pictures and not towards some main features of set-theoretical textbooks or British Rail timetables. The extent to which this can be accomplished without intuitive dissatisfaction will be clear or obscure *inter alia*.

We do not suggest that in discussing pictures it is entirely natural to make such a restriction. Obviously, in making it we leave out half the logic and psychology of most pictures. The point is that in plotting some of the paths of genetic *of*-ness, the street-serviceable notion of 'icon' is of considerable instrumental use. We will try to adapt the following in due course so as to deal with non-iconic symbols. This will entail some further adaptation to deal with overlap and fuzziness between the various symbol categories. It will be obvious from some of our efforts to preserve genesis or *of*-ness that this notion depends on persuading the reader to entertain colour-photographic nominalistic *icons*. It will also be clear that any worthwhile enquiry into the instrumentality of *of*-ness will depend on the recognition that, in so far as 'iconicity' is a lemma generated by 'geneticity', the relationship between the two notions is ridden with dilemmas.

A Supposed 'Independence'

The 'independence' of the descriptive content of a picture—its independence from the minds and interests of 'users' or 'producers'—is supposed by Kaplan to lie in the fact that 'morphologically identical' pictures, such as two prints from a single plate, or an 'identical' copy of a picture and the original etc, will be icons of all the same scenes, persons etc. Implicit in this supposition is the suggestion that the iconic content of a picture—which is connected to the 'descriptive' content— approaches aspects of the picture-*type* rather than the picture-*token*. We would say, however, that it is important not to underestimate the extent—if any—to which the concept of a *picture-type* may be parasitic upon the existence of common or conventional judgements of resemblance. The question also remains whether (eg) an iconic symbol will differ from (eg) a non-iconic symbol in ways which are not functions of *genetic* features of the picture. We do not suppose that the distinctions running through this text between type and token are necessarily clear intuitive categories. Type/token distinctions in respect of pictures conceived (at least partly) iconically (and certainly when they are conceived as 'representational') are perhaps a good deal more vexed and marginal than they are in respect of apparently conventional symbols. It is fairly obvious that *of* is supposed to involve some sort of 'Markovian' link between a picture and a bit of the world. With this in mind, it can be objected that the type/token icon/*of* business is *quite* clear—ie almost clear.

B Supposed 'Dependence'

The producer- or (in the case of symbols etc) 'user'-dependent nature of the genetic history (the 'causal' character) of a picture is supposed by Kaplan to lie in the fact that 'identical' pictures can be such that they have different causal histories, different 'real' objects. Two virtually identical pictures might be accidentally identical in so far as different objects had 'caused' them. A picture of a man walking up a hill might be indistinguishable from a picture of a man walking backwards down the same hill, though they would be *of* very different events. This skirts a normal problem for (eg) art history, where significant similarity (eg similarity which signifies 'influence') needs to be distinguished from accidental similarity or 'convergence'.

We would say that while it is within bounds of empirical-type discourse to connect (a) picture-type and iconicity; and while it is within bounds of empirical discourse to connect (b) genesis and picture-token; it is not necessarily within bounds of discourse critical to empiricism to make these connections exclusive. It is not clear that these connections are not functions of very large empirical assumptions. If you reject or begin to chip away at these assumptions (for instance, by introducing the concept of matching etc), it may well be, for example, that the sense of picture-type is deductively connected to 'intersubjective' judgements of resemblance or iconicity.

This is not too much of a worry. Obviously, we can understand that if two pictures 'describe' the one thing, they may be connected by *of*-ness to two different things. Someone might object that the sense of 'type' is attached here to the fact that pictures can *resemble* objects and presumably each other. The sense in which 'conventional', ie non-iconic, symbols ought to be said to describe does not involve any resemblance between them and what they describe, or any resemblance as such between the symbols themselves. This doesn't matter. John and JOHN may denote John as tokens of a type in the same way as U* and V** may denote a cat. The pictures don't really *resemble* one another. They are perhaps isomorphic in some way. What is worth considering for a moment, however, is whether a resemblance to John and 'John' are ever tokens of the same type.

This is not to say, of course, that intelligibility requires that iconicity does not go to features of the picture-type—somehow. The question remains how 'picture-type' is generated. It may be conjectured that the sense of iconicity → picture-type is within a range of empirical discourse which postulates a passive user of pictures and images and that 'user-independence' is secured as *empirical* 'user-independence'. This statement needs to be ramified by the remark that the ordinality of 'types' and the interrelationship of 'types' is historically produced. 'User-independence' is, among other things, to deny that ordinality. There may well be some realistic ordering of supervening, more complete types over others etc. There is a much larger critical nexus here. It may be argued that to see resemblance or icons as *at all* independent of users is to remove important aspects of picture generation from their genesis. What may be problematic is the pursuit of analogy between *denotation* and *resemblance* or iconicity. *Genesis* requires no sense of analogy.

*

**

Although at first sight the observation that (b) the genetic character of the picture is determined by (or goes to) aspects of the picture-token seems more intuitively secure than the suggestion that (a) iconicity goes to features of the picture-type, it probably isn't. (Deductive connectedness between the two observations does not entail symmetricality.) The genesis of a picture may not be capable of being assessed independently of questions of iconicity (or something like them) and—as a consequence of (a)'s being defended—independently of picture-type and etc. It is plainly an idealisation to suggest that the question of the causation of the produced picture is to be considered independent of iconic (or etc) features of that picture and hence independent of some possible assumptions about picture-type. This is strange territory. Nothing could seem more common-sensical than the suggestion that if 'p' is (iconically) a picture of a French general c. 1805 (p:f) or (iconically) a picture of an English general c. 1805 (p:g) but not both, it would be natural to expect a decision that 'p' is (g) to imply a different genesis for (p:g) than for (p:f). But what then?

The convention (*pace* Kaplan) concerning the genetic sense of *of* entails that, irrespective of questions of what it is iconically connected to, a picture is *of* what it is genetically connected to. This may be full of intuitive fissures, but it is still *very powerful* as an instrument for keeping your eye on the *material* character of pictures as produced. It may be no more than that. It seems intuitively obvious that the genetic history of a picture can determine its iconic (etc) features and not vice versa. What is not very clear is what are to be counted as the consituents of this genetic history—exactly how a picture's genetic link with reality is to be circumscribed.

A picture that is an icon of Attila the Hun may not have been generated by Attila the Hun in the genetic sense of *of*. Considerations of type and token aside, this statement is fraught with difficulty on an almost theological scale. A picture that was *generated* by Attila the Hun may have been generated via hearsay, fantasy and decay and, as a consequence or partial consequence, be iconically connected to Joe Jordan. How feeble could the causal chain become before Joe Jordan started to get *genetically* or at least *quasi-genetically* significant without abandoning or seriously mutilating our present conventions concerning genetic *of*? There are a lot of homework-type problems associated with this and similar or contrasting questions.

If you are considering the matter of iconicity, it is supposed here that you can do it independent of questions of genesis. This independence is, of course, not absolute: a picture may be iconically 'unlike' what it is *of* (genetically) precisely because of this genesis—and presumably (though this is substantially weaker (?)) a picture can be iconically 'like' what it is not *of* genetically as a consequence of its real genesis and so on.

It is supposed, in order to preserve the distinction between *of* and icon, that, in considering an iconic feature of a picture, you are not necessarily considering its genesis (you are '*matching*' or something). This does not entail that in considering a picture as iconic you are not participating in its genesis in some way. It is a moot point whether or not icon-genesis is any special category distinct from robust *of*-genesis. (An icon can be an icon of what it is not *of*.) The prevailing state of discourse is such as to provide one with very little clarity.

It seems you can't sort out 'description' without reference *both* to cause and to use. A description characterises something *to some end*. Because the causal chains between object and representation can be very complex and highly mediated by interests, concepts of use etc, specification of the object of the characterisation in terms of a given representation of that object will need to involve a sense of the initial contingency of attributions of cause and of iconicity.

For a given picture P, we can sustain for a while the convention that we have, on the one hand, some relative of resemblance (iconicness) and, on the other, its status as being genetically *of* something. We might say that an ideally 'simple' picture is one in which there is relatively little complication in the relations between the two, but it is hard to know where to find such a picture.

We proceed to rehearse a few more commonplaces about pictures.

(1) Obviously not all pictures which are supposed to be genetically *of* x are icons of x at all.

(2) Not all pictures which are supposed to be (genetically) *of* x are icons in some cultural circumstances.

(3) Equally obviously, not all pictures supposed to be icons are *of* that or those of which they are supposed to be icons, and further,

(4) a picture which does 'resemble' someone or something (is an icon) may not be *of* anyone or anything at all in the supposed genetic sense, but it will be *of* something in the sense that it will have some *material* genesis.

The lemma-ridden character of the relation between the pair iconicity and geneticity should by now be apparent. It seems, however, of some heuristic value to try to preserve the conjecture (*pace* Kaplan) that a picture may be genetically *of* no-one, nothing, one person, many persons, one thing, many things, while being an icon of no-one, nothing, one person, many persons, one thing, many things, for no-one or someone or most people, and with any degree of overlap between those, or those things, whom it is *of* and those whom it is an icon of for those it does the resembling or signifying.

At the moment we can see no way of going on that does not involve preserving this conjecture. This is not, however, to accord the conjecture the status of an indefeasible truth. It's better to have some conjectures than none at all.

If Mel describes x and Anne 'draws it', then the resulting picture is, in the genetic sense, *of* x, notwithstanding the apparent lack of iconicity in the picture which follows *as a consequence of this genesis*. If there was a drawing (genetically) *of* the original Banbury Parish Church which was copied by an artist with two left hands and his copy was dropped in the river and was found by someone whose heirs were amateur computer fanatics who transmitted a computer version of what they could make out of the drawing to another computer which reconstructed it on a TV screen which was watched by an old wino, intoxicated short of hallucination, who described it to an artist friend who painted a picture on the basis of the description, then, within the sense of genesis sketched so far, this last picture would have to be supposed to be genetically *of* the original parish church, no matter how 'undecipherable', and no matter what it appeared to be an icon of. It might be suggested that consequent judgements of 'realism' will be bounded by the reconstruction of the causal relations, rather than any iconic consideration in respect of any of the versions subsequent to the original.

Intuitively monstrous as this reconstruction might seem, its purport is worth preserving so as to have a faint glimmer of what's good and explanatory about some aspects of some correspondence theory in the face of the speculative hegemony of a coherence theory. What this says is that while it would be absurd to over-inflate *of*-ness—to make a genetic object a unitary cause (agent or condition) of a picture—the notion of genesis directs our attention to the world, to the problem of material causation and not to the patrician intricacies of an idealised cultural coherence. Of course, the prospects for correspondence may be dim, but the concepts lurking in its logical penumbra are illuminating. When Chomsky smashed Skinner to bits he did not suggest that speech production was uncaused. The lack of glue between a sign and the world does not make the world (which is *stratified* and *differentiated*) causally insignificant; does not make causal connections an unimportant historical and epistemological problem. Of course, causation and a 'correspondence theory' are not necessarily connected; it's just that some people who have been concerned with 'correspondence' have sustained some of the dialectical *problems* of genesis—not buried then in a bitty *cultural* algebra.

Let us suppose someone who, in 1979, sets out to paint a possibly religious picture. He conceives of this picture 'realistically' (etc, etc). One of his 'problems' is whether the conventional attributes of angels (eg wings) originated in something like (a) hallucination (hallucination ≡ the perception of what isn't there) (the non-clinical borderline between chemically induced hallucination and ideologically produced misperception is nothing if not fuzzy), or (b) is a perceptual mistake (eg seeing flowing garments as wings). If (a), then a picture of angels as they are conventionally described is (for puritanical readers of Kaplan) a picture genetically *of* nothing and no-one. But no-one would suggest—would they?—that this was a genetically empty picture. If (b), then the genetic cause is clear.

Of does not, of course, make it compulsory for angels to be real. Not only do we have the possibility that the picture is *of* models and attached or unattached wings, we also have other pictures. These pictures can also mark some genetic closure or node. At the same time, wouldn't an angel-entertaining 'realist' want to look for some existential credentials for his angels? He'd have to find some angelic being or be content with an existential *claim*.

Fuzziness notwithstanding, the closure that's imposed by the preservation of what may now seem like an over-rigorous sense of genesis is somehow better-than-trivial. Its better-than-trivial aspect has something to do with the link with reality it provides, in so far as it can be used to exclude the hypostasized conversation about pictures produced from internal necessities or internal images, visions etc. These images and necessities will not even qualify as Aristotelian material causes. The idea of a representation as produced production is not handled by a restricted use of Kaplan's genesis. We conjecture, however, that it is a *powerful* notion if adapted in suitable ways—that it provides a potential critique of those who want to hide behind idealisations and psychologised versions of material cause.

The extent to which *of* will accommodate highly complex or 'constructed' entities larger than or more complex than middle-sized dry goods is in question. That is, it is in question whether *of* can accommodate not just tables and chairs but also 'Scenes from the Massacre of Chios'. The idea of genesis raises the question of a picture's link with mind-independent reality. This is not to say that the idea of genesis can be used to provide answers to all the questions about what the conditions of a picture actually are. Nor is it a sufficient condition of the truth of any claim as to the veridicality or mendacity of any art.

Genetic *of*-ness is followed by lemmas. Iconicity, *of*-ness and their family are notions which have their feet in empiricism. When we've tried a bit longer to deal with some of the puzzles consequent upon the attempt to preserve a schematic or crystalline account of relations (the lacunae) between genetic *of*-ness and iconicity, it will be necessary for us or someone to examine them in relation to some of the powerful arguments of historical materialism. Among these upshots will be conditions of closure on genesis in iconic and non-iconic, symbolic and non-symbolic contexts and so on. A result of this examination should be the raising of such questions as to what extent the boundaries of icons and produced images and produced things of other kinds must collapse or to what extent must iconicity be in the margins of all discussion of genesis, and so forth. This cannot all be done at once. It will be appropriate to consider the matter of historical materialism and other closure conditions, other explanatory functions, against these schematic rehearsings in order to use these rehearsings as instruments to discover how it is that some closures on some genetic-type arguments and considerations and some closures on iconic and iconic-type arguments are to be defended or undefended within a broad realist proposal.

There is a dialectical relation between identification of genesis and identification of descriptive content. A strong sense of how a picture is *of* something can thus be expected to generate lemmas or anomalies (in a strict sense) with respect to identifications of or suppositions about its descriptive content. This, because of the comparatively greater material force and functionality of information about a picture's genesis. This may seem to go against those intuitions which are secured in and by 'on the street' identifications of a picture's iconic resemblance (to something). Nevertheless, the nomological priority of genetic explanation and the notion of a dialectical relation between that and identification of descriptive content should be preserved as restraining conditions upon the operation and autonomy of idealist concepts of representation; and by this we mean that it is an important condition of any realistic criticism of representation that genesis be recognised in general as a more powerfully explanatory concept than resemblance.

We have been trying to discuss *of*-ness while avoiding the shrilly materialist view that work which is not unscientific is directly caused by the material world or is firmly secured by some series of brute correspondences with it. We are taking the broadly transcendental-realist position that a search for genesis must entail recognition of actual tools, training, dispositions, interests etc, and that the search for genesis will *itself* involve making representations. This animates the other member of the dialectical pair: ie it makes clear that genesis cannot be sorted out independently of some sort of description. What is 'described' may circumscribe what can be looked for genetically. Logical construction and the stipulation (eg) that somehow the object which a picture is considered to be *of* shall serve as subject or something for the picture prevents confusion. We should take care though, lest this blinds us to instances—ie to actual genetic practice.

In 'Quantifying In', Kaplan introduces the special notion of *vividness*:

> In addition to the link with reality provided by the relation of resemblance the descriptive content of a picture determines its *vividness*. A faded picture showing the back of a man wearing a cloak and lurking in shadow will lack vividness. A clear picture, head on, full length, life size, showing finger prints, etc would be counted as highly vivid. What is counted as vivid may to some extent depend on special interests. To the clothier, nude portraits may be lacking in detail, while to the foot fetishist a picture showing only the left big toe may leap from the canvas. Though special interests may thus weight detail, I should expect that increase in detail always increases vividness. It should be clear that there are no necessary connections between how vivid a picture is and whether it is *of* anyone or whether it resembles anyone.[4]

A picture of Arthur Scargill would no doubt be vivid for Margaret Thatcher. If she knew it was *of* Arthur Scargill in a genetic sense, would it be more vivid than if it was merely an icon—ie resembled him (or something)? It seems we will have to consider the notion of vividness as some kind of practical index of the operation of our dialectical relation or else as an escape from criticism of it. This is to say that what is to count as vivid will differ in relation to actual practices and interests. These latter are not 'interests' in a merely trivial sense, but include such as reason, constraint, aim etc.

Arthur Scargill's causal connection (or not) with his picture notwithstanding, it might be expected that the notion of or experience of its vividness would go explicitly to features comprising the descriptive content of the picture, and to questions or assumptions about its genesis only secondarily and discursively. We would, however, say that a practice or an interest which is determining vividness will include the question of genesis if it is to have any reflective potential at all. This may be to say that to talk of a non-genetic practice 'determining vividness' is to put the cart before the horse. Does it mean that a practice or interest determines what *is* vivid, or what is (conventionally) *seen as* 'vivid'? Is reality as it were 'held up' or matched against criteria of vividness somehow instinct in or established by a practice or set of interests? We might want rather to say that a representational practice or interest must somehow be *produced*. This is to say that it may be a mistake to parse vividness as the psychological link with users in the context of icons seen as user-independent.

1(a) P1 is an icon of Arthur Scargill for Margaret Thatcher: P1 is vivid for Margaret Thatcher.

1(b) P1 is genetically *of* Arthur Scargill: P1 is vivid for Margaret Thatcher.

1(c) P1 is genetically *of* Arthur Scargill for Margaret Thatcher: P1 is vivid for Margaret Thatcher.

2(a) P2 is an icon of Arthur Scargill for Margaret Thatcher: P2 is vivid for Margaret Thatcher.

2(b) P2 is genetically *of* Clint Eastwood: P2 is vivid for Margaret Thatcher.

2(c) P2 is genetically *of* Clint Eastwood for Margaret Thatcher: P2 is not vivid for Margaret Thatcher.

3(a) P3 is not an icon of Arthur Scargill for Margaret Thatcher: P3 is not vivid for Margaret Thatcher.

3(b) P3 is genetically *of* Arthur Scargill: P3 is not vivid for Margaret Thatcher.

3(c) P3 is genetically *of* Arthur Scargill for Margaret Thatcher: P3 is vivid for Margaret Thatcher.

4(a) P4 is not an icon of Arthur Scargill for Margaret Thatcher: P4 is not vivid for Margaret Thatcher.

4(b) P4 is not genetically *of* Arthur Scargill: P4 is not vivid for Margaret Thatcher.

4(c) P4 is not genetically *of* Arthur Scargill for Margaret Thatcher: P4 is not vivid for Margaret Thatcher.

This table is not logically exhaustive. Among its general artificialities is the assumption that 1(a)–4(c) represent psychologically discrete encounters, that they do not overlap or impinge upon or influence one another. A further assumption is the one criticised to some extent in the foregoing, viz: that it is thoroughly possible to abstract iconic 'readings' of a picture from some variant of genetic-type inquiry or knowledge. Neither is this table concerned with questions of degree of vividness as might be expected to arise with different icons and so forth.

Clearly the table illustrates something. But it and its restrictions can only be defended in a practically empty universe.

We would expect, for example, that some at least marginal genetic presumptions would be made in actual instances of 1(a), 4(a) and perhaps others. We would expect that the addition of explicit or discursive positive genetic-type information would, in an instance of 1(a), lead to an increase(?) of vividness and that the addition of negative genetic-type information, in an instance of 1(a), would lead to a relative decrease of vividness, etc. How considerations of vividness would connect with *of* in the absence of information about *of*-ness is a bit hazy—unless we are going to conscript these interests such that pictures are pictures *of* things. Certainly, there are people who would do the other possible thing: they confuse the existence claim associated with the experience of vividness with the existence fact associated with *of*-ness.

Kaplan's notion of vividness is a bit intractable in other ways. It is hard to be convinced that increase in detail always leads to an increase in vividness—unless we can find some way of restricting implicit reductionism in our notion of detail. A ten-foot square hyper-realist portrait of Arthur Scargill is surely not vivid. Its 'detail' is formal, the picture was probably painted upside down—a fetish of airbrush, epidiascope and alienation. Roman Jakobson's and Claude Lévi-Strauss' stylistic analysis of Baudelaire's 'Les Chats'[5] is surely not *detailed*, even though it goes on page after page picking patterns from the poem. The status of intuitions, purposes and interests in the determination of detail is highly problematic. What is to count as an increase in detail *for* someone in his *internal* picture will not be exemplified by 'fingerprints'.

Vividness is almost clear intuitively. It does seem to be powerfully connected to genesis and icon. We are not sure how. The trouble with genesis in Kaplan's text is that it may be dangerously *phenomenalistic*. Its related notions similarly so. However, we *can* understand that two look-alike pictures can be *of* non-identical things, scenes or people. We *can* understand that two pictures which are *of* non-identical objects can look alike. We can also understand that two pictures *of* the same object can look different and so forth. We can understand it all within limits. It is 'clear'.

The fact that pictures can be vivid may well account for the relative casualness with which the logical structure of representation is treated. Kaplan's notion of vividness goes importantly to 'special interests'. It is associated with the descriptive content of a picture, though it does not involve any necessary connection with the naturalism of a picture or whether this is an icon of anyone or anything or whether it is *of* anyone. We would argue that vividness is a powerful concept, notwithstanding its troubles. What is interesting is the extent to which the high vividness (or something very like it) of a picture or pictures is held to be the principal reason for their 'realisticness' (or something very like it). Certainly, in much of the literature that purports to treat of 'realism' there is no clear differentiation between (produced) genetic considerations and those (produced) judgements of vividness which do not necessarily entail the genetic or denotative features of pictures. (We would say, however, that the hermeneutic that surrounds the problems of genetic conditions of representation will involve genesis as an historical function of vividness.)

It might be argued that pictures judged vivid by someone are not so much replete with detail as productive of (or contain) features which *match* the beliefs or interests of some onlooker or class of onlookers. (Compare the 'realism' of Lukács: 'Realism in art portrays the world in the sense that it enables man to perceive his own true nature.')

If we understand the observation that a picture p is vivid for T. J. Clark, then this involves the picture p's 'representing' what T. J. Clark is interested in. What T. J. Clark may be interested in may be actual or not, although usually he will claim that what he is interested in is actual. A picture's vividness is at least conceptually separated from its genesis and iconicity; ie we might say that there is some predicate of it which renders it vivid in relation to a user's interests but which is a function neither of its genesis nor of its iconicity. For a variety of historical reasons such conditions of vividness may be analytic in their contributions to rigour-bearing depictions, representations etc. This is not the lunatic assertion it may at first appear to be, since vividness and matching etc must involve some degrees of logical transitivity etc and some possibilities of cognitive content, to escape from accusations of relativism.

The productive or descriptive (or iconic) features may of course be of pictures which are *of* certain bits of the world and which are icons of other sorts of representations of them. But not necessarily. You cannot infer *of*-ness and inconicity or naturalism from vividness—and you can distinguish them from it.

But, presumably, 'good' pictures are usually vivid. It is highly likely that vivid pictures for someone or for some class or interest have a high plausibility for them. (Class naturalism? Bourgeois naturalism?) And vivid pictures might be expected to involve an ontological claim or to be thought to expect some sort of ontological commitment (but not knowledge as such).[6]

It would be hard to think of a picture as vivid unless its being vivid involves some sort of ontological commitment to what it is thought to describe for those for whom it is vivid. This may be hard to take—just sort of stipulative. We may seem to be restricting vividness to an artificially small class of pictures—pictures that seem to involve an existence claim in respect of what they describe on the part of those for whom they are vivid.

A picture that shows some sort of humanoid out of science fiction might be traceable or *of* something, might be thought to be an icon or a multiple icon, or it might be *of* other pictures, or *of* nothing, or etc. The picture might be vivid for someone but only if he, she or they are in some way ontologically committed to what is 'described'.

But what is described is not thought to exist by people who look at the covers of science-fiction books. It is hard to be categorical about this. We think that it is not an uncritical regurgitation of the philosophical analysis of fictions to suggest that a vivid picture should involve an existence claim in some possible world for someone. The extent to which the relations between this possible world and the actual world are thought to be specified will depend on the contextually determined logical limits.

The extent to which this purely 'internal' (to someone) existence claim is, or could be, a claim that whatever is vivid has ontological credentials in the actual world is of some interest. The blithe postulation of a well-marked possible world will not cope with all questions, anomalies etc.

Bearing in mind 'vivid', we return to *of*. Consider the following: A hyper-realist H is going to have a show at the A.N. Other Gallery. Boris Fish, the owner of the gallery and entrepreneur of hyper-realist painting, has informed the artist that the portrait he exhibited in the gallery artists' Summer Show was the subject of enormous interest on the part of the illiterate plutocrats who patronise his gallery. Could he possibly do ten more, just like it? H agrees. He photographs Bob, Carol, Ted, Alice, Jules, Jim, Tex etc with his perfectly functioning Hasselblad. His brilliant technician girlfriend develops the film and produces perfect 10 x 8 in colour prints. H sticks the prints in his epidiascope which enlarges the image to 10 x 8 ft, and proceeds to airbrush and fudge a hyper-realist picture complete with enlarged pores, blackheads, eyelashes and hair-roots.

H's 'picture of Bob' etc satisfies or seems to satisfy Kaplan's criteria of *of*-ness, resemblance and vividness. At the same time, it involves us in no undue metaphorical strain to say that H's 'picture of Bob' etc is *of* no-one, that it is only marginally iconic and that it is utterly lacking in vividness. It would be sufficient for him to have an adequately caparisoned doll. The metaphor is not strained. We could say that it is almost to be taken literally.

We may be able to accept—in a commonsensical or culturally bound phenomenalistic way(?)—the argument that H's picture of Bob is a picture such that Bob played an important part in 'the causal chain leading to its production'. We are nevertheless struck by the vacuity of the argument. In fact it seems to be the poor historiographical brother of 'The First World War was caused by the assassination of the Archduke Ferdinand at Sarajevo.' It is a vastly inferior argument to account for the picture when compared with the statement that the picture was produced—materially caused—by other hyper-realist pictures, by the pressure of the hyper-realist market, and that these material causes do not involve reference to Bob in any significant sense.

The point about the notion of genesis (not the only point, but it must be important) must be the question of the explanatory power of an account of the production of something. For Kaplan, at first sight, explanatory power may not seem to be of the essence. This is a pity. If you are considering how you got a name you could very well be explaining to yourself how you acquired it.

It is perhaps interesting to consider Kaplan's *of* in relation to W. B. Gallie's genesis. According to William Dray:

> In his general account of *genetic* explanation, Professor W. B. Gallie says . . . if a historian explains the rapid rise of Christianity by referring to its possession of the proselytizing platform of the Jewish synagogue . . . this does not commit him to arguing that the development was either necessary or probable. The force of the explanation is rather to show how Christianity got its opportunity. An everyday example of the same pattern would be the explanation of an angry retort by reference to the taunt which evoked it. Once again, there is no claim to show the retort to be deducible or predictable. It is rather that *but for* the taunt, 'the statement would remain unintelligible in the sense of lacking an appropriate historical context.'[7]

Now, it may seem that we could substitute 'Bob' for 'the taunt' and 'hyper-realist picture' for 'the retort' in the passage above. This will not, however, lead to a satisfactory result. We would argue that in order to get a satisfactory result what would have to be substituted for 'the taunt' in the above passage is a lengthy sentence concerning the interests of A. N. Other, art money and art market. Thus:

> An everyday example of the same pattern would be the explanation of a *hyper-realist picture* by reference to *the art market* (etc) which evoked it. Once again, there is no claim to show the *hyper-realist picture* to be deducible or predictable. It is rather that *but for* the art market (etc), 'the hyper-realist picture would remain unintelligible in the sense of lacking an appropriate historical context.'

What would artistic pictures be like if a Kaplan sense of the genesis of such pictures were not only true but important as an explanation—contributed something to a sense of material cause?

Everyone, or nearly everyone, can understand that a picture can be an icon of what it is not *of*, that pictures that 'look alike' can be *of* different actual objects, and that pictures that do not look icon-alike can be *of* the same actual objects etc. This all makes sense diagrammatically.

Of can have a strange stipulative *character*. We are suggesting that it is more or less than merely genetic. Stipulatively associate some pictures with perceptions of their objects and that's all you have—a dogmatic claim that some conjunction occurred sometime. This can be genetically empty. The hyper-realist's 'piece' is *of* Bob. The painting is associated with its object by some 'natural' stipulation. 'Weymouth Bay' by John Constable is also *of* its object—Weymouth Bay. Now we suggest that it is not wilfully obtuse to record the thought that this genetic association of the picture 'Weymouth Bay' with Weymouth Bay is to tell us something *quite different* about how 'Weymouth Bay' was produced than the stipulative association of the hyper-realist 'piece' with Bob. This would seem so even if the genetic connection between 'Weymouth Bay' and Weymouth Bay were via hearsay and drunken verbal description. Why is this?

160

We can further conjecture that *of* or rather the problem of *of*-like relations between pictures and their objects is central to any discussion of realism. (Far too much of the debate at Realism conferences and so forth is concentrated on (vague and laymanlike fixations with) the descriptive character of pictures and with 'semiological' updates of these; not enough attention is paid to the genetic character of pictures. Indeed, these aspects of pictures are often confused etc.)

The *genesis* of a photograph could include the camera factory in Germany or Japan. The *of*-ness of (eg) a photograph can provide an epistemologically significant closure on such a genetic discussion. It is (eg) *of* Arthur Scargill. *Of*-ness is stipulative in that it seems to license the stipulative association of a picture with another bit of the world. It is *not* a correspondence but a genetic relationship. What is complex and interesting is that the genetic significance of the stipulation will be a matter of enquiry for any picture or pictures. Within the limits of artificial intelligence, or of vulgar intuition, the epiphenomenal photograph can be insulated from absurdity. The epiphenomenal painting, it might be said, is close to being a category mistake. The painter is not a mechanism triggered by the tree or whatever he is painting. At least, you might want to say, 'Look at the painter for the "causes" of the painting. Look for *a structure*, not at the tree.' The point is that *of*-ness does not impose a Skinnerian metaphysics of cause; it stipulates some possible genetic closure.

Perhaps there are arguments for seeing symmetry between *of*-ness and genetic closure. Firstly, such a condition would dispose of behaviourists' (and others') reification. Secondly, closure is interest-bound rather than a mechanical conclusion from which *of*-ness is seen as produced. Thirdly, *of*-ness must be complex and must be intimately connected to the functions of closure.

In order to ask the right sorts of questions concerning the significance of the relation between genesis and *of*-ness to the problem of realism, a number of continuing difficulties must be faced, and if not brought to solution at least given some dialectical air. These difficulties continue largely in the locale of accusations that the Kaplanesque notion of *of* is phenomenalistic, empiricistic, behaviouristic or just vulgarly materialistic. A similar objection is (eg) that it makes one of a picture's possible links with the world the alleged fact that it is an epiphenomenon of it, or that the painter just mechanically and passively copies his object and so on. Another possible criticism is that anyone who conscripts Kaplan's *of*-ness into art discourse is trying to make some sort of glue with which to stick (some) signs to the world and vice-versa. Not many of these objections are easily met. The problems come thick and fast when it is remembered that *of*-ness is being considered not because of its psychological interest but primarily because of its historical and historiographical explanatory interest. It has to do with how something was produced.

We are suggesting, in adapting *of*-ness, that it is a special sort of restriction in arguments concerning the production of certain types of pictures or representations. This restriction is genetic. *Of*-ness has genetic status but it is not genetically sufficient. Genetic considerations are, as we have earlier mentioned, in some clear and vulgar ways distinct from considerations of (eg) iconicity and isomorphicness. The defensibility of a particular sort of genetic argument in analysis distinguishes some kinds of art production from other kinds. (And to put what we keep saying another way, we pursue this conjecture on the near conviction that the semiological self-restriction of many earnests of 'realism' has them worrying about whether pictures are *like* something or other or nothing, whereas what they should be worrying about or asking is whether pictures are *of* something or other or nothing. If you ask the latter question the genetic debate is *brought to the forefront;* and we can thus stifle the anxious squeaks of those whose interests are served by the high-minded suppression of informal fallacies.)

In order for a genetic explanation to be complete there would have to be a reduction of the various genetic disciplines (all the possible ways to account for things) to a single stratum, a complete description of all the individuals at that level. There would have to be an *antecedent* closure. This is absurd not because it is a megalomaniac dream but because it amounts to a condition of the impossibility of any meaningful enquiry not only into representation but into anything. The possibility of enquiry entails that what is enquired into is open. The high-bourgeois consumer account of the genesis of the masterpieces of, eg, Robyn Denny or Carl Andre at the Tate Gallery is dogmatically complete. Their genesis is fully explained and closed off on pain of curatorial suicide. Such a *dogmatic* closure is irrational, not merely self-serving or venal. This can be shown by showing what it would *presuppose* if its practitioners could be bothered to consider the upshots of their smugness.

A stipulative association of picture and object obviously suggests a closure of some kind. It does not suggest that a complete explanation is possible, however. *Of*-ness appears to have the merit of preserving some sort of alternative to a coherence theory of representation. That is, it directs attention and it directs enquiry to material causation; it is materially *intelligible* quasi-closure, not an arbitrary criterion of the credibility of some cultural interest.

Of-ness does not suggest that there is a complete genetic explanation of any picture. Neither does it suggest that this is a reasonable aim. What it does is suggest that for some kinds of representational work a quasi-closure is defensible and that this can lead to more, perhaps, than the examination of *structures of some kind,* but not just the examination of recorded experiences nor the trivial collection of recorded experiences by artists and their apologists.

The quasi-experimental character of some picture production is dependent upon the fact that the producer produces a closure which is intelligible, and that its intelligibility is rooted in some reality. *Of*-ness proposes and can be defended as a condition of such a closure.

One of the possible ways *of*-ness can be thought to mark a difference between realistic and non-realistic artistic work is that it is defensible and significant in accounting for the genesis of realistic pictures and arbitrary and marginal in accounting for other types. You can't always—can seldom ever—just tell by looking whether artistic work is idealistic or not. This last statement is so obvious as to have the status of a truism.

We recapitulate our conjecture and say that a closure of a possibly 'stipulative'—but not antecedent—kind is defensibly associated with *of* in instances of *realistic* pictures. That is, there may be a way to regard realistic pictures as, among other things, pictures whose genetic systems contain a 'closed' or rather partially closed, system. We may be able to regard a realistic picture as a picture whose termini are that picture and that which it is *of*. Such a system is not really closed, rather it is differentiated from other non-realist art practice in that it is limited or restricted in some way that is historically or *cognitively significant*, and not just structurally or because of an investment in dominance.

This is not to presume that human agency is not an important genetic question. What *of*-ness does is introduce a closure in the form of a conjecture and a set of lemmas as to what you can go on and say about that agency—what that agency is like. (A *greedy* painter's painting *of* something is perhaps not the same sort of genetic object as a greedy painter's painting *of* nothing.) Because of the 'realist' conjecture above and its lemmas, questions concerning agency may well differ in cognitively dramatic ways.

Whether or not *of*-ness distinguishes a particular kind of 'operation', as we appear to be suggesting, is far from clear. If we *are* suggesting such an operationism, then it should be clear that the relations which this implies are not seen as such as to require that a picture p being *of* x is both necessary *and* sufficient. We are not prohibited, for example, from having pictures of x which are 'irrational'; that is, presumably contrastive predicates may still be simultaneously applicable. From the point of view of a theory of types, we should not suppose that x's are primitive items, nor should we suppose that pictures of x's are modally simple things or relations. *Of*-ness does not suggest some variant of action by contact thought not to require explanation. We're not thinking in terms of a set of cog-wheel relations. The causal *agent* in the genetic sequence is the artist or artists, men and women as producers of produced production. The notion of producer is better understood than the notion of a producer of pictures *of* something.

Another objection to *of*-ness (which is connected variously to many others) is that it can only go to features of a very restricted class of pictures. Think of this as a theoretical argument in the sense that what is being objected to is the causal implication that there is some intelligibly equivalent Markovian-ness to be found in very long and attenuated genetic chains and in very short and apparently simple ones. That is, it may be thoroughly objectionable to suggest that a relation of *of*-ness established between a photographic print and a depicted object (where, eg, mediation and so forth are not all that complicated) is significantly like a relation of *of*-ness thought to be reconstructable in a very long, complex and highly mediated chain. Such an objection to *of*-ness amounts to saying that while it may be sort of commonsense to think of some very simple pictures as epiphenomena of the 'actual objects' of the world, it makes no sense to think this way of most pictures which are genetically the result of human activity, competences, cognitivity etc. It's not obvious whether this objection concerns some sort of implicit phenomenalism of *of*-ness. To accuse *of*-ness of phenomenalism may not be to say that it is genetically insignificant—although it would be if you thought that phenomenalism was incapable of accounting for anything. The objection may not be so much an accusation of phenomenalism but a suggestion that *of*-ness can't account for anything non-phenomenalistic—which is different.

The objection that *of*-ness makes pictures epiphenomena of actual objects is perhaps something to infiltrate Kaplan with. *Of*-ness is, however, not unavoidably phenomenalistic. It might be true that a genetic *of*-ness 'link' between a picture and reality could be seen as phenomenalistic; if, that is, the chain involved was sufficiently oversimplified. But what we have to defend is a claim for *of*-ness that it is a 'link' with the independently real world that a picture (etc) can have, and one which is distinct from a descriptive or denotative or iconic link, in some fairly important and clear ways. The logical character of *of*-ness is such that it continues to show through a lot of counter-exemplary fog. The link is phenomenalistic *only* if it's made that way—only if a phenomenalistic emphasis is gratuitously produced.

An elaboration of the criticism—viz that *of*-ness is only one of many candidates for consideration in trying to account for picture-production genetically—is well taken. But *of*-ness is at least a differently weighted candidate when one is dealing with some or some possible representational pictures. *Of*-ness is epistemologically significant. It is not a notion that points to some epiphenomenal residue. It is a special type of genetic category.

But this is not the end of the troubles of *of*-ness. Someone might object that *of* as a stipulative association (hyper-realism *and* John Constable) will cover a wider (looser) range of pictures than *of* as a genetically significant explanatory function (just John Constable). *Of* works on at least two levels of picture 'intelligibility'. These two levels are in some way unreconcilable. They belong to different types or levels of enquiry. One *of*-ness is just obscurantist. The trouble with an objection of this sort is that it is founded on a misunderstanding of the instrumentality of *of*-ness. While some pictures *of* something or other are 'only trivially so', and others not, this does not mark any subdivision of *of*-ness. The fact that for a hyper-realist 'portrait' *of* is a merely stipulative, explanatorily insignificant relation is indeed highly problematic. This 'insignificance' is due to the fact that there are other genetic considerations which are liable to obliterate the sense that the *of*-ness of such portraits is a (genetic) *link with reality*. Indeed, it can be argued that *of*-ness is here a condition of the critical obliteration of the hyper-realist's claim to any sort of realism. The fact that the hyper-realist portrait of Bob is *of* Bob and the fact that this stipulative association is no significant closure on accounts of its genesis is some indication that the portrait has no realistic character (unless we were to assent to the preservation of a stipulative quasi-denotative (dogmatic and boring) restriction on *of*-ness). We conjecture that the realistic or unrealistic character of a picture *of* something (eg hyper-realism v. Pissarro etc) is meaningfully contributed to by answers to the question, 'How significant is the *of*-ness of that picture in accounting for its genetic intelligibility?' Another way of putting this is in answer to the question, 'How significant is its *of*-ness in the production of a closure, given that any explanation of the genetic system in which it is produced is necessarily incomplete in so far as the system itself is open?'

Of is a link as a functional relation between a picture and some part of the world. The non-dogmatic aspects of the stipulative association between the two entail the cognitive conditions discussed earlier. Some pictures are *of* some part of the world, though this stipulative association *does not* seem to express one of their links with reality. Other pictures are *of* some part of the world, and this stipulative association *does* seem to express one of their links with reality. The detail and

164

truth-value of the stipulation are not the same in both cases. But this does not mean that we have to interpret *of* differently in each case. Indeed, the relevance of the very distinction between the cases is a pointer to the critical explanatory potential of our concept of *of*.

Of-ness is not just a relation between middle-sized dry goods. Not quite. It is indifferent with respect to homeomorphic, isomorphic, paramorphic representations. This does not mean it is empty. The fact that the double-helix representation of the DNA molecule is grounded in mechanical, not biophysical, models does not reduce its *of*-ness with respect to (all or some) DNA molecules. This is, of course, to extend Kaplan's *of*-ness—but not beyond intuitive facility. To say that a model is supposed to be *of* a DNA molecule is to say a bit more than that it is supposed to represent it or look like it or explain it. It is to say that it is in some way genetically tied to some actual (though presumably not real) object of science (or some real object that science studies) and not the product of mere fantasy or an imaginary object or some other object. The link between representation and some parts of external reality has its explanatory power etc in hypothesis-formation. The links are not themselves hypotheses. Hypotheses are not just noetic correspondences within the discourse of science. As actual though not real objects they are part of the production of scientific discourse.

Of is always potentially marginal or genetically vacuous. What positively distinguishes some representational pictures from others is the genetic significance of *of*-type relations in accounting for their character.

Of handles the possibility that two formally and at a certain level psychologically identical pictures could have different genetic links with reality. Of course, pictures of the same thing can have different genetic character etc, pictures *of* nothing could differ genetically etc. *Of*-ness is a link that a picture can have with reality. It can be suggested that it is a link that any realist picture must have. It is in order to point out the difference between a descriptive or iconic link of *of*-ness and a genetic link of *of*-ness that diagrammatic examples have been used above. These diagrammatic examples make 'a picture *of*' seem like 'based on a perception *of*'. This is fraught with anxieties about practical redundancy and logical collapse (as we have seen). *Of*'s apparent reducibility to some form of phenomenalism is the problem.

Actual instances of pictures do not very often just involve a decisive single or simple *of* in their genesis. At the same time, the genetic significance of an apparently reduced and primitive sense of *of* is of importance in distinguishing some categories of pictures. There is a more psychologically real circumstance such that *of* is involved and which can be thought to bear on some actual instances of pictures.

Picture-production is not passive perception-copying. It must be clear that perception *of* or mechanical conjunction of object and picture (or picturer) is by no means genetically sufficient for any recognisable pictures. It was never supposed to be. Perception *of* is a sort of genetic closure. *Of* can comprehend that virtual *absence* of the 'object' which is involved in a defensible sense of picture genesis. By 'virtual absence' we mean the following: If Courbet's 'The Stone-breakers' is *of* (or not *of* and not both) actual people, then that is, among other things, epistemologically significant. The occurrence of some specific bit of

165

stonebreaking in nineteenth-century France is not sufficient for 'The Stone-breakers'. The non-occurrence of that bit of stonebreaking is not sufficient for the rejection of an *of*-ness claim with respect to 'The Stonebreakers'. But if an *of*-ness claim is to be sustained, then the painting must be some significant genetic conjuncture, and the constituents of this genesis must be people and processes independent of the painting, and there must be part of this genesis independent of the producer of the painting. Furthermore, there must be some way in which it can be claimed that the picture *refers* to what it is *of*.

The ambiguity of the more or less conventional phrase 'plays a significant part in the (causal) genesis of the picture' can be thought to permit some sense of this 'virtual absence'. By 'virtual absence' we mean to emphasise the fact that pictures have a mediated genesis. We mean to bury the idea that the epistemological significance of *of* denotes the epiphenomenal-or-worse picture. 'Mediation' is not here supposed to throw fancy intellectual Lukácsian idealist notions into the discussion. Nor is mediation here supposed to be of some abstract form, isolating human agents and agency from each other and from external reality; historical agency is the mediation. By talking of a 'virtual absence' of the object we mean to point to the fact that pictures are produced production and that within the *of*-ness relation between a picture and an object other pictures and descriptions can be accommodated. Recent criticism of Stalinist left-wing usage of 'mediation' has suggested that such epistemological problems of pictures and reality are not subject-object interfaces or problems, but that mediation is simply a function of human agency in subject-subject relations.

We have tended to dwell on the problem of a very schematic *of*. Genetic credentials and the derivation of genetic credentials are of great epistemological significance. If 'The Stonebreakers' was transported without comment to Southern California, it could denote two Californian artistic persons collecting stones for their crib of a Richard Long. The painting's realistic status as having something to do with knowledge can only be extracted from its genetic attachment to some real peasants—whether it naturalistically denotes them or not.

If Courbet heard snatches of a report about a burial at Ornans and that's all he had to go on, then (some of) the genesis of 'Burial at Ornans' could be traced back from mouth to mouth or from 'mouth to eye' to the actual burial (eventually). This is not at all surprising. This tracing may seem to have very little to do with the significance of 'Burial at Ornans'. But if 'Burial at Ornans' is supposed to have anything to do with the class struggle in France, it will have to be linked to it by more than resemblance to people at a funeral and the presumption that the descriptive features of the picture are somehow discursive enough to produce or match knowledge. Of course, the picture may not be linked genetically to people at a funeral—it may be linked to a different event in the life of the country bourgeoisie and the burial may be a kind of metaphor. There is nothing genetically odd about that. The picture is *of* what it is *of*. Alternatively, it may be 'about' the rural proletariat in a metaphor that 'describes' the country bourgeoisie. If it's *of* the rural proletariat, it has to satisfy *of*-ness conditions. 'Serve as subject' is not that simple. It is no less *of* what it is *of* when what it is *of* is not the *primary* subject of the picture. *Title* and *subject* do not have to coincide; artist's subject and subject may well be a matter of genetic investigation etc. (We do not need to say

166

that what a picture is *of* must also be the subject of the picture in order to stop pictures just being *of* the artist. We can either stipulate that they shall not be *of* the artist or else include the artist in the list of those—usually many—things which the picture is *of*, stipulating that there are no realist pictures which are genetically *restricted* to being *of* the artist.)

Someone might object that the suggestion that Courbet's 'The Stonebreakers' is of artistic persons making a silly Richard Long sculpture is itself so silly, so lacking in plausibility, as to be able to mark no boundary between iconic 'naturalism' and *of*-ness. The objection has a certain merit—but not much. It is perhaps more genetically significant to say that Courbet was French, that he lived at a certain time and that the genesis of the *picture* is what was happening at the time he lived and his perception of it and his perception of truths about it. Maybe. But the production of certain resemblances by Courbet will not link his picture with reality genetically. We cannot infer realism from resemblance. Neither can we infer realism from the extruded heroic personality. The assertion that Courbet held such and such a social position or positions, that he had such and such a grasp on the character of society, and that these views were *true* and were knowledge as a sort of consequence cannot be true unless these views and the pictures which formed and were formed by them are genetically linked to a world which is independent of him and his pictures.

Unless 'realistic' pictures have *of*-ness as at least one of their properties, no decisive move can be made against a theory of mere pictorial coherence. To fail to pay attention to the genetic credentials of Courbet's pictures is to extrude a mysterious hero. To extrude the hero is to minimise or to obliterate the genetic (epistemological) credentials of his pictures.

A picture *of* E. P. Thompson is genetically tied to E. P. Thompson. This genetic tie is with a specific actual entity. For a picture to be tied thus to E. P. Thompson is not to have this or that genetic history predictable of it or glued to it by necessity. It is, rather, to say that it has a link with the actual E. P. Thompson such that the well-rehearsed distinction between *what* is produced and *how* it is produced is reduced in its range of application. E. P. Thompson stands as a significant contributor to 'how'? '*How*' must conceptually restrict '*what*' if representation is to be intelligible at all beyond the vagaries of coherence theory. Indeed, it might be argued that unless the genetic link with reality is supplied initially by something like *of*-ness, then all realistic projects must be unintelligible. If *of*-ness were not a powerful link between a picture and reality, if it were merely a fifth-rate genetic explanatory device, then realist projects would, it might be conjectured, degenerate as modernist art projects have degenerated—into super-mediated art-world projects susceptible to no intelligible closures, susceptible only to the arbitrary closures which are functions of the instrumental apologetics of the rest of the bourgeois cultural creation.

We do not say that there is a correspondence between pictures and the world. Rather that without *of* we cannot contemplate, let alone stress, the role that someone's knowledge might play in the production of pictures and representations.

It should not be assumed that we are trying to enshrine *of* in a world of contemplative social atoms. The individuality of the dramatis personae of most examples in the foregoing is accidental. Kaplan's text is more than touched with empiricism/positivism. We do not stress passive, disinterested contemplation—indeed we would say that it is an unworkable distortion of a link between a picture or representation and reality. On our account, *of* stipulates not a disinterested individual's perception of an object conceived as a middle-sized dry good, but a genetically significant part of the world independent of the picture and the mind of the artist coupled with or conjoined with a denotative or referential claim concerning that part of the world and the picture in question. The perceptual experience of an individual or a collective is by no means sufficient for the closure or confirmation (or disconfirmation) of an *of* claim in respect of a given picture. Our examples are no more than diagrams of a bit of *of*'s territory. Pictures (and many other sorts of representations) are not (of themselves) sufficiently discursive in their descriptive or semiotic aspects to establish links with reality in a materially significant way. This is the case notwithstanding the plethora of transitive objects which must be 'reality' for most putatively realistic pictures. *Of*-ness is a property (or a tendency) that pictures can have significantly and without recourse to an overweening empiricist epistemology. The discursive elaboration of an *of*-ness claim in respect of some picture will be a representational activity itself. This does not imply an idealist world. An *of*-ness claim is work. A picture is work on available materials circumscribed by available cultural resources. An *of*-ness claim will have material as well as efficient causes. A picture's *of*-ness, if it has any, will involve material (Aristotelian) causes as well as efficient ones.

We have made lemmatic presumptions that *of* involves the causal independence of that which a picture is *of*. What a picture is *of* is supposed to be agent and not patient. This supposition is too strong. We are by no means sure that asymmetrical agency is required. The ontological independence of the world which a picture pictures does not require the causal asymmetry of picture and world. The causal interdependence of a picture and what it is genetically *of* is not hard to think of. Trivially, a simper in a portrait may involve a genetic reference to a simpering person who simpered at the second sitting because other aspects of the portrait were flattering and etc—problematically. The causal or genetic interdependence of the process of picturing and what is pictured is obvious. *Of* does not imply uninterpreted or unreflected reality. *Of* is not super-correspondence. The status of the closure is not very often that of the intransitive *nature* of natural science.

Of is a notion transcendentally raised in pursuit of something very like the question, 'How is some limited sort of realist art possible?' It may be that (some) realist pictures are the intersections of defensible and accessible *of*-ness and descriptiveness. At least, these intersections (to which we could add vividness) will permit the strongest claims to realism. *Of* is cold comfort. It's cold out. A lot more work has to be done.

Some of the work to be done concerns the question of *of*'s transcendental character. We need to look at the question whether or not *of* is just a simply a priori requirement established *once* you've claimed something is a realistic representation, and meant something specific by that.

The genetic relation between many pictures and their objects is complex and mediated. The relation between many pictures and what they denote is complex and mediated. The relationship between many pictures' genesis and their descriptive content is very often complex if not so often mediated. We might say, *pace* Thompson, that all the difficulties are so immense that it has become apparent that reality and 'realism' must be totally distinct, but that it does not follow from this that we must establish what links them.[8]

Notes

1   In 'Quantifying In', first published in D. Davidson and J. Hintikka (eds), *Words & Objections: Essays on the Work of W. V. Quine* (Reidel, Dordrecht, Holland, 1969) pp. 178–214.

2   On this issue see 'Seven Strictures on Similarity'.

3   R. Taylor, *Art, An Enemy of the People* (Harvester Press, London, 1978) p. 85.

4   D. Kaplan, 'Quantifying In', reprinted in L. Linsky (ed), *Reference and Modality* (Oxford Readings in Philosophy series, OUP, London, 1971) pp. 112–44. References are to this printing. This reference p. 134.

5   R. Jakobson and C. Lévi-Strauss, 'Charles Baudelaire's Les Chats', in Lane (ed), *Structuralism: A Reader* (London, 1970).

6   Cf. Kaplan, loc. cit. n.4, p. 136.

7   W. B. Gallie, 'Explanation in History and the Genetic Sciences', in *Theories of History* (Glencoe, Ill., (1959). Quoted in William Dray, 'The Historical Explanation of Actions', in *The Philosophy of History* (Oxford Readings in Philosophy, London, 1974).

8   E. P. Thompson, *The Poverty of Theory and Other Essays* (London, 1978) p. 211.

IV
EXPRESSION

16   Expression

Nelson Goodman

Goodman's The Languages of Art *is subtitled* An Approach to a Theory of Symbols. *Elsewhere Goodman has argued against picturing the aesthetic attitude as 'passive contemplation of the immediately given, direct apprehension of what is presented, uncontaminated by any conceptualization, isolated from all echoes of the past and from all threats and promises of the future, exempt from all enterprise'. He criticizes 'the domineering dichotomy between the cognitive and the emotive' which has prevented us from seeing that 'in aesthetic experience the* emotions function cognitively ... *Emotion in aesthetic experience is a means of discerning what properties a work has and expresses.' He continues:*

> ... what we learn from and learn through a symbol varies with what we bring to it. Not only do we discover the world through our symbols but we understand and reappraise our symbols progressively in the light of our growing experience. Both the dynamics and the durability of aesthetic value are natural consequences of its cognitive character. Like considerations explain the relevance to aesthetic merit of experience remote from the work ... How our lookings at pictures and our listenings to music inform what we encounter later and elsewhere is integral to them as cognitive. The absurd and awkward myth of the insularity of aesthetic experience can be scrapped.

Goodman argues further that:

> Truth and its aesthetic counterpart amount to appropriateness under different names. If we speak of hypotheses but not works of art as true, that is because we reserve the terms 'true' and 'false' for symbols in sentential form. I do not say this difference is negligible, but it is specific rather than generic, a difference in field of application rather than in formula, and marks no schism between the scientific and the aesthetic ... The difference between art and science is not that between feeling and fact, intuition and inference, delight and deliberation, synthesis and analysis, sensation and celebration, concreteness and abstraction, passion and action, mediacy and immediacy, or truth and beauty, but rather a difference in domination of certain specific characteristics of symbols.
> ('Art and Inquiry' in Goodman, Problems and Projects, Bobbs-Merrill, 1972, reprinted in Frascina and Harrison, 1982.)

In the following excerpt from The Languages of Art *Goodman deals with the expressive characteristics of symbols, and thus with a series of issues central to the meaning and function of modern art as represented in prevailing accounts. The Modernist tradition in art criticism rests heavily on claims made for the expressiveness of modern works of art, though, as Goodman implies, these claims have more often been supported by the incorrigible evidence of 'feelings' than by adequate and testable hypotheses. In asserting that 'The properties a symbol expresses are its own property', Goodman takes a firm stand against those views of art which identify expressive meaning with the responses of the sensitive observer. He does acknowledge, however, that 'Verbal discourse is not least among the many factors that aid in founding and nurturing ... associations with certain other objects.' These associations themselves establish that relationship of reference to metaphorical properties which Goodman identifies with expression.*

In Goodman's text, metaphorical reference and expression are clearly distinguished from depiction and description. In Salvador Dali's painting of soft watches, for instance, the watches may express 'softness' (and what 'softness' itself refers to by association with other soft things) by virtue of the fact that softness is not *a property of watches as normally described and depicted. The property of softness is 'transferred' to the watches by metaphorical association with that property in some other thing or things, and thus can be said to be expressed in the painting. 'A thing can express only what belongs but did not originally belong to it.'*

Goodman's admonitions are cautions against the idle use of language in criticism and interpretation. They are not attempts to close the expressive power or range of art itself. Indeed he makes clear just why the 'metaphorical reach' of expressive symbols is likely to be hard to prescribe or delimit. Metaphor, as he observes, is distinguished by 'novelty and instability'.

Source: Languages of Art (Hackett Publishing Company 1976), pp. 85–95. First published 1968. Footnotes have been re-numbered. Reprinted by permission of Nelson Goodman and Hackett Publishing Company Inc., Indianapolis, Indiana.

What is expressed is metaphorically exemplified. What expresses sadness is metaphorically sad. And what is metaphorically sad is actually but not literally sad, ie comes under a transferred application of some label coextensive with 'sad'.

Thus what is expressed is possessed, and what a face or picture expresses need not (but may) be emotions or ideas the actor or artist has, or those he wants to convey, or thoughts or feelings of the viewer or of a person depicted, or properties of anything else related in some other way to the symbol. Of course, a symbol is often said to express a property related to it in one of these ways, but I reserve the term 'expression' to distinguish the central case where the property belongs to the symbol itself—regardless of cause or effect or intent or subject matter. That the actor was despondent, the artist high, the spectator gloomy or nostalgic or euphoric, the subject inanimate, does not determine whether the face or picture is sad or not. The cheering face of the hypocrite expresses solicitude; and the stolid painter's picture of boulders may express agitation. The properties a symbol expresses are its own property.

But they are acquired property. They are not the homely features by which the objects and events that serve as symbols are classified literally, but are metaphorical imports. Pictures express sounds or feelings rather than colors. And the metaphorical transfer involved in expression is usually from or via an exterior realm rather than the interior transfer effected in hyperbole or litotes or irony. A pretentious picture does not express the modesty that may be sarcastically ascribed to it.

Properties expressed are, furthermore, not only metaphorically possessed but also referred to, exhibited, typified, shown forth. A square swatch does not usually exemplify squareness, and a picture that rapidly increases in market value does not express the property of being a gold mine. Normally, a swatch exemplifies only sartorial properties while a picture literally exemplifies only pictorial properties and metaphorically exemplifies only properties that are constant relative to pictorial properties. [1] And a picture expresses only properties— unlike that of being a gold mine—that it thus metaphorically exemplifies as a pictorial symbol. Daumier's 'Laundress' so exemplifies and expresses weight but not any metaphorical property dependent upon the physical weight of the picture. In general, a symbol of a given kind—pictorial, musical, verbal etc—expresses only properties that it metaphorically exemplifies as a symbol of that kind.

Plainly, then, not every metaphorical statement about a symbol tells us what is expressed. Sometimes the metaphorical term is incorporated in a predicate that applies *literally* to the symbol, as in the modified metaphors noticed earlier or in the statement that a picture is by a painter in his cups. Sometimes the metaphorical property ascribed is possessed but not exemplified by the symbol or not constant relative to the required properties. And sometimes the metaphorical transfer involved is of the wrong kind. Only properties of the appropriate kind, metaphorically exemplified in the appropriate way, are expressed.

Though accuracy would often call for speaking of expression of predicates, I defer to a prissy prejudice by speaking throughout this section of expression of properties. [2] Yet by explaining expression in terms of the metaphorical exemplification of labels, I have risked the charge of making what a symbol expresses depend upon what is said about it—of leaving what a picture, for example, expresses to the accident of what terms happen to be used in describing the picture, and hence of crediting the expression achieved not to the artist but to the commmentator. This, of course, is a misunderstanding. A symbol must have every property it expresses; what counts is not whether anyone calls the picture sad but whether the picture is sad, whether the label 'sad' does in fact apply. 'Sad' may apply to a picture even though no one ever happens to use the term in describing the picture; and calling a picture sad by no means makes it so. This is not to say that whether a picture is sad is independent of the use of 'sad' but that given, by practice or precept, the use of 'sad', applicability to the picture is not arbitrary. Since practice and precept vary, possession and exemplification are not absolute either; and what is actually said about a picture is not always altogether

175

irrelevant to what the picture expresses. Among the countless properties, most of them usually ignored, that a picture possesses, it expresses only those metaphorical properties it refers to. Establishment of the referential relationship is a matter of singling out certain properties for attention, of selecting associations with certain other objects. Verbal discourse is not least among the many factors that aid in founding and nurturing such associations. If nothing more than selection takes place here, still selection from such a multitude of eligibles amounts, as observed earlier, to virtual constitution. Pictures are no more immune than the rest of the world to the formative force of language even though they themselves, as symbols, also exert such a force upon the world, including language. Talking does not make the world or even pictures, but talking and pictures participate in making each other and the world as we know them.

Nonverbal as well as verbal labels may be metaphorically exemplified, and the corresponding properties expressed, by symbols of any kind. A picture of Churchill as a bulldog is metaphorical; and he may stand as a symbol that exemplifies the picture and expresses the bulldoggedness thus pictorially ascribed to him. We must note carefully that the pictorial metaphor here has to do not with what the picture may exemplify or express but with what may exemplify the picture and express the corresponding property.[3]

Expression, since limited to what is possessed and moreover to what has been acquired at second-hand, is doubly constrained as compared with denotation. Whereas almost anything can denote or even represent almost anything else, a thing can express only what belongs but did not originally belong to it. The difference between expression and literal exemplification, like the difference between more and less literal representation, is a matter of habit— a matter of fact rather than fiat.

Yet the habits differ widely with time and place and person and culture; and pictorial and musical expression are no less relative and variable than facial and gestural expression. Aldous Huxley, upon hearing some supposedly solemn music in India, wrote:

> ... I confess that, listen as I might, I was unable to hear anything particularly mournful or serious, anything specially suggestive of self-sacrifice in the piece. To my Western ears it sounded much more cheerful than the dance which followed it.
> Emotions are everywhere the same; but the artistic expression of them varies from age to age and from one country to another. We are brought up to accept the conventions current in the society into which we are born. This sort of art, we learn in childhood, is meant to excite laughter, that to evoke tears. Such conventions vary with great rapidity, even in the same country. There are Elizabethan dances that sound as melancholy to our ears as little funeral marches. Conversely, we are made to laugh by the 'Anglo-Saxon attitudes' of the holiest personages in the drawings and miniatures of earlier centuries.[4]

The boundaries of expression, dependent upon the difference between exemplification and possession and also upon the difference between the metaphorical and the literal, are inevitably somewhat tenuous and transient. An Albers picture may pretty clearly *exemplify* certain shapes and colors and interrelations among them, while it merely possesses the property of being exactly 24½ inches high; but the distinction is not always so easily drawn. Again, the status of a property as metaphorical or literal is often unclear and seldom stable; for comparatively few properties are purely literal or permanently metaphorical. Even for very clear cases, ordinary discourse only sporadically observes the difference between expression and exemplification. Architects, for instance, like to speak of some buildings as expressing their functions. But however effectively a glue factory may typify glue-making, it exemplifies being a glue factory literally rather than metaphorically. A building may express fluidity or frivolity or fervor;[5] but to express being a glue factory it would have to be something else, say a toothpick plant. But since reference to a possessed property is the common core of metaphorical and literal exemplification, and the distinction between these is ephemeral, popular use of the term 'expression' for cases of both kinds is not very surprising or pernicious.

Music and dance alike may exemplify rhythmic patterns, for example, and express peace or pomp or passion; and music may express properties of movement while dance may express properties of sound. With respect to verbal symbols, ordinary usage is so undiscriminating that a word or passage may be said to express not only what the writer thought or felt or intended, or the effect upon the reader, or properties possessed by or ascribed to a subject, but even what is described or stated. In the special sense I have been discussing, though, a verbal symbol may express only properties it metaphorically exemplifies; naming a property and expressing it are different matters; and a poem or story need not express what it says or say what it expresses. A tale of fast action may be slow, a biography of a benefactor bitter, a description of colorful music drab, and a play about boredom electric. To describe, as to depict, a person as sad or as expressing sadness is not necessarily to express sadness; not every sad-person-description or -picture or every person-expressing-sadness-description or -picture is itself sad. And a passage or picture may exemplify or express without describing or representing and even without being a description or representation at all—as in the case of some passages from James Joyce and some drawings by Kandinsky.

Yet though exemplification and expression are distinct from, and run in the opposite direction from, representation and description, all are intimately related modes of symbolization. In these varied ways, a symbol may select from and organize its universe and be itself in turn informed or transformed. Representation and description relate a symbol to things it applies to. Exemplification relates the symbol to a label that denotes it, and hence indirectly to the things (including the symbol itself) in the range of that label. Expression relates the symbol to a label that metaphorically denotes it, and hence indirectly not only to the given metaphorical but also to the literal range of that label. And various longer chains of the elementary referential relationships of labels to things and other labels, and of things to labels, may run from any symbol.

To exemplify or express is to display rather than depict or describe; but as representation may be stereotyped or searching, and exemplification trite or telling, so may expression be platitudinous or provocative. A property expressed, though it must be constant relative to certain literal properties, need not coincide in extension with any easy and familiar literal description. Finding a disjunction of conjunctions of ordinary literal properties of pictures that is even approximately equivalent to metaphorical sadness would give us a good deal of trouble. The expressive symbol, with its metaphorical reach, not only partakes of the greenness of neighboring pastures and the exotic atmospheres of farther shores, but often in consequence uncovers unnoticed affinities and antipathies among symbols of its own kind. From the nature of metaphor derives some of the characteristic capacity of expression for suggestive allusion, elusive suggestion, and intrepid transcendence of basic boundaries.

Emphasis on the denotative (representative or descriptive), the exemplificatory ('formal' or 'decorative'), and the expressive in the arts varies with art, artist, and work. Sometimes one aspect dominates to the virtual exclusion of the other two; compare Debussy's *La Mer*, Bach's *Goldberg Variations*, and Charles Ives's *Fourth Symphony*, for instance; or a Dürer watercolor, a Jackson Pollock painting, and a Soulages lithograph. In other cases two or all three aspects, fused or in counterpoint, are almost equally prominent; in the film *Last Year at Marienbad*, the narrative thread, though never abandoned, is disrupted to let through insistent cadences and virtually indescribable sensory and emotional qualities. The choice is up to the artist and judgment up to the critic. Nothing in the present analysis of symbolic functions offers any support for manifestos to the effect that representation is an indispensable requirement for art, or is an insuperable barrier to it, or that expression without representation is the highest achievement of the human spirit, or that representation and expression alike corrupt exemplification, or so on. If representation is reprehensible or revered, if expression is exalted or execrated, if exemplification is the essence of poverty or purity, this must be on other grounds.

Some writers, according to their temperament, have regarded expression either as sacredly occult or as hopelessly obscure. Perhaps the foregoing pages have exposed the main factors fostering such admiration or exasperation: first, the extreme ambiguities and inconstancies of ordinary usage; second, the great multiplicity of labels that apply to any object; third, the variation in application of a label with the set of alternatives in question; fourth, the different referents assigned the same schema under different symbolic systems; fifth, the variety of metaphorical applications that a schema with a single literal application may have to a single realm under different types and routes of transfer; and finally, the very novelty and instability that distinguishes metaphor. The first four of these troubles beset the literal as well as the metaphorical use of terms; and the last two are symptomatic neither of uncontrolled caprice nor of impenetrable mystery but of exploration and discovery. I hope that chaos has been reduced, if not to clarity, at least to lesser confusion.

In summary, if a expresses b then: (1) a possesses or is denoted by b; (2) this possession or denotation is metaphorical; and (3) a refers to b.

No test for detecting what a work expresses has been sought here: after all, a definition of hydrogen gives us no ready way of telling how much of the gas is in this room. Nor has any precise definition been offered for the elementary relation of expression we have been examining. Rather, it has been subsumed under metaphorical exemplification, and circumscribed somewhat more narrowly by some additional requirements, without any claim that these are sufficient.[6] The concern has been to compare and contrast this relation with such other major kinds of reference as exemplification, representation, and description.

Notes

1   A property is thus constant only if, although it may or may not remain constant where the pictorial properties vary, it never varies where the pictorial properties remain constant. In other words, if it occurs anywhere, it also occurs whenever the pictorial properties are the same. The constancy here in question obtains within a given symbol system between the metaphorical extension of the expressed property and the literal extension of the basic pictorial properties: but a property thus constant also itself qualifies as a pictorial property ...

2   No difficulty or obscurity is removed by such pussyfooting; and the bolder course of defying prejudice and speaking forthrightly of expression of labels rather than properties is surely to be recommended.

3   Or express the picture itself, if we stop pampering prejudice.

4   In 'Music in India and Japan' (1926), reprinted in *On Art and Artists* (Meridian Books, New York, 1960) pp. 305–6.

5   A building may 'express a mood—gaity and movement in the whirly little Comedy Theatre, Berlin—or even ideas about astronomy and relativity like Mendlesohn's Einstein tower, or nationalism like some of Hitler's architecture', according to Richard Sheppard in 'Monument to the Architect?', *The Listener*, 8 June 1967, p. 746.

6   But some superficially odd cases meeting the stated requirements seem entitled to admission; many a work, I think, may quite appropriately be said to express eloquently its unintentional clumsiness or stupidity.

17   Hysteria as Communication

Thomas S. Szasz

Szasz is a practising psychoanalyst. In his published work he has consistently drawn attention to the actual or potential confusion between organic disease and pathological states on the one hand and socially defined deviance and hysterical representations on the other. His book, The Myth of Mental Illness, *as its title suggests, treats the concept of 'mental illness' as a kind of category mistake, and one which leads to a confusion of coercion with concern. In pursuit of adequate working concepts and distinctions, Szasz has employed logical, semantic and semiological analyses to the problems of psychiatry and psychoanalysis.*

The relevance of the following passage to the problems of art lies in its discussion of hysterical symptoms as forms of representation. It has been a persistent (and false) truism of modern art criticism that expressive or expressionist art offers a relatively unmediated access to the psychological states or dispositions of artists. ('The innovation of Action Painting was to dispense with the representation of the [psychic] state in favour of enacting it in physical movement.' Harold Rosenberg, 'Hans Hofmann: Nature into Action', Art News, *May 1957.) Another and related truism is that the content or subject matter of modern art has been enlarged by the acknowledgement and expression of psychological depth and diversity. Szasz's discussion of hysteria as a kind of language, and of hysterical symptoms or expressions as kinds of 'lies' ('strategic misrepresentations' might be a more appropriate term in the present context), encourages us to reinstate the concept of representation in analysis of the expressive symbols and styles of art. The recovery of meaning from expressive symbols in art can fruitfully be considered by analogy with the analysis of meaning in 'hysterical body signs' as suggested by Szasz.*

*The following passage relies on a distinction derived from the Semiotics of Charles Pierce (*Collected Papers, Harvard, *1934), and made earlier in Szasz's book, between 'iconic signs' (such as maps or photographs), 'which stand in a relation of similarity to the objects they designate', and 'conventional signs' or 'symbols' which 'usually do not exist in isolation, but are co-ordinated with each other by sets of rules, called the rules of language'. The suggestion is that we may consider hysterical symptoms as 'iconic signs of bodily illness' in a kind of* '*proto-language*' *used to promote certain beliefs and actions; ie as a kind of picturing on, or in terms of, the body, of the ways in which the patient* considers *himself sick, or wishes to be* seen *as sick. The function of therapy is then to transform or redescribe the representation of sickness into a verbal description which traces the* causes *of this representation, and which thus translates '*iconic*' sign into '*indexical*' sign; ie into one which '*acquires its function through a* causal connection *between object and sign*', as smoke can be said to signify fire. (The relation between '*iconic*' and '*indexical*' signs is further discussed by Art & Language in text 15.)*

Szasz stresses the distinction between the bodily symptoms (or indexical signs) of organic disease and the iconic symbolism *of hysterical body signs. In the former case diagnosis may be performed on the basis of medical-scientific knowledge and independently of social and biographical context. In the latter case what will be required is familiarity both with the personal circumstances and idiosyncracies of the patient and with the '"meanings" of the predominant patterns of "psychiatric symptoms" or difficulties in a given culture or situation'. The latter might be considered as the 'resources of expression' for hysterical states. There are clear analogies with the requirements for interpretation of both indexical and expressive signs and symbols in art.*

Szasz further distinguishes between 'discursive' and 'non-discursive' languages. 'Discursive' languages are those serving to transmit information in conventional form, to which judgements of truth or falsity may be directly applied. In 'non-discursive' languages, symbolization is 'idiosyncratic' and serves 'mainly the purpose of emotional expression'. We would take issue with Szasz's characterization of 'art, dance and the ritual' as characteristically non-discursive languages—though some *art is certainly non-discursive in character. It should be clear from Goodman's analysis (text 16) that expression is not so simply to be equated with non-discursiveness. What* is *relevant, however, is Szasz's relation of 'non-discursive' forms of expression to the need that communicants be 'attuned to each other' if translation into other idioms is to be feasible. The less 'discursive' the languages of art, we would say, the more the analytic techniques of the art critic will depend upon his or her being 'attuned' to the social, cultural and biographical contexts of the artist's activity.*

Szasz's text raises interesting problems concerning our perception and analysis of the relationship between representation and misrepresentation in expressive art, and between 'mistakes' (for example the 'accidental' effects of incompetence) and 'lies' (for example the deliberate *uses of distortion—as in the work of Picasso—the strategic confusion of 'use' with 'mention' of a style—as apparent in the work of Jasper Johns—and so on).*

A further relevant question is: under what methodological and conceptual framework do we correct an agent's account of his or her own reasons? This question is considered by MacIntyre in text 20, where he, like Szasz, points to the need for causal inquiry which is conceptually independent of agents' own explanatory discourses. Szasz uses the idea of rule-following as a frame of reference for hysteria and 'mental illness'. This introduces the questions: (1) What kinds of rules are in operation in hysteria and how do they influence behaviour?; and (2) What are the most relevant rules for understanding this behaviour?

Source: 'Hysteria as Communication', pp. 133–143 in *The Myth of Mental Illness* by Thomas S. Szasz, M. D. Copyright © 1961 Hoeber Medical, Division of Harper & Row, Publishers, Inc. By permission of Harper & Row, Publishers, Inc.

Hysteria as Non-discursive Language

Logic, mathematics, and the sciences employ language only, or predominantly, to transmit information. Indeed, probably because science is so intimately associated with the informative use of language, scientists and philosophers have repeatedly suggested that 'the essential business of language is to assert or deny facts' (Russell, 1922[1]). This is true, however, only for the language of science, mathematics, and logic, and is false for sign-using behaviour encountered in many other situations. As Rapoport (1954)[2] aptly observed:

> It is not necessary to look into books on philosophy to find words without referents. Any commencement speech, sermon, newspaper editorial, or radio commercial follows the same philosophic tradition of reinforcing the delusion that anything which is talked about is real: success, charity, public opinion, and four-way indigestion relief. Indeed, nothing is easier than to 'define' these noises so as to make it appear that they mean something.

These 'noises' of everyday speech, which have a great deal in common with the 'noises' of psychiatric symptoms, require that we consider the second principal function of language, namely, the expression of emotions, feelings, or desires. These expressions are, according to most modern students of language, not symbols for thought but symptoms of the inner life of the speaker. In *Philosophy in a New Key* (1942), Langer criticized this view and suggested that there was a necessity for a 'genuine semantic beyond the limits of discursive language'.[3] Although Langer made some tentative suggestions about the directions in which this semantic might be sought, particularly with respect to music and the visual arts, her work in this regard remained programmatic. One of my aims in this book is to implement this programme by providing a *systematic semiotical analysis of a language-form hitherto regarded as purely expressive, ie the language of certain bodily signs.*

Discursive and Non-discursive Languages

In addition to classifying languages according to their logical complexity, they may also be classified according to the degree of their discursiveness. *Discursiveness is a measure of the degree of arbitrariness of symbolization.* Mathematics and the languages of the various sciences serve the sole function of transmitting information. Non-discursive—or, more precisely, relatively slightly discursive— languages, on the other hand, serve mainly the purpose of emotional expression. Art, dance, and the ritual are characteristic examples. In these communications, symbolization is *idiosyncratic* rather than *conventional*.

In this connection Langer emphasized the special significance of the picture as symbol, noting that the photograph of a person does not describe the man who posed for it but rather presents a replica of him.[4] For this reason, non-discursive symbolism is often called *presentational.* It is evident, too, that while discursive symbolism has primarily a general reference, a presentational symbol refers to a specific, individual object. The former is thus eminently *abstract,* the latter exquisitely *concrete.* The word 'man' refers to every conceivable man—and even woman!—in the universe, but points to no specific person. The photograph of a man, on the other hand, represents and identifies a particular person.

In the earliest forms of written language, formal representation was achieved by means of iconic signs—that is, by hieroglyphs, which constitute a form of picture writing. According to Schlauch (1942),[5] the two simplest elements in written language are pictographs and ideographs. Both express their messages by means of pictures that *resemble* the object or idea to be conveyed. They could be regarded as the earliest prototypes of what we now call the analogic type of codification. *Kinesics* (Birdwhistell, 1949[6]) could thus be said to be a modern attempt to explore and understand *the hieroglyphics that a person writes, not on marble tablets, but on and with his own body.*

The advantages of discursive symbolism for transmitting information are known and generally appreciated. The question that now arises is whether non-discursive symbolism has any function besides that of expressing emotions? Indeed, it has several such functions.

Since verbal symbols *describe* the objects they denote in a relatively general, abstract fashion, the identification of a specific object requires much circumlocution (unless it has a *name,* which is a very special kind of discursive sign).

> For this reason [wrote Langer (1942)[7]] the correspondence between a word-picture and a visible object can never be as close as that between the object and its photograph. Given all at once to the intelligent eye, an incredible wealth and detail of information is conveyed by the portrait, where we do not have to stop to construe verbal meanings. That is why we use a photograph rather than a description on a passport or in the Rogues' Gallery.

It is evident, then, that so-called hysterical body signs, *as pictures,* bear a much greater similarity to the objects which they depict than do words describing the same objects.[8] To exhibit, by means of bodily signs—say, by paralyses or convulsions—the idea and message that one is sick is at once more striking and more informative than simply saying: 'I am sick.' *Body signs portray—they literally present and represent—in exactly what way the sufferer considers himself sick.* Thus, in the symbolism of his symptom, the patient could be said to present his own complaint and—albeit in a highly condensed form—even his autobiography. This is tacitly recognized by psychoanalysts who often treat the patient's presenting symptom—if he has one—as if it contained the whole history and structure of his 'neurosis'. When psychoanalysts say than even the simplest symptom can be understood fully only in retrospect, they mean that in order to understand the patient's 'symptom' we must be acquainted with all the historically unique aspects of his personality development and social circumstances.

The situation in regard to cases of typical organic disease is quite different. The patient's symptom—say, angina pectoris (due to coronary insufficiency)— is not autobiographical; in other words, it is not personal and idiosyncratic, at least not characteristically so. Instead, the symptom is anatomically and physiologically determined. The structure of the body defines, within limits, its function. Substernal pain cannot be the sign of, say, a ruptured ovarian cyst. Knowledge of pathological anatomy and physiology thus makes it possible to infer the 'meaning' of the 'messages' of certain bodily symptoms. To make similar inferences from iconic symbolism, however, it is of no use to be familiar with the language of medicine. What is needed, instead, is familiarity with the personality of the sign-user, including his family background, personal history, religion, occupation, and so forth. Accordingly, although so-called psychiatric symptoms are idiosyncratic (in the sense that they are personal), they may be shown to exhibit certain patterns of regularity. These will depend on the patient's personal and social experiences— in brief, on what he has learned as a human being. The experienced or intuitive psychotherapist is one who is familiar with the 'meanings' of the predominant patterns of 'psychiatric symptoms' or difficulties in a given culture or situation.

It is to be expected, then, that the non-discursive or presentational form of symbolism should readily lend itself to the expression and communication of so-called psychiatric problems. Such problems pertain to personal difficulties that are, by nature, concrete experiences. Human beings have troubles with their mothers, fathers, brothers, and so forth as *individuals—* as *concrete human beings.* They do not suffer from the effects of Oedipal complexes or sexual instincts as abstractions. It follows, then, that iconic body signs have the advantage of fitting specifically the objects to which they refer. Such signs and most 'psychiatric symptoms' do not, like the symbols of ordinary language, have a general reference, but point rather to specific individuals or events. The transformation (for it cannot properly be called translation) of presentational symbols into conventional signs (ordinary words), such as occurs in the course of psychoanalysis and some forms of psychotherapy, must thus be seen as itself constituting a process of personality change. This does not necessarily mean that verbalization is the most significant feature of psychological 'treatment'. Nor should this idea be confused with the early psychoanalytic notion of 'catharsis'. On the contrary, a semiotical analysis of psychiatric operations should enable us to see more clearly, and to describe more accurately, the precise mechanisms by which talking often helps people to cope with their problems in living.

The Non-discursiveness of Hysteria

To illustrate that the communicative aspects of hysterical symptoms are incomprehensible in terms of the logic of everyday speech, let us consider some of Freud's clinical observations (. . .). Remarking on the differences between organic and hysterical pains, Freud (Breuer and Freud, 1893–5[9]) wrote:

> I was struck by the indefiniteness of all the descriptions of the character of her pains given me by the patient, who was nevertheless a highly intelligent person. A patient suffering from *organic pains* will, unless he is *neurotic in addition*, describe them *definitely and calmly*. He will say, for instance, that they are shooting pains, that they occur at certain intervals, that they seem to him to be brought on by one thing or another. Again, when a *neurasthenic describes his pains*, he gives an impression of being engaged in a difficult intellectual task to which his strength is quite unequal.

He is clearly of the opinion that *language is too poor to find words for his sensations* and that these sensations are something unique and previously unknown, of which it would be quite impossible to give an exhaustive description. [Italics added.]

Freud's account shows how exceedingly difficult it is for the patient to find words for his so-called sensations. The same holds true for patients expressing bodily feelings associated with psychiatric syndromes other than hysteria (eg hypochondriasis, schizophrenia, depression). This phenomenon has been generally explained by assuming that the patient has unusual or peculiar feelings, difficult to put into words; or by attributing it to a general impoverishment in the patient's use of verbal language. Let me suggest still another explanation. The symptom—say, a pain or bodily feeling—may be part of a symbol system, albeit not of a discursive type. The difficulty in expressing the 'feeling' in verbal language is due to the fact that non-discursive languages do not lend themselves to translation into other idioms, least of all into discursive forms. The referents of non-discursive symbols have meaning only if the communicants are attuned to each other. This is in harmony with the actual operations of psychoanalysis: analytic technique rests on the tacit assumption that we cannot know—in fact, must not even expect to know—what troubles our patients until we have become attuned to them.

The Informative Function of Iconic Body Signs

To what extent, or precisely how, can non-discursive languages be used to transmit information? This question has occupied philosophers and students of signs for some time. More particularly, the informative function of a special type of non-discursive language, namely, of so-called hysterical body signs, has long been of interest to psychiatrists. Although hysteria has been approached *as if it were a language*, it has never been systematically so codified. Let us therefore consider the *informative uses of iconic body signs as a system of non-discursive language.* [10]

In general, the informative use of language depends on the referents of its symbols. The radical positivist view, probably rarely held today, maintains that non-discursive languages have no referents at all: messages framed in this idiom are held to be meaningless. A more balanced and, I think, today more widely accepted philosophical position regards the difference between discursive and non-discursive languages as a matter of degree rather than kind. Hence, non-discursive languages, too, have referents and cognitive meaning.

Rapoport,[11] for example, suggested that the referents of non-discursive symbols are the 'inner states' of the communicants. Although Rapoport recognized that non-discursive languages have referents, he nevertheless adhered to a traditional 'out there—in here' distinction between them. He thus regarded discursive referents as ideally suited for conveying information, and non-discursive referents as having the function of transmitting a feeling state from one person to another. The latter is a familiar phenomenon in clinical psychiatry, and also in the arts.

It is true, of course, that non-discursive communication is simple and concrete. Still, it is *not merely* a communication of the sender's inner experience. Let us consider, in this connection, the example of people fleeing a burning theatre. The panicky behaviour of some members of the audience may signify— even to someone who neither sees flames nor hears anyone shout 'Fire!'—*more* than mere panic. At first, perhaps, one may respond to the purely affective function of body language: 'People around me are afraid, panicky: I, too, *feel* panicky.' Yet, closely connected with this, there is a communication of a quasi-cognitive message: 'I am in danger! I must flee to save myself, or otherwise make sure that I shall be safe (eg by checking whether a danger really threatens).'

I cite this case to show that the referent *inside* a communicant—say, his affect—cannot be completely severed from the experiencing person's *relationship to the world about him.* This is because affects are at once private—'inner referents', and public—indices of relationships between ego and object(s), self and others (Szasz, 1957[12]). Affects are thus the primary link between inner, private experiences—and outer, publicly verifiable, occurrences. Herein lies the ground for assigning more than only subjective, idiosyncratic meanings to the referents of non-discursive languages. Accordingly, the limitation of iconic body signs does not lie solely in the subjectiveness of the experience and its expression—that is, in the fact that no one can feel another's pain; it lies, rather, in the fact that such signs present a picture—say, of a person writhing in pain— which, standing alone, has a very limited cognitive content.

The study of *gestures* is pertinent in this connection. Gesture is the earliest faculty of communication, the 'elder brother of speech' (Critchley, 1939[13]). This developmental fact is consistent with the relatively primitive cognitive use to which this form of communication may be put, and with the equally primitive learning (imitation, identification) which it subserves. In semiotical terms, gesture is a highly iconic system of signs, verbal speech is only very slightly iconic, while mathematics is completely non-iconic.

Concrete, action-oriented gestures are manifestations of an early stage in the maturational history of the human being as a *social animal.* The ability to wait, to defer action, to inhibit impulses, are aspects of psychosocial maturation. Together, as they are displayed in the increasingly complex uses of symbols, they constitute the differences between child and adult.

Hysteria, Translation, and Misinformation

When hysterical body signs are used to transmit information, they exhibit the same limitations as do non-discursive languages generally. Weakly discursive languages cannot be readily translated into more strongly discursive ones. When such translation is attempted, the possibilities for error are enormous, since virtually *any* discursive rendition of the original message will, in a sense, be false! There are two basic reasons, then, why hysterical symptoms so often *misinform*: one is the linguistic difficulty, just noted, of rendering non-discursive symbolism into discursive form; the other is that the message may actually be intended for an internal object and not for the recipient who actually receives and interprets it.

Misinformation is bound to be generated whenever a communication framed in the idiom of iconic body signs is interpreted in the language of medicine.

Typical is the case of the patient who 'says' that he is sick by means of hysterical panto-mime, but whose communication the physician interprets by making a diagnosis. Since in the special scientific idiom of medicine 'sickness' means a disorder of the body, the patient's original message will necessarily be mistranslated.

Of course, misinformation—whether it be a mistake or a lie—may be communicated by means of ordinary language as well as by iconic body signs. We speak of a lie when the misinformation is considered to serve the speaker's interests and when it is believed that he has sent the false message deliberately. A mistake, by contrast, is an error made indifferently. Hence, there can be no such thing as a 'deliberate mistake', but mistakes out of ignorance or lack of skill (conditions which might themselves be the results of deliberate planning) can occur.

In describing this contrast between lying and making a mistake I have deliberately avoided the concept of consciousness. The traditional psychoanalytic idea that so-called conscious imitation of illness is 'malingering' and hence 'not illness', whereas its allegedly unconscious simulation is itself 'illness', that is, 'hysteria', creates more problems than it solves. I think it is more useful to *distinguish between goal-directed and rule-following behaviour on the one hand, and indifferent mistakes on the other.* In psychoanalytic theory there is no room for indifferent mistakes—because it is tacitly assumed that all action is goal-directed. It then follows that a person's failure to perform adequately cannot be due to his ignorance of the rules of the game or to his lack of skills in playing it. Instead, the failure itself is regarded as a goal, albeit an unconscious one. This perspective, and the therapeutic attitude it inspires, are exceedingly useful. Yet it is obvious that not all human error is of this purposive kind. To insist on this view is to deny the very possibility of genuine error.

By reintroducing the distinction between goal-directed misinformation and indifferent error into psychiatry and psychoanalysis, I believe we shall be able to clarify many problems in human behaviour. In the case of hysteria, for example, Freud himself emphasized the quasi-rational, goal-directed nature of the process. In short, *it is more accurate to regard hysteria as a lie than as a mistake.* People caught in a lie usually maintain that they were merely mistaken. The difference between mistakes and lies, when discovered, is chiefly pragmatic.[14] From a purely cognitive point of view, both are simply falsehoods.

Notes

1   Bertrand Russell, Introduction to L. Wittgenstein's *Tractatus Logico-Philosophicus* (Routledge & Kegan Paul, London, 1922) p. 8.
2   A. Rapoport, *Operational Philosophy: Integrating Knowledge and Action* (Harper & Row, New York, 1954) p. 18.
3   Langer, *Philosophy in a New Key* (1942) p. 70.
4   Langer, 1942, pp. 76–7.
5   M. Schlauch, *The Gift of Language* (Dover, New York, 1955).
6   R. L. Birdwhistell, 'Contribution of Linguistic-Kinesic Studies to the Understanding of Schizophrenia', in A. Auerbach (ed), *Schizophrenia: An Integrated Approach* (Ronald Press, New York, 1959) Chapter 5, pp. 99–124.
7   Langer, 1942, p. 77.

8   Treating certain forms of behaviour as pictures, used to communicate messages, also helps us to comprehend such everyday acts as wearing certain articles of clothing (eg caps, jackets, the use of pipes, etc). Such 'dressing up' behaviour is like saying: 'I belong to this group', or 'I am so and so' (as a means of self-identification, eg 'I am a Harvard man'). Uniforms, of course, are used deliberately to bestow a specific identity or role on a person, such as 'You are in the navy, now', or 'You are an officer', etc. In all these situations we deal with the social uses of iconic signs.

9   J. Breuer and S. Freud, 'Studies on Hysteria' (1893–5), in *The Standard Edition of the Complete Psychological Works of Sigmund Freud,* Vol II (Hogarth Press, London, 1955) p. 136.

10   This analysis will apply to phenomena variously labelled 'hysteria', 'hypochondriasis', 'schizophrenia', and so forth. The distinguishing feature is the use of *body signs* and their *iconicity*. The labels of traditional psychiatric nosology are of no use in ascertaining where or when we may encounter such signs.

11   Rapoport, 1954.

12   T. S. Szasz, *Pain and Pleasure: A Study of Bodily Feelings* (Basic Books, New York, 1957).

13   M. Critchley, *The Language of Gesture* (Edward Arnold, London, 1939) p. 121.

14   What is meant by this is that we hold people responsible for lies but not, as a rule, for mistakes. We touch here on the immense problem of the observer's *attitude* towards various forms of personal conduct for it depends largely on how behaviour is *judged* whether it will be rewarded, ignored, punished, treated as illness, etc.

18   Abstract Expression

Art & Language

According to Art & Language, 'The following notes are the consequence of an attempt to "re-read" or adapt Nelson Goodman's account of expression in art in the light of some of the upshots of the so-called causal theory of reference.' As representative of the 'core idea' of this theory Art & Language quotes W. D. Hart.

> For a singular term used by a speaker to refer to an object (or for a speaker to refer to an object by using a term) it is necessary that his use of this term is the last link in some causal chain tracing back to, at least, the initial dubbing of the object with that term, or more interestingly, to some person's interacting with the object. ('Causation and Self Reference' in Dancy (ed), Papers in Language and Logic, 1979)

The issue of expression and the causal theory of reference is related to the legacy of those problems discussed in Art & Language's 'Portrait of V. I. Lenin' (text 15). In addressing these issues Art & Language aim 'to approach the special kind of "contradiction" associated with Marx's analysis and critique of capital in a context of symbolic or meaningful things'. In spirit and in implication the essay is critical of the art world's normal tendency 'to drive wedges between exegetical, critical or interpretive discourse on the one hand, and such matters as causal and historical inquiry on the other'. In particular the text demonstrates why we should be wary of conflating or identifying statements of the kind, 'This picture makes me feel sad' with others of the kind, 'This picture expresses sadness' (or 'This picture is sad'). The first is an autobiographical statement of the type Szasz (text 17) labels 'non-discursive'. The second is a claim made about the picture and is open to interrogation and correction.

Goodman observes that 'Talking does not make the world or even pictures, but talking and pictures participate in making each other and the world as we know them.' He also writes of the 'selection' made in verbal discourse that it 'amounts ... to virtual constitution'. Art & Language suggests that such analyses as Goodman's maintain a fastidious distance from the reality of art discourse, and that this distance can only be closed by inquiring further into the relation between 'talking' and 'pictures' and by asking whose talking does the

191

constituting. This will entail causal inquiry not simply into the conditions of production of expression in art, but also into the conditions of production of statements about expressive content or meaning.

Source: Art-Language vol. 5, no. 1, Banbury, October, 1982, pp. 1–21. This material has been edited. © Art & Language.

[. . .] What follows is a discussion about such claims as 'Painting *p* expresses sadness *s*.' It is suggested that a paradigm of such a claim involves the idea that '*s*' must be causally connected or be causally implicated in the production of the picture. This paradigm is a schematic representation of one of the conditions of an emancipatory critique of the conceptions or interpretations of artists, critics, and aestheticians. It also sets conditions in respect of the emancipatory potential of (or in) various kinds of art and criticism. The idea of causal implication breaks through the hermeneutic circle of 'understanding' and makes it clear that the community of enthusiasts involved in art's hermeneutic circle *constitute* the actual material they deal with.

It might seem that while a claim as to the figurative reference of a picture, its iconic descriptive features, is corrigible in certain important circumstances by reference to its genetic character, to *of*, a claim as to expressive reference is not. We would say either that this is not necessarily the case, or, more interestingly, that a person's statement that *p* expresses *s* must be corrigible on causal-type grounds. (Note however that the corrigibility of the figurative reference of a picture should not exclude other conditions of corrigibility based on knowledge of social causes etc. To exclude social and etc causes is to serve up an extreme model of *of*. If it is recognised that objects pictured are frequently complex, and if one drops or weakens the stipulation that the object pictured must serve as subject for the picture, some interesting possibilities of overlap, even identity between the genetic character of a picture and its social causes etc, are forthcoming.)

There are a number of possible meanings of statements like 'This picture *p* expresses sadness *s*.' What is meant by this statement is often 'This picture *p* makes me feel sadness *s*,' sometimes 'This picture *p* is thought by me (and etc) to express sadness *s*,' sometimes in the sense that 'What is depicted (eg a person) is sad', sometimes 'This picture *p* has the expressive effect of sadness *s*,' etc, etc. These various possibilities go to various conceptions as to the sort of symbol *p* is, as to the dependence or independence of expression with respect to the onlooker, and so on.

Let us consider first the critical circumstance in which '*p* expresses *s*' is taken to mean '*p* expresses *s* irrespective of (or possibly in respect of) any (or some) cognitive or emotional state *s* caused by the symbol *p* in the critic.' In practice, what often happens is that critics establish expressive meanings by virtue of their own stipulative power. They constitute the possibilities of the 'fixing of reference' so to speak. What occurs in this mechanism is the conventionalisation of, or near conventionalisation of, expressive symbols. The force of the idea of expression gets lost. (This is not to say, however, that expressive symbols are never deposited in a culture as conventions. And obviously expressive things are symbolic; they form part of or are a system of signification.)

What is lost or obscured is the indexicality of expressive symbols. Or rather, the fact that, at some point, the *claim* that *p* expresses *s* entails the indexicality of *p*—its causal character. There is a tendency in criticism to make an abstraction of the expression relation. The constitutiveness of the critic's account renders it incorrigible.

Apart from obscuring the underlying causal implications of an expression claim, the incorrigibility of interpretation licenses the scandals and obscurities which we have dealt with elsewhere [see text 23]. The obfuscation or rather 'loss' of the causal implications of expression claims is itself a reactionary tendency—in so far as it tends to reinforce prevailing interpretations or to entail cognitively empty battles for critical power. The causal-reference-fixing *power* of the critic supplants the inquisitive causal implications of the expressive claims.

There are a number of illusions attached to this. It may be argued that this substitution is nothing to worry about, because (a) the critic's recovery of expressivity or his apprehension of *p*'s expression *s* has the causal matter embedded in it, and (b) it is embedded in it as *corrigible*.

But the interpretation-fixing power of the critic and the non-cognitive nature of the conditions of change of interpretation require that the causal claim is not so much embedded as blocked in critical discourse. The corrigibility of a claim on causal grounds will depend upon those causal grounds' substantiveness with respect to the claim. If the claim is 'conventionalised', constitutive and adequate, it will remain a circle.

Another related reason that the loss of the causal implications of an expression claim may be thought to be insignificant is that, somehow, the critic is only responding to a symbol whose expression is sedimented in his psycho-biological being. This argument won't do. Among other things it requires a number of possible illusions to sustain it. The claim that *p* expresses *s* is potentially truth-functional. It is a matter of irrelevance to this whether the interpretation of the symbol is sedimented etc or not (though of course, the claim to truth value will be a contingent social product).

It can be argued further that this argument is in general grounded on a mistake. The fact that everyone in the history of the world takes or has taken ☹ to express sadness (to be caused by sadness or something) is no guarantee of the truth of the statement that ☹ expresses (is caused by) sadness. Further, the constant conjunction of ☹ and the judgement that it expresses sadness is neither here nor there so far as the mechanism of the (expressive) production of ☹ is concerned.

This type of argument seems to be *grounded* in an abstraction already performed in the causal implications of '*p* expresses *s*.'

A close relative of the sedimentation argument is the argument that there is some universal human tendency to make the judgement that ☹ expresses sadness. And this tendency is supported by the fact that occurrences of ☹ and judgements that it expresses sadness are constantly conjoined. This argument won't wash. It is empiricist and fake. Judgements that *p* expresses *s* are determined in open systems—they are multiply and plurally caused. No universal law-like human tendency is demonstrated by this argument.

The psycho-biology type arguments are, in the absence of substantive scientific and conceptual enquiry, means whereby the critic naturalises his sensibility. His sensibility is not supposed to be a contingent social product but a law-like human tendency. The naturalisation (and the supposedly consequent universalisation) is fraudulent. The stipulative power of the critic is not to be transformed into an emancipatory possibility by these means. The logic of critical discourse is such as to block enquiry into the conditions of the production of '*p* expresses *s*' itself, in so far as that statement is a terminus in respect of causal enquiry as to *how* '*p* may express *s*' and whether it does or does not. The causal mechanism, relocated and transformed in the critic, loses its causal character and protects the critic himself from causal enquiries.

Let us now consider such statements as 'This picture *p* expresses sadness *s*' and others like 'This picture *p* makes me feel sadness *s*.' These statements are distinct. The aesthetics of the sensitive and 'detached' (however 'interested') observers tend to keep these statements glued together. Their job is to turn 'This picture *p* makes me feel sadness *s*; into 'This picture *p* expresses sadness *s*,' by the stipulative force deriving from their status *as* 'sensitive (etc) observers'.

A number of possible illusions and reinforcements are required to sustain the stipulative force of the critic/sensitive in respect of 'sad feelings'. One of the main ones is a variant of the empiricist illusion that the conjunctural constancy of an expressive effect and a certain symbol is an indication of a 'law-like' human (biological?) tendency. The critic's (or the human race's) possible universal tendency to 'feel sadness' or to feel sadness expressed when confronted with ☹ is not to be identified with the fact that the critic or the human race frequently or constantly feels sadness when confronted with ☹ .

Of course, '*p* makes me feel sadness, and '*p* expresses sadness' may overlap in use, but for the purpose of our discussion of pictures, and if we are to be able to secure any possibility of meaning in talk of expression, we need to show that their conflation is at least a potential falsehood. In fact we don't even need to try. It is a logical falsehood to equate them, let alone an 'empirical' one. It is an 'empirical' mistake because it conflates a real part of the process of the production of pictures to the experience of those persons privileged to interpret them out loud. Or, more precisely in this case, the critic is in a position to treat what are the results of his experience as if they are or were real properties of the picture's production process. Of course they are—but not *that* process. This type of conflation is endemic to our art and criticism. The difficulty it instantiates is endemic to the logic of expression. Plainly, to talk about how one of Van Gogh's pictures might act as a paradigm of sadness-expressed *is* a different matter from talking about how Sensitive Nigel's experience might act as a condition of a paradigm of sadness-expressed. (And this notwithstanding the true statement that meaning can only be understood, not measured.)

The critic's role is protected by various mechanisms for the suppression of the possibly contradictory conditions of critical production. There is the illusion of the monolithic cognitivity of the conditions of criticism: the critic's rationale for a given description or a theorisation of a picture is the critic's reason for so describing it (this is a potentially dangerous illusion in art). (Another one is the possible illusion that the mechanism of the production of (art or) criticism is precisely the critic's reason or means of giving an account of his criticism.) There are sundry genetic deformations and homologies. They are ideological contingencies. They produce silence from the uninitiated—silence, irrespective of whether or not the uninitiated do in fact say something.

The sometimes categorically different roles played by the various possible producers of 'expression', in an often inadequately theorised art discourse, have little attention paid to the relations of priority between these various roles. This tendency is exhibited by many philosophical aestheticians and critics. People write about 'expression' at a high level of abstraction, without paying much heed to the material substrates which determine the correct (categorically and so forth) application of expression concepts.

A curious variant is exhibited by those who would claim to be sustained by quite different presumptions; that is, those who would claim to be significant amenders of the marxist tradition. In general, aesthetic and critical discourse is authoritarian. Its categories, including the category of expression, are reproduced and manipulated according to the presumption that the conceptions of the agents concerned are substantially incorrigible. In the case of expression it is *what* is expressed that takes precedence over *how* something is or may be expressed. The *how* is, in general, confined to a search for some *grounds* for a putative effect which are no more than rules for the priority of the interpretation over competing alternatives. Aesthetic and critical controversy continues to reduce to squabbles over translation problems. And the searched-for grounds are bounded by an antecedent acceptance of the conceptions of and in the reported experience of the critic: a self-authenticating hermeneutic circle not susceptible to emancipatory critique, yet produced in culture as an emancipatory paradigm: an arbitrary cacophony taken as the paradigmatic liberation of the human spirit. That a face or picture expresses *s* is taken as sufficient grounds for its being deemed to 'express *s*'. In the absence of a causally based critique of this interpretation, we are left with a Wittgensteinian or Winchian world—a set of quasi-rules. (These are augmented in some cases by an arbitrary and ethnocentric 'substrate'—Paretian residues, 'universal conditions' etc. It's difficult to see how the 'marxist' (eg) Timpanaro's material substrates differ significantly from the pre- or sub-economic residues of the anti-marxist Pareto: sexual instinct, hunger, gratification etc.) The tendency of these new worlds is to employ the hermeneutic circle in the reinforcement of the interpretations of an unreflective section engaged at its 'dialectical' best in an illocutionary struggle for power in a palace of its own invention.

The more patrician aestheticians are frequently content to affirm a conceptual or, at best, normic link between certain features of pictures and what they are supposed to express, a mystery mediated by Mind's various appearances. Goodman, for example, discussing expression as a metaphorical property of works of art in *Languages of Art* writes:

I don't want to go into the matter of specific occurrences of sadness or emotion and

195

their relationships with works of art. I want to consider these, so to speak, more abstract circumstances in which you describe a painting as expressing an emotion.

He may be putting the explanatory (and the conceptual) cart before the horse. The matter of expressive occurrence of expression concepts is not at all at home in our more mundane intuitions. It doesn't follow from that, of course, that Goodman is claiming that it is. We are not suggesting that. But in a circumstance where you have no apparatus, no conceptual tools to speak of, and where most of the materials you have are speculative materials in any case, it is often best to consider your more robust intuitions and to see how these are expressed in talk about a mechanism, or how they attest to a mechanism or attest to something real rather than something thought actual because it occurs in the 'experience' of aestheticians.

Our ordinary ways of thinking and talking about expression have the character of being causally grounded. They invoke the notion of a causal mechanism in some relevant way, and in so doing they do not completely undermine the surmise that expression is referential (and whether or not it is well founded, a causal theory of reference does exist). It might indeed be argued that at some points expression looks almost paradigmatically referential, in so far as it is one of the most paradigmatically cause-infested notions when viewed in terms of our ordinary intentions. We might argue that it has been a consequence if not a function of the concept of aesthetic experience that expression and cause have been prised apart in our understanding of pictures. It may well be a consequence, if not a function, of a historical materialist view of art that the two are brought back together—and brought more in line with our ordinary intuitions.

We start with the suggestion that we normally talk about expression (a) in the context of the expression of belief (which is the ordinary way), and (b) in the context of expression of emotion in the face, gestures, social behaviour, the manifestation of symbols and so forth. But we are not yet distinguishing between contexts of expression which are 'conventional' and those which are not. ☹ 'conventionally' expresses sadness. ☺ does not. For our purposes however it is an 'open' question whether this conventional expression of sadness is what it is supposed to be, whether it is an act, a fake, a representation, etc. We do not yet claim to have established the distinctions between pictures or portraits which (eg) show emotion, and emotion shown in the way that a portrait is painted, or abstract painting showing emotion, or landscape expressing emotion etc.

What we can say, though, is that many people's intuitions would be satisfied if you were to say that what is meant by saying that a painting expresses sadness is that sadness plays some part in a causal chain or sequence leading to the production of the picture. No more than that. Now that can obviously mean many things or be fulfilled in many ways. It could mean—without restricting it in a semantical kind of way—that the sadness was the artist's, or that it was the sitter's (in the case of the portrait), or that it was the artist's friend's (eg if he came and wept all over the artist when he was painting the picture). Such a loose understanding of cause fails, for instance, to distinguish or deal with a case in which the sadness is, so to speak, faked: eg where someone who is extremely happy produces a painting which expresses sadness. It does not get us near a criterion of 'sincerity', for example, and that may seem like a danger for a causal theory of expression. A provisional answer to that objection is that you cannot have a very adequate sense that sadness is 'faked' unless you have some sense of the (contingent) role of some sadness in the first place (eg you can't fake sadness without *some* sort of preoccupation with sadness having acted as a cause of what you did or made). In other words, without a genetically significant paradigm you cannot have a relevant concept of dissembling or bullshit, and without a causal component to a theory of expression you can't unmask it. Without a 'genetic' or causal theory of expression, it would be hard to see how we could have actors. How would an actor's 'representation' of sadness be understood as just that and not as an expression of *his* sadness (when it wasn't)?

In order to create conditions of enquiry we need to think up lots of examples of pictures which are alleged to 'express', lots of ways in which they might be thought to 'express', and lots of anomalies in which the matter of the causal role can be significant (even if you can't trace it). We need to sort out where the causal or genetic component really comes in. We should ask in which sense the causal role is presumptively present, or whether it has to exist as a kind of inquisitive theme, or whether it can be made to disintegrate by virtue of our asking certain questions or by the recognition of certain boundary conditions, and so on. The anomalies may be the most fruitful. (Goodman seems to have got enchanted by the fact that while there *are* so many anomalies, love is love, hunger is hunger, etc.) There is a neglect of material specificity. As Kate Soper points out:

> One must, for example, be able to differentiate between the biological instinct of hunger regarded as an attribute that holds universally, and *this* hunger for *this* kind of food, consumed in *this* kind of way; the latter can only be explained as a materialisation of particular historical relations; it is not a mere *form* of abstract hunger and cannot therefore be conceptualised in the same terms. ('Marxism, Materialism and Biology', in *Issues in Marxist Philosophy,* Harvester Press, 1979.)

Materialist reductionists and people of a commonsensical nature might object that all this stuff about the causal role of emotional and/or cognitive states is systematically misleading. Central-state materialism is fake.

But a causal role for emotional and cognitive states is compatible with the idea of expression of belief. Beliefs may indeed apply to groups of persons and even, at the limit, to 'societies'. But they are pre-eminently attributes of persons. Persons possess minds, and persons possessing minds manipulate symbols; but what they do in manipulating those symbols is to express their beliefs. And it's people's beliefs that can cause them to act. (Whether or not we may be talking at some level of the maximising of utilities etc, etc, let us call them beliefs for the sake of it.) Presumably also those beliefs are their dispositions, mental states etc. We can assert dogmatically that psychology is an autonomous science of the mind, although it may be conditioned by and may intersect other conditions. The causation we are talking about in the case of beliefs is trans-categorical rather than corpuscular. In talking of beliefs, dispositions and states we wish to consider them as causes of behaviour—social behaviour—and this will include such activities as the making of marks and inscriptions, colouring-in etc. Such a notion of causation allows due importance to the question of agency. Aestheticians find it easy to dispose of artists as agents and to treat them rather as their own patients.

197

To say that the statement '*p* expresses sadness' implicates (some) sadness causally significant in (the system of) the production of the picture is to say little in detail. The claim is corrigible in so far as it is possible that no sadness was causally implicated. But if the statement is really to the effect that the viewer takes *p* to express sadness, things are apparently more difficult because the viewer may be making no genetic claim at all—taking *p* to be a *symbol* of sadness, etc, etc. But is this version not corrigible in so far as the former one is? If we mean 'expresses *s*', don't we mean *caused* by *s*, notwithstanding actors and so forth?

A more difficult case will be one in which we don't know what *p* expresses. Do we take it that it expresses nothing? If we find out that *s* was causally implicated, do we then say that '*p* expresses *s*'? Obviously not. Some structural features (or, etc) of *p* must also *refer* to *s*—in some sense recognisable to Goodman.

Of course, the idea that expression is causal does not obliterate the fact that *p* will have material causes and other causes and that a claim that it expresses *s* will itself have material and other causes. We are discussing the methodological tendencies of a highly schematic paradigm.

Another objection might be that in drawing attention to causes one is in principle liable to confusion in a regress of causes: further and further reductions; that postulating sadness as a cause is arbitrary in the sense that it is a high-level, redescribable state of an individual and so on. In answer to this we would say that the world has different levels—that reality is at least stratified, that some reductions and redescriptions are feasible and that, eg, sadness may be thought of as an emergent property of mind and that some properties of mind are irreducible to their material constituents. Sadness is psychological. And the mind is not reducible by (eg) central-state materialism.

Nor are we suggesting that the statement '*p* expresses *s*' requires, prima facie, inquiry into the causes of *s*. Whether or not the *s* was generated by a bad breakfast may be of no immediate relevance or interest. But it might be of interest circumstantially.

The mechanism of the production of a picture *p* will be an open system (*p* will be multiply and plurally caused). That is to say that any *p* or any feature or structural aspect of *p* will be caused both by many competing causes and by many causes entirely compatible—or at least not likely to rule each other out. Such causal systems will not be *chains* linked together like crochet. The products of history or nature are not accounted for by such 'two-dimensional' models. If someone says 'George', and then goes on to predicate something of George, you are entitled to ask how they got George as a name—who or what they are using it to single out. You need to know whether they are using George as the name of the person who just climbed over the wall or whether they're using it as the name of the person who just knocked on your door. Without knowing, you can't know whom the predicate is supposed to refer to. One of the ways to discover is to identify how their causal histories are distinct: how some 'story' will serve to link the act of predication to some specific George. This is to ask how the reference of the name George is fixed. But to know this is not to rule out the possibility that someone—or some other 'story'—may change the reference. In the case of sadness, suppose you're asking, 'How is a claim to the effect that *p* expresses sadness fixed?' If the cause of the sadness-effect turns out to be the state of the person who is looking at the picture, then so be it if it is indeed so. We do not deny that the reference can be so fixed. We merely say that we have not been talking paradigmatically about that kind of mechanism. Our discussion presupposes that 'expression' implies cause. [. . .]

It might be argued by some psychology-enchanted persons (and it may indeed be true) that there is an effected property of faces (for example) such that we read them as sad. But that is neither here nor there in respect of this matter, because whether or not you happen to have the psychological equipment to read a face as sad is irrelevant to the issue of whether or not that face is authentically sad, since 'authentically sad' means that the person pulling the face *is* sad, at some level of a stratified world of which he or she is a part. Obviously we have to consider actors pretending to be sad, and expressing sadness thereby, etc, etc. This means that you can't make it a necessary condition of a person being on the stage expressing sadness that he or she *is* sad. All we would require, to satisfy the interests of a causal-type theory of reference, is that there should be some genealogical trace back to some sadness, and that not necessarily 'direct'. We might say that the minimal condition is that someone should have to know how to fake sadness, since this would presuppose that he had sadness as a paradigm. It would presuppose of the person who knew how to pull a sad face not necessarily even that they had experienced sadness, but that they had experienced or taken a face to be sad, and, in that sense, made an inference from some case in which a real sadness had furnished the paradigm. In other words, to say this face is sad means that this face is caused (however indirectly) by a person being sad. So there is a causal connection of some kind involved, *pace* a causal theory of reference.

We are not saying that all you have to do when you come up to a picture is ask, 'Was the artist sad when he painted it or wasn't he?' and if not sling the thing out of the window. Not at all. We are trying to figure out how far the causal connection—even the simple type that we have schematised—is of importance as a kind of logical component of any judgement of expressivity in respect of a picture *p*; ie we are suggesting that some or most substantive claims of the form '*p* expresses *s*' are claims about the mechanism that produced the picture. We are further suggesting that such a claim of this form *ought*—for a certain class of cultural products at least (pictures rather than symphonies, some modern pictures rather than (some) old pictures, etc, but not exhaustively or exclusively)—to amount to a claim compatible with the possibility of a limited naturalist and realist social science, and that the hermeneutic survival of some art activity is compatible with such a possibility, and that the Têtes Molles of most of the perpetrators of art and criticism are conditioned by a circumstance incompatible with such a possibility. We are not claiming that this causal-type argument will settle matters of expressivity, which are analogues or subsets of such things as perlocutionary and illocutionary force. And the general or universal concepts, Sadness, Loneliness etc will have, no doubt, material substrates of various kinds. And perhaps more interestingly some adequate distinction will have to be made between the vivid expression of prima facie trivial or 'weak' emotion and the leaden or inadequate expression of prima facie apocalyptic emotions. 'Prima facie' because, of course, it is possible to express something 'badly' or to fail for various causes 'to express anything', or anything that is a potential cause of symbol-production which is present or actual emotional or cognitive state, and so on—and because it is a possibility that symbols with a certain effect (say vivid effect) may, *qua* expressive symbols, involve the imputation of 'strong' emotion to the producer(s). This may be wrong, but it's not that easy to push to this margin. The perlocutionary force of a set of symbols will, if it is an *expressive* force, involve reference to what is or was felt (etc) by the producer (although the producer of the expressive effect may be the hearer/spectator).

At stake is what you would have to do in order to show that a judgement was wrong, where the causal connection had furnished a logical component of the judgement that *p* expresses *s*. Presumably not all judgements of this type are absolutely wrong. There are some extreme vagaries and ambiguities and so forth associated with judgements in respect of such properties as *s* (ie sadness). We do not dispute this or claim to abbreviate the difficulties. But there does not seem to be any good reason to be frightened of the possible corrigibility of such judgements where they can be said to be entangled with the conceptions of agents.

The sad face is not a particularly odd case of expression. It's a very ordinary use of expression that we employ when we talk about it. It's distinct from theatrical and aesthetic uses. But it is at least true to say than one circumstance in which you can mean that a painting expresses sadness is when you intend to say that the artist was sad in producing it. That is, so to speak, the caught-red-handed case, the plead-guilty case. Of course the others are far less open and shut, and even that one is often likely to be 'confirmed' or supported in a circumstantial way, unless you have been able to conduct some kind of psychological test on the artist while he was painting, in order to establish that he was in a so-called 'sad' state. Various degrees of circumstantial confirmation might count. If you knew that his cat had just been run over you would be more likely to accept the judgement that his picture expresses sadness than if you knew he'd just won the pools. And there would be other considerations to take into account at the same time: for example if he had just won the pools and at the same time you regarded him as someone of an extraordinarily melancholy disposition you would still tend to accept the idea that he was sad (at the death of the cat). Abstract sadness is sadness. Sadness is sadness. But compare sadness at the loss of a profitable tenancy with sadness at the destruction of the livelihood of millions, and both or either of these kinds with hunger—hunger for caviar compared with hunger for meat torn with tooth and claw. And note how bourgeois aesthetics . . . makes empty abstractions out of this possibility.

Within that simplistic circumstance there is another sort of case which might seem more problematic, and which is located in the difference between, say, a Mark Rothko painting and a picture 'of' a sad person. In fact this is not too much of a problem. It is dealt with, in the trivial instance of the picture of the sad person, by saying that it is *of* whoever it is *of*, and if they were sad then they express sadness. If it's not *of* anybody or you don't know that it is *of* anybody, and you are interested in the expression of sadness, then you might make the presumption at some level that it is *of* somebody and that they may have been sad and etc. But there could be a picture showing a happy face which in no causally significant sense involved the face expressing sadness, but where there were structural features of the picture which expressed sadness. The case of the abstract painting might be related to this. An abstract painting may or may not share some structural features of 'expressive' faces, may be sombre, may be excessively animated and etc. Its expressivity will involve a tacit or explicit claim as to a causally significant sadness implicated in the process of its production etc.

There are, of course, many circumstances in which a lot is known or thought about the 'how' and the 'what' of a picture; a very determinate reading is made and, at the same time, a very indistinct idea as to what is *expressed* is produced and vice versa. A speaker can produce a semantically clear English sentence and remain more than enigmatic with respect to his emotional (and other aspects of his mental) state etc. All the different layers involved are relatively autonomous in certain respects. The cognitive function involved in such reading is something we can come to later.

A 'normal' occurrence might be a picture of a landscape, painted, let's say, when the artist was perfectly happy, but which nevertheless is seen as expressing sadness, by virtue, perhaps, of some 'conventional' or other reference. [. . .] Let's say that it expresses sadness somehow independently of its containing any iconically described features supposed to be capable of expressing such feelings, and independently of direct causation from a mental state to a state of the world in terms of what's scribbled on it or in it. How might this come about? In the case of, say, Van Gogh, we can argue that the 'personality of Van Gogh' is very important in the context of expressing sadness. We might also consider the extent to which the ascription of a causal connection between his paintings and his sadness is significant in fixing the possibilities for other pictures which do not have a genetic character so strongly associated with expression of sadness—or anything else, possibly.

Let a landscape by Van Gogh be thought to be sad, and let that be paradigmatic. His sadness is thought to be causally responsible at least for the expressive features. Those features will be a causal redescription. And there will be a material substrate or substrates of Van Gogh's condition even though this may not comport to an adequate application of the concept 'sadness'. The material substrate will conceivably, in this case, be circumstantially evidencing— if you're looking for evidence—as well as grounding the correct application of the concept or, as in the case of sadness, grounding the particular sense of what this sadness is, etc. Indeed, certain features of the Van Gogh may have become paradigms of expressive brushwork, colour and so forth. This possibility does not detract at all from the genetic character of expression.

Whether sad faces make you feel sad or not (or whether Einfühlung is true or not—and it doesn't matter in this case whether Einfühlung *is* true), if the inference that one makes in respect of faces is the sort of inference that one makes in general in talking about something expressing sadness, then if it just so happens that a person who has never seen a Van Gogh says that a picture (which happens to be by Van Gogh) expresses sadness, you can take him to be asserting that sadness was causally significant in the production of that picture. Or if you happen to be struck deeply (eg) by Gestalt theory and you believe that where somebody 'sees a sad face' what this means is that the face is interpreted in some way as expressing sadness, then OK, that's fine too: we just say that the Van Gogh works that way according to some psychological mechanism which need not be specified in detail in what is essentially a methodological argument. The mechanism of symbol-storage and recognition will include as part of its cognitive substance a statement schematised by the form '*s* caused *p*.'

In the case where you don't know whether someone has seen a Van Gogh or not, you might try to find out what the genetic sequence was back to some conceivably adequate circumstance—in other words, back to some circumstance in which the expressive properties of a picture of the type Van Gogh was fixed for them. Back to '*s* caused *p*.'

In a great deal of chat about art it's clear that the method of inquiry stops a long way short of what would be adequate to express this non-unique and unsurprising implication of a claim that '*p* expresses *s*.' Writing about the 'Night Café' Van Gogh declared that he intended to express men's passions by means of red and green. On the face of it he could do no such thing. But give some half-well-read student the picture to look at and ask what it expresses and he will say, 'Men's passions'. There is a categorical jump, from talking about what are the conceivable material conditions of one's taking a painting to express sadness, to what is the residual, causal meaning of the statement that painting *p* expresses sadness. They are distinct and stratified, although they may be connected. In the case of the 'Night Café', conversation about what is expressed should take account both of the circumstances of art-world discourse that made it seem plausible for Van Gogh to assert such an ambition in such terms, and of the fact that the student has read Van Gogh's letters and thus had the expressive properties of the picture fixed, or at least suggested, in advance.

But this possibility does not detract from the residual significance of the causal connection between some passion and some picture. Let's say a person is hungry. We can all empathise the pangs of hunger up to a point. But to say that someone is 'expressing' hunger, we need to know that he is hungry or that his features (etc) can trace their ancestry back to a circumstance in which '*h* caused <*p*' or not; that is a circumstance in which an internal state of an individual (usually) might be said to have caused<*p*. (We don't all have a bit of the universal 'hunger' that we share. And if someone starts going on about those 'universals' in experience that we are all supposed to share—'birth and copulation and death' etc, etc—it's worth asking how he formed his set, and why certain things got left out.)

We don't see how there can be any objective circumstances save causal ones in which pictures can be said to express sadness. Non-causal circumstances seem all highly ethnocentric. If you want to say that a picture within a certain community expresses sadness then it seems that the only relevant way you can account for differences in community is by saying that there are different ways of fixing the references of such things and different circumstances in which those references are fixed: different histories of the references of symbols. Expression is a partial subset of reference, and that involves you at some point in a form of reduction to the expression, face, belief or whatever. You can rarely just stick discursively with the producer's *sadness* as such. ('Producer' can mean 'artist' or 'sitter' here, *mutatis mutandis*.) That's one of the questions that has to be asked: Do you stay with the artist or do you go beyond him, and where do you go? You can 'go beyond the producer' in all sorts of ways. You can search for material and efficient conditions of his state *s*; you can search for redescriptions and analyses of *s* and its conditions; and you can accept the causal analysis of expression and look for the conditions of the production of picture *p*. They will still amount to causal implication in the claim that *p* expresses *s*.

The alternative to a criticism corrigible in causal terms is a cultural circle in which authoritative figures fight for an absurd pre-eminence as they cast uneasy glances at the emancipatory spiral.

Our argument is compatible with Goodman's 'semantic' analysis of expression in 'abstract' circumstances [. . .] What Goodman's analysis does not do (perhaps does not purport to do) is adequately to account for the fact that certain people and certain skills, or alleged skills, do the fixing on behalf of other people, thereby creating genetic conditions for them; in other words certain people create causal sequences or conditions for others' ascriptions of sadness in pictures. We also need to recognise that certain psychology-enchanted persons underestimate the class-and-ideology causes. They fail, in fact, to recognise the difference between the in-principle falsifiable claim that picture *p* expresses sadness and the more marginally corrigible (or differently corrigible) claim to the effect that 'I feel sad in front of this picture.' We are back to our starting point and the claim that interpretative and critical discourse are confused, or rather that interpretative and what passes for critical discourse are split apart from causal and historical enquiry. What the sensitive explainer does is to say that the interpretative discourse—ie the 'what I feel'—*is* the historical and causal enquiry; ie that it *is* what picture *p* expresses.

It is perhaps to keep his hands clean of this kind of ideological dispute that Goodman uses the concepts of metaphor and label. For this is indeed the way by which expressive qualities do get fixed. The aesthetician is inclined to operate in a world in which the operations of the connoisseur are accepted as *faits accomplis*. The latter is accustomed to saying 'This is what I feel' without any sense of the need to ground what he feels in what he knows, and this is a part of the mechanism by which references do in fact get fixed, and by means of which pictures are said to be sad. Goodman and Gombrich *et al* deal—albeit fastidiously—with the given state of the discourse.

Our hands are dirty anyway. So we can say, 'We shouldn't mess around with these allegedly abstract categories. Goodman might have asked why he had to have a metaphor.' The reason he had to have a metaphor is that pictures cannot be caused to be sad, whereas people can. So at some point you are left with the fact that agents are involved, and that expression goes paradigmatically to particular agents.

There are, no doubt, psychological mechanisms to be discovered which amount to material substrates of something like what are called states of mind. They will be in competition with and collusion with ideological, psychological substrates and so forth.

The redescribability of states of mind does not detract from the proposition that expression has to be expression *of* something. That means that what is expressed is a state or states of mind, or something connected thereto. But an expressing symbol (also) refers to what caused it to be produced. That is, either (a) an implicit genesis to the relevant state of mind is produced in virtue of the claim that a certain symbol does express (eg) *s* (this genesis implies no natural closure), or (b) the production of a 'sad' face or a 'sad' picture is an act of referring, of 'dubbing' or reference-fixing or (possibly) both. The more interesting is (a), but there are some conceptual problems associated with the idea of a causal interaction between an individual and his state of mind as referring to that state of mind in addition to (or conflated with) the causal interaction which leads to the individual's symbolic behaviour. They may not be inseparable, however. Is it not possible to assume that a sad face expresses sadness *s* in being caused by *s* (as a mental state), and that in so far as it is symbolic behaviour (if it is), then it refers to that mental state also? Running around like a chicken with its head off can be just caused by panic; it can also express it if it is symbolic and caused, etc.

The critic's 'expresses' claims are corrigible with reference to the causal implications (however ancestral) of all such claims. They are also corrigible in so far as the critic is himself an agent. His conceptions are corrigible on causal grounds. To say that is perhaps to offer to dirty one's hands.

The 'abstract' circumstance is little more than a failure to understand why it is that physiognomy *is* paradigmatic in discussions of expression. It is paradigmatic because we do better than cobble up constant conjunction when we are ordinarily talking about causes. When we say that *p* expresses *s*, we are, if we are not to produce gratuitous idealisations, saying that an individual *i* is expressing *s* in *p*, and that *p* also is symbolic and has the property of also referring to *s*. The really exotic (or rather interesting) question is whether or not *s*'s being the cause of *p* is the same thing as *p* referring to *s*.

The emancipatory potential of art is minimal. But if art discourse is to have *any* such potential, it must depend upon the possibility that the circle of interpretation can be broken in a causal discourse which is a moment in the unfolding of what it describes. But causality is vanity. The real project is to do without it: to make do with nothing.

V
COMMUNITIES AND INTERESTS

19   The Twentieth-Century Dilemma

C. B. Macpherson

Macpherson's influential book, The Political Theory of Possessive Individualism, *emphasizes the individualistic basis of seventeenth-century English political theory and the identification of this individualism with possession. His aim was to substantiate a view that 'the central difficulties of liberal-democratic thought from John Stuart Mill to the present might be better understood if they were seen to have been set by the persistence and deep-rootedness of that [unifying] assumption' which he describes as 'possessive individualism'.*

The assumptions of possessive individualism are summarized by Macpherson as follows.

1   *What makes a man human is freedom from dependence on the wills of others.*
2   *Freedom from dependence on others means freedom from any relations with others except those relations which the individual enters voluntarily with a view to his own interest.*
3   *The individual is essentially the proprietor of his own person and capacities, for which he owes nothing to society . . .*
4   *Although the individual cannot alienate the whole of his property in his own person, he may alienate his capacity to labour.*
5   *Human society consists of a series of market relations . . .*
6   *Since freedom from the wills of others is what makes a man human, each individual's freedom can rightfully be limited only by such obligations and rules as are necessary to secure the same freedom for others.*
7   *Political society is a human contrivance for the protection of the individual's property in his person and goods, and (therefore) for the maintenance of orderly relations of exchange between individuals regarded as proprietors of themselves.*

According to Macpherson these assumptions inhere in a market society and are most clearly articulated in the work of Thomas Hobbes and John Locke. They also characterize the work of later philosophers whose concept of human nature as essentially individualistic recognizes that that is indeed man's nature under the market. 'The assumptions of possessive individualism', he writes, 'have been retained in modern liberal theory, to an extent not always realized. Yet they have failed as foundations of liberal-democratic theory. The trouble is not that they have been kept after they had ceased to correspond to our society. They still do correspond to our society and so must be kept.' Macpherson believes however that it is now 'impossible ... to derive a valid theory of obligation from the assumptions' of possessive individualism, as a consequence of the change in possessive market society which has come about with 'the emergence of working-class political articulacy'. Hence the 'twentieth-century dilemma'.

In the concluding section of his book, which follows, Macpherson considers how it has happened that though 'the assumptions remain indispensable... no sufficient principle of obligation can now be derived from them', and 'what prospects are left for liberal-democratic theory'.

It is of interest to relate prevailing liberal-democratic views of the practice and meaning of art to the possessive individualist notions of individuals as 'proprietors of themselves' and of humanity as entailing 'freedom from dependence on the wills of others'. These views are particularly influential in the sphere of art education, where a high priority tends to be placed upon the achievement of 'self-expression' and the realization of personal 'creative potential'. The development of an individualistic style is generally taken as a measure of such achievement and realization. On the other hand it is a strong feature of the values normally placed upon modern art that its production is not subordinate to 'the laws of the market'. If Macpherson is correct in his diagnosis of the 'twentieth-century dilemma', we could expect just such a hiatus between the actual conditions of production of art (which must be those of a market society) and the theories employed to justify and evaluate individualistic practice.

Macpherson posits a loss of cohesion in the basis for liberal-democratic justification of political obligation, and attributes this to the development of political articulacy in the working class. If we perceive a similar loss of cohesion in the basis for liberal-democratic justification of cultural and aesthetic commitment, might this be attributable to the development of articulacy within a social section characterized by different cultural commitments and interests? Such an analysis might certainly help to explain those conditions of divergence and contradiction which appear to prevail in the discourses and practices of the modern world of art.

It may be noted that Macpherson's account of the twentieth-century dilemma in political theory is compatible in many ways with MacIntyre's analysis of the modern conditions of moral debate (see our introduction to text 5).

Source: The Political Theory of Possessive Individualism: Hobbes to Locke (Oxford University Press, 1962), pp. 271–277. Footnotes have been deleted. © Oxford University Press 1962. Reprinted by permission of Oxford University Press.

[. . .] The assumptions of possessive individualism are peculiarly appropriate to a possessive market society, for they state certain essential facts that are peculiar to that society. The individual in a possessive market society *is* human in his capacity as proprietor of his own person; his humanity does depend on his freedom from any but self-interested contractual relations with others; his society does consist of a series of market relations. England, and the other modern liberal-democratic nations, are still, in the twentieth century, possessive market societies. Why, then, should not modern liberal-democratic justificatory theory, to the extent that it contains these assumptions, be satisfactory? Why should not the possessive individualist theory of the English utilitarian tradition, which is essentially the theory of Hobbes as amended by Locke in the matter of the self-perpetuating sovereign, be a satisfactory demonstration of the political obligation of the individual to the liberal state? And why should not that theory, further amended as it was in the nineteenth century by the admission that wage-earners were free men, be adequate now for the liberal-democratic state? We can best deal with these questions by collecting from our earlier analysis the conditions on which a possessive individualist theory can be an adequate theory of political obligation.

I have argued that to get a valid theory of political obligation without relying on any supposed purposes of Nature or will of God (which we may call an autonomous theory of political obligation), one must be able to postulate that the individuals of whom the society is composed see themselves, or are capable of seeing themselves, as equal in some respect more fundamental than all the respects in which they are unequal. This condition was fulfilled in the original possessive market society, from its emergence as the dominant form in the seventeenth century until its zenith in the nineteenth, by the apparent inevitability of everyone's subordination to the laws of the market. So long as everyone was subject to the determination of a competitive market, and so long as this apparently equal subordination of individuals to the determination of the market was accepted as rightful, or inevitable, by virtually everybody, there was a sufficient basis for rational obligation of all men to a political authority which could maintain and enforce the only possible orderly human relations, namely, market relations.

I have argued also that in a possessive market society a further condition is required for a valid theory of obligation of the individual to a non-self-perpetuating sovereign body (and hence for a theory of obligation to any kind of liberal state). The further condition is that there be a cohesion of self-interests, among all those who have a voice in choosing the government, sufficient to offset the centrifugal forces of a possessive market society. This condition was fulfilled, in the heyday of the market society, by the fact that a political voice was restricted to a possessing class which had sufficient cohesion to decide periodically, without anarchy, who should have the sovereign power. As long as this condition was fulfilled there was a sufficient basis for an autonomous theory of obligation of the individual to a constitutional liberal state. This second condition, like the first, was fulfilled until about the middle of the nineteenth century.

Thereafter, both conditions ceased to be met. Although possessive market relations continued to prevail in fact, their inevitability became increasingly challenged as an industrial working class developed some class consciousness and became politically articulate. Men no longer saw themselves fundamentally equal in an inevitable subjection to the determination of the market. The development of the market system, producing a class which could envisage alternatives to the system, thus destroyed the social fact (acceptance of inevitability of market relations) which had fulfilled the first prerequisite of an autonomous theory of political obligation.

The second prerequisite condition was similarly affected. Although the society continued to be class divided, and the possessing class continued to be cohesive, its cohesion ceased to fulfil the prerequisite when the possessing class had to yield its monopoly of power by admitting the rest of the society to the franchise. With the democratic franchise, there was no longer that assurance of cohesion, among all those with a political voice, which had been provided by class interest during the time when only one class had had the franchise.

It may be argued that the continued existence of liberal-democratic states in possessive market societies, since that time, has been due to the ability of a possessing class to keep the effective political power in its hands in spite of universal suffrage. But while this may suffice to keep a liberal state going, it savours too much of deception to be an adequate basis for a moral justification of liberal democracy.

It may be argued also that the continued existence of liberal-democratic states into the twentieth century, after the cohesion of a possessing governing class had given way to the uncertain cohesion of the democratic franchise, was made possible by a sort of class cohesion on an international level. The democratic franchise came in the nineteenth century in advanced capitalist countries. By the time it came, these countries stood, in relation to the backward peoples, in somewhat the same relation as the possessing class had stood towards the non-possessing class within the advanced market societies. But while the cohesion of a possessing nation may have provided some substitute for the previous cohesion of a possessing class, this too was an inadequate basis for a moral justification of liberal democracy. In any case, with the emergence of colonial peoples to national independence, this basis is now rapidly disappearing.

A temporary substitute for the old cohesion has sometimes been provided in our century by war. But, apart from the fact that the cost of this cohesion is a weakening of liberal institutions, few would rest a moral justification of liberal democracy on a premise of continual war. In any case, the technical conditions of war are now such that war on a scale sufficient to bring the required cohesion within one warring nation would destroy the nation. Thus none of the factors which together may be said to have operated to keep liberal-democratic states going in possessive market societies, after the disappearance of the old basis of cohesion, has provided or can provide a satisfactory justifying theory.

The dilemma of modern liberal-democratic theory is now apparent: it must continue to use the assumptions of possessive individualism, at a time when the structure of market society no longer provides the necessary conditions for deducing a valid theory of political obligation from those assumptions. Liberal theory must continue to use the assumptions of possessive individualism because they are factually accurate for our possessive market societies. Their factual accuracy has already been noticed, but the point will bear repetition. The individual in market society *is* human as proprietor of his own person. However much he may wish it to be otherwise, his humanity does depend on his freedom from any but self-interested contractual relations with others. His society does consist of a series of market relations. Because the assumptions are factually accurate, they cannot be dropped from a justificatory theory. But the maturing of market society has cancelled that cohesion, among all those with a political voice, which is a prerequisite for the deduction of obligation to a liberal state from possessive individualist assumptions. No way out of the dilemma is to be found by rejecting those assumptions while not rejecting market society, as so many theorists from John Stuart Mill to our own time have done on the ground that the assumptions are morally offensive. If they are now morally offensive they are none the less still factually accurate for our possessive market societies. The dilemma remains. Either we reject possessive individualist assumptions, in which case our theory is unrealistic, or we retain them, in which case we cannot get a valid theory of obligation. It follows that we cannot now expect a valid theory of obligation to a liberal-democratic state in a possessive market society.

The question whether the actual relations of a possessive market society can be abandoned or transcended, without abandoning liberal political institutions, bristles with difficulties. In the measure that market society could be abandoned, the problem of cohesion would be resolved, for the problem was defined as the need for a degree of cohesion which would counteract the centrifugal force of market relations. But there would still be the problem of finding a substitute for that recognition of a fundamental equality which had originally been provided by the supposed inevitable subordination of everyone to the market. Could any conceivable new concept of fundamental equality, which would be consistent with the maintenance of liberal institutions and values, possibly get the wide acknowledgement without which, as I have argued, no autonomous theory of political obligation can be valid?

We may take some comfort from the fact that the two problems, of cohesion and of equality, do not now have to be solved in that order. The question whether the actual possessive market relations of a given liberal-democratic state can be abandoned or transcended has now become of secondary importance. For a further change in the social facts has supervened. The very factor, namely, technical change in the methods of war, that has made war an impossible source of internal cohesion, has created a new equality of insecurity among individuals, not merely within one nation but everywhere. The destruction of every individual is now a more real and present possibility than Hobbes could have imagined.

From this, the possibility of a new rational political obligation arises. We cannot hope to get a valid theory of obligation of the individual to a single national state alone. But if we postulate no more than the degree of rational understanding which it has always been necessary to postulate for any moral theory of political obligation, an acceptable theory of obligation of the individual to a wider political authority should now be possible. Given that degree of rationality, the self-interested individual, whatever his possessions, and whatever his attachment to a possessive market society, can see that the relations of the market society must yield to the overriding requirement that, in Overton's words, which now acquire a new significance, 'humane society, cohabitation or being, . . . above all earthly things must be maintained'.

The new equality of insecurity has thus changed the terms of our problem. Twentieth-century technology has, so to speak, brought Hobbes and the Levellers together. The problems raised by possessive individualism have shrunk: they can perhaps now be brought to manageable proportions, but only if they are clearly identified and accurately related to the actual changes in the social facts. Those changes have driven us again to a Hobbesian insecurity, at a new level. The question now is whether, in the new setting, Hobbes can again be amended, this time more clearly than he was by Locke.

20 The Idea of a Social Science

Alasdair MacIntyre

     MacIntyre's explicit aim in the following article is 'to express dissent from the position taken in Mr Peter Winch's book whose title is also the title of this essay'. Winch's The Idea of a Social Science *(Routledge and Kegan Paul, London, 1958) was published nine years before the first printing of MacIntyre's essay. The latter is thus not so much a review as a critique of interconnecting methods and assumptions within certain types of social-scientific study, for which Winch's work is taken as representative. The argument addresses questions of interpretation and use of such concepts as 'reason', 'motive', 'cause', 'intention' and 'rule', and compares the conceptual and methodological frameworks within which these concepts are differently related and distinguished.*

     As represented by MacIntyre, Winch's concept of social-anthropological study may be summarized as follows. To study a community is to study rule-governed behaviour. The rules of a given form of social life provide the context within which the motives, reasons and decisions of an agent may be seen to explain his actions. These rules determine both 'the range of reasons and motives open to a given set of agents and hence also the range of decisions open to them'. For the anthropologist therefore, 'Their rules, not his, define the object of his study.' The account of a community's system of rationality will be derived only from those concepts available within that community and these will be learned by learning its language. The limits of the community's language, then, will set the conceptual limits of any social-scientific representation of that community. This excludes causal inquiry and explanation (for example, of any agent's actions) which rests upon concepts available to the social scientist but not to members of the community under study. If the native's account of why he carries a stone in a forked stick is that it is his soul, then that reason is adequate in social-scientific explanation. To object that souls are not such as to be carried in forked sticks is to commit a methodological foul, since 'Understanding in terms of rule-following and causal explanation have mutually exclusive subject-matters.' As MacIntyre observes, this rules out the application of such concepts as those of 'ideology' and 'false-consciousness', since these presuppose

213

the availability of a causal account of reasons which is at odds with any which the members of a society would be able to give for their own actions. MacIntyre counters Winch's prescriptions with an admonition drawn from Walter Goldschmidt: 'Do not ask what an institution means for the agents themselves, ask what necessary needs and purposes it serves.'

We would assert that the conceptual vocabulary of art history and art criticism implies a set of unspoken commitments and methodological assumptions regarding the social anthropology of the art community. These are commitments to its framework of rules and to the meanings of its language. Certain normal practices in art history and art criticism may thus be seen as compatible with Winch's theoretical model. The adequacy of agents' reasons in explanation may be seen as taken for granted, for instance, in the use made of such concepts as 'artistic intention', 'inner necessity', 'personal vision', and 'self-expression' and so on. The need for critical redescription and paraphrase of such terms, we would suggest, entails causal inquiry and explanation of the type for which MacIntyre argues. What is required for such inquiry to be feasible is that an independent conceptual framework be available to thought. To qualify as independent such a framework will have to underwrite a description of 'necessary needs and purposes' which deploys terms other than those constitutive of meaning in the art community's own discourse.

Source: Proceedings of the Aristotelian Society, supplementary volume xli, 1967. Reprinted by courtesy of the editor of the Aristotelian Society. © 1967 The Aristotelian Society. This material has been edited and footnotes have been re-numbered.

[. . .]

1

Wittgenstein says somewhere that when one gets into philosophical difficulties over the use of some of the concepts of our language, we are like savages confronted with something from an alien culture. I am simply indicating a corollary of this: that sociologists who misinterpret an alien culture are like philosophers getting into difficulty over the use of their own concepts.

This passage (p. 114) epitomizes a central part of Winch's thesis with its splendid successive characterization of the figure baffled by an alien culture; a savage at one moment, he has become a sociologist at the next. And this is surely no slip of the pen. According to Winch, the successful sociologist has simply learned all that the ideal native informant could tell him; sociological knowledge is the kind of knowledge possessed in implicit and partial form by the members of a society rendered explicit and complete (p. 88). It is not at first entirely clear just how far Winch is at odds in this contention with, for example, Malinowski, who insisted that the native Trobriander's account of Trobriand society must be inadequate, that the sociologists' account of institutions is a construction not available to the untutored awareness of the native informant.[1] For Winch of course is willing to allow into the sociologist's account concepts 'which are not taken from the forms of activity which he is investigating; but which are taken rather from the context of his own investigation', although he adds that 'these technical concepts will imply a prior understanding of those other concepts which belong to the activities under investigation.' Perhaps this might seem sufficient to remove the apparent disagreement of Winch and Malinowski, until we remember the conclusion of Malinowski's critique of the native informant's view. The sociologist who relies upon that view, he says,

> ... obtains at best that lifeless body of laws, regulations, morals, and conventionalities which *ought* to be obeyed, but in reality are often only evaded. For in actual life rules are never entirely conformed to, and it remains, as the most difficult but indispensable part of the ethnographer's work, to ascertain the extent and mechanism of the deviations.[2]

This makes two points clear.

First, Malinowski makes a distinction between the rules acknowledged in a given society and the actual behaviour of individuals in that society, whereas Winch proclaims the proper object of sociological study to be that behaviour precisely as rule-governed. The second is that in the study of behaviour Malinowski is willing to use notions such as that of mechanism which are clearly causal; whereas Winch warns us against comparing sociological understanding with understanding in terms of 'statistics and causal laws' and says of the notion of function, so important to Malinowski, that it 'is a quasi-causal notion, which it is perilous to apply to social institutions' (p. 116).

It does appear, therefore, that, although Winch and Malinowski agree in seeing the ideal native informant's account of his own social life as incomplete by comparison with the ideal sociologist's account, they do disagree about the nature of that incompleteness and about how it is to be remedied. My purpose in this essay will be to defend Malinowski's point of view on these matters against Winch's, but this purpose can only be understood if one reservation is immediately added. It is that in defending Malinowski's views on these points I must not be taken to be endorsing Malinowski's general theoretical position. I have in fact quoted Malinowski on these matters, but I might have quoted many other social scientists. For on these matters Malinowski speaks with the consensus.

2

> A regularity or uniformity is the constant recurrence of the same kind of event on the same kind of occasion; hence statements of uniformities presuppose judgements of identity. But ... criteria of identity are necessarily relative to some rule: with the corollary that two events which count as qualitatively similar from the point of view of one rule would count as different from the point of view of another. So to investigate the type of regularity studied in a given inquiry is to examine the nature of the rule according to which judgments of identity are made in that inquiry. Such judgments are intelligible only relatively to a given mode of human behavior, governed by its own rules (pp. 83–4).

This passage is the starting-point for Winch's argument that J. S. Mill was mistaken in supposing that to understand a social institution is to formulate empirical generalizations about regularities in human behaviour, generalizations which are causal and explanatory in precisely the same sense that generalizations in the natural sciences are. For the natural scientist makes the relevant judgements of identity according to *his* rules (that is, the rules incorporated in the practice of his science); whereas the social scientist must make his judgements of identity in accordance with the rules governing the behaviour of those whom he studies. *Their* rules, not *his*, define the object of his study.

> So it is quite mistaken in principle to compare the activity of a student of a form of social behavior with that of, say, an engineer studying the working of a machine. If we are going to compare the social student to an engineer, we shall do better to compare him to an apprentice engineer who is studying what engineering—that is, the activity of engineering—is all about (p. 88).

What the type of understanding which Winch is commending consists in is made clearer in two other passages. He says that, although prediction is possible in the social sciences, it 'is quite different from predictions in the natural sciences, where a falsified prediction always implies some sort of mistake on the part of the predictor: false or inadequate data, faulty calculation, or defective theory' (pp. 91–2). This is because 'since understanding something involves understanding its contradictory, someone who, with understanding, performs X must be capable of envisaging the possibility of doing not-X' (p. 91). Where someone is following a rule, we cannot predict how he will interpret what is involved in following that rule in radically new circumstances; where decisions have to be made, the outcome 'cannot be *definitely* predicted', for otherwise 'we should not call them decisions'.

These points about prediction, if correct, reinforce Winch's argument about the difference between the natural sciences and the social sciences. For they amount to a denial of that symmetry between explanation and prediction which holds in the natural sciences. (It has been argued often enough that this symmetry does not hold in the natural sciences; Professor Adolf Grünbaum's arguments in Chapter 9 of the *Philosophy of Space and Time* seem a more than adequate rebuttal of these positions.) But when we consider what Winch says here about decision, it is useful to take into account at the same time what he says about motives and reasons. Winch treats these as similar in this respect: that they are made intelligible by reference to the rules governing the form of social life in which the agent participates. So Winch points out that 'one can act "from considerations" only where there are accepted standards of what is appropriate to appeal to' (p. 82) and argues against Ryle that the 'law-like proposition' in terms of which someone's reasons must be understood concerns not the agent's disposition 'but the accepted standards of reasonable behavior current in his society' (p. 81).

From all this one can set out Winch's view of understanding and explanations in the social sciences in terms of a two-stage model. An action is *first* made intelligible as the outcome of motives, reasons, and decisions; and is then made *further* intelligible by those motives, reasons, and decisions being set in the context of the rules of a given form of social life. These rules logically determine the range of reasons and motives open to a given set of agents and hence also the range of decisions open to them. Thus Winch's contrast between explanation in terms of causal generalizations and explanations in terms of rules turns out to rest upon a version of the contrast between explanations in terms of causes and explanations in terms of reasons. This latter contrast must therefore be explored, and the most useful way of doing this will be to understand better what it is to act for a reason.

Many analyses of what it is to act for a reason have written into them an incompatibility between acting for a reason and behaving from a cause, just because they begin from the apparently simple and uncomplicated case where the action is actually performed, where the agent had one and only one reason for performing it, and where no doubt could arise for the agent as to why he had done what he had done. By concentrating attention upon this type of example, a basis is laid for making central to the analyses a contrast between the agent's knowledge of his own reasons for acting and his and others' knowledge of causes of his behaviour. For clearly in such a case the agent's claim that he did X for reason Y does not seem to stand in need of any warrant from a generalization founded upon observation; while equally clearly any claim that one particular event or state of affairs was the cause of another does stand in need of such a warrant. But this may be misleading. Consider two somewhat more complex cases than that outlined above. The first is that of a man who has several quite different reasons for performing a given action. He performs the action; how can he as agent know whether it was the conjoining of all the different reasons that was sufficient for him to perform the action or whether just one of the reasons was by itself alone sufficient or whether the action was overdetermined in the sense that there were two or more reasons, each of which would by itself alone have been sufficient? The problem arises partly because to know that one or other of these possibilities was indeed the case entails knowing the truth of certain unfulfilled conditionals.

A second case worth considering is that of two agents, each with the same reasons for performing a given action; one does not in fact perform it, the other does. Neither agent had what seemed to him a good reason or indeed had any reason for not performing the action in question. Here we can ask what made these reasons or some subset of them productive of action in the one case, but not in the other. In both these types of case we need to distinguish between the agent's having a reason for performing an action (not just in the sense of there being a reason for him to perform the action, but in the stronger sense of his being aware that he has such a reason) and the agent's being actually moved to action by his having such a reason. The importance of this point can be brought out by reconsidering a very familiar example, that of post-hypnotic suggestion.

Under the influence of post-hypnotic suggestion a subject will not only perform the action required by the hypnotist, but will offer apparently good reasons for performing it, while quite unaware of the true cause of the performance. So someone enjoined to walk out of the room might, on being asked why he was doing this, reply with all sincerity that he had felt in need of fresh air or decided to catch a train. In this type of case we would certainly not accept the agent's testimony as to the connection between reason and action, unless we are convinced of the untruth of the counter-factual, 'he would have walked out of the room, if no reason for doing so had occurred to him' and the truth of the counter-factual, 'he would not have walked out of the room, if he had not possessed some such reason for so doing.' The question of the truth or otherwise of the first of these is a matter of the experimentally established facts about post-hypnotic suggestion, and these facts are certainly expressed as causal generalizations. To establish the truth of the relevant generalization would entail establishing the untruth of the second counter-factual. But since to establish the truth of such causal generalizations entails consequences concerning the truth or untruth of generalizations about reasons, the question inevitably arises as to whether *the possession of a given reason* may not be the cause of an action in precisely the same sense in which hypnotic suggestion may be the cause of an action. The chief objection to this view has been that the relation of reason to action is internal and conceptual, not external and contingent, and cannot therefore be a causal relationship; but although nothing could count as a reason unless it stood in an internal relationship to an action, *the agent's possessing a reason* may be a state of affairs identifiable independently of the event which is *the agent's performance of the action.* Thus it does seem as if the possession of a reason by an agent is an item of a suitable type to figure as a cause, or an effect. But if this is so then to ask whether it was the agent's reason that roused him to act is to ask a causal question, the true answer to which depends upon what causal generalizations we have been able to establish. This puts in a different light the question of the agent's authority as to what roused him to act; for it follows from what has been said that this authority is at best prima facie. Far more of course needs to be said on this and related topics; but perhaps the argument so far entitles us to treat with scepticism Winch's claim that understanding in terms of rule-following and causal explanations have mutually exclusive subject-matters.

This has obvious implications for social science, and I wish to suggest some of these in order to provide direction for the rest of my argument. Clearly if the citing of reasons by an agent, with the concomitant appeal to rules, is not necessarily the citing of those reasons which are causally effective, a distinction may be made between those rules which agents in a given society sincerely profess to follow and to which their actions may in fact conform, but which do not in fact direct their actions, and those rules which, whether they profess to follow them or not, do in fact guide their acts by providing them with reasons and motives for acting in one way rather than another. The making of this distinction is essential to the notions of *ideology* and of *false consciousness*, notions which are extremely important to some non-Marxist as well as to Marxist social scientists.

But to allow that these notions could have application is to find oneself at odds with Winch's argument at yet another point. For it seems quite clear that the concept of ideology can find application in a society where the concept is not available to the members of the society, and furthermore that the application of this concept implies that criteria beyond those available in the society may be invoked to judge its rationality; and as such it would fall under Winch's ban as a concept unsuitable for social science. Hence there is a connection between Winch's view that social science is not appropriately concerned with causal generalizations and his view that only the concepts possessed by the members of a given society (or concepts logically tied to those concepts in some way) are to be used in the study of that society. Furthermore, it is important to note that Winch's views on those matters necessarily make his account of rules and their place in social behaviour defective.

3

The examples which Winch gives of rule-following behaviour are very multifarious: games, political thinking, musical composition, the monastic way of life, an anarchist's way of life, are all cited. His only example of non-rule-governed behaviour is 'the pointless behavior of a berserk lunatic' (p. 53), and he asserts roundly 'that all behavior which is meaningful (therefore all specifically human behavior) is *ipso facto* rule-governed'. Winch allows for different kinds of rules (p. 52); what he does not consider is whether the concept of a rule is perhaps being used so widely that quite different senses of *rule-governed* are being confused, let alone whether his account of meaningful behaviour can be plausibly applied to some actions at all.

If I go for a walk, or smoke a cigarette, are my actions rule-governed in the sense in which my actions in playing chess are rule-governed? Winch says that 'the test of whether a man's actions are the application of a rule is . . . whether it makes sense to distinguish between a right and a wrong way of doing things in connection with what he does.' What is the wrong way of going for a walk? And, if there is no wrong way, is my action in any sense rule-governed? To ask these questions is to begin to bring out the difference between those activities which form part of a coherent mode of behaviour and those which do not. It is to begin to see that although many actions must be rule-governed in the sense that the concept of some particular kinds of action may involve reference to a rule, the concept of an action as such does not involve such a reference. But even if we restrict our attention to activities which form part of some coherent larger whole, it is clear that rules may govern activity in quite different ways. This is easily seen if we consider the variety of uses to which social scientists have put the concept of a role and role concepts.

Role concepts are at first sight peculiarly well fitted to find a place in the type of analysis of which Winch would approve. S. F. Nadel wrote that 'the role concept is not an invention of anthropologists or sociologists but is employed by the very people they study', and added that 'it is the existence of names describing classes of people which makes us think of roles.' It would therefore be significant for Winch's thesis if it were the case that role concepts had to be understood in relation to causes, if they were to discharge their analytic and explanatory function.

Consider first a use of the notion of role where causal questions do not arise. In a society such as ours there are a variety of roles which an individual may assume or not as he wills. Some occupational roles provide examples. To live out such a role is to make one's behaviour conform to certain norms. To speak of one's behaviour being governed by the norms is to use a sense of 'governed' close to that according to which the behaviour of a chess player is governed by the rules of chess. We are not disposed to say that the rules of chess or the norms which define the role of a head-waiter constrain the individual who conforms to them. The observation of the rules constitutes the behaviour and what it is; it is not a causal agency.

Contrast with this type of example the inquiry carried on by Erving Goffman in his book *Asylums.* One of Goffman's concerns was to pose a question about mental patients: how far are the characteristic patterns of behaviour which they exhibit determined, not by the nature of the mental disorders from which they suffer, but by the nature of the institutions to which they have been consigned? Goffman concludes that the behaviour of patients is determined to a considerable degree by institutional arrangements which provide a severely limited set of possible roles both for patients and for the doctors and orderlies with whom they have to deal. Thus the behaviour of individual patients of a given type might be explained as the effect of the role arrangements open to a person of his type. In case it is thought that the role structure of mental hospitals only has a causal effect upon the patients because they are *patients* (and the implication might be that they are not therefore rational agents but approach the condition of the exception Winch allows for, that of the berserk lunatic) it is worth noting that Goffman's study of mental hospitals is part of a study of what he calls 'total institutions'. These include monasteries and armed services as well as mental hospitals. A successful terminus to his inquiry would therefore be the foundation of generalizations about the effects upon agents of different types of character of the role structure of such different types of institution.

If Winch were correct, and rule-governed behaviour were not to be understood as causal behaviour, then the contrast could not be drawn between those cases in which the relation of social structure to individuals may be correctly characterized in terms of control or constraint and those in which it may not. Winch's inability to make this contrast adequately in terms of his conceptual scheme is the counterpart to Durkheim's inability to make it adequately in terms of his; and the resemblance of Winch's failure to Durkheim's is illuminating in that Winch's position is, roughly speaking, that of Durkheim turned upside-down. Durkheim in a passage cited by Winch insisted, first, 'that social life should be explained, not by the notions of those who participate in it, but by more profound causes which are unperceived by consciousness' and, secondly, 'that these causes are to be sought mainly in the manner according to which the associated individuals are grouped'.[3] That is, Durkheim supposes, just as Winch does, that an investigation of social reality which uses the concepts available to the members of the society being studied, and an investigation of social reality which utilizes concepts not so available and invokes causal explanations of which the agents themselves are not aware, are mutually exclusive alternatives. But Durkheim supposes, as Winch does not, that the latter alternative is the one to be preferred. Yet his acceptance of the same dichotomy involves him in the same inability to understand the different ways in which social structure may be related to individual action.

Durkheim's concept of *anomie* is the concept of a state in which the constraints and controls exercised by social structure have been loosened and the bonds which delimit and contain individual desire have therefore been at least partially removed. The picture embodied in the Durkheimian concept is thus one according to which the essential function of norms in social life is to restrain and inhibit psychological drives. For Durkheim, rules are an external imposition upon a human nature which can be defined independently of them; for Winch, they are the guidelines of behaviour which, did it not conform to them, could scarcely be human. What is equally odd in both is the way in which rules or norms are characterized as though they were all of a kind. Durkheim is unable to recognize social structure apart from the notions of constraint and control by the structure; Winch's concept of society has no room for these notions.

Just as Winch does not allow for the variety of relationships in which an agent may stand to a rule to which his behaviour conforms, so he does not allow also for the variety of types of deviance from rules which behaviour may exhibit. I quoted Malinowski earlier on the important gap between the rules professed in a society and the behaviour actually exhibited. On this Winch might well comment that his concern is with human behaviour as rule-following, not only with mere professions of rule-following, except in so far as professing to follow rules is itself a human and (for him) *ipso facto* a rule-following activity. Moreover he explicitly allows that 'since understanding something involves understanding its contradictory, someone who, with understanding, performs X must be capable of envisaging the possibility of doing not-X'. He makes this remark in the context of his discussion of predictability; and what he does not allow for in this discussion is that in fact the behaviour of agents may exhibit regularities of a Humean kind and be predictable just as natural events are predictable, even though it can also be characterized and in some cases must also be characterized in terms of following and deviating from certain rules. That this is so makes it possible to speak not only, as Malinowski does in the passage quoted earlier, of mechanisms of deviation, but also of mechanisms of conformity. Of course those who deviate from the accepted rules may have a variety of reasons for so doing, and in so far as they share the same reasons their behaviour will exhibit rule-following regularities. But it may well be that agents have a variety of reasons for their deviance and yet deviate uniformly in certain circumstances, this uniformity being independent of their reasons. Whether in a particular case this is so or not seems to me to be an empirical question and one which it would be well not to attempt to settle *a priori*.

I can put my general point as follows. We can in a given society discover a variety of systematic regularities. There are the systems of rules which agents professedly follow; there are the systems of rules which they actually follow; there are causal regularities exhibited in the correlation of statuses and forms of behaviour, and of one form of behaviour and another, which are not rule-governed at all; there are regularities which are in themselves neither causal nor rule-governed, although dependent for their existence perhaps on regularities of both types, such as the cyclical patterns of development exhibited in some societies; and there are the interrelationships which exist between all these. Winch concentrates on some of these at the expense of the others. In doing so he is perhaps influenced by a peculiarly British tradition in social anthropology and by a focus of attention in recent philosophy.

The anthropological tradition is that centred on the work of Professor E. E. Evans-Pritchard, work which exemplifies the rewards to be gained from understanding a people first of all in their own terms. Winch rightly treats Evans-Pritchard's writing as a paradigm case of a social scientist knowing his own business, but neglects the existence of alternative paradigms.[4] [. . .]

Secondly, in Winch's account the social sciences characterize what they characterize by using action descriptions. In his stress upon these, Winch follows much recent philosophical writing. It is on what people *do* and not what they *are* or *suffer* that he dwells. But social scientists are concerned with the causes and effects of *being unemployed, having kin relations of a particular kind, rates of population change,* and a myriad of conditions of individuals and societies, the descriptions of which have a logical character other than that of action descriptions. None of this appears in Winch's account.

4

The positive value of Winch's book is partly as a corrective to the Durkheimian position which he rightly castigates. But it is more than a corrective because what Winch characterizes as the whole task of the social sciences is in fact their true starting-point. Unless we begin by a characterization of a society in its own terms, we shall be unable to identify the matter that requires explanation. Attention to intentions, motives, and reasons must precede attention to causes; description in terms of the agent's concepts and beliefs must precede description in terms of our concepts and beliefs. The force of this contention can be brought out by considering and expanding what Winch says about Durkheim's *Suicide* (p. 110). Winch invites us to notice the connection between Durkheim's conclusion that the true explanation of suicide is in terms of factors outside the consciousness of the agents themselves such that the reasons of the agents themselves are effectively irrelevant and his initial decision to give the term 'suicide' a meaning quite other than that which it had for those agents. What is he inviting us to notice?

A number of points, I suspect, of which one is a central insight, the others in error. The insight is that Durkheim's particular procedure of giving to 'suicide' a meaning of his own *entails* the irrelevance of the agent's reasons in the explanation of suicide. Durkheim does in fact bring forward independent arguments designed to show that reasons are either irrelevant or inaccessible, and very bad arguments they are. But even if he had not believed himself to have grounds drawn from these arguments, he would have been unable to take reasons into account, given his decision about meaning. Durkheim arbitrarily equates the concept of *suicide* with that of *doing anything that the agent knows will bring about his own death* and thus classifies as suicide both the intended self-destruction of the Prussian or English officer who shoots himself to save the regiment the disgrace of a court martial and the death in battle of such an officer who has courageously headed a charge in such a way that he knows that he will not survive. (I choose these two examples because they both belong to the same category in Durkheim's classification.) Thus he ignores the distinction between *doing X intending that Y shall result* and *doing X knowing that Y will result.* Now clearly if these two are to be assimilated, the roles of deliberation and the relevance of the agent's reasons will disappear from view. For clearly in the former case the character of Y must be central to the reasons the agent has for doing X, but in the latter case the agent may well be doing X either in spite of the character of Y, or not caring one way or the other about the character of Y, or again finding the character of Y desirable, but not desirable enough for him for it to constitute a reason or a motive for doing X. Thus the nature of the reason *must* differ in the two cases, and if the two cases are to have the same explanation the agent's reasons can scarcely figure in that explanation. That is, Durkheim is forced by his initial semantic decision to the conclusion that the agent's reasons are in cases of what agents in the society which he studies would have called suicide (which are included as a subclass of what he calls suicide) *never* causally effective.

But there are two further conclusions which might be thought to, but do not in fact, follow. It does not follow that all such decisions to bring actions under descriptions other than those used by the agents themselves are bound to lead to the same *a priori* obliteration of the explanatory role of reasons; for this obliteration was in Durkheim's case, as I have just shown, a consequence of certain special features of his treatment of the concept of suicide, and not a consequence of any general feature of the procedure of inventing new descriptive terms in social sciences. Secondly, from the fact that explanation in terms of reason ought not to be excluded by any initial decision of the social scientist, it does not follow that such explanation is incompatible with causal explanation. Here my argument in the second section of this essay bears on what Winch says about Weber. Winch says that Weber was confused because he did not realize that 'a context of humanly followed rules . . . cannot be combined with a context of causal laws' without creating logical difficulties, and he is referring specifically to Weber's contention that the manipulation of machinery and the manipulation of his employees by a manufacturer may be understood in the same way, so far as the logic of the explanation is concerned. So Weber wrote, 'that in the one case "events of consciousness" do enter into the causal chain and in the other case do not, makes "logically" not the slightest difference.' I also have an objection to Weber's argument, but it is in effect that Weber's position is too close to Winch's. For Weber supposes that in order to introduce causal explanation he must abandon description of the social situation in terms of actions, roles, and the like. So he proposes speaking not of the workers being paid, but of their being handed pieces of metal. In so doing Weber concedes Winch's point that descriptions in terms of actions, reasons, and all that falls under his term 'events of consciousness' cannot figure in causal explanations without a conceptual mistake being committed. But in this surely he is wrong.

Compare two situations: first, one in which managers minimize shop-floor trade-union activity in a factory by concentrating opportunities of extra overtime and of earning bonuses in those parts of the factory where such activity shows signs of flourishing; and then one in which managers similarly minimize trade-union activity by a process of continual transfers between one part of the factory and another or between different factories. In both cases it may be possible to explain the low level of trade-union activity causally by reference to the managers' policies; but in the former case the reasons which the workers have for pursuing overtime and bonuses can find a place in the explanation without it losing its causal character and in both cases a necessary condition of the managers' actions being causally effective may well be that the workers in question remain ignorant of the policy behind the actions. The causal character of the explanations can be brought out by considering how generalizations might be formulated in which certain behaviour of the managers can supply either the necessary or the sufficient condition or both for the behaviour of the workers. But in such a formulation one important fact will emerge; namely, that true causal explanations cannot be formulated—where actions are concerned—unless intentions, motives, and reasons are taken into account. That is, it is not only the case as I have argued in the second section of this essay that a true explanation in terms of reasons must entail some account of the causal background; it is also true that a causal account of action will require a corresponding account of the intentions, motives, and reasons involved. It is this latter point that Durkheim misses and Winch stresses. In the light of this it is worth returning to one aspect of the explanation of suicide.

In modern cities more than one study has shown a correlation between the suicide rate for different parts of the city and the proportion of the population living an isolated, single-room apartment existence. What are the conditions which must be satisfied if such a correlation is to begin to play a part in explaining why suicide is committed? First it must be shown that at least a certain proportion of the individuals who commit suicide live in such isolated conditions; otherwise (unless, for example, it was the landlord of such apartments who committed suicide) we should find the correlation of explanatory assistance only in so far as it pointed us toward a common explanation of the two rates. But suppose that we do find that it is the individuals who live in such isolated conditions who are more likely to commit suicide. We still have to ask whether it is the pressure on the emotions of the isolation itself, or whether it is the insolubility of certain other problems in conditions of isolation which leads to suicide. Unless such questions about motives and reasons are answered, the causal generalization 'isolated living of a certain kind tends to lead to acts of suicide' is not so much an explanation in itself as an additional fact to be explained, even though it is a perfectly sound generalization and even though to learn its truth might be to learn how the suicide rate could be increased or decreased in large cities by changing our housing policies.

Now we cannot raise the questions about motives and reasons, the answers to which would explain why isolation has the effect which it has, unless we first of all understand the acts of suicide in terms of the intentions of the agents and therefore in terms of their own action descriptions. Thus Winch's starting-point proves to be the correct one, provided it is a starting-point. We could not even formulate our initial causal generalization about isolation and suicide, in such a way that the necessary question about motives and reasons could be raised later, unless the expression 'suicide' and kindred expressions which figured in our causal generalizations possessed the same meaning as they did for the agents who committed the acts. We can understand very clearly why Winch's starting-point must be substantially correct if we remember how he compares sociological understanding with understanding a language (p. 115). The crude notion that one can first learn a language and then secondly and separately go on to understand the social life of those who speak it can only flourish where the languages studied are those of peoples whose social life is so largely the same as our own that we do not notice the understanding of social life embodied in our grasp of the language; but attempts to learn the alien language of an alien culture soon dispose of it. Yet the understanding that we thus acquire, although a necessary preliminary, is only a preliminary. It would be equally harmful if Winch's attempt to make of this preliminary the substance of social science were to convince, or if a proper understanding of the need to go further were not to allow for the truth in his arguments.

5

These dangers are likely to be especially inhibiting in the present state of parts of social science. Two important essays by anthropologists, Leach's *Rethinking Anthropology* and Goldschmidt's *Comparative Functionalism*[5] . . . focus upon problems to which adherence to Winch's conclusions would preclude any solution. At the outset I contrasted Winch with Malinowski, but this was in respects in which most contemporary social scientists would take the standpoint quoted from Malinowski for granted. We owe also to Malinowski, however, the tradition of what Goldschmidt calls 'the detailed internal analysis of individual cultures' with the further comparison of institutional arrangements in different societies resting on such analyses. This tradition has been criticized by both Leach and Goldschmidt; the latter believes that because institutions are defined by each culture in its own terms, it is not at the level of institutions that cross-cultural analyses will be fruitful. The former has recommended us to search for recurrent topological patterns in, for example, kinship arrangements, with the same aim of breaking free from institutional ethnocentrism. I think that both Leach and Goldschmidt are going to prove to be seminal writers on this point and it is clear that their arguments are incompatible with Winch's. It would therefore be an important lacuna in this essay if I did not open up directly the question of the bearing of Winch's arguments on this topic.

Winch argues, consistently with his rejection of any place for causal laws in social science, that comparison between different cases is not dependent on any grasp of theoretical generalizations (pp. 134–6), and he sets limits to any possible comparison by his insistence that each set of activities must be understood solely in its own terms. In so doing he must necessarily reject for example all those various theories which insist that religions of quite different kinds express unacknowledged needs of the same kind. (No such theory needs to be committed to the view that religions are and do no more than this.) Indeed in his discussion of Pareto (pp. 104–11) he appears to make such a rejection explicit by the generality of the grounds on which he rejects Pareto's comparison of Christian baptism with pagan rites. I hold no brief for the theory of residues and derivations. But when Winch insists that each religious rite must be understood in its own terms to the exclusion of any generalization about religion or that each social system must be so understood to the exclusion of any generalization about status and prestige, he must be pressed to make his grounds precise. In his later discussion of Evans-Pritchard, one aspect of Winch's views becomes clear; namely, the implication of his remark that 'criteria of logic are not a direct gift of God, but arise out of, and are only intelligible in the context of, ways of living or modes of social life' (p. 100). Winch's one substantial point of difference with Evans-Pritchard in his treatment of witchcraft among the Azande is that he thinks it impossible to ask whether the Zande beliefs about witches are true.[6] We can ask from within the Zande system of beliefs if there are witches and will receive the answer 'Yes'. We can ask from within the system of beliefs of modern science if there are witches and will receive the answer 'No'. But we cannot ask which system of beliefs is the superior in respect of rationality and truth; for this would be to invoke criteria which can be understood independently of any particular way of life, and in Winch's view there are no such criteria.

This represents a far more extreme view of the difficulties of cultural comparison than Goldschmidt, for example, advances. Both its extreme character and its error can be understood by considering two arguments against it. The first is to the effect that in Winch's view certain actual historical transitions are made unintelligible; I refer to those transitions from one system of beliefs to another which are necessarily characterized by raising questions of the kind that Winch rejects. In seventeenth-century Scotland, for example, the question could not but be raised, 'but are there witches?' If Winch asks, from within what way of social life, under what system of belief was this question asked, the only answer is that it was asked by men who confronted alternative systems and were able to draw out of what confronted them independent criteria of judgement. Many Africans today are in the same situation.

This type of argument is of course necessarily inconclusive; any historical counter-example to Winch's thesis will be open to questions of interpretation that will make it less than decisive. But there is another important argument. Consider the statement made by some Zande theorist or by King James VI and I, 'there are witches' and the statement made by some modern sceptic, 'there are no witches.' Unless one of these statements denies what the other asserts, the negation of the sentence expressing the former could not be a correct translation of the sentence expressing the latter. Thus if we could not deny from our own standpoint and in our own language what the Azande or King James assert in theirs, we should be unable to translate their expression into our language. Cultural idiosyncracy would have entailed linguistic idiosyncracy and cross-cultural comparison would have been rendered logically impossible. But of course translation is not impossible.

Yet if we treat seriously, not what I take to be Winch's mistaken thesis that we cannot go beyond a society's own self-description, but what I take to be his true thesis that we must not do this except and until we have grasped the criteria embodied in that self-description, then we shall have to conclude that the contingently different conceptual schemes and institutional arrangements of different societies make translation difficult to the point at which attempts at cross-cultural generalization too often become little more than a construction of lists. Goldschmidt and Leach have both pointed out how the building up of typologies and classificatory schemes becomes empty and purposeless unless we have a theory which gives point and criteria to our classificatory activities. Both have also pointed out how, if we compare for example marital institutions in different cultures, our definition of 'marriage' will either be drawn from one culture in terms of whose concepts other cultures will be described or rather misdescribed, or else will be so neutral, bare, and empty as to be valueless.[7] That is, the understanding of a people in terms of their own concepts and beliefs does in fact tend to preclude understanding them in any other term. To this extent Winch is vindicated. But an opposite moral to his can be drawn. We may conclude not that we ought not to generalize but that such generalization must move at another level. Goldschmidt argues for the recommendation: do not ask what an institution means for the agents themselves, ask what necessary needs and purposes it serves. He argues for this not because he looks for functionalist explanations of a Malinowskian kind, but because he believes that different institutions, embodying different conceptual schemes, may be illuminatingly seen as serving the same social necessities. To carry the argument further would be to raise questions that are not and cannot be raised within the framework of Winch's book. It is because I believe writers such as Goldschmidt are correct in saying that one must transcend such a framework that I believe also that Winch's book deserves close critical attention.

Notes

1   Bronislaw Malinowski, *The Sexual Life of Savages in North-Western Melanesia* (Harcourt, Brace & Jovanovich, New York, 1932; Routledge & Kegan Paul, London, 1932) pp. 425–9.
2   Malinowski, 1932, pp. 428–9.
3   Durkheim, review of A. Labriola's *Essays on Historical Materialism* (Giard & Brière, Paris, n.d.) in *Revue Philosophique*, xliv, 1897, pp. 645–51.
4   In 'Understanding a Primitive Society', *American Philosophical Quarterly*, i:4, 1964, pp. 307–24.
5   Walter Goldschmidt, *Comparative Functionalism* (University of California Press, Berkeley, 1966).
6   *American Philosophical Quarterly,* i:4, 1964, p. 309.
7   See Kathleen Gough, 'The Nayars and the Definition of Marriage', in P. B. Hammond (ed) *Cultural and Social Anthropology* (Macmillan, New York, 1964); E. R. Leach, 'Polyandry, Inheritance and the Definition of Marriage with Particular Reference to Sinhalese Customary Law', in *Rethinking Anthropology* (Athlone Press, London, 1966); and Goldschmidt, 1966, pp. 17–26.

21 Paradigms, Tacit Knowledge and Incommensurability
Thomas S. Kuhn

In his book The Structure of Scientific Revolutions, *first published in 1962, Kuhn proposed a new interpretation of the cognitive authority of science. He argued that this authority was vested not in the rules which govern scientific inquiry, but in the constitution of that scientific community which recognizes, ratifies and validates the results of inquiry. He supported his proposal with a general account of the history of science, drawing attention to specific moments when scientific results were obtained, developed and abandoned. His key notion is that of the paradigm. It is central to his whole view of science, and it is elastic. Kuhn introduced paradigms as 'universally recognized scientific achievements that for a time provide model problems and solutions to a community of practitioners', though he also employed the term in other, connected senses.*

The book provides a description of how change occurs in systems of scientific belief. In 'normal science' past achievement is used as a model or guide to the formulation and solution of problems; progress thus takes place, as it were, within the established paradigm. At moments of 'scientific revolution' however there is a 'paradigm shift' as one set of models is replaced by another, following a period of 'communication breakdown' within the practice of science.

Reprinted below are extracts from the 36-page 'Postscript—1969' appended to the second (1970) edition of The Structure of Scientific Revolutions. *At the outset Kuhn acknowledges that several difficulties of his original text 'cluster around the concept of a paradigm'. These he is concerned to disentangle. His discussion proceeds from the observation that:*

> *. . . in much of the book the term 'paradigm' is used in two different senses. On the one hand, it stands for the entire constellation of beliefs, values, techniques, and so on shared by the members of a given community. On the other, it denotes one sort of element in that constellation, the concrete puzzle-solutions which, employed as models or exemplars, can replace explicit rules as a basis for the solution of the remaining puzzles of normal science.*

The first sense of the term, which Kuhn calls sociological, refers to the 'disciplinary matrix' of a community of specialists. In the second sense paradigms are 'shared examples'.

Regarding the latter Kuhn asks how a student of science learns to 'design the appropriate version' of certain law-like symbolic generalizations (or formulae) in order to interrelate a certain set of mechanisms or processes in any one of a variety of physical situations. His answer is that this entails perceiving an analogy between different problem situations; the formula 'has functioned as a tool, informing the student what similarities to look for, signaling the gestalt in which the situation is to be seen' (cf Hanson's discussion of 'the conceptual organisation of the visual field' in text 8). To acquire 'the same gestalt as other members of his specialists' group' is to assimilate 'a time-tested and group-licensed way of seeing'. Yet Kuhn asserts that the generalizations can 'begin to function' only once something relevant has been learned 'about the situations that nature does and does not present'.

> *That sort of learning is not acquired by exclusively verbal means. Rather it comes as one is given words together with concrete examples of how they function in use; nature and words are learned together . . . What results . . . is 'tacit knowledge' which is learned by doing science rather than by acquiring rules for doing it.*

From a philosophical point of view, Kuhn's text raises issues relevant to concepts of seeing (that), speaking (of) and sharing within the context of an interest in knowledge. From a methodological point of view his work is of most interest in its concentration on the means by which a shared practice is originated, sustained and criticized. His emphasis on science as shared material practice runs counter to the prevailing view (as represented, for instance, by Karl Popper) of science as shared 'thought'. As historiography Kuhn's text is catastrophist in nature: change is conceived of as dramatic, radical and discontinuous. His sociology is limited to the internal dynamics of community, which is effectively perceived in a state of insulation. By contrast with his view of scientific change as revolutionary, this identification of paradigms in terms of the procedures of an isolated community implies a relatively conservative image of science and the scientist.

Various questions may be raised by testing Kuhn's ideas for their application to the practice, history and criticism of art. Is the development of art best characterized in terms of the continuity of certain autonomous values (as it is within the Modernist critical tradition), or rather in terms of a series of catastrophic shifts which change the meaning and practice of 'art' itself? Can we isolate an 'art community'—either of practitioners or, say, of connoisseurs, or of both conjoined—in terms of a shared 'disciplinary matrix', composed of 'symbolic generalizations', 'metaphysical paradigms', 'values' and 'exemplars'? How relevant is Kuhn's account of the 'communication breakdown' preceding a paradigm shift to the conditions of change in art-critical and art-theoretical discourse? According to Kuhn, one symptom of such a breakdown is that members of scientific communities 'may suddenly find themselves responding to the same stimulus with incompatible descriptions and generalizations. . . . Part of the difference is prior to the application of the languages in which it is nevertheless reflected.' This at least suggests one way in which we might compare conditions and accounts of scientific and artistic change. Another comparison might be made in terms of the concept of 'tacit knowledge', which Kuhn derives from

Michael Polanyi's Personal Knowledge *(1958), where it receives its most thorough explication. It seems entirely appropriate to apply to the practice of art the idea of development of tacit or intuitive knowledge through the ways in which 'nature and words are learned together' in the context of exemplars and symbolic generalizations.*

Source: The Structure of Scientific Revolutions (2nd edition, Chicago University Press, 1970), 'Postscript – 1969', sections 2, 4, 5, 8, 7, pp. 181–187, 191–198, 200–204, 208–210. This material has been edited and footnotes have been deleted. Reprinted by permission of the University of Chicago Press. © 1962, 1970 by The University of Chicago.

[. . .]

2. Paradigms as the Constellation of Group Commitments

Turn now to paradigms and ask what they can possibly be. My original text leaves no more obscure or important question. One sympathetic reader, who shares my conviction that 'paradigm' names the central philosophical elements of the book, prepared a partial analytic index and concluded that the term is used in at least twenty-two different ways. Most of those differences are, I now think, due to stylistic inconsistencies (eg Newton's Laws are sometimes a paradigm, sometimes parts of a paradigm, and sometimes paradigmatic), and they can be eliminated with relative ease. But, with that editorial work done, two very different usages of the term would remain, and they require separation. The more global use is the subject of this subsection; the other will be considered in the next.

Having isolated a particular community of specialists . . . one may usefully ask: What do its members share that accounts for the relative fulness of their professional communication and the relative unanimity of their professional judgments? To that question my original text licenses the answer, a paradigm or set of paradigms. But for this use, unlike the one to be discussed below, the term is inappropriate. Scientists themselves would say they share a theory or set of theories, and I shall be glad if the term can ultimately be recaptured for this use. As currently used in philosophy of science, however, 'theory' connotes a structure far more limited in nature and scope than the one required here. Until the term can be freed from its current implications, it will avoid confusion to adopt another. For present purposes I suggest 'disciplinary matrix': 'disciplinary' because it refers to the common possession of the practitioners of a particular discipline; 'matrix' because it is composed of ordered elements of various sorts, each requiring further specification. All or most of the objects of group commitment that my original text makes paradigms, parts of paradigms, or paradigmatic are constituents of the disciplinary matrix, and as such they form a whole and function together. They are, however, no longer to be discussed as though they were all of a piece. I shall not here attempt an exhaustive list, but noting the main sorts of components of a disciplinary matrix will both clarify the nature of my present approach and simultaneously prepare for my next main point.

One important sort of component I shall label 'symbolic generalizations', having in mind those expressions, deployed without question or dissent by group members, which can readily be cast in a logical form like $(x)(y)(z)\phi(x,y,z)$. They are the formal or the readily formalizable components of the disciplinary matrix. Sometimes they are found already in symbolic form: $f = ma$ or $I = V/R$. Others are ordinarily expressed in words: 'elements combine in constant proportion by weight,' or 'action equals reaction.' If it were not for the general acceptance of expressions like these, there would be no points at which group members could attach the powerful techniques of logical and mathematical manipulation in their puzzle-solving enterprise. Though the example of taxonomy suggests that normal science can proceed with few such expressions, the power of a science seems quite generally to increase with the number of symbolic generalizations its practitioners have at their disposal.

These generalizations look like laws of nature, but their function for group members is not often that alone. Sometimes it is: for example the Joule-Lenz Law, $H = RI^2$. When that law was discovered, community members already knew what H, R, and I stood for, and these generalizations simply told them something about the behaviour of heat, current, and resistance that they had not known before. But more often, as discussion earlier in the book indicates, symbolic generalizations simultaneously serve a second function, one that is ordinarily sharply separated in analyses by philosophers of science. Like $f = ma$ or $I = V/R$, they function in part as laws but also in part as definitions of some of the symbols they deploy. Furthermore, the balance between their inseparable legislative and definitional force shifts over time. In another context these points would repay detailed analysis, for the nature of the commitment to a law is very different from that of commitment to a definition. Laws are often corrigible piecemeal, but definitions, being tautologies, are not. For example, part of what the acceptance of Ohm's Law demanded was a redefinition of both 'current' and 'resistance'; if those terms had continued to mean what they had meant before, Ohm's Law could not have been right; that is why it was so strenuously opposed as, say, the Joule-Lenz Law was not. Probably that situation is typical. I currently suspect that all revolutions involve, among other things, the abandonment of generalizations the force of which had previously been in some part that of tautologies. Did Einstein show that simultaneity was relative or did he alter the notion of simultaneity itself? Were those who heard paradox in the phrase 'relativity of simultaneity' simply wrong?

Consider next a second type of component of the disciplinary matrix, one about which a good deal has been said in my original text under such rubrics as 'metaphysical paradigms' or 'the metaphysical parts of paradigms'. I have in mind shared commitments to such beliefs as: heat is the kinetic energy of the constituent parts of bodies; all perceptible phenomena are due to the interaction of qualitatively neutral atoms in the void, or, alternatively, to matter and force, or to fields. Rewriting the book now I would describe such commitments as beliefs in particular models, and I would expand the category models to include also the relatively heuristic variety: the electric circuit may be regarded as a steady-state hydrodynamic system; the molecules of a gas behave like tiny elastic billiard balls in random motion. Though the strength of group commitment varies, with non-trivial consequences, along the spectrum from heuristic to ontological models, all models have similar functions. Among other things they supply the group with preferred or permissible analogies and metaphors. By doing so they help to determine what will be accepted as an explanation and as a puzzle-solution; conversely, they assist in the determination of the roster of unsolved puzzles and in the evaluation of the importance of each. Note, however, that the members of scientific communities may not have to share even heuristic models, though they usually do so. I have already pointed out that membership in the community of chemists during the first half of the nineteenth century did not demand a belief in atoms.

A third sort of element in the disciplinary matrix I shall here describe as values. Usually they are more widely shared among different communities than either symbolic generalizations or models, and they do much to provide a sense of community to natural scientists as a whole. Though they function at all times, their particular importance emerges when the members of a particular community must identify crisis or, later, choose between incompatible ways of practicing their discipline. Probably the most deeply held values concern predictions: they should be accurate; quantitative predictions are preferable to qualitative ones; whatever the margin of permissible error, it should be consistently satisfied in a given field; and so on. There are also, however, values to be used in judging whole theories: they must, first and foremost, permit puzzle-formulation and solution; where possible they should be simple, self-consistent, and plausible, compatible, that is, with other theories currently deployed ... Other sorts of values exist as well—for example, science should (or need not) be socially useful—but the preceding should indicate what I have in mind.

One aspect of shared values does, however, require particular mention. To a greater extent than other sorts of components of the disciplinary matrix, values may be shared by men who differ in their application. Judgments of accuracy are relatively, though not entirely, stable from one time to another and from one member to another in a particular group. But judgments of simplicity, consistency, plausibility, and so on often vary greatly from individual to individual. What was for Einstein an insupportable inconsistency in the old quantum theory, one that rendered the pursuit of normal science impossible, was for Bohr and others a difficulty that could be expected to work itself out by normal means. Even more important, in those situations where values must be applied, different values, taken alone, would often dictate different choices. One theory may be more accurate but less consistent or plausible than another; again the old quantum theory provides an example. In short, though values are widely shared by scientists and though commitment to them is both deep and constitutive of science, the application of values is sometimes considerably affected by the features of individual personality and biography that differentiate the members of the group.

... Because I insist that what scientists share is not sufficient to command uniform assent about such matters as the choice between competing theories or the distinction between an ordinary anomaly and a crisis-provoking one, I am occasionally accused of glorifying subjectivity and even irrationality. But that reaction ignores two characteristics displayed by value judgments in any field. First, shared values can be important determinants of group behavior even though the members of the group do not all apply them in the same way. (If that were not the case, there would be no *special* philosophic problems about value theory or aesthetics.) Men did not all paint alike during the periods when representation was a primary value, but the developmental pattern of the plastic arts changed drastically when that value was abandoned. Imagine what would happen in the sciences if consistency ceased to be a primary value. Second, individual variability in the application of shared values may serve functions essential to science. The points at which values must be applied are invariably also those at which risks must be taken. Most anomalies are resolved by normal means; most proposals for new theories do prove to be wrong. If all members of a community responded to each anomaly as a source of crisis or embraced each new theory advanced by a colleague, science would cease. If, on the other hand, no one reacted to anomalies or to brand-new theories in high-risk ways, there would be few or no revolutions. In matters like these the resort to shared values rather than to shared rules governing individual choice may be the community's way of distributing risk and assuring the long-term success of its enterprise.

Turn now to a fourth sort of element in the disciplinary matrix, not the only other kind but the last I shall discuss here. For it the term 'paradigm' would be entirely appropriate, both philologically and autobiographically; this is the component of a group's shared commitments which first led me to the choice of that word. Because the term has assumed a life of its own, however, I shall here substitute 'exemplars'. By it I mean, initially, the concrete problem-solutions that students encounter from the start of their scientific education, whether in laboratories, on examinations, or at the ends of chapters in science texts. To these shared examples should, however, be added at least some of the technical problem-solutions found in the periodical literature that scientists encounter during their post-educational research careers and that also show them by example how their job is to be done. More than other sorts of components of the disciplinary matrix, differences between sets of exemplars provide the community fine-structure of science. All physicists, for example, begin by learning the same exemplars: problems such as the inclined plane, the conical pendulum, and Keplerian orbits; instruments such as the vernier, the calorimeter, and the Wheatstone bridge. As their training develops, however, the symbolic generalizations they share are increasingly illustrated by different exemplars. Though both solid-state and field-theoretic physicists share the Schrödinger equation, only its more elementary applications are common to both groups. [. . .]

4. Tacit Knowledge and Intuition

. . . Reference to tacit knowledge and the concurrent rejection of rules isolates another problem that has bothered many of my critics and seemed to provide a basis for charges of subjectivity and irrationality. Some readers have felt that I was trying to make science rest on unanalyzable individual intuitions rather than on logic and law. But that interpretation goes astray in two essential respects. First, if I am talking at all about intuitions, they are not individual. Rather they are the tested and shared possessions of the members of a successful group, and the novice acquires them through training as a part of his preparation for group-membership. Second, they are not in principle unanalyzable. On the contrary, I am currently experimenting with a computer program designed to investigate their properties at an elementary level.

About that program I shall have nothing to say here, but even mention of it should make my most essential point. When I speak of knowledge embedded in shared exemplars, I am not referring to a mode of knowing that is less systematic or less analyzable than knowledge embedded in rules, laws, or criteria of identification. Instead I have in mind a manner of knowing which is misconstrued if reconstructed in terms of rules that are first abstracted from exemplars and thereafter function in their stead. Or, to put the same point differently, when I speak of acquiring from exemplars the ability to recognize a given situation as like some and unlike others that one has seen before, I am not suggesting a process that is not potentially fully explicable in terms of neuro-cerebral mechanism. Instead I am claiming that the explication will not, by its nature, answer the question, 'Similar with respect to what?' That question is a request for a rule, in this case for the criteria by which particular situations are grouped into similarity sets, and I am arguing that the temptation to seek criteria (or at least a full set) should be resisted in this case. It is not, however, system but a particular sort of system that I am opposing.

To give that point substance, I must briefly digress. What follows seems obvious to me now, but the constant recourse in my original text to phrases like 'the world changes' suggests that it has not always been so. If two people stand at the same place and gaze in the same direction, we must, under pain of solipsism, conclude that they receive closely similar stimuli. (If both could put their eyes at the same place, the stimuli would be identical.) But people do not see stimuli; our knowledge of them is highly theoretical and abstract. Instead they have sensations, and we are under no compulsion to suppose that the sensations of our two viewers are the same. (Sceptics might remember that color blindness was nowhere noticed until John Dalton's description of it in 1794.) On the contrary, much neural processing takes place between the receipt of a stimulus and the awareness of a sensation. Among the few things that we know about it with assurance are: that very different stimuli can produce the same sensations; that the same stimulus can produce very different sensations; and, finally, that the route from stimulus to sensation is in part conditioned by education. Individuals raised in different societies behave on some occasions as though they saw different things. If we were not tempted to identify stimuli one-to-one with sensations, we might recognize that they actually do so.

Notice now that two groups, the members of which have systematically different sensations on receipt of the same stimuli, do *in some sense* live in different worlds. We posit the existence of stimuli to explain our perceptions of the world, and we posit their immutability to avoid both individual and social solipsism. About neither posit have I the slightest reservation. But our world is populated in the first instance not by stimuli but by the objects of our sensations, and these need not be the same, individual to individual or group to group. To the extent, of course, that individuals belong to the same group and thus share education, language, experience, and culture, we have good reason to suppose that their sensations are the same. How else are we to understand the fulness of their communication and the communality of their behavioral responses to their environment? They must see things, process stimuli in much the same ways. But where the differentiation and specialization of groups begins, we have no similar evidence for the immutability of sensation. Mere parochialism, I suspect, makes us suppose that the route from stimuli to sensation is the same for the members of all groups.

Returning now to exemplars and rules, what I have been trying to suggest, in however preliminary a fashion, is this. One of the fundamental techniques by which the members of a group, whether an entire culture or a specialists' sub-community within it, learn to see the same things when confronted with the same stimuli is by being shown examples of situations that their predecessors in the group have already learned to see as like each other and as different from other sorts of situations. These similar situations may be successive sensory presentations of the same individual—say of mother, who is ultimately recognized on sight as what she is and as different from father or sister. They may be presentations of the members of natural families, say of swans on the one hand and of geese on the other. Or they may, for the members of more specialized groups, be examples of the Newtonian situation, of situations, that is, that are alike in being subject to a version of the symbolic form $f = ma$ and that are different from those situations to which, for example, the law-sketches of optics apply.

Grant for the moment that something of this sort does occur. Ought we say that what has been acquired from exemplars is rules and the ability to apply them? That description is tempting because our seeing a situation as like ones we have encountered before must be the result of neural processing, fully governed by physical and chemical laws. In this sense, once we have learned to do it, recognition of similarity must be as fully systematic as the beating of our hearts. But that very parallel suggests that recognition may also be involuntary, a process over which we have no control. If it is, then we may not properly conceive it as something we manage by applying rules and criteria. To speak of it in those terms implies that we have access to alternatives, that we might, for example, have disobeyed a rule, or misapplied a criterion, or experimented with some other way of seeing. Those, I take it, are just the sorts of things we cannot do.

Or, more precisely, those are things we cannot do until after we have had a sensation, perceived something. Then we do often seek criteria and put them to use. Then we may engage in interpretation, a deliberative process by which we choose among alternatives as we do not in perception itself. Perhaps, for example, something is odd about what we have seen . . . Turning a corner we see mother entering a downtown store at a time we had thought she was home. Contemplating what we have seen we suddenly exclaim, 'That wasn't mother, for she has red hair!' Entering the store we see the woman again and cannot understand how she could have been taken for mother. Or, perhaps we see the tail feathers of a water-fowl feeding from the bottom of a shallow pool. Is it a swan or a goose? We contemplate what we have seen, mentally comparing the tail feathers with those of swans and geese we have seen before. Or, perhaps, being proto-scientists, we simply want to know some general characteristic (the whiteness of swans, for example) of the members of a natural family we can already recognize with ease. Again, we contemplate what we have previously perceived, searching for what the members of the given family have in common.

These are all deliberative processes, and in them we do seek and deploy criteria and rules. We try, that is, to interpret sensations already at hand, to analyze what is for us the given. However we do that, the processes involved must ultimately be neural, and they are therefore governed by the same *physico-chemical* laws that govern perception on the one hand and the beating of our hearts on the other. But the fact that the system obeys the same laws in all three cases provides no reason to suppose that our neural apparatus is programmed to operate the same way in interpretation as in perception or in either as in the beating of our hearts. What I have been opposing in this book is therefore the attempt, traditional since Descartes but not before, to analyze perception as an interpretive process, as an unconscious version of what we do after we have perceived.

What makes the integrity of perception worth emphasizing is, of course, that so much past experience is embodied in the neural apparatus that transforms stimuli to sensations. An appropriately programmed perceptual mechanism has survival value. To say that the members of different groups may have different perceptions when confronted with the same stimuli is not to imply that they may have just any perceptions at all. In many environments a group that could not tell wolves from dogs could not endure. Nor would a group of nuclear physicists today survive as scientists if unable to recognize the tracks of alpha particles and electrons. It is just because so very few ways of seeing will do that the ones that have withstood the tests of group use are worth transmitting from generation to generation. Equally, it is because they have been selected for their success over historic time that we must speak of the experience and knowledge of nature embedded in the stimulus-to-sensation route.

Perhaps 'knowledge' is the wrong word, but there are reasons for employing it. What is built into the neural process that transforms stimuli to sensations has the following characteristics: it has been transmitted through education; it has, by trial, been found more effective than its historical competitors in a group's current environment; and, finally, it is subject to change both through further education and through the discovery of misfits with the environment. Those are characteristics of knowledge, and they explain why I use the term. But it is strange usage, for one other characteristic is missing. We have no direct access to what it is we know, no rules or generalizations with which to express this knowledge. Rules which could supply that access would refer to stimuli not sensations, and stimuli we can know only through elaborate theory. In its absence, the knowledge embedded in the stimulus-to-sensation route remains tacit.

Though it is obviously preliminary and need not be correct in all details, what has just been said about sensation is meant literally. At the very least it is a hypothesis about vision which should be subject to experimental investigation though probably not to direct check. But talk like this of seeing and sensation here also serves metaphorical functions . . . We do not *see* electrons, but rather their tracks or else bubbles of vapor in a cloud chamber. We do not *see* electric currents at all, but rather the needle of an ammeter or galvanometer. Yet in the preceding pages . . . I have repeatedly acted as though we did perceive theoretical entities like currents, electrons, and fields, as though we learned to do so from examination of exemplars, and as though in these cases too it would be wrong to replace talk of seeing with talk of criteria and interpretation. The metaphor that transfers 'seeing' to contexts like these is scarcely a sufficient basis for such claims. In the long run it will need to be eliminated in favor of a more literal mode of discourse.

The computer program referred to above begins to suggest ways in which that may be done, but neither available space nor the extent of my present understanding permits my eliminating the metaphor here. Instead I shall try briefly to bulwark it. Seeing water droplets or a needle against a numerical scale is a primitive perceptual experience for the man unacquainted with cloud chambers and ammeters. It thus requires contemplation, analysis, and interpretation (or else the intervention of external authority) before conclusions can be reached about electrons or currents. But the position of the man who has learned about these instruments and had much exemplary experience with them is very different, and there are corresponding differences in the way he processes the stimuli that reach him from them. Regarding the vapor in his breath on a cold winter afternoon, his sensation may be the same as that of a layman, but viewing a cloud chamber he sees (here literally) not droplets but the tracks of electrons, alpha particles, and so on. Those tracks are, if you will, criteria that he interprets as indices of the presence of the corresponding particles, but that route is both shorter and different from the one taken by the man who interprets droplets.

Or consider the scientist inspecting an ammeter to determine the number against which the needle has settled. His sensation probably is the same as the layman's, particularly if the latter has read other sorts of meters before. But he has seen the meter (again often literally) in the context of the entire circuit, and he knows something about its internal structure. For him the needle's position is a criterion, but only of *the value* of the current. To interpret it he need determine only on which scale the meter is to be read. For the layman, on the other hand, the needle's position is not a criterion of anything except itself. To interpret it, he must examine the whole layout of wires, internal and external, experiment with batteries and magnets, and so on. In the metaphorical no less than in the literal use of 'seeing', interpretation begins where perception ends. The two processes are not the same, and what perception leaves for interpretation to complete depends drastically on the nature and amount of prior experience and training.

5. Exemplars, Incommensurability, and Revolutions

[. . .] To understand why science develops as it does, one need not unravel the details of biography and personality that lead each individual to a particular choice, though that topic has vast fascination. What one must understand, however, is the manner in which a particular set of shared values interacts with the particular experiences shared by a community of specialists to ensure that most members of the group will ultimately find one set of arguments rather than another decisive.

That process is persuasion, but it presents a deeper problem. Two men who perceive the same situation differently but nevertheless employ the same vocabulary in its discussion must be using words differently. They speak, that is, from what I have called incommensurable viewpoints. How can they even hope to talk together much less to be persuasive. Even a preliminary answer to that question demands further specification of the nature of the difficulty. I suppose that, at least in part, it takes the following form.

The practice of normal science depends on the ability, acquired from exemplars, to group objects and situations into similarity sets which are primitive in the sense that the grouping is done without an answer to the question, 'Similar with respect to what?' One central aspect of any revolution is, then, that some of the similarity relations change. Objects that were grouped in the same set before are grouped in different ones afterward and vice versa. Think of the sun, moon, Mars, and earth before and after Copernicus; of free fall, pendular, and planetary motion before and after Galileo; or of salts, alloys, and a sulphur–iron filing mix before and after Dalton. Since most objects within even the altered sets continue to be grouped together, the names of the sets are usually preserved. Nevertheless, the transfer of a subset is ordinarily part of a critical change in the network of interrelations among them. Transferring the metals from the set of compounds to the set of elements played an essential role in the emergence of a new theory of combustion, of acidity, and of physical and chemical combination. In short order those changes had spread through all of chemistry. Not surprisingly, therefore, when such redistributions occur, two men whose discourse had previously proceeded with apparently full understanding may suddenly find themselves responding to the same stimulus with incompatible descriptions and generalizations. Those difficulties will not be felt in all areas of even their scientific discourse, but they will arise and will then cluster most densely about the phenomena upon which the choice of theory most centrally depends.

Such problems, though they first become evident in communication, are not merely linguistic, and they cannot be resolved simply by stipulating the definitions of troublesome terms. Because the words about which difficulties cluster have been learned in part from direct application to exemplars, the participants in a communication breakdown cannot say, 'I use the word "element" (or "mixture", or "planet", or "unconstrained motion") in ways determined by the following criteria.' They cannot, that is, resort to a neutral language which both use in the same way and which is adequate to the statement of both their theories or even of both those theories' empirical consequences. Part of the difference is prior to the application of the languages in which it is nevertheless reflected.

The men who experience such communication breakdowns must, however, have some recourse. The stimuli that impinge upon them are the same. So is their general neural apparatus, however differently programmed. Furthermore, except in a small, if all-important, area of experience even their neural programming must be very nearly the same, for they share a history, except the immediate past. As a result, both their everyday and most of their scientific world and language are shared. Given that much in common, they should be able to find out a great deal about how they differ. The techniques required are not, however, either straightforward, or comfortable, or parts of the scientist's normal arsenal. Scientists rarely recognize them for quite what they are, and they seldom use them for longer than is required to induce conversion or convince themselves that it will not be obtained.

Briefly put, what the participants in a communication breakdown can do is recognize each other as members of different language communities and then become translators. Taking the differences between their own intra- and inter-group discourse as itself a subject for study, they can first attempt to discover the terms and locutions that, used unproblematically within each community, are nevertheless foci of trouble for inter-group discussions . . . Having isolated such areas of difficulty in scientific communication, they can next resort to their shared everyday vocabularies in an effort further to elucidate their troubles. Each may, that is, try to discover what the other would see and say when presented with a stimulus to which his own verbal response would be different. If they can sufficiently refrain from explaining anomalous behavior as the consequence of mere error or madness, they may in time become very good predictors of each other's behavior. Each will have learned to translate the other's theory and its consequences into his own language and simultaneously to describe in his language the world to which that theory applies. That is what the historian of science regularly does (or should) when dealing with out-of-date scientific theories.

Since translation, if pursued, allows the participants in a communication breakdown to experience vicariously something of the merits and defects of each other's points of view, it is a potent tool both for persuasion and for conversion. But even persuasion need not succeed, and, if it does, it need not be accompanied or followed by conversion. The two experiences are not the same, an important distinction that I have only recently fully recognized.

To persuade someone is, I take it, to convince him that one's own view is superior and ought therefore supplant his own. That much is occasionally achieved without recourse to anything like translation. In its absence many of the explanations and problem-statements endorsed by the members of one scientific group will be opaque to the other. But each language community can usually produce from the start a few concrete research results that, though describable in sentences understood in the same way by both groups, cannot yet be accounted for by the other community in its own terms. If the new viewpoint endures for a time and continues to be fruitful, the research results verbalizable in this way are likely to grow in number. For some men such results alone will be decisive. They can say: I don't know how the proponents of the new view succeed, but I must learn; whatever they are doing, it is clearly right. That reaction comes particularly easily to men just entering the profession, for they have not yet acquired the special vocabularies and commitments of either group.

Arguments statable in the vocabulary that both groups use in the same way are not, however, usually decisive, at least not until a very late stage in the evolution of the opposing views. Among those already admitted to the profession, few will be persuaded without some recourse to the more extended comparisons permitted by translation. Though the price is often sentences of great length and complexity . . . many additional research results can be *translated* from one community's language into the other's. As translation proceeds, furthermore, some members of each community may also begin vicariously to understand how a statement previously opaque could seem an explanation to members of the opposing group. The availability of techniques like these does not, of course, guarantee persuasion. For most people translation is a threatening process, and it is entirely foreign to normal science. Counter-arguments are, in any case, always available, and no rules prescribe how the balance must be struck. Nevertheless, as argument piles on argument and as challenge after challenge is successfully met, only blind stubbornness can at the end account for continued resistance.

That being the case, a second aspect of translation, long familiar to both historians and linguists, becomes crucially important. To translate a theory or worldview into one's own language is not to make it one's own. For that one must go native, discover that one is thinking and working in, not simply translating out of, a language that was previously foreign. That transition is not, however, one that an individual may make or refrain from making by deliberation and choice, however good his reasons for wishing to do so. Instead, at some point in the process of learning to translate, he finds that the transition has occurred, that he has slipped into the new language without a decision having been made. Or else, like many of those who first encountered, say, relativity or quantum mechanics in their middle years, he finds himself fully persuaded of the new view but nevertheless unable to internalize it and be at home in the world it helps to shape. Intellectually such a man has made his choice, but the conversion required if it is to be effective eludes him. He may use the new theory nonetheless, but he will do so as a foreigner in a foreign environment, an alternative available to him only because there are natives already there. His work is parasitic on theirs, for he lacks the constellation of mental sets which future members of the community will acquire through education.

The conversion experience that I have likened to a gestalt switch remains, therefore, at the heart of the revolutionary process. Good reasons for choice provide motives for conversion and a climate in which it is more likely to occur. Translation may, in addition, provide points of entry for the neural reprogramming that, however inscrutable at this time, must underlie conversion. But neither good reasons nor translation constitute conversion, and it is that process we must explicate in order to understand an essential sort of scientific change.

The Nature of Science

[. . .] To one last reaction to this book, my answer must be of a different sort. A number of those who have taken pleasure from it have done so less because it illuminates science than because they read its main theses as applicable to many other fields as well. I see what they mean and would not like to discourage their attempts to extend the position, but their reaction has nevertheless puzzled me. To the extent that the book portrays scientific development as a succession of tradition-bound periods punctuated by non-cumulative breaks, its theses are undoubtedly of wide applicability. But they should be, for they are borrowed from other fields. Historians of literature, of music, of the arts, of political development, and of many other human activities have long described their subjects in the same way. Periodization in terms of revolutionary breaks in style, taste, and institutional structure have been among their standard tools. If I have been original with respect to concepts like these, it has mainly been by applying them to the sciences, fields which had been widely thought to develop in a different way. Conceivably the notion of a paradigm as a concrete achievement, an exemplar, is a second contribution. I suspect, for example, that some of the notorious difficulties surrounding the notion of style in the arts may vanish if paintings can be seen to be modeled on one another rather than produced in conformity to some abstracted canons of style.

This book, however, was intended also to make another sort of point, one that has been less clearly visible to many of its readers. Though scientific development may resemble that in other fields more closely than has often been supposed, it is also strikingly different. To say, for example, that the sciences, at least after a certain point in their development, progress in a way that other fields do not, cannot have been all wrong, whatever progress itself may be. One of the objects of the book was to examine such differences and begin accounting for them.

Consider, for example, the reiterated emphasis, above, on the absence or, as I should now say, on the relative scarcity of competing schools in the developed sciences. Or remember my remarks about the extent to which the members of a given scientific community provide the only audience and the only judges of that community's work. Or think again about the special nature of scientific education, about puzzle-solving as a goal, and about the value system which the scientific group deploys in periods of crisis and decision. The book isolates other features of the same sort, none necessarily unique to science but in conjunction setting the activity apart.

About all these features of science there is a great deal more to be learned. Having opened this postscript by emphasizing the need to study the community structure of science, I shall close by underscoring the need for similar and, above all, for comparative study of the corresponding communities in other fields. How does one elect and how is one elected to membership in a particular community, scientific or not? What is the process and what are the stages of socialization to the group? What does the group collectively see as its goals; what deviations, individual or collective, will it tolerate; and how does it control the impermissible aberration? A fuller understanding of science will depend on answers to other sorts of questions as well, but there is no area in which more work is so badly needed. Scientific knowledge, like language, is intrinsically the common property of a group or else nothing at all. To understand it we shall need to know the special characteristics of the groups that create and use it.

22   Culture and History

Barry Barnes

In this second excerpt from Barnes' book (see text 11) the discussion departs from an assertion of the instrumental character of knowledge. This raises the question of whether there is 'a single permanent corpus of genuine knowledge' to which we gain increasing access through the exercise of rationality, or whether, on the other hand, all knowledge is relative, the representation of knowledge being determined in different ways by different cultures so that no objective critical comparison can be made between different views of reality. (On this question see also MacIntyre, text 20.)

Barnes considers and rejects various arguments against relativism and concludes that 'Knowledge cannot be understood as more than the product of men operating in terms of an interest in prediction and control shaped and particularised by the specifics of their situations. It is not the unique possession of any culture or type of culture.' This argument, however, is an argument for 'the sociological equivalence of different knowledge claims'. Barnes points to the need for a distinction between sociological and evaluative accounts of beliefs: '. . . as a methodological principle we must not allow our evaluation of beliefs to determine what form of sociological account we put forward to explain them'. On the other hand, 'The naturalistic equivalence of the knowledge of different cultures is merely a finding, something which happens to be the case.' We can still evaluate and compare natural scientific knowledge on the basis of whether or not its predictions are successful in given circumstances. 'Everything of naturalistic significance would indicate that there is indeed one world, one reality, "out there", the source of our perceptions if not their total determinant, the cause of our expectations being fulfilled or disappointed, of our endeavours succeeding or being frustrated.' Barnes' point, however, is that 'this reality should not be identified with any linguistic account of it, or, needless to say, with any way of perceiving it, or pictorial representation of it.' He concludes by questioning why we should expect our 'linguistic and cognitive capabilities' to be such as to produce convergence in representations of reality.

As Barnes observes, the problem of the validity of knowledge is not generally seen as relevant to the consideration of paintings and other artistic forms of

243

representation. We can still ask, though, how pictorial representations, however divergent, might be considered as testifying to some form of learning in the face of reality, where learning is seen as related to an interest in prediction and control within some specific community. Prompted by Kuhn (text 21) we could also ask whether a form of 'tacit' or 'intuitive' knowledge might not be at work in artistic representation, opaque to questions of validity only so long as it remains untranslatable into linguistic propositions or formulae. In such an event 'validity' might depend upon an evaluation of the practice—the doing—of art rather than analysis of its results. One substantive question raised by the relationship between Barnes' text and Kuhn's is whether such an evaluation would have to be sociological. Could we envisage an evaluation of intuition in terms of its 'truth' or its 'realism'? Even if so, that evaluation would itself be unlikely to be more than another, perhaps matching intuition, informed by a sense of what 'doing art' involved or had involved. The possibility seems worth pursuing, however. It might at least allow us some tentative purchase on the evaluation of art which was free on the one hand from talk about 'embeddedness in history' and on the other from noises about 'quality'.

Source: Interests and the Growth of Knowledge (London, Routledge and Kegan Paul PLC, 1977), Ch. 1 'The Problem of Knowledge', Section 3, 'Culture and History', pp. 19–26. Footnotes have been deleted.

[. . .] All knowledge is actively produced by men with particular technical interests in particular contexts; its significance and its scope can never be generalised to the extent that no account is taken of those contexts and interests. Mannheim made this point in the abstract, but never successfully incorporated it into his concrete work. Lukács and Habermas also stressed it, but solely as a basis for large-scale speculation; they both overlooked the character of scientific knowledge as the product of a historical development. Ivins and Gombrich are the only authors so far cited whose understanding of cultural change provides a sufficient basis for a general conception of knowledge. Only they appreciated the way that representations are always built out of pre-existing cultural resources, and hence have always to be explained as developments within an ongoing cultural tradition. Only they gave detailed examples of how cultural forms actually have developed and changed over time.

It is tempting to suggest that concrete, specific investigation is essential to an adequate general understanding of the character of knowledge and the way that it grows and changes. Familiarity with specific instances would seem a necessary, although certainly not a sufficient, condition of such an understanding. But there is probably a further reason why Gombrich, in writing a detailed commentary on particular pictorial representations, produced a work of greater general theoretical insight than Habermas's cosmological speculations. Gombrich's essay had no need to address the problem of validity; the paintings and other representations he considered were not for the most part thought of as knowledge at all. Habermas, on the other hand, wrote as an epistemologist: validity was his central problem; to pronounce upon the merit and the scope of possible forms of knowledge was his explicit intention.

If genuine knowledge is uniquely determined by the actual, presently existing relationship between the knower and the known, the subject(s) and the objects(s) of knowledge, such problems can be approached with confidence. Only one corpus of genuine knowledge can emerge from the rational perception of reality (as 'positivists' would have it), or the rational investigation of reality in terms predetermined by interests. Such a corpus can be used as a criterion in detecting and criticising error and ideology, and as an end-point for an hypothesised progressive movement in the growth of knowledge. The characteristic epistemological activity of passing judgment upon the knowledge claims of others is thus automatically justified. The most that men can actually hope to achieve in the way of knowledge is conceivable as a final, finished corpus. But if knowledge must *also* be the product of given cultural resources, if rational men must generate knowledge on the basis of what is already thought and believed, then the evaluation of knowledge becomes altogether more problematic.

If old knowledge is indeed a material cause in the generation of new, then man's rationality alone no longer suffices to guarantee him access to a single permanent corpus of genuine knowledge; what he can achieve will depend upon what cognitive resources are available to him, and in what ways he is capable of exploiting such resources. To begin to understand the latter involves abandoning simplistic theories of learning, and undertaking a detailed examination of knowledge generation. To discover the former involves examining knowledge generation in its social context, as part of the history of a particular society and its culture; rational men in different cultures may represent reality in different, even contradictory ways. Hence, the evaluation of knowledge claims is shot through with difficulties; in particular the existing knowledge on the basis of which new knowledge is generated, the culturally given component, can never be independently checked; its origins and justifications in the past are largely inaccessible, nor is there an Archimedean point without the domain of culture, from which to make an assessment of it. To many, this raises the daunting spectre of relativism; for they rightly perceive that standards formulated to judge knowledge must be themselves manufactured from existing resources and historically contingent, if the above account is correct. Small wonder that epistemological writings rarely get directly to grips with these themes.

The problem of relativism should not be of direct concern to a sociological study, and the issues involved cannot in any case be properly considered in the present context. It should suffice us simply to adopt the instrumental ideal of knowledge we have arrived at, and proceed. However, there is a good deal of sociological interest in the problem of relativism, and its discussion does raise some points of naturalistic interest, so a very brief digression on the issue is in order.

For those who wish to avoid relativism, the trouble with the above account is that it offers no naturalistic basis for the objective evaluation of competing knowledge claims, and for the view that knowledge is progressive. Let us then consider whether its essentials can be retained, but its relativistic implications eliminated. Two attempts to do this will be examined; both prove to be unsatisfactory but it is interesting to see why this is so. The first attempt involves postulating that the rational processes by which men learn suffice to produce a convergence in the knowledge of different cultures. Although men have to use their existing knowledge and concepts to make the world intelligible and hence to learn about it, in learning they modify their knowledge in the direction of an ideal final form. They have indeed to start somewhere, but that starting point does not affect where they will eventually end up. A sculptor has to start with a given block of marble when he takes a figure, and the initial shape of the block may continue to influence his work as he proceeds, but we credit him with the ability eventually to realise his figure, whatever initial block he chooses.

This interesting possibility has been very thoroughly investigated by philosophers of science in the inductivist tradition, who would have welcomed its confirmation. So far, their work has produced no grounds for assuming a tendency to such convergence, and the general indication is that no such grounds can be expected to emerge. We must take it, as a provisional, revisable answer to this empirical question, that the cognitive processes which routinely are involved in learning do not suffice to shake off the effect of the given, culturally variable, starting point from which they proceed.

A second possibility is to concentrate upon the cultural resources out of which new knowledge is produced, and question whether these given resources are *merely* conventionally meaningful and consensually sustained. New knowledge, it is agreed, is actively produced from existing knowledge, without necessarily any regard for appearances, or the random flow of phenomena as they are experienced generally. But this is because men are seeking to capture the constantly operating underlying agencies which generate appearances, the real continuing mechanisms at work in the world. To do this they imagine, or create out of existing knowledge, theories about the world—putative mechanisms and agencies, held to exist, and to explain why things are as they are. And then they actively intervene in the course of events to check their theories. Since many mechanisms and forces are thought to exist, they prevent the operation of some, and calculate the effect of others, so that the effect of the mechanism they wish to check becomes apparent. Given that this is what men do, and find profitable, the world must surely be made up of continuing mechanisms and agencies as men imagine. And given that existing knowledge, which postulates particular agencies, is predictively successful, these agencies must surely bear some resemblance to those which really exist.

When scientists attempt to further our understanding of the human body they exploit existing accounts of muscular and skeletal organisation, theories of organic function, and so on. When they investigate chemical compounds and their structures they utilise taken-for-granted knowledge of stable electronic configurations and orbitals. When members analyse their own society they deploy given notions like the 'power' of unions or political groupings, or the 'interests' of classes or occupational groups. In all these cases, knowledge may be developed and extended from a taken-for-granted base. But the base is not arbitrary and *merely* conventional; to have gained acceptance as existing knowledge, it must have come close to describing real existing mechanisms and powers underlying appearances, and presumably it must therefore be capable of describing them more closely still if it is further articulated in the course of active investigation. This gives us a kind of modified correspondence theory of truth: knowledge is not made up of facts which correspond with appearances; it is always a set of given theories, which are evaluated to the extent that they correspond with the powers and mechanisms constantly operative in the world and thus basically constitutive of reality. Our concepts are thus putative real universals which may eventually be modified and developed until they are indeed real universals. They are not just any set of signs and conventions.

There is much to be said for such a position. It is correct to say that the very structure of the knowledge which men produce presumes that reality is constituted in terms of enduring agencies and mechanisms; this is how knowledge gains its essential coherence, and why its verbal component is viably a finite system of symbols. It is also correct to insist that existing knowledge, the material cause of new knowledge, will always embody already the results of learning, and to this extent be more than arbitrary. But neither of these points suffices to discriminate and evaluate different conflicting bodies of knowledge.

Clearly, any group of men believing in some set of real universals can take these universals as the best available rendition of reality, and use them to evaluate different beliefs. We can and do evaluate in this way, but so do those in other cultures, and so did our intellectual ancestors. If we are to regard our evaluations as special, we must be able to show that our favoured real explanatory mechanisms and agencies are inherently superior to or better grounded than anybody else's, that they really are closest to the real state of things. It is the evident lack of any way of doing this which deprives our own beliefs about the basic character of reality of any value as justified independent standards for the evaluation of knowledge claims generally.

Men in different cultures and societies have understood reality in a wide variety of ways, invoking diverse causative agencies and powers allegedly at work in the universe. In simple, tribal, societies, quasi human agencies—spirits or personified forces—have often been invoked to explain natural events and human fortunes. But despite assiduous investigation on the part of social anthropologists, we have no firm evidence that such beliefs are inherently unstable, nor is it clear that men who rationally endeavour to predict and control reality within such anthropomorphic cultures must eventually transcend their received perspective and recognise that their scheme of things is erroneous.

It might be thought, nonetheless, that the anthropological record is not sufficiently powerful evidence in this context. Tribal beliefs are sometimes alleged not to be related to attempts to predict and control reality at all, but to be primarily related to other interests (Douglas[1]). Hence, it is appropriate to reinforce the argument by reference to the culture of the natural sciences, the primarily instrumental interests of which can scarcely be doubted.

It is well known that as scientific knowledge has developed numerous mechanisms and theories have been postulated and successively set aside. This is, indeed, why so many philosophers of science have struggled to maintain a fact/theory distinction, and to base their justificatory rhetoric on the accumulation of facts. But there has also been a good deal of informal faith placed in the progressive quality of this sequence of theories and mechanisms. Recent historical studies, however, in particular those of T. S. Kuhn[2], effectively undermine this faith; they demonstrate that fundamental theoretical transitions in science are not simply rational responses to increased knowledge of reality, predictable in terms of context-independent standards of inference and evaluation. Such transitions make very good sense as responses to perceived practical problems, or as correlates of technical and procedural reorganisation within particular scientific communities. They are intelligible enough when referred to actual situations where new findings or new instrumentations are emerging. To this extent, they certainly are not manifestations of scientific irrationality, or mysterious emotional reorientations. But they do not possess the kind of general features which would be required by the progressive realism we are considering: it cannot be said that there is less of reality left to explain after such a transition, or that part of the world is finally explained, or even necessarily that scientists perceive themselves as having fewer problems afterwards. Nor are we ever in a position to say that scientists could not properly have done other than they did. We simply do not find, when actual instances are studied, that the case for a particular theoretical change can be established in context-independent terms. It is never unambiguously clear that existing theories could not have reasonably been maintained, or that yet other theories might not have been produced with just as much to recommend them.

Progressive realism is one of the ideal accounts of scientific knowledge which has it moving toward something, in this case a description of the real existing mechanisms in the world. There are now several independent strands of work which imply that such theories are misconceived, and that all knowledge generation and cultural growth should be regarded as endlessly dynamic and susceptible to alteration just as is human activity itself, with every actual change or advance a matter of agreement and not necessity. Even the long-standing Popperian tradition provides an adequate feel for these points; it provides many examples of the dialectical character of science, and the way it feeds upon an ever expanding number of self-generated problems, producing more work for itself with every accomplishment (rather than less, through disposing of 'part of reality'). Imre Lakatos's brilliant study of the history of Euler's Theorem[3] is an outstanding illustration of how much there is to be learned from this tradition. But two recent general approaches to semantic change, which cannot be discussed here, convey even more clearly the merits of such a view. One is the interaction view of metaphor, and the fully general account of meaning and meaning change it involves. The other is the ethnomethodological treatment of the indexical and reflexive properties of verbal utterances. Although apparently distinct independent academic traditions are involved, there are interesting parallels between them, which derive from their common reliance on the late work of Ludwig Wittgenstein.

The upshot of all this is that our current scientific models and mechanisms are likely to be seen at some future time as part of what is an endlessly unfolding chain of such mechanisms, constructed and eventually abandoned (or stripped of their ontological standing) as the activity of knowledge generation proceeds. Clearly then our present theories should stand symmetrically with earlier scientific theories, and for that matter with any other instrumentally oriented knowledge, in all sociologically relevant respects. The diverse real universals postulated at different times and in different cultures and contexts, should be regarded alike as inventions of the mind, sustained to the extent that they are instrumentally valuable in the settings where they are found. There is no means of going further and ranking or evaluating them in a way which does not simply *assume* the priority of one or other of them.

Knowledge cannot be understood as more than the product of men operating in terms of an interest in prediction and control shaped and particularised by the specifics of their situations. It is not the unique possession of any particular culture or type of culture. Wherever men deploy their cultural resources to authentic tasks of explanation and investigation indicated by their interests, what they produce deserves the name of knowledge. It deserves sociological study (and naturalistic or scientific study generally) as a typical example of knowledge. There is no more strictly defined conception which would discriminate say between 'scientific' knowledge, and other kinds, and justify different forms of sociological investigation in the two cases. We can study the process of knowledge generation, and fill out our general understanding of how it unfolds, by observing *any* culture wherein change is occurring under the impetus of an interest in prediction and control.

What then of the problem of relativism? The first thing to be said of this is that whatever conclusions are reached on the matter should not count against the preceding discussion. If one is interested in exploring and extending the possibilities of naturalistic thought and investigation, one does not turn back because its consequences prove unpleasant. If we cannot find any naturalistic basis for differentially evaluating the knowledge of different cultures, then that is that. If epistemologists and ontologists face problems as a consequence, they must simply be accepted. What matters is that we recognise the *sociological* equivalence of different knowledge claims. We will doubtless continue to evaluate beliefs differentially ourselves, but such evaluations must be recognised as having no relevance to the task of sociological explanation; as a methodological principle we must not allow our evaluation of beliefs to determine what form of sociological account we put forward to explain them.

It is sometimes felt that such arguments must be rejected simply because they represent a concession to relativism. Relativism is often opposed in sociology as a matter of passion and commitment, even by those who recognise the lack of any good arguments for their case. It is felt that to do otherwise is to provide a licence for any kind of nonsensical thought, and to display a lack of interest in what the world is really like.

Although there is no need to offer concessions to such an unsatisfactory position, it should be emphasised that the merits of relativism as a philosophical position are not argued for here. Nobody is enjoined to value all knowledge equally, or to choose which they will employ with a coin or a die. The prejudice of the argument is rather thoroughly naturalistic; it is naturalism which is being employed and advocated. The naturalistic equivalence of the knowledge of different cultures is merely a finding, something which happens to be the case. To be sure, it implies the conventional status of naturalism itself, but this is no disaster. It does not imply the abandonment of naturalism in favour of a frantic search for necessity elsewhere. One can choose to continue with the relevant activities.

Naturalism, moreover, implies the most intensely serious concern with what is real, and a particular, concretely relevant conception of it is actually advocated here. Everything of naturalistic significance would indicate that there is indeed one world, one reality, 'out there', the source of our perceptions if not their total determinant, the cause of our expectations being fulfilled or disappointed, of our endeavours succeeding or being frustrated. But this reality should not be identified with any linguistic account of it, or, needless to say, with any way of perceiving it, or pictorial representation of it. Reality is the source of *primitive causes*, which, having been pre-processed by our perceptual apparatus, produce changes in our knowledge and the verbal representations of it which we possess. All cultures relate symmetrically to this reality. Men in all cultures are capable of making reasonable responses to the causal inputs they receive from reality—that is, are capable of learning. That the structure of our verbal knowledge does not thereby necessarily converge upon a single form, isomorphous with what is real, should not surprise us. Why ever should we expect this to be a property of our linguistic and cognitive capabilities?

Notes

1 M. Douglas, *Purity and Danger* (Routledge and Kegan Paul, London, 1966).
2 T. S. Kuhn, *The Structure of Scientific Revolutions*, second edition (University of Chicago Press, Chicago and London, 1970).
3 I. Lakatos, 'Proofs and Refutations', *British Journal of the Philosophy of Science*, 14, 1963, pp. 1–25, 120–39, 221–45, 296–342.

23   Author and Producer Revisited

Art & Language

The title of this article refers to 'The Author as Producer', an address delivered by the German critic Walter Benjamin at the Institute for the Study of Fascism, in Paris in April 1934. (For an edited version see Frascina and Harrison, 1982.) Benjamin sought to argue through the relationship between (political) tendency and (artistic) autonomy in the context of a contemporary debate about the role and obligations of the socialist writer in bourgeois society. As he expressed the dichotomy:

> On one hand, *the correct political line is demanded of the poet;* on the other, *it is justifiable to expect his work to have quality . . . The connection can be asserted dogmatically. You can declare: a work that shows the correct political tendency need show no other quality. You can also declare: a work that exhibits the correct tendency must of necessity have every other quality.*

Benjamin takes the latter position but by inversion modifies the bases of judgement of 'correct tendency'. 'The correct political tendency of a work includes its literary quality because it includes its literary tendency.' *Pointing to the easy assimilation of 'socialist' styles and themes within the evaluative and economic systems of bourgeois culture, he argues for an emphasis rather upon the* position *of the work within 'the relations of production of its time' and upon the position of the author or artist as a* type *of producer within those relations. As he asserts, '[The work of] the author who has reflected deeply on the conditions of present-day production will never be merely work on products but always, at the same time, on the means of production.' Benjamin associates the 'literary relations of production' with the 'literary* technique' *of a work. 'A political tendency', he continues, 'is the necessary, never the sufficient condition of the organizing function of a work.' This organizing function is in part instructive.*

> *What matters therefore is the exemplary character of production, which is able first to induce other producers to produce, and second to put an improved apparatus at their disposal. And this apparatus is better the more consumers it is able to turn into producers, that is, readers or spectators into collaborators . . .*

251

Art & Language considers the relationship between 'artist-as-author' and 'artist-as-producer' within the context of Marx's critique of the capitalist mode of production and of his theory of historical materialism (see Assiter, text 12). The article also addresses the question of the 'recovery of meaning' from art as it is affected by analysis of the relationship between author (or artist or thinker) and producer. The contention is that any process of recovery of meaning (for example any interpretation of art) will be determined by assumptions *about the nature of this relationship. These assumptions may be misrepresentations necessary for the existence of that (eg social-economic) structure which generates them. (This connects to the Marxist notion of 'ideology' and the related notion of 'false consciousness'.) The suggestion is that assumptions made about the artist-as-author may be such as to block inquiry into the role of the artist-as-producer — ie into the artist's position in the relations of production—and thus to frustrate a causal analysis of the ways in which this position may affect the nature of the artist's products. In pointing to the constitutive nature of discourse about the artist-as-artist, Art & Language has recourse to MacIntyre's critique of Winch's social anthropology (text 20) and to the discussion there offered of the need for an independent conceptual framework in causal explanation.*

The possibility of reinstatement of the artist-as-producer is associated by Art & Language with the explanatory interests and potential of what T. J. Clark has called 'the meanings of the dominated'. (See Clark, 'Preliminaries to a Possible Treatment of Olympia *in 1865', edited version printed in Frascina and Harrison, 1982.) These 'meanings' are symbolized by Art & Language in the formula 'He did it for the money.' The suggestion is that the task of the critic is 'to produce interpretations which are not, or do not entail misrepresentations of the mechanisms of production . . . Discourse on meaning', it is claimed, 'must have an apparently second-order discourse concerning the fixing of meaning. That meaning is inconceivable without the mechanisms of its being fixed.'*

Source: Art-Language vol. 5, no. 1, Banbury, October, 1982, pp. 20–31. © Art & Language.

Such relationships as those between author and producer, and between the cognitive and non-cognitive determinants of modern art, remain enigmatic. Marx began two projects of inquiry. One of them was the analysis and critique of the capitalist mode of production in *Capital*, and the other was Historical Materialism, notably in the Preface to the *Critique of Political Economy*. The two are not integrated in Marx's work except in marginal conjunctions. The enigma of the relationship between author and producer, and more particularly (and *a fortiori*) of the relationship between artist and producer, lives in the margins between these two projects of inquiry. It is not to be found just at one level.

For instance, given a particular formation (call it Art) which is conceived as relatively autonomous, there will be the problem of the contradictions which may or do exist 'in' that formation, and which are or may be Marxian contradictions. These contradictions involve a misrepresentation of the base (itself also relatively autonomous) in the superstructure or ideology of that relatively autonomous formation (Art). This misrepresentation is in turn a *necessary condition* of the base. In this case the enigma involves the nature of the connection between author and producer in such a 'world'.

Alternatively, given the thesis of the relative autonomy and specific efficacy of the various superstructures *vis-à-vis* the Marxian thesis of 'determination in the last instance' (eg by the need to provide the means of subsistence), there is the problem of the producer's (and the author's) status as a denizen of this thesis.

These two 'levels' intersect where the enigma of author and producer is considered as a condition of inquiry into the recovery of meaning. This is to say that the relationship between the world analysed and criticised in *Capital* on the one hand, and the relatively autonomous world of art on the other, will have to be studied, in respect of the possibility that Marxian-type contradictions exist in both, by anyone who suspects that the discourses of art are constitutive misrepresentations of the mechanisms of production of art, and consequently mystifications of the concrete conditions of its signification.

The apparent logical problem that the producer and the thinker might be identical, or that the one might be causally—ie intransitively and asymmetrically—connected to the other, is informed by the critique of the capitalist mode of production. Irrespective of that apparent logical problem there is the question of the recovery of meaning according to the project of historical materialism. We need to consider what part is played in the recovery of meaning by the relationship between producer and thinker, and by the determinations upon that relationship. One problem is that while such considerations will themselves be determined by some 'real' (eg causal) connection between producer and thinker, they will also be determined, residually, by those *assumptions* about the nature of producer/thinker relations which are functions of the relatively autonomous formation, and which are misrepresentations of that 'real' connection.

The question of the character of the relation between the (mis)representations in art discourses, and the question of the nature of the specificity and the limited autonomy of various art practices, await a satisfactory analysis of the relations between author and producer. It is all very well for commentators to enjoin artists to understand their own struggle within the ideological and productive apparatuses, but without an explicit attempt to grasp the materials (including the conceptual materials) with which a technical transformation may be at least dimly thought, we are left with no more than conviction and sentiment.

The structures that might be thought basic to modern art (modern art conceived as some set of relatively autonomous formations) are not identifiable as a formality. In respect of the preceding discussion of 'levels', we may identify two possible positions (among others): (1) that the real structures of art lie precisely within bourgeois ideology — itself explicable as a misrepresentation of real economic structures — and that the misrepresentations *within* art are misrepresentations of that ideology, for which they nevertheless produce necessary conditions; ie art is both a part of the mechanism by which the real economic structures are misrepresented, *and* a necessary condition of the ideology which misrepresents them; (2) that the structures basic to art (conceived etc) are autonomous in some other sense than that which would be attributable to their basic structures being in bourgeois ideology (as above), and that the misrepresentations and the necessity involved are in terms of homologues, partial identities, functions etc of the 'system determining in the last instance'.

What we have to say does not presume to adjudicate between these (or other) positions. Of course, the relation author/producer must be contingently deformable-in-thought in respect of some substantive adjudication of these and related questions. That a relation of some author/producer sort will exist as a function of structural relations is not in dispute. But, as we have suggested, 'author' and 'producer' are also reflexive afflictions of misrepresentation. Let us therefore note that in the following, 'author', 'thinker', 'artist', 'producer' etc do not necessarily go to historical materialist intensions or to the intensions of *Capital*.

We might accept that there is an interpretation of historical materialism that does not *reduce* artist (author) to producer. Alison Assiter suggests that the same individual can be designated by (eg) the terms 'Policeman' and 'Thinker'. But what these express is a *contingent* identity, referring to different 'time slices' of the same individual. She further argues that the possibility of that individual as Policeman exercises some conditioning power over the same individual as Thinker; and this is not inimical to the sense of *identity* she expatiates. According to this interpretation, while there is no tendency to *reduce* artist to producer, the producer nevertheless determines or conditions the artist. (The 'gouging careerist with a retrospective at X now' determines and conditions and refers to the same individual who 'fearlessly exposes American Imperialism on behalf of CND'.)

Assiter's article does resolve, or rather suggest, a solution to some of the apparent inconsistencies of historical materialism concerning the author/producer relationship. What Assiter fails to theorise is that the conditioning 'power' of the producer may well be misrepresented in superstructural accounts of the author's practice. What we wish to establish is this. Although the activity or practice of an *author* could be, and often is, a generated misrepresentation — a necessary condition — of the practice of the *producer*, the possibility of contradiction in the *representation* of the author/producer relationship does not exist in virtue of the causal 'identity' relationship between author and producer as suggested by Assiter. The contradiction exists in virtue of *structurally* generated (etc) misrepresentations of whatever phenomenal form.

What is therefore needed is a project of analysis and critique *vis-à-vis* the possibility that contradiction will be involved in the *representation* of the author/producer relationship. To resolve the antinomies of the identity/non-identity of author and producer in causal terms is to suggest such a project. The fact that modern art's ontogenesis depends, as much as its philogenesis, upon the productive activity of its interpreters and consumers need not worry us. That modern art is multiply and plurally caused, and multiply and plurally produced, is a real complexity, not an indication that co-production does not involve misrepresentation.

The problem of the misrepresentation of the producer in author discourse can be split into: (1) the question of claims explicitly made in interpretive discourse

254

concerning generative (producer) structures; (2) the question of implicit or residual claims concerning such structures; and (3) the question of the blocking effect of author discourse *vis-à-vis* inquiry necessitated by (1) and (2). These and related problems are difficult and underanalysed. What is also difficult and underanalysed is the prescriptive potential of such questions with respect to 'productive' art practice relative to the various possible distributions of function involved in them.

These misrepresentations and contradictions are not monolithic. But they are endemic. Very little work has been done to figure out some of the implications of possible answers to (1)–(3), and to sort out just how much the interpretive discourse entails residual claims about some sort of producer or mechanism of production, the truth value of which will be a ground of the truth of the interpretive claim. (Consider expression claims, for example.) Very little work has been done to analyse the power of interpretive discourse to produce or describe illicit closures in the system of production of art. Very little work has been done on the question of the prevailing assumptions concerning the characterisation of, and the relation between, the various cognitive and non-cognitive conditions of art, and so on.

These problems have been marginalised in favour of discourses which look for contradictions in the self-image of the author as author, ie in the very contingency which renders these contradictions untranslatable with respect to others. This assertion is filled out by the description we have offered of the anthropologist on the Trobriand Island. Briefly, if the limits of a language are taken to be the limits of a word, and if agents' reasons are taken as adequate in causal explanation, then both causal inquiries and translation problems (eg in the study of a 'community' by an 'anthropologist', or of a 'movement' by an art historian) will reduce to mere reinforcements of a professional self-image already adopted; ie the one by means of which anthropologist and islanders were joined into one propitious constituency in the first place. To suggest that the anthropologist-as-producer determines the anthropologist-as-author in a radically different 'world' from that in which the islander-as-producer determines the islander-as-author (eg speaker), is to step outside the world of the anthropologist's author-discourse. The contradictions which this suggestion reveals are at a level such that they cannot be resolved within that discourse, if they can be recognised at all. Their marginalisation is therefore a necessary condition of the maintenance of the anthropologist's (or artist's, historian's, critic's etc) profession.

This is not to suggest that there is an Archimedean point outside our language and time. The recovery of meanings, whether producer's meaning or not, is done, inescapably, in the 'language' available. But this does not mean that interpretations are not themselves practically conditioned and caused, and that they cannot therefore be scrutinised by cognitive adequacy or explained. What it does mean is that the examination of the generative conditions of the 'languages', and analysis of their causal conditions, will generate second-order discourses (and n-order discourses) which may or may not include those meanings, but which might amount to a condition of their possibility. 'This is a portrait of a woman and all that goes with that' (that is to say, all that is entailed by that), will be susceptible to some sort of critique if it can be shown that it is a portrait of a man. It would be susceptible to critique if it could be shown that the mode of representation was causally implicated in, and a causal product of the subjection of women (a necessary misrepresentation). 'This painting expresses an inner torment, a spontaneous bursting forth of the dreams of the artist' will be susceptible to critique if it can be shown that the artist knocked it off to please a collector known to have preference for a similar painting owned by somebody else, etc. 'This painting describes the rural bourgeoisie' will be susceptible to critique if it can be shown . . . etc, etc. These are familiar and oversimplified ciphers for various sorts of intuitively acceptable examples.

Introduce a picture P1 into discourse as referring to x, which it is not *of* (it is *of* y), and introduce a picture P2 as referring to y (it is *of* x). What happens to the meaning? P1 will be used to 'refer' to y 'conventionally' (that is, in virtue of some circumstances fixing its reference and etc), P2 to x. Dropping of the stipulation that what a picture is *of* must serve as subject will make things fairly interesting. The system of signification of P1 and P2 will become an open one, one for analysis in causal terms. But P1 'refers' to y (not x), and P2 'refers' to x (not y) if that is what analysis turns up. Unless the signification of P1 and P2 is to remain circular, or entirely logocentric (in the sense that the islander's reasons, expressed in the islander's language, are taken as adequate in explanation of action in a world itself adequately constituted by that language alone), the causal-type analysis will be indispensable. The dropping of the subject-matter stipulation opens the question of *of*, or rather of reference, to substantive investigation as an open system.

Of course, ideas are ideas. To say that art is produced is not to *reduce* it to something entirely determined by the economic, nor to a mere expression of the economic. Furthermore, we assert its relative autonomy. Indeed, 'basic' to certain formations will be certain *practices*. These will involve beliefs and so forth. And these in turn will involve representations of other practices and forms and so forth. We are not concerned to seem to theorise the absolute priority of the economic. We are concerned to point out that the world of art produces contradictions (that is, misrepresentations of its basic structures), and that these are necessary for those basic structures, and furthermore that given the relativity of relative autonomy these may themselves be misrepresentations, or entail misrepresentations of structures basic to capitalism etc. These misrepresentations involve contradictions of a special sort. And they are to be understood causally.

We are further concerned to suggest that the 'meanings of the dominated' may go to non-cognitive productive mechanisms which are, or entail, a causally grounded critique of the conceptions (misrepresentations) of art. We use 'He did it for the money' as a 'symbol' for the 'dead' account produced by the dominated and in part entailed by Marx's economic and historical work, or if not entailed by it, defensible in respect of its substantive project.

We offer a picturesque illustration in support of the preceding discussion, and one which unites talk of subject matter and *of*-ness to consideration of author/producer relations and to those considerations of competence which are symptomatic of the relations between practices (which involve beliefs) and broader superstructural formations (which also involve beliefs).

By those with a commitment to the conditions of competence relevant to the French Salon, the Impressionists were criticised in the mid 1870s on the grounds that their representations were *technically* incompetent. Monet and Renoir had enrolled in the early 1860s in the atelier of Charles Gleyre, who was a normally successful ('competent') exhibitor at the Salon. Gleyre painted pictures with moralising and classical subjects. His technical means of representation were conventional signifying features associated with such subject matter: 'rounded' modelling, a 'gradual' chiaroscuro etc. In conventional mid-nineteenth century practice the use of bitumen was regarded as a more or less indispensable means to the production of appropriate pictorial 'effects'. The use of bitumen leads over the course of time to a wrinkling of the paint surface, or, if fast drying agents are used, to crazing and cracking. Monet and Renoir avoided the use of what was known by at least the mid 1860s to be an unstable medium. The development of an alternative technical means of representing light/dark contrasts was reflexively related within their practice to an interest in different types of subject. Whatever other judgements might have been made, their paintings were more technically competent than those of many more successful exhibitors at the Salon, at least in the sense that they were less likely to deteriorate in time.

The point is that a (largely inarticulated) assessment of the inappropriateness of (what was taken to be) their subject matter was articulated as a negative judgement on their execution. A response to the critical implications of their *avoidance* of explicit moralising and classicising themes was misrepresented in critical discourse as a recognition of technical incompetence; and this judgement of technical incompetence was itself an implicit misrepresentation of the actual technical incompetence of that practice from which assumptions about decorum in subject matter were in fact derived.

Talk of the 'meanings of the dominated' was not originally raised in relation to Monet and Renoir. It was used by T. J. Clark in the interests of discriminating between the 'effectiveness' of Courbet and Manet respectively. But the notion may actually gain in critical reference and purport by being prised apart from the interests of Realism and conscripted rather in a search for the conditions of realism.

Plainly, in respect of the above account we could say that the issues of competence, subject matter, practice etc, were to be arbitrated in very different ways according to which were identified as the cognitive and which the non-cognitive mechanisms of production of the pictures concerned, and that this identification was implicated in those assumptions about artist/producer relations which were entrenched in the dominant discourse; ie that within which the respective practices of Salon and Impressionism were to be discriminated. Recognition of Gleyre's incompetence as a producer (of technically defective pictures) did not moderate assessment of his competence as a 'painter' (of moral and classical subjects); while the assessment of Monet's and Renoir's relative incompetence as painters (of 'proper' pictures) was not moderated by recognition of their competence as producers (of technically durable paintings).

An account of art will achieve an interpretation of its meaning whether or not this involves explicit claims about the mechanism of its production. What a non-circular, 'non-contradictory' account (in the sense of contradiction adumbrated above) is liable to do is to describe another level — to go to another stratum of reality (ie to go outside the Island for its terms and referents and concepts). 'Art' is not paintings and their meanings, but the how of their production and a critique of its mechanisms. There is a sense in which it is not possible to think the second-order discourse which renders art's constitutive account of itself concretely corrigible as a first-order one.

The conditions of the 'meanings of the dominated' are class society. This does not mean that the dominated do not have some account of the meanings of the dominating. Indeed, it can be argued that the possibility of an adequate representation of the meanings of the dominating will depend upon the recognition on the part of the dominated that their meanings may go to an analysis and a critique of the conditions of a special sort of contradiction.

The meanings of the dominated will not be (are not) broadly comparable (categorically, existentially, methodologically) with the meanings of the dominating. This must be obvious. Of course, it is also obvious that some actual 'meanings of the dominated' will be identical, functional, homologous, etc, with the meanings of the bourgeois subsection privileged to produce interpretations. If they do, they do, and those interpretations will go to the determination of the meanings of the dominated by the meanings of the dominating. The sense in which the meanings of the dominated *must* differ from the meaning of the dominating is in virtue of the class interests of the latter. It may also be argued that the class position of the dominated, the real life of the dominated, the practice of the dominated, will tend towards a description or an attempted description of some subset of the set of real conditions of production of the meanings of the dominating.

All we are really saying is that the 'dead' materialism of the working class *vis-à-vis* the antics of the bourgeoisie frequently has explanatory power—power as a subset of an analysis and critique of the system of misrepresentation which bourgeois culture is. The *cognates* of 'He did it for the money' are not as readily exhausted as are those crude forms of economic determinism it may be taken to stand for. Such a claim is not *necessary* for the truth of *Capital* or for the truth of historical materialism. It is merely a way of pointing out that the meanings of the dominated will *have* to be sought in their characterisation as a (speciously or temporarily) second-order discourse, and further that the meanings of the dominated may *actually* be sought in part in a second-order discourse already in production. The search for the meanings of the dominated cannot be engaged in on the basis of a linguistic fallacy, nor of any other entailment of Trobriand Islanderhood.

The task for those who would criticise and demystify Modernism and its partners is to produce an analysis and critique which renders the Modernist's account corrigible. The task will be not so much to bring the conditions of interpretation 'closer' to the conditions of production — although this is a way of thinking about it — as to produce interpretations which are not, or do not entail, misrepresentations of the mechanisms of production. This means of course that an analysis/critique will have to be produced which is capable of showing modern art's discourse as producing misrepresentations, and also of showing the *necessity* of this. Such a critique will not render all explanations of artistic work reducible to the equivalent of 'He did it for the money.' 'It' will be over-determined — multiply and plurally caused. The matter of how much (eg) Edgar Degas paid his models is not in itself crucial. It is rather a paradigm of how someone is going to approach his work, and of the kinds of questions he is going to ask in order to characterise it as a type of production. Asking how Degas' work was produced entails asking how the co-producer of his work exists or existed. If someone interprets Degas, then they are going to have to be seen as part of the same world as that in which he paid his models. If you can't understand that world, then neither can you understand how someone interprets Degas' work. You will still merely be present at the congregational constitution of 'Art'.

Discourse on meaning must have an apparently second-order discourse concerning the fixing of meaning. That meaning is inconceivable without the mechanism of its being fixed. And paraphrastic or remote conception, meaning or reference is just that: a condition of the second-order, or n-order discourse. And this sort of meaning will be the 'meaning of the dominated'.

We assert that the being of art is in virtue of its doing . . . something. And this is in virtue of its being a result of human agency, and so forth. T. J. Clark was right — in a sense. The 'meanings' of the dominated are not to be found as an alternative relation of signifier and signified, but within the explanatory historical discourse which situates possible artistic meanings in an agency — a social, causal agency. Historical materialism, it might be said, 'contains' in some form what Clark wants to call the meanings of the dominated. The meanings of the dominating are a sub-set of the meanings of the dominated, in so far as the former is a Trobriand Islander whose constitutive accounts are potentially under the causal explanation and hence critique of the dominated.

We are saying that the meanings of the dominated will recognise, install one might say, the contradictions of the present. What we mean by this is that the dominated can or must implicate their meanings in the emancipatory potential of a second-order or n-order causal, analytical, historical-materialist discourse. Of course, there can or could be art work addressed to this possibility — or not. It may be imagined that a work could indicate, perhaps, or cause reflection on the materials of which culture is made, in so far as they are subject to non-constitutive, non-certifying description.

But what of explanation? As M. Foucault says, 'The interests of the oppressed are best expressed in their own words.' Yes. But in talking of art, in finding meaning in art, a set of Aristotelian material conditions operates. Little knowledges. These are power. This power is to be unmasked if the means (or interests) of the oppressed are to be emancipated from those Aristotelian material conditions which are (eg) ideological or 'contradictory'.

24 Some General Features of Language

Noam Chomsky

In this second excerpt from Reflections on Language, *Chomsky reasserts his view of the language faculty as biologically determined and pursues his critique of empiricist and behaviourist psychology, and of their implications for social theory. A rational view of the limits on human cognitive capacity, he argues, is a necessary protection against the attractions of that type of presumptuous and pseudo-scientific hypothesis which 'serves so well the needs of dominant coercive ideologies'. As an illustration of the thesis that 'humans may develop their capacities without limit, but never escaping certain objective bounds set by their biological nature', he offers a vivid if tentative characterization of production in Modernist culture.*

In seeking an explanation for the appeal of empiricism Chomsky points both to the historically specific nature of the problems empiricist theory was developed to address, and to the tendency to confuse a (progressive) concern for empirical test with a (reactionary) commitment to empiricist doctrine. He also criticizes that empiricist misreading of Marx (exemplified by Gramsci) which identifies Marxism with the supposedly *progressive view that 'human nature is the totality of historically determined relations'. Such a view of human nature, Chomsky suggests, 'removes all barriers to coercion and manipulation by the powerful', and leaves the field clear for 'intellectual ideologists of whatever political persuasion'. By contrast, Chomsky emphasizes the connection between rationalist thought and a tradition of concern for human freedom. 'Creativity', he asserts, 'is predicated on a sytem of rules and forms, in part determined by intrinsic human capacities. Without such constraints, we have arbitrary and random behaviour, not creative acts.'*

If Chomsky is right in his views — if the faculty and development of language is a model of human cognitive faculties and development in general — then what he has to say will be directly relevant to our means of visual apprehension and expression. A rational view of these as limited by genetic, biological and epistemological constraints will similarly offer some protection against attractive but pretentious and coercive attitudes and beliefs. Such a view will also provide some resistance to those currently fashionable theories which represent human 'signifying practices' as entirely determined by and contingent upon the 'social production of meaning', and which locate the 'sites of meaning production' not within any biologically defined concept of the human, but within abstract concepts of 'culture', 'society' and 'history'. Despite the claims to emancipatory potential made by those who employ them, such theories may be seen as falling under the range of Chomsky's critique.

Source: Reflections on Language (Fontana, London 1976), Ch. 3, 'Some General Features of Language', pp. 123–134. Reprinted by permission of William Collins Sons & Company, and Random House, Inc. This material has been edited.

[. . .] The study of language falls naturally within human biology. The language faculty, which somehow evolved in human prehistory, makes possible the amazing feat of language learning, while inevitably setting limits on the kinds of language that can be acquired in the normal way. Interacting with other faculties of mind, it makes possible the coherent and creative use of language in ways that we can sometimes describe, but hardly even begin to understand.

If we undertake the study of humans as organisms in the natural world, the approach I have outlined seems entirely reasonable. Given the role of language in human life and probably human evolution, and given its intimate relations to what I have been calling 'common-sense understanding', it would not be very surprising to discover that other systems within cognitive capacity have something of the character of the language faculty and its products. We should anticipate that these other cognitive systems too set limits on human intellectual achievement, by virtue of the very structure that makes it possible to acquire rich and comprehensive systems of belief and knowledge, insight and understanding . . .

I would like to stress again that these conjectures should not seem in any way surprising to the natural scientist. Rather, they conform reasonably well to what is known about how the brain works in other domains, say, the construction of visual space, or more generally, our concept of physical space and the objects in it. Furthermore, as a number of biologists have pointed out, something of the sort is to be expected on simple evolutionary grounds. Citing Lorenz, Gunther Stent points out that Darwinian considerations offer a 'biological underpinning' to a kind of Kantian epistemology, but in addition, these considerations concerning the evolutionary origin of the brain explain 'not only why our innate concepts match the world but also why these concepts no longer work so well when we attempt to fathom the world in its deepest scientific aspects,' thus perhaps posing a 'barrier to unlimited scientific progress'.[1] The reason, simply, is that there is no reason to suppose that the capacities acquired through evolution fit us to 'fathom the world in its deepest scientific aspects'. He also warns that 'it is important to give due recognition to this fundamental epistemological limitation to the human sciences, if only as a safeguard against the psychological or sociological prescriptions put forward by those who allege that they have already managed to gain a scientifically validated understanding of man.' A warning that we might well bear in mind in a period when pseudo-scientific pretense serves so well the needs of dominant coercive ideologies.

Notice that these quite natural views on the scope and limits of knowledge set no finite limits on human progress. The integers form an infinite set, but they do not exhaust the real numbers. Similarly, humans may develop their capacities without limit, but never escaping certain objective bounds set by their biological nature. I suspect that there is no cognitive domain to which such observations are not appropriate.

Suppose that the social and material conditions that prevent free intellectual development were relieved, at least for some substantial number of people. Then, science, mathematics and art would flourish, pressing on towards the limits of cognitive capacity. At these limits, as noted earlier, we find various forms of intellectual play, and significant differentiation among individuals who vary little within the domain of cognitive capacity. As creative minds approach the limits of cognitive capacity, not only will the act of creation be limited to a talented few, but even the appreciation or comprehension of what has been created. If cognitive domains are roughly comparable in complexity and potential scope, such limits might be approached at more or less the same time in various domains, giving rise to a 'crisis of modernism', marked by a sharp decline in the general accessibility of the products of creative minds, a blurring of the distinction between art and puzzle, and a sharp increase in 'professionalism' in intellectual life, affecting not only those who produce creative work but also its potential audience. Mockery of conventions that are, ultimately, grounded in human cognitive capacity might be expected to become virtually an art form in itself, at this stage of cultural evolution. It may be that something of the sort has been happening in recent history. Even if correct, such speculations would not lead us to deny that there is surely a vast creative potential as yet unexplored, or to overlook the fact that for most of the human race, material deprivation and oppressive social structures make these questions academic, if not obscene. As Marx wrote in his early manuscripts, echoing Humboldt, animals 'produce only under the compulsion of direct physical needs, while man produces when he is free from physical needs and only truly produces in freedom from such need.' By this criterion, human history has barely begun for the majority of mankind.

If the approach to the study of cognitive capacity outlined earlier is a proper one, then we can hope to develop a theory of human nature in its psychological aspects. The possibility of such a theory has often been denied. This denial is implicit in the scholastic doctrine that the mind contains nothing beyond what the senses convey. One might read a similar conclusion into the various efforts in the modern period to relate human reason and the scope of human intelligence to the weakness of instinct, an idea that can be traced at least to Herder . . . Empiricist and later behaviorist psychology are firmly grounded in the doctrine that there is no non-trivial theory of human nature. Or more accurately, that such a theory is limited to the physical organs of the body, with the sole exception of those parts of the brain involved in higher mental functions. I will return directly to some of the ramifications of this doctrine.

I think it is fair to say that these empiricist views are most plausible where we are most ignorant. The more we learn about some aspect of human cognition, the less reasonable these views seem to be. No one would seriously argue today, for example, that our construction of perceptual space is guided by empiricist maxims. The same, I think, is true of the language faculty, which relates more closely to the essential nature of the human species. I suspect that the empiricist position with regard to higher mental functions will crumble as science advances towards an understanding of cognitive capacity and its relations to physical structures.

The claims of empiricism have often been put forth, not as speculation, but as established fact, as if they must be true or have been demonstrated. Such claims must be evaluated on their merits, but if they are found to be without support, plain wrong, or seriously exaggerated, as I believe invariably proves to be the case, then it is appropriate to search elsewhere for an explanation for their appeal and power.

In part, the commitment to empiricist doctrine in the human sciences is a reaction to the speculative character of earlier work, its lack of firm empirical foundation. Surely this has been true of the study of language. There is, however, an obvious gap in reasoning. We can agree that classical rationalist and empiricist doctrines should be recast (or perhaps replaced) so as to be more directly susceptible to empirical test, and that empirical evidence should be brought to bear, as far as possible, in determining their validity. Those who fashioned the traditional doctrines would not have quarreled with this principle. Descartes and Hume and Kant were grappling with problems at the borders of scientific knowledge, problems that are both conceptual and empirical, and sought such evidence as they could muster to justify their theoretical speculations ... But from a justifiable concern for empirical confirmation, we cannot argue to a commitment to empiricist doctrine. Rather, empiricist and rationalist theories alike must be cast in a form in which they are subject to confirmation, and this task seems no more difficult in one case than in the other. I have tried to suggest how these theories can be so reformulated, without doing violence to certain basic leading ideas (though others must be discarded), and have argued further that where we have any glimmerings of understanding, we are led to theories with a distinctively rationalist character.

But the conflict between rationalist and empiricist doctrines, and the grip of the latter on the modern temper, cannot be explained solely on the 'intrinsic' grounds just mentioned. As Harry Bracken (1973[2]) has emphasized:

> The empiricist/rationalist debates of the seventeenth century *and* of today are debates between different value systems or ideologies. Hence the heat which characterizes these discussions.

The issues have changed from the seventeenth century to today, though there may well be some common threads. Complicating the matter further, the issues and conflicts can be perceived along many dimensions and in quite different ways. But the social and ideological context has always been critical, a fact often noted. Locke's epistemology, as John Yolton shows, was developed primarily for application to religious and moral debates of the period; 'the vital issue between

264

Locke and his critics [on the doctrine of innateness] was the grounds and foundations of morality and religion' (Yolton, 1956³). Throughout the modern period, not to speak of earlier eras, such questions lie in the background of seemingly arcane philosophical controversies and often help explain their issue.

Classical British empiricism arose in often healthy opposition to religious obscurantism and reactionary ideology. Its appeal, perhaps, resides in part in the belief that it offers a vision of limitless progress in contrast to the pessimistic doctrine that humans are enslaved by an unchangeable nature that condemns them to intellectual servitude, material deficit, and eternally fixed oppressive institutions. Thus, it might be understood as a doctrine of progress and enlightenment.

This may also be the reason for the appeal of empiricist ideology in Marxist thought, a commitment that has often been expressed in the most extreme forms. Gramsci went so far as to argue that 'the fundamental innovation introduced by Marxism into the science of politics and history is the proof that there does not exist an abstract, fixed and immutable "human nature"' . . . but that human nature is the totality of historically determined social relations' (Gramsci, 1957⁴)—a statement that is surely false, in that there is no such proof, and a questionable reading of Marx. In his introduction to Jean Itard's study of the Wild Boy of Aveyron, Lucien Malson asserts categorically that 'the idea that man has no nature is now beyond dispute'; the thesis that man 'has or rather is a history', nothing more, 'is now the explicit assumption of all the main currents of contemporary thought,' not only Marxism, but also existentialism, behaviorism, and psychoanalysis. Malson too believes that it has been 'proven' that the term 'human nature' is 'completely devoid of sense'. His own critique of 'psychological heredity' aims to 'destroy . . . the notion of human nature' by demonstrating that there are no 'mental predispositions [present in the embryo] which are common to the species or to man in general'. To be sure, there are inherited biological characteristics, but not in the area in which man 'displays his peculiarly human qualities'. 'The natural in man is due to inborn heredity, the cultural to his acquired heritage,' with no contribution from 'psychological heredity' (Malson, 1972⁵).

Such claims are not untypical of left-wing opinion, a fact that demands explanation, since plainly there is no compelling empirical argument to buttress them. The explanation, I think, is the one just given: it has been assumed that empiricist doctrine is fundamentally 'progressive', as in certain respects it was in an earlier period.

There are quite independent issues that must be clearly distinguished in considering a doctrine put forth as a theory of human nature, or of the lack of any such distinctive nature. Is it correct, or at least plausible? What were its social and political implications at certain historical periods in fact? How were these implications perceived? To what extent (if at all) did these implications, as perceived, contribute to the reception of the doctrine? What (if anything) does this tell us about the commitments of those who defend it? All these questions arise in the case of the advocacy by the revolutionary left of empiricist principles, in particular the doctrine that human nature is nothing but a historical product and thus imposes no limits and suggests no preferred directions for social change.

I have been discussing, so far, only the question of truth and plausibility; there is, I believe, little of either. As a problem of intellectual and social history, the matter is complex. Empiricism has indeed served as a doctrine of progress and enlightenment. It is closely associated with classical liberal thought, which has been unable to survive the age of industrial capitalism.[6] What remains of value in classical liberal doctrine is, in my opinion, to be found today in its most meaningful form in libertarian socialist concepts of human rights and social organization. Empiricism rose to ascendancy in association with a doctrine of 'possessive individualism' that was integral to early capitalism,[7] in an age of empire . . . Bracken has [. . .] developed the theme that

> . . . the anti-abstractionism and anti-empiricism of Cartesianism are connected with concern for human freedom. More generally, the rationalist model of man is taken to support an active and creative mind which is neither impressed from 'outside' to 'inside' nor considered to be malleable . . . Cartesian thought constitutes a vigorous effort to assert the dignity of the person . . . [In contrast] the empiricist blank tablet account of learning is a manipulative model . . .[8]

I think that this is an accurate perception, on both conceptual and historical grounds. As for the latter, I have commented elsewhere on the roots in Cartesian thought of Rousseau's opposition to tyranny, oppression, and established authority; and at a greater remove, Kant's defense of freedom, Humboldt's precapitalist liberalism with its emphasis on the basic human need for free creation under conditions of voluntary association, and Marx's critique of alienated fragmented labor that turns men into machines, depriving them of their 'species character' of 'free conscious activity' and 'productive life', in association with their fellows.[9]

[. . .] The question whether 'the human mind [is] to be regarded simply as a responsive cog in the mechanism of nature', as in empiricist doctrine, or as 'a creative, determinative force' is a crucial one, which arises in many forms in the context of the debate over various models of mind (Wood, 1972[10]).

Kant described 'man's inclination and duty to *think freely*' as 'the germ on which nature has lavished most care'.[11] A concern for this 'species character' lies at the core of Cartesian thought and animates an intellectual tradition (not the only one) that derives in part from it, not limiting itself, however, to the inclination and duty to think freely, but also affirming the need to produce freely and creatively, to realize one's full potentialities, to revolt against oppression, and to take control of the institutions of economic, political and social life.

The doctrine that the human mind is initially unstructured and plastic and that human nature is entirely a social product has often been associated with progressive and even revolutionary social thinking, while speculations with regard to human instinct have often had a conservative and pessimistic cast. One can easily see why reformers and revolutionaries should become radical environmentalists, and there is no doubt that concepts of immutable human nature can be and have been employed to erect barriers against social change and to defend established privilege.

But a deeper look will show that the concept of the 'empty organism', plastic and unstructured, apart from being false, also serves naturally as the support for the most reactionary social doctrines. If people are, in fact, malleable and plastic beings with no essential psychological nature, then why should they not be controlled and coerced by those who claim authority, special knowledge, and a unique insight into what is best for those less enlightened? Empiricist doctrine can easily be molded into an ideology for the vanguard party that claims authority to lead the masses to a society that will be governed by the 'red bureaucracy' of which Bakunin warned. And just as easily for the liberal technocrats or corporate managers who monopolize 'vital decision-making' in the institutions of state capitalist democracy, beating the people with the people's stick, in Bakunin's trenchant phrase.

The principle that human nature, in its psychological aspects, is nothing more than a product of history and given social relations removes all barriers to coercion and manipulation by the powerful. This too, I think, may be a reason for its appeal to intellectual ideologists, of whatever political persuasion. I have discussed elsewhere[12] the striking similarity in the doctrines evolved by authoritarian socialists and ideologists of state capitalism, those who constitute 'a secular priesthood claiming absolute authority, both spiritual and lay, in the name of unique scientific knowledge of the nature of men and things' (Berlin, 1972[13]), the 'new class' of technical intelligentsia, who hope to bring about 'the reign of *scientific intelligence*, the most aristocratic, despotic, arrogant and elitist of all regimes'.[14] The 'empty organism' doctrine is a most natural one for them to adopt.

Creativity is predicated on a system of rules and forms, in part determined by instrinsic human capacities. Without such constraints, we have arbitrary and random behavior, not creative acts. The constructions of common sense and scientific inquiry derive no less from principles grounded in the structure of the human mind. Correspondingly, it would be an error to think of human freedom solely in terms of absence of constraint. Bakunin once remarked that 'the laws of our own nature . . . constitute the very basis of our being' and provide 'the real condition and the effective cause of our liberty'. A libertarian social theory will try to determine these laws and to found upon them a concept of social change and its immediate and distant goals. If, indeed, human nature is governed by Bakunin's 'instinct for revolt' or the 'species character' on which Marx based his critique of alienated labor, then there must be continual struggle against authoritarian social forms that impose restrictions beyond those set by 'the laws of our own nature', as has long been advocated by authentic revolutionary thinkers and activists.

It is reasonable to suppose that just as intrinsic structures of mind underlie the development of cognitive structures, so a 'species character' provides the framework for the growth of moral consciousness, cultural achievement, and even participation in a free and just community. It is, to be sure, a great intellectual leap from observations on the basis for cognitive development to particular conclusions on the laws of our nature and the conditions for their fulfilment; say, to the conclusion that human needs and capacities will find their fullest expression in a society of free and creative producers, working in a system of free association in which 'social bonds' will replace 'all fetters in human society'.[15] There is an important intellectual tradition that stakes out some interesting claims in this regard. While this tradition draws from the empiricist commitment to progress and enlightenment, I think it finds still deeper roots in rationalist efforts to establish a theory of human freedom. To investigate, deepen, and if possible substantiate the ideas developed in this tradition by the methods of science is a fundamental task for libertarian social theory. Whether further investigation will reveal problems that can be addressed or mysteries that will confound us, only the future can tell.

If this endeavor succeeds, it will refute Bertrand Russell's pessimistic speculation that man's 'passions and instincts' render him incapable of enjoying the benefits of the 'scientific civilization' that reason can create (Russell, 1924[16]), at least if we understand 'passions and instincts' (as Russell sometimes did) to include the 'instincts' that provide the basis for the achievements of the creative intellect, as well as the 'instinct of revolt' against imposed authority—in some measure, a common human attribute. Rather, success in this endeavor might reveal that these passions and instincts may yet succeed in bringing to a close what Marx called the 'prehistory of human society'. No longer repressed and distorted by competitive and authoritarian social structures, these passions and instincts may set the stage for a new scientific civilization in which 'animal nature' is transcended and human nature can truly flourish.

Notes

1   Gunther S. Stent, 'Limits to the Scientific Understanding of Man', *Science*, 187, 1975, pp. 1052–7.

2   Harry M. Bracken, 'Minds and Learning: The Chomskian Revolution', *Metaphilosophy*, 4, 1973, pp. 229–45.

3   John W. Yolton, *John Locke and the Way of Ideas* (Oxford University Press, London, 1956) p. 68.

4   Antonio Gramsci, *The Modern Prince and Other Writings* (International Publishers, New York, 1957) p. 140.

5   Lucien Malson, *Wolf Children and the Problem of Human Nature* (Monthly Review Press, New York, 1972) p. 9–12, 35, translation of *Les Enfants Sauvages* (Union Générale d'Editions, Paris, 1964).

6   On the collapse of liberal doctrine in the nineteenth century, cf Karl Polanyi, *The Great Transformation: The Political and Economic Origins of Our Time* (Beacon Press, Boston, 1957) and Rudolph Rocker, *Anarchosyndicalism* (Secker & Warburg, London, 1938). For a fuller discussion of my own views on the matters discussed here, cf Noam Chomsky, *American Power and the New Mandarins* (Pantheon Books, New York, 1969) Chapter 1; Chomsky, *For Reasons of State* (Pantheon Books, New York, 1973) Chapters 8 and 9.

7   On this matter, see C. B. Macpherson, *The Political Theory of Possessive Individualism* (Oxford University Press, London, 1962).

8   Bracken, *Berkeley* (Macmillan, London, 1974) pp. 16, 156; Bracken, 1973.

9   Chomsky, 1973, Chapters 8 and 9.

10 Ellen M. Wood, *Mind and Politics* (University of California Press, Berkeley, 1972) pp. 29, 38, 174.

11 Kant, 'An Answer to the Question "What is Enlightenment?"', in H. Reiss (ed), *Kant's Political Writings* (Cambridge University Press, London, 1970) p. 59.

12 Cf references in Note 6 and elsewhere.

13 Isaiah Berlin, 'The Bent Twig', *Foreign Affairs*, 51, 1972, pp. 11–30.

14   Bakunin, 'The International and Karl Marx', in Sam Dolgoff, *Bakunin on Anarchy* (Knopf, New York, 1972) p. 319. The other remarks of Bakunin cited will also be found here. For further discussion of such views and the various forms they have taken, and the realization of some of these prophetic insights, see Chomsky, 1973.

15   The terms are Humboldt's. Cf Chomsky, 1973, Chapter 9.

16   Bertrand Russell, *Icarus, or the Future of Science* (Kegan Paul, London, 1924).

Index A: Names

Action Painting, 181
Adkins, A., *Merit and Responsibility*, 49, 56, n4
Albers, J., 176
Albert Memorial, the, 21
Althusser, L., xx, xxi, xxvii n15; xxviii n16; 121
  'Ideology and Ideological State Apparatuses
    (Notes towards an Investigation)', *Lenin and
    Philosophy and Other Essays* xxviii n17, n18
American Philosophical Quarterly, 227, n4, n6
Andre, C., 162
Arendt, H., 56
Aristotle, 41, 53, 70, 71, 98, 128
  Metaphysics I, 51, *XII*, 54
  Posterior Analytics, 99 n2
Aristotelian theory of a definition, 54, acquisition of
    knowledge, 95, causes, 154, 168, conditions,
    259
Arnauld, A., *The Art of Thinking: Port-Royal Logic*
    99 n13
Art and Language, xx, xxiii, 145, 146, 252
  re text 15 'Portrait of V.I. Lenin', xxii, 145–146,
    182, 191
  re text 18 'Abstract Expression', xvii, 10, 26,
    146, 191–192
  re text 23 'Author and Producer Revisited', xv,
    xvi, xvii, xix, 37, 114, 193, 251–252
  *Portrait of V.I. Lenin in the Style of Jackson
    Pollock*, 145
Artforum, xxv n5
Art History, xxvi n7
Art-Language, 145
Art Monthly, xxvi n7, xxvii n11, xxviii n26
Art News, 181
Arts yearbook, xxv n4
Assiter, A., re text 12 'Philosophical Materialism or
    the Materialist Conception of History', xvii, xx,
    xxii, 113–114, 252
Auerback, A. (ed), *Schizophrenia: An Integrated
    Approach*, 188 n6
Avicenna, 133
Azande, the, 225–226

Bach, J.S., 7, 22
  Goldberg Variations, 178

Bakunin, M.A., 267
  'The International and Karl Marx', 269 n14
Baldwin, M., 145, see Art and Language
Barnes, B., re text 11 'Conceptions of Knowledge',
    xii, xxiii, 101–102, 113, 126, 139, 243
  re text 22 'Culture and History', xii, xix, 102,
    243–244
  Interests and the Growth of Knowledge, 101, 243
Barthes, R., xx, xxvii n15
Baudelaire, C., 'Les Chats', 157
Baxandall, M., re text 14 'The Cognitive Style', xvii,
    10, 139–140
  *Painting and Experience in Fifteenth Century
    Italy*, 139
Beethoven, L. von, 88
Bell, C., xii, xv, xvii, 25–26, 31–34, 47, 114
  Art, 25, 35 n7, n8, n9, n12, n12, n14
Benjamin, W., 125
  'The Author as Producer', 251
Berlin, I., 'The Bent Twig' 267, 268 n13
Berkelian tradition, 96, idealist, 114
Bernini, G., 13
Bewick, T., 131
Birdwhistell, R.L., 'Contribution of Linguistic-
    Kinesic Studies to the Understanding of
    Schizophrenia', 184, 188 n6
Bloch, E., 'Discussing Expressionism', xxvi n8
[Bloomfield, J.], *Class, Hegemony and Party*, 121
    n16
Bloomsbury, 25, 41
Bloor, D., *Knowledge and Social Imagery*, xxvii
    n14
Bohn, H.G., 128
Bohr, N., 233
Bosse, A., 129
Botticelli, S., *Birth of Venus*, 27
Bower, T.G.R., 96
  'Object Perception in Infants', 99 n9
Bracken, H.M., 266
  Berkeley, 268 n8
  'Minds and Learning: The Chomskian Revolution',
    264, 268 n2
Bradley, F.H., 41, 42
Bragg, L., 74

Brahe, T., 70–73, 76, 78–79
Brahms, J., *Second Symphony*, 27
Brain, W.R., 71
  Recent Advances in Neurology, 83 n2
Breuer, J., and Freud, S., *Studies on Hysteria*, 185,
  189 n9
British Journal of the Philosophy of Science, 250 n3
Bruner, J.S. and Koslowski, B., 'Visually Preadapted
  Constituents of Manipulatory Action', 96, 99
  n10
Brunfels, *Herbal ('Herbarum vivae eicones')*, 136
Buddhist carving, 5
Butor, M., *Inventory*, 17 n4
  'Rothko: The Mosques of New York', 16

Carrit, E.F.,23
  An Introduction to Aesthetics, 19
Carroll, L., 63
  Alice's Adventures in Wonderland, 19, 20
Cartesian . . . , 20, 95, 266
Cavell, S., *Must We Mean What We Say?* 17 n1
Cézanne, P., 23, 28, 34
Chomsky, N., 154
  re text 10 *'On Cognitive Capacity'*, xxii, xxiii, 93–
    94
  re text 24 *'Some General Concepts of Language'*,
    xxi, xxii, xxiii, 94, 261–262
  American Power and the New Mandarins, 268 n6
  For Reasons of State, 268, n6, n9, 269, n14, n15
  Reflections on Language, 93, 261
Christ, 41; Christianity, 42
Clark, T.J., 158, 257, 259
  'Preliminaries to a Possible Treatment of *Olympia*
    in 1865', 252
Claudius, 22
Cohen, G.A., 119, 120
  Essays in Honor of E.H. Carr, 121 n15
[Coleridge, S.T.], *Kubla Khan*, 20
Collingwood, R.G., 28, 54, 55
  The Principles of Art, 35, n6, 54, 56, n5
Comedy Theatre, Berlin, 179 n5
Compton, M., (ed) *Toward a New Art: Essays on
  the Background to Abstract Art 1910–20*, xxvii
  n13
Constable, J., 69, 70, 164
  Weymouth Bay, 160
Copernicus, 239
Courbet, G., 257
  Burial at Ornans, 149, 166
  The Stonebreakers, 165–167
Coward, R. and Ellis, J., *Language and Materialism:
  Developments in Semiology and the Theory of
  the Subject*, xxviii n19, n20, n21
Croce, B., xv, xvii, 3–4, 22, 25–26, 26–31, 33–34
  Aesthetic, 22, 27, 29, 34 n1 n2, n3
Crateuas, 128
Critchley, M., *The Language of Gesture*, 187, 189
  n13
Crusoe, 75
Cudworth, R., 95
  *Treatise Concerning Eternal and Immutable
    Morality*, 99 n3
  True Intellectual System of the Universe, 99 n5

Dalton, J., 235, 239
Dali, S., 174
Dancy, *Papers in Language and Logic*, 191
Dante, 7

Darwinian . . . , 262
Das Wort, xxvi n8
Daumier, H., *Laundress*, 175
David, J.L., 7
Davidson, D. and Harman, F. (eds), *Semantics of
  Natural Languages*, 121 n13
Davidson, D. and Hintikka, J. (eds), *Words and
  Objections: Essays on the Work of W.V.
  Quine*, 169 n1
Debussy, C., *La Mer*, 178
Degas, E., 259
[Delacroix, E.], *Scenes from the Massacre of Chios*,
  155
Denny, R., 162
Derrida, J., xx
Descartes, R., 237, 264
Diderot, D., *Encyclopaedia*, 130
Dionysius, 128
Dolgoff, S., *Bakunin on Anarchy*, 269 n14
[Dostoyevsky, F.,], *The Brothers Karamazov*, 20
  Crime and Punishment, 19
Douglas, M., 247
  Purity and Danger, 250 n1
Dray, W., 160
  The Historical Explanation of Actions, 169 n7
Duhem, P., 74
  La théorie physique, 83 n5
Dürer, A., 178
Durham Cathedral, 23
Durkheim, E., 220–224 passim
  'Review of A. Labriola's *Essays on Historical
    Materialism*', 227 n3
  Suicide, 222
Dyce, W., 5

Einstein, A., 80, 232, 233
Eimas, P.D., Signeland, E.R., Jusczyck, P., Vigorito,
  J., 'Speech Perception in Infants', 96, 99 n8
Ellis, J., Coward, R.E., *Language and Materialism*,
  xxviii n19, n20, n21
[Eliot, T.S.], 'The Love-Song of J. Aldred Prufrock',
  20
Engels, F., 119, 120
  Anti-Dühring, 117
  'Letter to Bloch', 117, 121, n7
Engels, F., & Marx, K., *The German Ideology*,
  xxviii n22, 114, 121, n1, n2, n3, n10, n11
  The Holy Family, 121 n9
  Selected Works, 121 n7, n8, n12
Etty, W., 5
Euler's Theorem, 248
Evans, T. (ed), 'A Conversation with Clement
  Greenberg', xxvi n7, xxvii n11
Evans-Pritchard, E.E., 221, 225
Expressionism, xxvi, n8

Florence, 29
Foreign Affairs, 268 n13
Foucault, M., xx, xxvii n15, 259
Fourdrinier, 131
Foxe's Martyrs, 130
Frascina, F. and Harrison, C. (eds), *Modern Art
  and Modernism: a Critical Anthology*, xxv n2,
  n4, xxviii n26, 173, 251, 252
Frege, G., 39, 119
  'On Sense and Reference', 121 n14
French Revolution, 130
Freud, S., xxi, xxiii, xxviii n24

The Standard Edition of the Complete Psychological Works of Sigmund Freud, 189 n9
Freud, S., Breuer, J.C., *Studies on Hysteria*, 185, 189 n9
Fried, M., 9, 16
'Three American Painters: Kenneth Noland, Jules Olitski, Frank Stella', xxv n5, 17 n3
Frith, W.P., *Paddington Station*, 32
Fry, R., xi–xv passim, xviii, xxvi n10, 32, 42
Art and Life, xi, xv
Vision and Design, xxv n1, 35 n10
Fuchs, *Herbal ('De Stirpium Historia')*, 136–138
Fullmauer, H., 136

Gadd, D., *The Loving Friends*, 43 n3
Gainsborough, T., 12
Galen, 133
Galileo, 71, 72, 76, 79, 80, 239
Dialogue Concerning the Two Chief World Systems, 83 n1
Gallie, W.B., 160
'Explanation in History and the Genetic Sciences', 169 n7
'Gart der Gesundheit', 133, 134
Ged, W., 131
[Gibbon, E.], *The Decline and Fall of the Roman Empire*, 19, 20
Giotto, 7
Gleyre, C., 257
Goffman, E., *Asylums*, 219
Goldschmidt, W., 214, 225–227
Comparative Functionalism, 225, 227, n5
Goldwater, R., 7
Gombrich, E., 106, 203, 244
Art and Illusion: a Study in the Psychology of Pictorial Representation, xxiii, xxviii n25, 102, 106, 139
Goodman, N., 191, 195–198 passim, 203
re text 9 'Seven Strictures on Similarity', xiii, xix, xxii, 85–86, 146, 169 n2
re text 16 'Expression', xvii, xxv, 26, 173–174, 182
'Art and Inquiry', 173
The Languages of Art, 85, 173, 174, 195
Problems and Projects, 173
Gough, K., 'The Nayars and the Definition of Marriage', 227 n7
Gould, J., 50, 53
The Development of Plato's Ethics, 49, 56 n2
Goya, F. de, 16, 21
Gramsci, A., xx, xxi, xxviii n16, 261, 265
The Modern Prince and Other Writings, 265, 268 n4
Greek art, epic poetry, xxviii n23; philosophy on knowledge, 47–56; science 127–129, 131, 133
Greenberg, C., xii–xiii, xv, xvii, xxv n5, xxvi n7, xxvi n9, 3–4, 9, 10
re text 1 'Complaints of an Art Critic', xv, xvii, 3–4
'Abstract, Representational and so forth', xxvii n12
Art and Culture: critical essays, xxv n3, xxvi n8, xxvii n12
'Avant-Garde and Kitsch', xxvi n8
'Modernist Painting', xxv n4, xxvi n9
'Towards a Newer Laocoon', xxvi n7, n9
Gregory, R., 96
'The Grammar of Vision', 99 n11

'Grete Herbal', 134–135
Grünbaum, A., *Philosophy of Space and Time*, 216

Habermas, J., 107, 244–245
Hall, S., 120
'Rethinking the "Base-and-Superstructure" Metaphor', 121 n16, n17, n18, n19
Hamlet, 75
Hammond, P.B. (ed), *Culture and Social Anthropology*, 227 n7
Hanson, N.R., re text 8 'Observation', xviii, xxiii, 58, 69–70, 102, 113, 139, 230
Patterns of Discovery, 69, 70
Harrison, C., 'The Ratification of Abstract Art', xxvii n13, see also Art and Language
Harrison, C., Frascina, F. &., *Modern Art and Modernism: A Critical Anthology*, xxv n2, n4, xxviii n26, 173, 251, 252
Hart, W.D., 'Causation and Self-Reference', 191
Hayez, F., 5
Hegel, G.W.F., 41 Hegelian . . ., 114
Herder, J.G. von, 263
Hindu sculpture, 5
Hintikka, J., re text 6 'Knowing How, Knowing That, and Knowing What . . .', xiv, 47–48
Hintikka, J., Davidson D. & (eds), *Words and Objections: Essays on the Work of W.V. Quine*, 169 n1
Hitler's architecture, 179 n5
Hobbes, T., 207, 209, 211, 212
Hogarth, W., 21, 33
[Homer], *Iliad*, 48
Odyssey, 50
Hook, S., *Towards an Understanding of Karl Marx*, 121 n6
Humboldt, W. von, 263, 266, 269 n15
Hume, D., 40, 264, Humean . . ., 221
Huxley, A., 176
'Music in India and Japan', 179 n4

Impressionism, ists, 9, 257
Indian music, 176
Ingres, J.A.D., 8
Itard, J., *The Wild Boy of Aveyron*, 265
Ives, C., *Fourth Symphony*, 178
Ivins, Jr., W.M., 105, 106, 125, 126, 244
re text 13 'The Blocked Road to Pictorial Communication' and 'The Road Block Opened', xviii, xxiii, 70, 102, 125–126
Prints and Visual Communication, 105, 125

Jaeger, W., 56
Jakobson, R. and Lévi-Strauss, C., 'Charles Baudelaire's "Les Chats" ', 157, 169 n5
James VI and I, 226
Jastrow's duck-rabbit, 59, see also duck-rabbit
Jehovah, 41
Johns, J., 182
Joule-Lenz Law, 232
Joyce, J., 177
Ulysses, 20, 21
Jusczyck, P., see Eismas, P.D., *et al*

Kandinsky, W., 177
Kant, I., xii, 41, 96, 264, 266, Kantian epistemology, 262
'An Answer to the Question "What is Enlightenment?" ' 268 n11

Kaplan, D., 145, 147, 148, 150, 152, 153, 154, 156–161 passim, 163, 165, 167
'Quantifying In', 156, 169 n1, n4, n6
Keats, J., 75
Kepler, J., 70–73, 76, 78–79 Keplerian orbits 234
Keynes, J.M., 40, 41, 42
Kline, F., 7
Koenig, F., 131
Köhler's hexagons, 66, 67
Koslowski, B., Bruner, J.S. &, 'Visually Preadapted Constituents of Manipulatory Action', 96, 99 n10
Kripke, S., 118
'Naming and Necessity', 121 n13
Kristeva, J., xx
Kuhn, T.S., 229–230, 248
re text 21 'Paradigms, Tacit Knowledge and Incommensurability', xii, xv, xviii, xxiii, 10, 37, 58, 101, 229–231, 244
The Structure of Scientific Revolutions, 101, 229, 250 n2

Labriola, A., *Essays on Historical Materialism*, 227 n3
Lacan, J.H., xx; xxvii n15
Lakatos, I., 248
Proofs and Refutations', 250 n3
Lakatos, I. and Musgrave, T. (eds), *Criticism and the Growth of Knowledge*, 101
Lake, B., *re text 4 'A Study of the Irrefutability of Two Aesthetic Theories*, xiv, xv, xvii, 3, 4, 10, 25–26
Lane, M., (ed) *Structuralism, A Reader*, 169 n5
Langer, S., 184
Philosophy in a New Key, 183, 184, 188, n3, n4, n7
Larisey S.J., P., 17 n5
Larrain, J., *Marxism and Ideology*, xxviii n16
'*Latin Herbarius*' 133
Leach, E.R., 225, 226
'Polyandry, Inheritance and the Definition of Marriage with Particular Reference to Sinhalese Customary Law', 227 n7
Rethinking Anthropology, 225, 227 n7
Lee, V., *Anthropomorphic Aesthetics*, 24 n1
Leibniz, G.W. v., 95
Discourse on Metaphysics, 99 n4
Leonardo da Vinci, *Mona Lisa*, 81
after – , 'Dimensions of a horse', 143
Lessing, G.E., *Laocöon*, 21
Levellers, the, 212
Lévi-Strauss, C., xx, xxvii n15, and Jakobson, R., 'Charles Baudelaire's "*Les Chats*" ', 157, 169 n5
Linsky, L. (ed), *Reference and Modality*, 169 n4
Listener, the, 99 n11, 179 n5
Llangollen Methodist Chapel, 23
Locke, J., 71, 207, 209, 212, –'s epistemology, 264–265
Lodge, D., xxvi n9
Long, R., 166, 167
Lorenz, K., 262
Lotze, *Microcosmos*, 24 n1
Louis, M., 15, 16
Lovejoy, A., O., 'Kant and the English Platonists', 99 n5, n6
Lukács, G., xxvi n8, 158, 244, Lukácsian . . ., 116
Lyly, P., 22

McCarthy, D., 40
MacIntyre, A., *re text 5 'Emotivism'*, xv, xvii, 10, 25, 37–38, 208
re text 20 'The Idea of a Social Science', xvii, xxii, 25, 182, 213–214, 243, 252
Macpherson, C.B., 297–208
re text 19 'The Twentieth Century Dilemma', 207–208
The Political Theory of Possessive Individualism, 207, 268 n7
Malinowski, B., 214–215, 221, 225, 227
The Sexual Life of Savages in North-Western Melanesia, 227 n1, n2
Mallarmé, S., xxiv
'The Impressionists and Edouard Manet', xxviii n26
Malson, L., *Wolf Children and the Problem of Human Nature*, 265, 268 n5
Manet, E., 257
Mannheim, K., 104–105, 110, 244
Ideology and Utopia, 104, 105
Manuels Roret, 131
Markovian . . ., 150, . . . 163
Marx, K., xxi, xxii, xxiii, xxviii n16, n23, n24, 113–121 passim, 191, 252, 256, 261, 263, 265–268 passim
Capital, 252, 253, 254, 258
A Contribution to the Critique of Political Economy, xxviii n23, 117, 118, 252
Economic and Philosophical Manuscripts, 114, 121 n4
The Eighteenth Brumaire of Louis Bonaparte, 120
Theses on Feuerbach, xxviii, 113, 117
Marx, K., and Engels, F., *The German Ideology*, xxviii n22, 114, 121 n1, n2, n3, n10, n11
The Holy Family, 121 n9
Selected Works, 121 n1, n8, n12
Marxism, xxi, xxii, 116, 261 265; Marxist theory, thought, xx–xxiii passim, 121, 253, 265; Marxists, 113, 117, 218
Matisse, H., 8, 12, 14, 15, 16
'*La Fenêtre (Le Rideau Jaune)*', 14
'*La Fenêtre Ouverte*', 14, 15
'*La Porte Fenêtre*', 14
Mayer, A., 136
Mendelsohn, E., *Einstein Tower*, 179 n5
Metaphilosophy, 268 n2
Metrodorous, 128
Mill, J.S., 207, 211, 215
Modernism, xi–xv, xviii–xx, xxii, xxiii, xxv n5, xxvi n9, 25, 37, 258, 261; 'crisis of –', 263; 'Post –', xiii, see also aesthetics, modernist; art, modernist; art criticism, modernist, art history, modernist
Molière, J.B.P. de, *Tartuffe*, 20
Monet, C., 257
Moore, G.E., 40, 41, 42, 43
Principia Ethica, 40, 41
More, H., *Antidote Against Aetheism*, 99 n7
Moussorgsky, M.P., *Boris Goudonov*, 21
Moxon, J., Mechanick Exercises, 129–130
Mozart, W.A., 7, 28
Munch, E., 8
Musgrave, T., Lakatos, I. & (eds), *Criticism and the Growth of Knowledge*, 101

Nadel, S.F., 219
[Necker cube], 77, 78

Newman, B., 5
Newton, I., 80, –'s Laws, 231, 236
    Opticks, 72, 83 n4
Nicholson, B., 33
Nietzsche, F., xxiii, xxviii n24

Oedipus complex, 185
Ohm's Law, 232
Orton, F. and Pollock, G., 'Avant-Gardes and
    Partisans Reviewed', xxvi n7
Orwell, G., xxvi n9
Osric, 22
Overton, R., 211

Papillon, J.M., *Traité*, 129–130
Pareto, V., 195, 225
Partisan Review, xxvi n7, n8
Passmore, J., *re text 3 'On the Dreariness of
    Aesthetics'*, 19–20
Paul, St., 41, 42
Penelope, 50
Penny Cyclopaedia, 131
Perception, 99 n9, n10
Picasso, P., 28, 182
    Guernica, 27
Pierce, C., *Collected Papers*, 181
Pisanello, A., *Studies of a Horse*, 142
Pissarro, C., 164
Plato (Platonic) 41, 48–56 passim, 95
    dialogues, 49, 52, 53: *'Laches'*, 52, 53,
    'Charmides', 48, 52–53, *'Ion'*, 48, *'Meno'*, 51,
    53, *'Euthyphro'*, 48, *Apologia*, 49, 50, 51,
    'Gorgias', 52, *'Republic' I*, 48, *IV*, *V*, 55,
    VII, 51, *'Euthydemus'*, 48, *'Theaetetus'*, 51
Pliny the Elder, 127, 128, 129, 131, 133
    Natural History, 127
Pliny the Younger, 126
Polanyi, K., *The Great Transformation: The Politi-
    cal and Economic Origins of Our Time*, 268 n6
Polanyi, M., *Personal Knowledge*, 231
Pollock, J., 7, 178
Pollock, G., Orton, F., &, 'Avant-Gardes and Par-
    tisans Reviewed', xxvi n7
'Pop Goes the Weasel', 23
Popper, K., xii, 230, Popperian tradition, 248
    The Logic of Scientific Discovery, xxvi n6, 101
Poussin, N., 15
'Pseudo-Apuleius', 132, 133, 135
Ptolemy, 70, Ptolemaist, 71
Pyreicus, 21

Radical Philosophy, xxviii n21, 113
Ramsden, M., 145, see Art and Language
Raphael, 6
Rapoport, A., 186
    *Operational Philosophy: Integrating Knowledge
    and Action*, 183, 188 n2, 189 n11
Read, H., *Art Now*, 35 n5
Realism, xix, xxvi n8, 161, 257
Rée, J., xxii
    'Marxist Modes', xxviii n21
Reiss, H. (ed), *Kant's Philosophical Writings*, 268
    n11
[Renais, A.], *Last Year at Marienbad*, 178
Renoir, P.A., 257
'Revue Philosophique', 227 n3
Robert, L., 131
Rocker, R., *Anarchosyndicalism*, 268 n6

Rockwell, N., 6
Rodin, A., 13
Rosa, S., 7
Rosenbaum, S.P. (ed), *The Bloomsbury Group*, 43
    n2
Rosenberg, H., 'Hans Hofmann: Nature into Action',
    181
Ross, D. (trans), Aristotle's *Metaphysics*, 51
Rothko, M., 10, 12, 16, 200
    'Four Seasons' series, 16
Rousseau, J. J., 266
Ruskin, J., 8
Russell, B., 81, 95, 96, 268
    Human Knowledge: Its Scope and Its Limits, 99
    n1
    Icarus, or the Future of Science, 268, 269 n16
    Intro. to L. Wittgenstein's *Tractatus Logico-
    Philosophicus*, 183, 188 n1
Ryle, G., 39, 216

Salon, the, 257
Saussure, F. de, xx, xvii n15
Scargill, A., 156–157, 161
Schapiro, M., 'On Some Problems in the Semiotics
    of Visual Art: Field and Vehicle in Image
    Signs', 17 n2
Schlauch, M., *The Gift of Language*, 184, 188 n5
Schrödinger Equation, 234
Science, 99 n8, 268 n1
Semiotica, 17 n2
Shakespeare, W., 22
    Macbeth, 20
    The Tempest, 16
Shelley, P.B., *Defense of Poetry*, 28, 35 n4
Sheppard, R., 'Monument to the Architect?', 179 n5
Sidgwick, A., 42
Signealnd, E., see Eismas, P.D., *et al*
Simplicius, 76, 79
Skinner, B.F., 99 n12, 154, 161
Snell, B., *The Discovery of the Mind*, 48, 49, 56 n1,
    n3
Socrates (Socratic) 48–56 passim
Soper, K., 'Marxism, Materialism and Biology', 197
Soulages, P., 178
Speckle, H.R., 136
Spencer, H., 41, 42
Stalin, J.V., 116, Stalinist . . . xxviii n16, 166
    Dialectical Materialism, 117, 121 n5
    Works, 121 n5
Stent, G.S., 262
    'Limits to the Scientific Understanding of Man',
    268 n1
Stephen, L., 42
Sterne, J.P., *Nietzsche*, xxviii n24
Stevenson, C.L., 38
    Ethics and Language, 43 n1
Stobbaerts, J., 5
Strachey, L., 40, 41, 42
Szasz, T.S., *re text 17 'Hysteria as Communi-
    cation'*, 181–182, 191
    The Myth of Mental Illness, 181
    Pain and Pleasure: A Study in Bodily Feelings,
    187, 189 n12
Taylor, R., *Art, An Enemy of the People*, 169 n3
Thatcher, M., 156–157
Thompson, E.P., 167, 169
    The Poverty of Theory and Other Essays, xxviii
    n16, 169 n8

Thomson, J., 88
Time, 8
Times, The, 131
Timpanaro, S., 195
Tolstoy, L.N., 7
Trobriand Island, 214, 255, 256, 258, 259
Tycho, see Brahe

Van Eyck, 15
Van Gogh, V., 27, 194, 201–202
  Night Café, 202
Velasquez, D.R. de S., 7, 12
Vigorito, J., see Eismas, P.D., *et al*
Vlastos, G., 50, 53

Waldmeuller, F.G., 5
Weber, M., 223
Weiditz, H., 136
Wheatstone bridge, 234
Whistler, J.A.M., 30
Whitehead, A.N., 130
Winch, P., 213–227 passim, 252, 'Winchian world',
  195
  The Idea of a Social Science, 213
  'Understanding a Primitive Society', 227 n4

Wisdom, 77, 81
  'Gods', 83 n7
Wittgenstein, L., xxii, xxiii, 32, 57, 58, 69, 81, 82,
  85, 214, 248, 'Wittgensteinian World', 195
  re text 7 'Seeing and Seeing as', 57–58, 69, 75
  Philosophical Investigations, 57, 58, 69, 83 n6,
  n8, n9
  Tractatus Logico-Philosophicus, 35 nll, 57, 83
  n8, n10, 188 n1
Wollheim, R., *re text 2 'The Work of Art as Object'*,
  xii, xv, 9–10
  Art and Its Objects, 9
Wood, E.M., *Mind and Politics*, 266, 268 n10
Woolf, L., 41, 42
Woolf, V., 40, 42
Whorfian fallacy, 55

Xenophanes, 51

Yolton, John, 264
  John Locke and the Way of Ideas, 265, 268 n3
Yorick, 75

Zande, see Azande

Index B: Concepts

abstract art, abstraction, xi, xii, xxv, xxvi n7, xxvii n13, 5, 7, 69–70, 200–201
'abstract circumstances', 196, 203
academic art, 5
'academics, the', xii
aesthetic approach, 22, 173; — considerations, 19, 22, 23; — contemplation, emotion, xxvii n10, 25, 31–32, 33; — criteria, evaluation, judgement, xi, xii, xv, xvii, xxv, xxvii n11, 3–6, 9, 10, 14, 19, 22, 23, 34, 37, 48, 102, 127, 173, 234; — experience, xiii, xvii, xxviii n23, 5, 19–20, 24, 34, 41, 173, 196; — kinds, doctrine of, 22; — objects, 34; — philosophy, 20; — properties, 22, 23; — quality, qualities, xxiv, 19, 125, 251
aesthetic theories, aesthetics, 19–24, 25–35, bourgeois —, 200, language of — 33, modernist —, 37
affects, 187
alienation, 267, 207
'anomie', 220
anthropology, social, xx, xxii, 25, 213–227, 252, 255, 256, 258, 259
apocalypticism, 40, 41
architecture, 20, 21, 22, expression and exemplification in, 177, 179 n5
'arete', 48, 49, 50, 53
art, as experience, 10, 25, 47, (intuitive knowledge) 26–31, 244; as expression, 4, 127, expression in —, xi, xviii, 10, 16, 23, 26, 173–179, 182, 183, 191–204, see also expression . . .
art, modern, xi, xii, 140, 174, 208, 252, 253, 254, 258, dominant theory of, material character of, 9–17; modernist —, xi, xii, xv, xvii, 3, 5, 11, 167; see also value judgement re art
art, and beauty, 21, 41; — and cognition, xiii, xiv, xxv, 225, 263; — and 'language', xxi, 23, 26, 28, 34, 94, 105, 182, 183, 186; — and science, 70, 173
art for art's sake, 24, see also autonomy, of art
art community, xv, xvii, 191, 195, 214, 230, 253, 256, — market, xvii, 160, 208
art criticism, theory, xi, xix, xx, xv, 3–8, 9, 10, 25,

47, 48, 214, 230; modern —, 181; modernist —, xi–xix passim, xxiii, xxvi n10, 3–8, 9, 37, 47, 70, 174, 230, 258
art history, xvii, xviii, xix, xx, xxiii, xxiv, 5, 70, 85, 105, 139, 151, 214, 230, 241; modernist —, xi, xvi, xvii, xxiii
artist — as/and — producer, 114, 163, 251–259
'aspect-blindness', 58, '— phenomena', 78, see seeing and . . . assemblage, 11
astronomy, 70–73, 129
attitude, expressions of, see expression; moral judgements
'aura', 125
author — as/and producer, 251–259
autonomy, of aesthetic experience, xvii; — of art, xi, xii, xiii, xvi, xvii, xviii, 6–7, 14, 230, 252, 253, 256; — of base/superstructure, 253; — of science, xiv, 101
avant-garde, ism, vanguardism, xiii, xxvi n7, n8, 6

base/superstructure, xxi, 117, 118, 120, 121, 253
beauty, 17, 21, 23, 41, '— of the horse', 141
behaviour, empiricist approach to, 93, 97–98, 216; patterns, 'internal states' in —', 93, 97; rationalist approach to —, 97; 'science of —', 98; distinction between goal directed and rule following . —, 182, 188; sign using —, 183, 189 n8, see hysteria as communication; social —, 197, explanation: reasons and causes, 217–218, rule governed —, 213, 215–221
behaviourism, 265, see also psychology, behaviourist
beliefs, expression of, 196, 197; evaluation of —, knowledge claims, 243, 245, 247, 249; scientific —, see paradigms, as disciplinary matrix; knowledge . . .
biological determination, on language, 93, 94, 261; — of cognitive capacities, systems, xxiii–xxiv, 93–94, 96, 261–262, 262–263; — on scientific inquiry, 267; — on visual apprehension, expression, 261
body signs, hysterical, iconic, informative functions of, see hysteria as communication

book illustration, 125–138

botany, 125, 128–129, 131–133

bourgeoisie, the, 21, 258; bourgeois aesthetics, 200; — cultural creation, 167; — culture, 258; — ideology, 254; 'meanings of the —', 258; — naturalism, 158; — society, 251; ' —' theory, xxii

capital, ism, ist, 191, 252, 253, 256, 266, 267

cartography, 108, see maps

'cartharsis', 185

causal inquiry and explanation, xii, xiv, xvi, xxiii, xxv, xxvii n14, 10, 25, 26, 35, 182, 252, 254, 255, 256, 259; re expression and expression claims, 191–204; re realism in representation, 145–169; re social science, 213–214, 215–218, 225

causes, 59, 65, 67, 154, 161, 168, 197, 203, 245, 250

class, 130, 131, 140, 141–142, 158, 203, 208, 209–210, 246, 258, 267, — struggle, 117–118, 166, see also bourgeoisie; proletariat

classification, 85, 106, 126, 143, 226

closure, xiv–xviii, xxiii–xxv passim, 146, 161–163, 255, see also criticism, stipulative power of

cognition, cognitive capacity, structures, systems, xxiii–xxiv, 93–99, 261–268; cognitive capabilities, processes, resources, 243, 245, 246, 250; — conditions, determinants, mechanisms, 252, 255, 256, 257; — functions, 102, 107, 173, 201; — states, 197

'cognitive style, the', 10, 139–143

'coherence theory', 154, 162, 167

collage, 11

'common sense', 41, 94, 96, 262, 267

communication, hysteria as, 181–189

communication, pictorial (prints), importance of exact repeatability of, 125–138

'communication breakdown', 229, 230, 239–240

community, see art community, language community, scientific community

competence, xi, xviii, 48, 256–257

congruency, 61, 63, see seeing and seeing as

connoisseurship, 125, 203, 230

contemplation, disinterested, 168, 173, see also aesthetic contemplation; knowledge, contemplative and sociological accounts of

content, xii, 4, 6–7

contradiction, 58, 191, 252–259 passim

'correspondance theory', 154, 247

craft, paradigm theory of, re knowledge, 48–56 passim; — skills, science, 110–111

creativity, xxiv, 21, 208, 261, 263, 266, 268

'crisis of modernism', 263

criticism, xviii, xxv, 145–146, 155, 195, 203, 252, see also art criticism, theory, art criticism, theory, modernist; — stipulative power of, 192–196, 203

culture, see Modernism; — and knowledge, 243–250; cultural achievement, 267; — change, growth, 244, 248; — creation, 167; '— production' xix; '—studies', 37

dance, 176, 177, 182, 183

'decorative', the 178

denotation, denotative, 86, 176–178, 184

description, 11; action —, 221; verbal —, and knowledge, 103, 105, 110

description, perception/visual experience, interpret-

ation, see seeing and . . .

description, similarity, representation, 86–87, 174, see also iconicness, descriptiveness, resemblance, re realism

determinism, xxi, 113, 117–118, 119, 120, 121, 253, 254, 256, 258

'disciplinary matrix', 229, re art community, 230, see also paradigms, as disciplinary matrix

discourse, second-order, 252, 255, 258, 259; verbal —, and expression, 174, 176, 191

'dominated, dominating, meanings of the ', 252, 256, 258–259

duck-rabbit, 59–64 passim

'*dynameis*', 55

economic determinism, see determinism

'effects', 3–4, 7–8, 25–26, 38, see also art, as experience, art as expression; moral judgements

'*einfühlung*', 201

'*elenchus*', 48, 50, 53

emotion, aesthetic, see aesthetic contemplation, emotion; expression of —, 182, 183, 186, 197–198, see also art as expression; expression in art

emotive-cognitive, dichotomy, 173

emotivism, xv, 25, 37–43

'*empeiria*', 47, 51

empiricism, ist doctrine re human nature, 261–267

enquiry, see causal inquiry and explanation; genesis as an explanatory concept

'*epistemai*', 48, 50

'*episteme*', 47–56 passim

epistemology, 102, 126, 168, 245, 249, 262, 264

ethics, 19, 23, 40–41

ethnomethodology, 248

evaluative judgements, doctrine of, see emotivism; see also aesthetic criteria; evaluation, judgement, value judgement re art; — re science, values; beliefs, evaluation of —

exemplars, 229, 231, 234, 236, 238, 239, 242, re modernism xv, re art community, 230, see paradigms, as shared examples

existentialism, 265

experience, s, inner world of, 20; — and knowledge, 103; — and physical states, 71, see also art as —

experience (apprehension, aspect, awareness, perception, sensation), visual, 41, 96–97, 102, 103, 139, 143, 261, see also observation; perception; seeing and . . .

explanation, of art, xii, xvi, xvii, xviii, xxiii, xxiv; — in natural sciences, 216, 233; — in social sciences, 216, reasons and causes 217–218; zeitgeist —, 128, see also causal inquiry and explanation; genesis as an explanatory concept; 'strong programme'

expression, 173–174; a definition, 178; possession and —, 174–176; — as exemplification, 174–178; metaphor in —, 174–178, 195, 203; — of sounds, 175, of feelings, 175–176, 183, 186, of thought, 62; verbal discourse, symbols and —, 176, 177, 191; denotation and —, 176; habituation, 176; specificity of —, 176; — and stipulative power of criticism, 192–196, 203; 'abstract circumstances', 196, 203; theatrical —, 197, 199, 200; — and states of mind, 203–204 see also art as expression; expression in art; effects; hysteria as communication; psychobiology

Index B: Concepts

expression, causal theory of reference, 191–204
'expression', self—', 208, 214

'false consciousness', 213, 218, 252, see ideology
'family resemblances', 85, see seeing and seeing as; similarity . . .
feelings, expression of, see expression, moral judgements
figuration, figurative art, reference, xxv, 5, 11, 192
flatness, xii, xiii, xv, 29, see also surface, priority, possession of, re painting
form, xi, 4, 6–7, 22, 'significant —', 25, 31–34
'formal', the, 178
formal considerations, 19, 22
formalism, 4, 6, 8, 58
franchise, democratic, 210, see also liberal democratic theory
freedom, 207, 208, 211, 266, 267, 268, see also 'possessive individualism'
functionalism, 213, 215, 223

genesis as an explanatory concept re realism, 145–169, see also 'of'
gestalt theory, 20
'good', re art, aesthetics, 7, 19–24; re moral judgements, 38–42
grammar, 93, 98; '— of vision', 97

herbals, 131–138
hieroglyphs, 82, 184
historical materialism, see materialism, historical
historicism, 128
history of art, see art history . . .
human nature, 97, 207, 220, empiricist doctrine, theory of, 261–267
human relations, society, 207, 209, 212, 268
hyper-realist painting, 157, 159–160, 164
hysteria as communication, 181–189

iconic signs, see signs, iconic . . ., iconicness, descriptiveness, resemblance, re realism; semiology; symbols, iconic iconicness, descriptiveness, resemblance, re realism, 145–169, 192
ideology, xxi, xxii, 203, 213, 218, 245, 252, 253, 259, 261, 263, 265, 267, 'visual —', xix, 102
incommensurability, 37, 239
individualism, see 'possessive individualism'
'inner picture', 61
inquiry, see causal inquiry and explanation
instrumentalism, 243, 245, 247, 248–249
intellect, distinct from senses, 98
intellectualism, 49, 50, 54
intelligentsia, technical, 267
intention, 7, 10, 213
'internal states', 97
'interest', xiv, xviii, xxiii; — and knowledge, 103, 107, 109, 243–247 passim, 249; — and similarity 85; — and vividness, 156, 158
intuition, ism, xxiv, 40–41, 43, 244
isomorph, ism, 148, 149, 151, 161, 165, see also iconicness, descriptiveness, resemblance, re realism, similarity

'kitsch', xiii, xxvi n8
knowledge, xi, xiv, xvi, xviii; xix; xxiii, xxiv, xxv, xxvii n14; —, knowing how, knowing that, and knowing what, 47–56; — and seeing, 69–70, 75–80, 230, 235–238; innate acquisition of,

93, 95–98, 262, biological constraints on, 262–263; contemplative and sociological accounts of, generation and production, 101–111, 243–250, see also beliefs; cognition; epistemology; 'material life' and 'consciousness'
knowledge, intellectual', 26; 'intuitive —', art as, 26–31, 244; scientific —, xiv, 79, 101, 107, 108, 110–111, 229–242, 243, 244, 247, 249; 'tacit —', 230, 234/235, 244

language, species characteristic and cognitive capacity, xxiii–xxiv, 93–94, 97–98, 261, 262, 264; moral —, 40; '— game', 64, philosophical investigation of, 57, 214; influence on observation, seeing, 77, 79–83; formative force of —, 176; discursive and non-discursive —, 182, 183–187; — and social scientific inquiry, 213–214, 224; '— community', 240–241, see also art and 'language'; linguistic . . .
liberal democratic theory, dilemma of, 207–212
linguistic concepts and discrimination, 139–140, see also seeing and . . .; — description, 126; — materials on seeing, see seeing and . . .; — mechanism, art as a, 26, 34; — universals, 98; — and cognitive capabilities, 243, 250, see also language . . .
literature, xxvi n7, n9, 6, 20, 21, 23, 24; 'doctrine of literary kinds', 22; 'literary relations of production, technique', 251
'logos', 51

maps, 81–82, 83, 108, 181
market, see art market, possessive market relations, — society
matching, 151, 152, 158
material base, see base/superstructure
material character of art, 9–17
'material life' and 'consciousness', 113, 114, 118–119
materialism, central-state, 197–198
materialism, historical, xvii, xx, xii–xxiii, 37, 113–121, 155, 196, 252, 253, 254, 258, 259; philosophical —, xxii, 116, 121
'materialization', 64
mathematics, 32, 104, 110–111, 183, 263
meaning, re art, 7, 8, 23, 102, 174, 191–192, 193, 194, 208, recovery of, 252–259; re emotivism, 38–40, 42–43; re philosophy, 47, 57–58, 69, 82, 248; re psychiatry, 182, 185
meaning, metaphor and, 248; picture theory of —, 82; 'social production of —', 102, 262
means of production, see production, means of
mechanism, see functionalism
mechanisms of production, see production, mechanisms of
medicine, 133, 142, 185, 187–188
medium, xxvi n7, 12, 13, 32
memory, 51
mental illness, 181–182, see hysteria as communication
metaphor, and meaning, 248; — and similarity, 84, 88; — in expression; 174–178, 195, 203
'metaphysical paradigms', 232, re art, xv, re art community, 230, see paradigms, as disciplinary matrix
metaphysics, 19, 21, 23
mind, 94, 95, 96, 98, 195, 197, 198, 203–204, 262, 266, 267
misinformation re hysteria, mistake or lie, 182, 188,

278

translation 187–188
misrepresentation, 135, 182, 252–259
'mode of production', 116, capitalist, 252, 253, see also capital, ism ist
models, 229, see paradigms, as standard examples, puzzle-solving
moral consciousness, 267; — conduct, skill, knowledge, 49–50; — culture (modern), 25, 37–43, 208; — justification re liberal democracy, 210; —judgements (expressions of attitude, feeling, preference) 38–39, 42–43, re art, xxv, see also ethics
music, 6, 20, 21, 22, 23, 24, 78, 173, 176, 177, 183

name, its objects, its users, 145, 147, 160, 198
naming, expressing, 177
nationalism, 179 n5
natural being, man as a, 114–116
naturalism, 85 86–87, 116, 158, 167
needs, 113, 114–116
'normal science', 229, 232, 239, 241, see also puzzle-solving; scientific revolution
'nouveau mélange', xxii
'number', 61

obligation, theory of political, 207–208, 209–212
observation, 69–83, 113, 126, 139, 235–238, see also seeing and . . .; perception
'of', genetic, 145–146, 147–168, 256
'opticality', xii, xxv n5

'paideia', 56
painting, classical, 127, descriptive, 32, 34, illusionist, 5, see also hyper-realist painting; priority, possession of, surface of, 9–17, see also flatness; styles of — 65
paradigm,s, 54, 55, 56, 58, 74, 101, 108, 221, 229–230; — as community commitments, 231–234, 242; — as disciplinary matrix, 231–234; — as standard examples, 234, 235
'paradigm shift', in science, 229, in art discourse, 230
patronage, 140, 141–142
perception, 26–27, 103–106, 141, 237, 243, psychology of —, 105, see also observation; seeing and . . .
philosophy, xii, xxiii, 57, 127, 249; aesthetic —, 19; —, on knowledge, 95; classical —, on knowledge, 47–56; — of language, 57, 214; — of seeing, 57–68; — of science, xxiii, 101, 231, 232, 246, 247, see also materialism, philosophical
photography, 8, 66, 82, 106, 110, 125, 126, 161, 163, 181, 184
physicality, material character of art, 9–17
picture — duck, rabbit, 59–64 passim; — face, 60, 68; — object, 60, 61; — puzzle, 61; — token, type, 147, 150–152
'picture "of" ', 165, 168, see 'of'
picturing, and language using, 79–83; — and talking, 175–176, 191
poetry, 28
'possessive individualism', 207–212, 266, re art, 208
'possessive market relations, — society', 207–212
power, xx, 209–210, 246–247, 254, 255
prediction, explanation and, re social and natural sciences, 216
prediction, and control, re knowledge, 107–111,

243–244, 247, 249; —, and similarity, 88–89
preference, expressions of, see moral judgement,s
prints (exactly repeatable pictorial statements) and communication, 125–138
producer, 114, artist-author — as/and —, 251–259
production, means of, 251; mechanisms of —, 252; organisation of —, 115; relations of —, xvi, 251, 252; — and consumption, 115–116; — and reproduction, 113, 117; — in modernist culture, 261; pictures-as-produced —, 166; productive activities, 113; see also mode of production
proletariat, 118
psychiatry, 181, 186, 188; psychiatric nosology 189 n10; psychiatric syndromes, 186
psychoanalysis, xx, xxi, xxii, 181, 188, 265; psychoanalytic diagnosis, 182; psychoanalytic theory, 188; psychoanalytic treatment, 181, 184, 185, 186
psycho-biology, re expression, 193–194
psychology, xx, xxiv, 9, 197; — and knowledge, 104; — and science, 101; — of perception, 105; empiricist, behaviourist, 261, 263
psychotherapy, 182, 185
purity, xii, xxvi n7, 5
puzzle-solving, scientific, 229, 233, 242

quality, aesthetic, see aesthetic quality, qualities
quality, in art, xi, xv, xix, xxiv, xxvi n7, 3–8 passim, 244, 251, art history as history of, 5

rabbit-duck, see duck-rabbit
rationalism,ist,s, 93, 96, 97, 98, 261, 264, 267–268
realism,ist,ic re art, representation, xix, 85, 86–87, 106, 145–169, 244, 257
'realism, progressive' re knowledge, 248, see also 'strong programme'
reality, re knowledge, xxi, 103, 106, 111, 243–244, 245, 247, 248, 250; links between a picture and —, 31, 146–147, 164–165, 168–169
reasons, and causes, in social science, 213–214, 217–218
reduction, 5
'reference', 'sense' and, 39
reference, chains of, re expression, 177; causal theory of —, re expression, 191–204; and representation, 82, 86
relations of production, see production, relations of
relativism, xxv, 158, 243, 245–250 passim
repetition, and similarity, 88
replication, and similarity. 87
representation, visual, xi, xiii, xiv, xv, xviii, xix, xxiii, 7, 10, 16, 69–70; — and copying, 63, 81–82; —, description, similarity, 86–87; —, re contemplative and sociological accounts of knowledge, 101–111; and knowledge, 243, 244, 250; —, re empirical observation, rational classification, 126–138; — and the representational skills of observers, 139–143; causal inquiry re realism in —, 145–169; — and description, exemplification re expression, 177–178; see also hysteria as communication; realism,ist,ic, re art, representation; reference and —
resemblance, see iconicness, descriptiveness, resemblance re realism; isomorph,ism; similarity; symbols, iconic, and similarity
revolt, instinct for, 267, 268

revolution, 118, 121, 128, 130, 234, 141:
  scientific —, see 'normal science'; scientific
  revolution
'right', 41
ritual, 181, 182
'role concepts', 219–220
rules, re language, 58, 181; re social behaviour, 182,
  188, 213, 215–221

science, xii, 48, 52, 247; art and —, 70, 173;
  autonomy of —, xiv, 101; cognitive authority of
  —, 229; dialectical character of —, 248; history
  of —, 229; philosophy of —, xxiii, 101, 231,
  232, 246, 247
scientific belief, see paradigms, as disciplinary
  matrix, see also scientific knowledge; —
  community, 229–230, 231–234, 239, 242; —
  development, change, 229, 230, 238–239,
  241–242, see also 'normal science', scientific
  revolution; — education, 230, 234, 242; —
  explanation, 216; — knowledge, xiv, 79, 101,
  107, 108, 110–111, 229–242, 243, 244, 247,
  248, 249; — laws, 232; — research, 107; —
  revolution, 229, 230; — techniques, 229, see
  paradigms, as disciplinary matrix; — theories,
  231, 233, 234, 240; — values, 229, see paradigms, as disciplinary matrix.
' "scientific intelligence", reign of', 267
sculpture, 5, 7, 8, 24
seeing, and seeing as, 57–68, 69, 75–76, 78–79,
  110, 140; — and seeing that, 69, 76–80; — and
  knowledge, 76–77, 79–80, 83; — and observation, 75–76, 79–80, 235–238; — and sensation, 237–238; — and verbal contextualisation
  73–75, 'seeing-talk', 77; —: pictures and
  language, 77–83; — 'theory-laden', 69, 75, 235;
  — community licensed, 230, 236, 237, see also
  perception
semiology, xiii, xx, xxi, 161, 162; semiotics, 146,
  147, 149, 168, of psychiatric operations, see
  hysteria as communication; see also signs . . .;
  signification; symbols
'sense' and 'reference', 39
'sense-datum', perception and knowledge, 95–96;
  ' — ' pictures, 72, 80, see also observation
'significant form', 25, 31–34
signs, conventional, 181, 183, 185; iconic —, 181–
  182, 184, 189 n8, iconic body —, 184–188, see
  semiology; symbols
signification, 58, 149, 193, 253, 256, 259, 'signifying practices', xix, see hysteria as communication; iconicness, descriptiveness, resemblance
  re realism; semiology; signs; symbols, iconic . . .
similarity, xii, 73, 85–86, 139, 148–151, 160; strictures on —, 86–92; similarity relation, 235–237,
  239, see also iconicness, descriptiveness, resemblance re realism; isomorph,ism; symbols, iconic,
  and similarity
skill, xi, xiv, xxiii, 21, 22; ' — ' and 'knowledge' in
  classical philosophy, 47–53 passim; pictorial,
  visual skills —: business —, medical —, pious
  —, polite —, see cognitive style

social action, 42; — anthropology, see anthropology,
  social; — behaviour, see behaviour, social; —
  conventions, 21; — forces, processes, xxi, xxiv;
  — institutions, 23; — theory, 261, 267, 268
'social realism', xix
sociology, 102–103, 104, 110; — of knowledge,
  xxvii n14, 101–111, 126, 243–250; the idea of
  social science, 213–227
'sophia', 48
species characteristics, human, xxiii–xxiv, 93, 94,
  97, 98, 261, 164, 266–268; —, botanical, 128,
  136–138
'strong programme', xxvii n14
structuralism, xx–xxii, xxvii–xxviii n15
style, xxiii, 22, 65, 146, 181, 182, 241, 242, see
  also 'cognitive style, the'
'subject, the', xxi
subject matter, xi, xii, xix; —, competence, practice,
  256–257; illustrated —, 7–8
suicide, 222–224
superstructure/base, see base/superstructure
surface, priority, possession of, re painting, 9–17, see
  also flatness
'symbolic generalisations', 230, 231–232, re art
  230–231, see paradigms, as disciplinary matrix
symbols, iconic, and similarity, 85, 86–87; —, re
  expression, 173–179 passim, 181–182, 183,
  184; indexical —, 181–182, 193, see also iconicness, descriptiveness, resemblance re realism;
  semiology; signification; similarity

'tacit knowledge', see 'knowledge, tacit'
talking and picturing, see picturing and language
  using
taste, xxvii n11, 6, 7, 10, 140, 241
technique, literary, 251; scientific —, see paradigms,
  as disciplinary matrix
'tekhne', 48–49, 51
teleology, 'telos', 47, 54–56
'three-dimensional seeing', 66–67
'time-slices', 114, 119, 254
translation, 182, 184, 187–188, 195, 240–241, 255
'trompe l'oeil', 106

'use', re meaning of terms, concepts, utterances, 39–
utilitarianism, 41–42, 209

value judgement, re art, xii, xvii, xxvii n11, 37, 47–
  48, 234, 244, see also aesthetic criteria,
  evaluation, judgement; — re science, 233–234,
  see also beliefs, evaluation of
values, 11, 12, academic —, xix, tactile — 141;
  scientific —, xv, 229, 233, re art, xv, 230, see
  also paradigms, as disciplinary matrix
virtue, 47–48, 49, 50, 53
'visual field', 69, 75, 230
'visual impression', 61, see also experience
  (apprehension, aspect, awareness, perception,
  sensation), visual
vividness, 145, 147, 156, 159, 168, 200

war, 210, 211, 212
witchcraft, 225–226